D1823140

The Israeli Military and the Origins of the 1967 War

This new book examines the relationship between the Israeli armed forces, the government and the origins of the 1967 war. It analyses the effect of the Israel Defence Forces (IDF) on Israel's defence policy between 1963 and 1967, against the backdrop of developments in the Middle East, and Israeli decision-making immediately preceding the Six Day War in June 1967. A watershed event in the Arab–Israeli conflict, the war has had a profound effect on the development of the Palestinian problem and the character of Israel over the past four decades.

Making extensive use of original documents, including protocols of meetings of the general staff and the government, discussions between the Prime Minister, Minister of Defence and the Chief of Staff, as well as testimonies by IDF generals, this volume sheds new light on the dramatic tension between the army and the Israeli government in the weeks preceding the conflict and the army's intervention in diplomatic initiatives. It also discloses the steps taken by the US Administration and its fluctuating policies during the crisis: from firm opposition to a pre-emptive Israeli strike, to support for such an operation.

This book will be of great interest to students of Middle Eastern politics, strategic studies, Israeli politics and military history in general.

Ami Gluska lectures in history and political science at the Hebrew University of Jerusalem and the Ashkelon Academic College. In 2005 he won the Yitzhak Sadeh prize for his book *Eshkol, Give the Order!* of which the present book is a translation. Formerly, he served in the IDF and held a number of senior positions in the ministries of defence and public security.

Middle eastern military studies
Series Editors: Barry Rubin
Interdisciplinary Center Herzliya, Israel

The Israeli Military and the Origins of the 1967 War
Government, armed forces and defence policy 1963–1967
Ami Gluska

The Israeli Military and the Origins of the 1967 War

Government, armed forces and defence policy 1963–1967

Ami Gluska

Routledge
Taylor & Francis Group

LONDON AND NEW YORK

First published 2007
by Routledge
2 Park Square, Milton Park, Abingdon, Oxon OX14 4RN

Simultaneously published in the USA and Canada
by Routledge
270 Madison Ave, New York, NY 10016

Routledge is an imprint of the Taylor & Francis Group, an informa business

Transferred to Digital Printing 2009

© 2007 Ami Gluska

Typeset in Sabon by Wearset Ltd, Boldon, Tyne and Wear

All rights reserved. No part of this book may be reprinted or
reproduced or utilized in any form or by any electronic,
mechanical, or other means, now known or hereafter invented,
including photocopying and recording, or in any information
storage or retrieval system, without permission in writing from
the publishers.

British Library Cataloguing in Publication Data
A catalogue record for this book is available from the British
Library

Library of Congress Cataloging in Publication Data
A catalog record for this book has been requested

ISBN10: 0–415–39245–4 (hbk)
ISBN10: 0–415–54511–0 (pbk)
ISBN10: 0–203–96596–5 (ebk)

ISBN13: 978–0–415–39245–7 (hbk)
ISBN13: 978–0–415–54511–2 (pbk)
ISBN13: 978–0–203–96596–2 (ebk)

For my wife Shuli and our children Einat, Ittai and Orit

'The Israeli army is called a "defense force" but it is not a defensive army.... The Sinai campaign (1956), the reprisal acts and the raids across the border were purely offensive operations, and were of decisive value.... Not only the actions which were actually carried out but also the IDF's prevailing conception is offensive.... The most significant technical expression of the new approach ... is the absence of fortifications and fencing along the country's borders. Although the Government's policy is, politically speaking, essentially defensive – those responsible for the armed forces have refrained from adopting defensive measures. Their response to Arab provocation has been counter-attacks, raids on enemy bases, transferring the war to the Arab countries ... to put it simply: the IDF is a characteristically offensive army as regards theory, planning and execution, in body and spirit.'

Major-General Moshe Dayan, April 1967

Contents

Illustrations

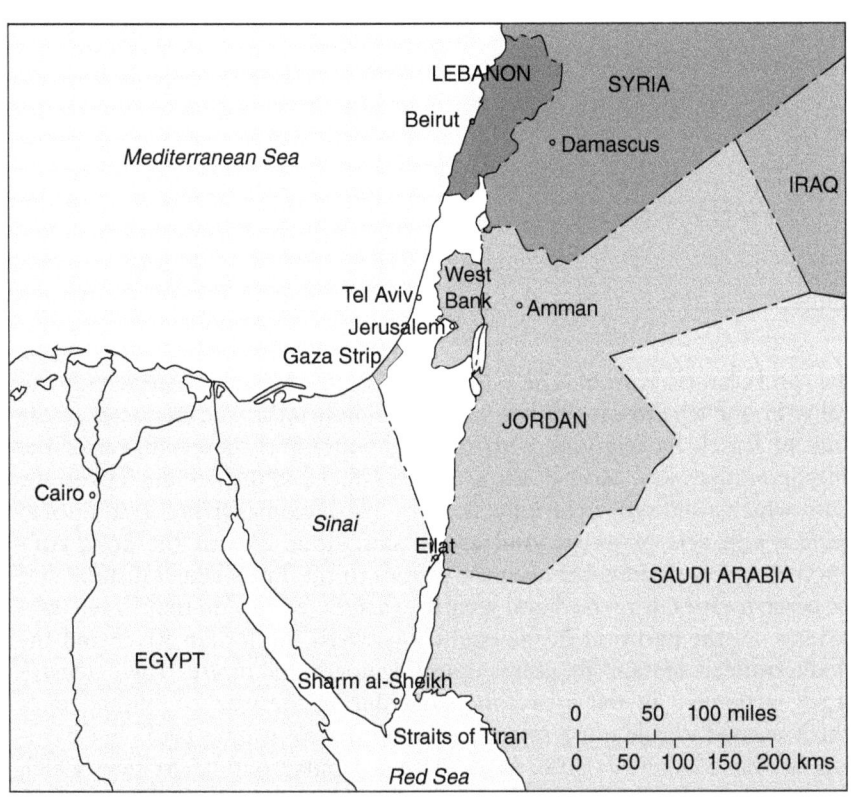

Map 1 Israel and its neighbours – pre-1967 borders.

Preface

The Arab–Israeli war of 1967 transformed the Middle Eastern political reality in one fell swoop and left a profound imprint on the character of the State of Israel, its relations with its neighbours and the evolution of the Palestinian question. Most of the events in Israel and the Middle East in the years which followed were influenced by its outcome. It begat additional warfare and acts of terror, and at the same time created the basic conditions for negotiations between the parties to the Arab–Israeli dispute and for peace treaties. It revived and greatly exacerbated the internal Israeli controversy on the partition of the country between the Jordan River and the Mediterranean Sea and its political and demographic future. The extensive Israeli settlement in the area conquered during the war established facts which seemed to rule out a return to the borders of 4 June 1967, but partition of the country in accordance with a similar outline to that which existed before the Six Day War remained the starting point for any discussion of a permanent settlement between Israel and the Palestinians.

The third military confrontation between Israel and the Arabs (after 1948 and 1956) was the direct result of the tension stemming from Arab opposition to the establishment of Israel and their refusal to accept the outcome of the 1948 war, of Egypt's desire to erase Israel's achievements in the 1956 war and of the proclaimed Arab commitment to restoration of the rights of the Palestinians. The Six Day War has been researched from various angles but no satisfactory answer has as yet been provided to a crucial query: How did a war, which none of the parties involved apparently wanted or planned for, nonetheless occur? The puzzling fact is not that the Arab-Israeli dispute once again erupted in war but that the decision-makers appear to have lost control of the situation.

Ostensibly, the facts are known: from 1966 on, Syria, which always claimed to be the standard-bearer of authentic Arab nationalism and the leader of the struggle against Israel, favoured a strategy of 'a popular struggle' and backed the guerrilla warfare or – as Israelis saw it – 'hostile terrorist activity' of the Palestinian organizations against them. In spring 1967, due to the intensification of this activity, the Soviet Union claimed that Israel was planning to launch an attack on Syria. Egypt hastened to flex its muscles in Sinai in order to deter Israel. From then on events proceeded under their own momentum and ran out of control. This version of events, however, does not supply a full historical explanation for the events which generated the crisis. The question of what led to war remains, therefore, unanswered.

This book attempts, on the basis of primary source material in Israel, to elucidate the way in which events proceeded on the Israeli side, with emphasis on the relations between military and political leaders. Its subject is the army's influence on Israel's security policy and its contribution to the downhill slide into war.

It does not aspire to be a comprehensive study of the roots of the Six Day War or to analyse the complex processes which led to war, but is, rather, focused on a specific angle: namely, how Israel's military command and political leadership reacted to the country's security problems between 1963 and 1967, and how their reactions affected the escalation of the conflict. Various other perspectives on the situation – inter-Arab, Egyptian, Syrian, Palestinian or international – deserve separate attention. To the extent that this book touches on them, it is usually from the inside viewpoint of the Israeli General Staff and the government.

The crucial question is: How did it happen that the State of Israel suddenly found itself at war, in total contradiction to the intentions of the government? Was Israel an innocent victim of the crisis evoked by President Nasser's decision to bring his army into Sinai and to bar Israel from free shipping? Or did Israel itself play a part in the escalation?

There is little doubt that in 1967 Israel had no desire for war.[1] The civilian leadership had no motive for wanting it. Levi Eshkol's government was moderate and most of his ministers were opposed to military activism. Confronted with serious problems of basic security, it allocated considerable resources to the security establishment. The objective was to preserve Israel's deterrent capacity, to equip the IDF and to enhance its qualitative advantages in order to forestall hostilities. The IDF, subject to the government's authority, was called upon to provide a solution which would avoid escalation and involvement in hostilities. Yitzhak Rabin, a measured and cautious Chief of Staff, bowed to the authority of the government, as did his senior officers, and enjoyed the confidence of the government. What, then, went wrong?

The basic underlying assumption of this study is that the possible explanation should be sought in perusal of the discussions, stances, decisions and activities of the military and political leadership relating to the security problems which Israel faced in the four-year period preceding the outbreak of war. The answer may lie in the built-in tension between the military and political echelons in crisis situations. In the absence of effective political alternatives for dealing with these situations, a government has no choice but to rely on the army and the influence of the latter increases. The aggressively oriented military leaders may then exert pressure on the political leadership to approve military measures or expand military action beyond the limits intended by the civilian decision-makers. This study will attempt to show that this was in fact the case.

This study attempts to cast new light, from the Israeli angle, on the historical process which led to the Six Day War. No previous study has penetrated the round-table discussions of the IDF general staff or the government sessions held during May and June 1967. The intention is not to provide a revised version of the Six Day War events or to refute known historical facts, but rather to illuminate events from a new angle and, hopefully, to offer a richer perspective and better understanding of the historical process. The book surveys the period between Israel's founding-father David Ben-Gurion's final resignation in June 1963 and the outbreak of war on 5 June 1967.

The Arab states

In the four years leading up to the Six Day War, Nasser's star was on the wane. The original aim of Nasserism, which won its place in the international arena from 1955 under Nasser's charismatic leadership, was to respond to the challenges and dilemmas facing the Arab world in its confrontation with the superior power of the West. As a messianic movement, non-religious but with Islamic contents and symbols, Nasserism held out the promise of salvation through an all-embracing revolution which would produce a new Arab society and a new Arab individual. Nasser set the goals of his country and the entire Arab world far beyond the dispute with Israel.

Consequently, and in light of the lessons of the Sinai Campaign, Nasser suspended the active conflict with Israel after the Sinai Campaign, and ordered the total cessation of guerrilla activities. While he never abandoned his commitment towards the Palestinians, he deferred implementation to the distant time when the Arab world would unite, undergo a social and technological revolution, and prepare the political and military instruments which would ensure Arab victory.

Two obstacles to the achievement of Nasser's aims vis-à-vis Israel were Syria, which seceded in 1961 from the union with Egypt and demanded war immediately, and Palestinian elements, which, inspired by the struggle and success of the FLN in Algeria, began to rally for guerrilla warfare against Israel.

But above all, Nasser's plans were frustrated by the waning of his personal influence and of the messianic fervour of Nasserism in the Arab world. His response to the dissolution of the union with Syria was radicalization of Egypt's internal and external policies, which entailed intervention in the Yemen war and in the internal affairs of other Arab states. From 1962 on, the Nasserist movement was at a standstill and rhetoric could no longer conceal failure. The impressive progress in economic development at the beginning of the 1960 to 1965 five-year plan had ceased. The slowdown of agricultural progress, the vast investments in military might and the elephantine bureaucracy were all sources of internal difficulties. Thanks to Nasser's policy of 'positive neutrality', aimed at exploiting rivalries between the Great Powers for Egypt's benefit, the Soviet Union had succeeded in its efforts to infiltrate the region. When President Lyndon Johnson expressed US censure of Nasser's strategies by halting the large-scale dispatch of surplus foodstuffs to Egypt, the latter's dependence on the Soviet Union increased.[2]

A different reason for Nasser's troubles was his position as one of the leading figures of the declining non-aligned bloc of nations, which from the outset was less powerful than it appeared. Lacking real power and a firm social and economic infrastructure, stability and modern technology, it could not consolidate its status. In 1964 to 1966 the bloc also suffered the loss of some of its prominent leaders, through the death of Jawaharlal Nehru of India and the overthrow of Ahmed Sukarno in Indonesia, Kwame Nkrumah in Ghana and Ahmed ben-Bella in Algeria.

The dispatch of a large Egyptian force to Yemen in 1962 with the aim of extending Egyptian hegemony to the oil-rich Persian Gulf also entrapped Nasser. By 1967 he was dragged deeper and deeper into the Yemeni mud. King Faisal of Saudi Arabia established a front of conservative pro-Western states to check Nasserism. The rivalry between the Powers in the region was related to the polarity between the revolutionary and conservative Arab regimes, and Egypt–US relations were further strained.

By spring 1967 Nasser's situation was considered desperate.[3] It was undoubtedly this predicament which impelled him to adopt new measures to rehabilitate his standing and leadership in the Arab world by compelling even his sworn adversaries to rally behind him. The only issue on which there was an ostensible pan-Arab consensus was the dispute with Israel. The Soviet Union, fearful for its foothold in Syria, served as the catalyst.

Did Nasser intend to instigate an armed conflict with Israel when he moved his forces into Sinai? It is generally agreed that he was borne on the swift current of events he precipitated and the fervour he roused, and that Israel was faced with a grave dilemma – capitulation or war? The other Arab states, both conservative and revolutionary, were taken totally by surprise but hastened to rally to the Egyptian standard, some eagerly and others having no alternative. The dynamics of the situation – the mass psychosis, concentration of forces and Egyptian blockage of the Tiran Straits – rendered war inevitable. Israel, haunted by Holocaust memories, gripped with existential panic and a sense of total isolation, felt forced to deal the first blow.

The Powers and the UN

The rivalry between the Great Powers played a vital part in the evolution of the Arab–Israel conflict, and it has been claimed that the 1967 war was the outcome of power struggles within the Kremlin. While the United States and the USSR were indeed battling for influence, it is not likely that they wanted to fan the flames since they usually directed their efforts at avoidance of direct confrontation. This was also the view of the Israeli Intelligence bodies at the time. It is, however, true that the conflicting interests and mutual suspicion of the Great Powers and their political and military support for the two sides complicated the situation and influenced decision-making. While the attitude of the United States towards Israel was complex, because of Washington's relations with other countries of the region, the policy of the Soviet Union was consistently one-sided, highly critical of and hostile towards Israel.[4]

The UN played a modest role in the evolution of the conflict. The UN Truce Supervision Observers' force on the Israel–Syrian border had little impact on events. The UN Emergency Force in Sinai was relieved of its duties on the Israel–Egyptian border due to a hasty decision by the UN secretary-general at a time when its presence was vital. Nasser's proclamation of the Blocking of the Tiran Straits while the UN secretary-general was on his way to Cairo served to demonstrate the limited impact of the international body on peace-keeping.[5]

Documentation

This study is based on primary source material which has not previously been utilized for historical research purposes. The main sources are the files of the IDF's History Department, General Staff protocols and discussions of senior forums. They have been supplemented by secondary, non-confidential material: press reports, minutes of seminars and personal interviews. I believe that the weekly sessions of the IDF's General Staff forum provide the most accurate picture of the evolving situation, the Intelligence assessments and the general mood of the senior command. They also reflect the attitude of the General Staff towards the government and the differences of opinion between them. It is important to note that the Prime Minister and Minister of Defence attended some of the more important meetings of the General Staff.

It should be noted that, due to limitations in the documentation at my disposal, the first half of the book focuses mainly on the military, while the standpoint of the politicians is reflected in the military documentation or in the external and secondary sources. The second half, however, which deals with the May–June 1967 crisis, is based on an abundance of primary sources relating both to the General Staff and the government, and offers a more balanced picture.

A semantic comment

While I deal in the wider sense with military–civil relations against the background of the security issues of the time, and the main references are to the General Staff and the government, this should be taken in most cases as relating to more limited groups: the Chief of Staff, and Chiefs of Intelligence and Operations versus the Ministerial Committee on Security Affairs. In many cases, the protagonists are the Chief of Staff and the Prime Minister and Minister of Defence.

Acknowledgements

The English version of this book, whose Hebrew edition was issued in 2004 by Ma'arakhot-Misrad Ha-Bitahon, is appearing with the generous aid of the Ashkelon Academic College. I owe a debt of gratitude to the President of the College Professor Moshe Mani, the Vice-President for Academic Affairs Professor Shimon Sharvit, the Director-General Adv. Pinhas Haliwa, the Head of Academic Administration Mr Zeev Vadas and the Head of the Political Science Department Dr Shmuel Tzabag. I would also like to express my appreciation to my teachers and colleagues at the Hebrew University of Jerusalem, and in particular Professor Uri Bialer, who supervised my Ph.D. thesis, and Professor Gideon Shimoni, Professor Benjamin Kedar and Professor Allon Kadish. My thanks also to my good friends Professor Avner Cohen, Dr Moti Golani, Dr Isabella Ginor and Gideon Remez for their recommendations and encouragement.

The research which generated this book required access to documents which had not yet been opened to the public, many of them classified, in army, state and private archives. I would like to note in particular the assistance extended to me by the staff of the IDF History Department and the Air Force History Branch, and the generosity of Miriam Eshkol, widow of Prime Minister Levi Eshkol, who placed his rich private archive at my disposal. All photographs included in this book were purchased from the Israeli Government Press Office.

The translation was carried out by Chaya Galai, who, in her skill, insight and experience, provided me with helpful advice and illuminating comments.

To the editor of the series, Professor Barry Rubin, I owe my contacts with Routledge. His accessibility whenever I communicated with him, his rapid reactions, efficient treatment, wise guidance and important advice, helped to remove various obstacles and errors, and contributed to the quality of the book. Many thanks also to my good friend Uri Maydan for his great technical help.

And above all, my love and gratitude go out to my wife Shuli and my children Einat, Ittai and Orit, for their support and faith in me all along the way.

Introduction

The crushing of the two Judaean revolts against the Romans, in the first and second centuries CE, marked the end of Jewish military efforts for nearly two millennia. When the first uprising (66–70 CE) concluded in catastrophic defeat and the destruction of Herod's Temple in Jerusalem, the last of the Jewish zealots, led by Elazar Ben Yair, took refuge at Masada on the Dead Sea shore and, after a lengthy siege, chose to commit suicide with their families rather than fall into enemy hands. The outcome of the second revolt (131–135 CE), led by Bar Kochba, was even more calamitous; the Jewish community was annihilated in a bloodbath and the Romans expunged even the name of Judaea, renaming the province Palestina (after the Philistines who had lived on the coast between Gaza and Ashdod about a millennium earlier). Jerusalem became the Roman city of Ilia Capitolina and a shrine for Jupiter was built on Temple Mount.

As a result of these traumatic events, the central trend in Jewish thought was marked by a strong aversion to military activity. Ancient military leaders, such as the Hasmoneans who triumphed over the Selucid forces and won independence or leaders of the abortive uprisings against the Romans, were not glorified in the Holy Scriptures, the Mishnah and the Talmud, and throughout the centuries-long exile, the Jewish dream of the return to their homeland 'Eretz Israel', expressed in prayer and literature, was devoid of military implications. It was to be achieved by divine intervention when the Messiah arrived.

The Zionist movement emerged at the end of the nineteenth century in the era of nascent nationalism. The vision of establishing a Jewish state in Eretz Israel, as expounded by its founder Theodore Herzl, also lacked all military implications. The early Zionists believed, naively, that the nations of the world would grant the Jews a 'charter' over their promised land, and that the Arab inhabitants of the country would welcome the Jews with open arms for bringing them the message of progress.[1] Herzl failed in his efforts to gain the charter, but after his death another Zionist leader, Chaim Weizmann, won a guarantee from the British government (The Balfour Declaration of 2 November 1917) that it would 'view with favour' the establishment of a national home for the Jewish people in Palestine, then still partly under Ottoman rule. During the First World War, Jewish volunteer battalions were established in the British army, one of which took part in the occupation of the country. These units, however, were disbanded soon after the war. In 1922 the League of Nations entrusted the mandate over Palestine to Great Britain.

The illusion that the Palestinians would calmly accept the transformation of their country into a national home for the Jewish people was soon dispelled by violent anti-Jewish riots which occurred in 1920, 1921 and 1929. They culminated in the Arab revolt of 1936 to 1939, which erupted against the background of a wave of Jewish immigration from Eastern Europe and especially Germany, in the wake of Hitler's rise to power. In late 1920, in response to Arab violence, the Jewish community (the Yishuv) established the semi-clandestine Haganah defence organization, which became subject to the authority of the Zionist leadership. In 1931 the Hagana ranks were split when a group – which later took the name Irgun Zvai Leumi (National Military Organization) and was associated with the opposition Revisionist Party – seceded in protest against the Haganah's policy of restraint. The Haganah received de facto recognition from the Mandate government and many of its members were recruited into British-run auxiliary police units. Charles Orde Wingate, a young, talented British officer who was an ardent advocate of Zionism, was appointed to train a special unit of young Jewish fighters for action against Arab terror.

In 1939, when war was imminent, the British government, in an effort to win Arab support, published a White Paper which drastically restricted Jewish immigration and proclaimed its intention to establish a state within a decade. There were half a million Jews in Palestine at the time and more than double that number of Arabs. The Jewish leaders were shocked by this volte-face, but when war broke out they felt obliged to cooperate with Britain in the fight against Nazism. Thousands of young Jews from the community (Yishuv) volunteered for service in the British army and towards the end of the war a Jewish Brigade was established within the British army. In 1941, when it was feared that German forces were about to invade the Middle East from the north through the Caucasus and from the south through Egypt, the British helped to establish elite units (the Palmach) within the Haganah to conduct guerrilla warfare against the Germans. Two years later, however, after the battles of Stalingrad and el-Alamein, when fears of a German invasion had faded, the British abandoned the initiative. The Palmach remained operative, funded by the Jewish Agency and kibbutz movement, and became the Haganah's crack force. Its young fighters later rose to senior ranks in the Israel Defence Forces. In 1967 most of the General Staff were graduates of the Palmach.

Wingate's Special Night Squads and the Palmach units represented a new generation of 'sabras' (native-born Jews), with a militant activist approach, reflecting the growing realization that the Zionist movement could not achieve its objectives without resorting to force. The transition within the Zionist movement from a defensive to an offensive ethos was by no means simple and was accompanied by internal conflict and bitter disputes, particularly between the forceful chairman of the Jewish Agency David Ben-Gurion and the ageing president of the World Zionist Organization Chaim Weizmann.

The dispute was resolved after the Second World War when the Labour government in Britain continued to adhere to the 1939 White Paper policy. In the post-Holocaust Jewish community the prevailing mood was militant and a struggle was launched to open the country's gates to mass immigration of refugees from Europe. The Irgun, the Lehi (Lohamei Herut Yisrael – Israel Freedom Fighters), an even more radical organization which seceded from the Irgun, and for a time the Haganah as well, waged a military campaign, which included acts of terror against the British authorities. The moderate Weizmann was deposed from the presidency of the World Zionist movement and Ben-Gurion led the Yishuv in the vital stage of the struggle for statehood.

In 1947 the British government decided – in light of the continuing violence, international pressure on the refugee question and its failure to achieve a compromise between Jews and Arabs – to submit the issue to the UN for resolution. On 29 November 1947, the UN General Assembly passed a resolution partitioning the country into two states – Jewish and Arab – and internationalizing the Jerusalem area. The Palestinians and the Arab states categorically rejected the resolution, and fighting broke out between armed Arab groups, reinforced by volunteers from the neighbouring Arab countries, and the Jewish military organizations. On 14 May 1948, Ben-Gurion proclaimed the establishment of the State of Israel at a session of the National Council, and in response the armed forces of Egypt, Syria, Jordan, Iraq and Lebanon invaded the Jewish state on the following day. The Israel Defence Force was established in the course of the war on the foundations of the Haganah. After bitter fighting, it repelled the invaders while expanding the territory of the Jewish state beyond the borders of the UN partition resolution. During the hostilities, Ben-Gurion forced the Palmach, Etzel and Lehi to disband in order to create a sovereign unified armed force unconditionally subordinate to the civilian authority.

The war ended in 1949 with the signing of armistice agreements between Israel and Egypt, Jordan, Lebanon and Syria. When the war ended, Israel controlled some 75 per cent of the area of the country (as against 55 per cent allocated to the Jewish state by the UN), while the Palestinian state had not come into existence due to Arab opposition. Jordan took over the West Bank, Egypt seized the Gaza Strip, and

Jerusalem was divided between Israel and Jordan. Some 700,000 Palestinian refugees left the State of Israel. After the war, Israel took in an even larger number of Jewish refugees from the Arab countries, but the issue of the Palestinian refugees remained at the core of the Arab–Israel conflict. Infiltration of Palestinians into Israel to perpetrate acts of revenge, sabotage and terror was the main cause of the escalation which led to the 1956 and 1967 wars.

Civil–military relations

A number of researchers have studied the Israeli military, its operations and history.[2] The question of the armed forces' relationship to the civilian leadership is one of particular interest.

The first crisis between the military command and the civilian leadership occurred during the 1948 War of Independence,[3] and, as this book will show, tension broke out again on the eve of the Six Day War. The subordination of the army to the political leadership was never questioned at any stage, but as early as the 1950s the army was carrying out reprisal operations on a scope beyond that approved by the government.

As the security situation deteriorated between 1963 and 1967, the gap between the aspirations of the army and the intentions of the civilian leadership widened. The IDF wanted maximum freedom of action in order to solve Israel's security problems in its own way and there were occasions when it permitted itself to interpret the wishes of the political echelons in a liberal operational fashion. In other words, the senior command believed that their task was to influence government policy and guide the civilian authorities into more activist and offensive paths of action. Years later, this approach was expressed unequivocally by a then member of the General Staff General Ariel Sharon, in an interview marking the thirtieth anniversary of the Six Day War:

> In a democracy there is a division of functions: the politicians examine all the options while the role of the army is to present the military option.... In general, one cannot expect the politicians to be more daring than the military. The latter must stamp their feet, and the politicians must be aware of the full range of political options.[4]

In the 1950s, it was this attitude which impelled the Chief of Staff, Major-General Moshe Dayan, to exert pressure on Prime Minister and Minister of Defence David Ben-Gurion to launch a pre-emptive strike against Egypt. Dayan believed that he bore equal responsibility with the politicians for national security and that it was incumbent on him to guide the country's political leaders towards the right policy as he perceived it. This situation led to the 1956 Sinai Campaign. In 1967 as well, though under entirely different circumstances, the army did not stand by idly waiting for the government to decide but played an active part and brought heavy pressure to bear in favour of a pre-emptive strike.[5]

Security theory and security policy

Israel's security theory is 'the basic and constant national programme of preparedness, deployment and war in defence of the national existence of the State of Israel'.[6] In the period under discussion, this was based on the conviction that the state faced an existential threat, under conditions of critical inferiority as regards quantity, territory and resources, and that the conflict could not be resolved by political or military means. This meant that the Israeli economy and infrastructure needed to be ready to confront emergencies and the majority of the national manpower needed to be trained and prepared for security tasks. The buildup of military force was mainly aimed at preparing a trained striking force, well equipped and infused with fighting spirit, capable of conducting decisive offensive warfare on enemy soil, with military superiority based on the quality of the fighting men, swift movement and concentrated effort.

Security policy implies 'the translation of security theory into everyday language' within the framework of dynamic political and military developments and processes, as demanded by national needs. If indeed, as Major-General Israel Tal claims, Israel's security theory may be regarded as 'one of the pinnacles of military thinking',[7] the same cannot be said of its security policy. In the period under consideration, it did not achieve its supreme aim – deterrence and prevention of war – and in the final analysis it expedited the outbreak of hostilities. As we shall see, the military leadership contributed to the failure of security policy, and Chief of Staff Yitzhak Rabin accepted responsibility for this failure.

The Israeli government was unanimous in its desire to maintain the status quo, but was not of one mind on other issues. Prime Minister and Minister of Defence Levi Eshkol was torn between the dovish majority in his government – including most of the Mapai (moderate socialist Israel Workers Party) ministers, and the representatives of the National Religious Party, Mapam (radical socialist) Party and the Independent Liberals – and the hawkish minority, consisting mainly of the left-wing Ahdut Haavoda ministers. The influence of the activist minority was enhanced by the military background and experience of the Ahdut Haavoda ministers Yigal Allon, Yisrael Galili and Moshe Carmel. These three, and Allon and Carmel in particular, concurred entirely with the assessments provided by Rabin, who was now a permanent participant in government meetings dealing with security.

Existential dread – and public faith in the army

The army's major influence on security policy stemmed, first and foremost, from the existential dread which was a basic component of the Israeli collective consciousness. Borne out of the historical experiences of the Jewish people, the recent trauma of the Holocaust, fresh memories of the 1948 Arab invasion and constant awareness of the proximity of a hostile border – this dread fluctuated in intensity but never vanished. It was particularly acute in the critical stages of the War of Independence and intensified again as a result of the 1955 'Czech arm deal' between the Soviet Union and Egypt and the deterioration of the security situation on the borders. It abated after the Sinai Campaign and rose to new heights on the eve of the Six Day War.[8]

In early June 1967 the American administration was aware of Israel's fears. In a missive to US ambassadors in the Arab states, Secretary of State Dean Rusk noted that the United States could not order Israel not to fight and stressed succinctly the psychological aspects of the situation: 'The "Holy War" psychology of the Arab world is matched by the apocalyptic psychology within Israel.'[9]

Israel's conduct before the Six Day War cannot be comprehended without understanding that this dread was a central factor in the thinking of the policy-makers[10] and in the consolidation of the standing of the army in society and the shaping of its objectives and actions. At the basis of Israel's security policy lay a dread of annihilation which was shared by many military men.[11] They feared catastrophic losses (the accepted estimate was 10,000 dead, and one source anticipated 100,000![12]), and Egyptian deployment of poison gas (as had occurred in Yemen)[13] or some secret weapon.[14] The government eventually accepted the army's view that failure to launch a pre-emptive attack would create an existential threat graver than that entailed in launching a strike.

Existential dread was also one of the major reasons for the 'sanctification' of the IDF, perceived as a value in its own right. The 'politicidal' attitude of the Arabs towards Israel and their incessant belligerent proclamations of intent to annihilate the 'Zionist entity' touched a sensitive nerve in Israeli society. Any item of information about the equipping of Arab armies with Soviet weaponry or some new military development shook Israeli nerves (ground-to-ground missiles or chemical and biological weapons in Egypt with the aid of German scientists evoked a particularly hysterical reaction in Israel). Consequently, Israeli society chose to place its trust totally in the IDF to the point where it was almost beyond and above criticism of any kind. The army, for its part, internalized these expectations and responded to them, and regarded itself as committed to and capable of providing a military solution to every problem.

In a 1997 interview, Ariel Sharon drew a critical comparison between the views of the senior command in 1967 and the situation three decades later, when senior officers conceded that the solution to terror was political and not military.

> 'When I served in the army', he declared, 'I don't recall a single instance when the commanding officer said that the only possible solution to the mission entrusted to him was political rather than military. A commander who made such a statement in Ben-Gurion's day would have been thrown out of the army in an instant'.[15]

The total confidence in the armed forces can also explain the generous allocation of national resources for security purposes[16] even – and perhaps in particular – by a government as moderate as that headed by Levi Eshkol. The majority of the ministers was innocent of any military pattern of thinking or desire to change the political and territorial status quo by force, and were anxious to maintain the relative calm and not to disturb the equilibrium. However, they gave the senior command whatever it wanted in order to maintain security and prevent hostilities. On the eve of the Six Day War, in the course of an acrimonious confrontation with several generals who demanded an immediate order to go to war, Eshkol, who wanted time for political manoeuvring and stressed the need for patience, addressed them bluntly:

> You need more weapons? OK. You wanted 100 aircraft? You got them. You wanted tanks. You got them so that we can win if it becomes necessary. You didn't get all that so that we could get up one day and say: 'Now we can destroy the Egyptian army – and we'll do it'.... Deterrence doesn't mean that one has to act.... I believe that deterrent force should be capable of waiting and enabling exploration of all other possibilities.... This may irritate the generals, who have been trained all their lives for attack, for war, but we [the government] talked of deterrence [to prevent war].... Are we to live on our swords all our lives'!?[17]

The government's approach to security policy during this period was basically preventive,[18] aimed at averting the subverting of Israel's security and vital interests and maintaining effective deterrent power in order to forestall war. This approach was one of the main reasons why civilian supervision of the army was so ineffective, in particular as regards operational planning. Since the army perceived itself as answerable to the government and accepted supreme civilian authority, the government did not deem it necessary to issue directives to the army and to define, at the strategic level, the objectives of the war (which in any case was to be avoided). Thus, in effect, strategic and operative planning was left entirely in the hands of the army. Even when war was imminent and the army urged that a pre-emptive attack be launched, neither the government nor the Ministerial Committee on Security held a single strategic debate on the objectives of the war or perused the army's operative plans.

Ben-Gurion vs. Eshkol; Eshkol vs. Rabin

It was Ben-Gurion who determined the pattern of relationships between the army and the defence establishment on one hand and the civilian political establishment on the other. His proclaimed objective, as noted above, was to detach the army from politics and to turn it into the executive arm, under the exclusive authority of the government as wielded by the Minister of Defence. Ben-Gurion's stamp on the security establishment and his identification with the IDF created a unique link between himself and the army in the public consciousness, and he was perceived as its father-figure. His abrupt resignation (in June 1963; see below) evoked considerable unease in the army and certain senior officers even appealed to him emotionally to change his mind.[19]

However, Eshkol's subsequent entry into the Ministry of Defence was smooth. He was not revolutionary by nature and acted with circumspection. At first, he consulted Ben-Gurion on every important issue – senior army appointments, for example.[20] The General Staff soon came to the conclusion that it would be easier to work with Eshkol, whose style was open and flexible, than with the authoritative Ben-Gurion. The army now had direct and frequent access to government institutions.

The Chief of Staff, and often the heads of Intelligence and Operations as well, became regular participants in sessions of the Ministerial Committee on Defence and sometimes attended government sessions as well. The Knesset's Foreign Affairs and Security Committee began to play an effective role and the inner circle of those informed on security matters widened. Important security issues were discussed by Mapai's ministerial forum (Sareinu) and the political council of the Alignment (Maarach) – established in 1964 as an amalgamation of Mapai and Ahdut Haavoda.[21]

In the present context, it is important to note that Eshkol's easygoing style enabled the IDF to extend its influence, with clear operative implications. The CO of the IAF (Israel Air Force), for example, was amazed at the ease with which Eshkol approved photo reconnaissance flights, unlike Ben-Gurion.[22] This situation enhanced Rabin's position and influence on matters pertaining to security policy, and had a positive impact on his relations with the Minister of Defence and with the government.

This was not the first time that a Chief of Staff had been on close terms with the minister; Dayan probably wielded stronger influence over Ben-Gurion than did Rabin over Eshkol.[23] However, Rabin's relations with the Prime Minister set a precedent. Eshkol bowed to Rabin on security issues and allowed him direct and constant access to the government, to the point where the latter gradually gained quasi-ministerial status[24] and became a popular and 'political' figure, overshadowing Eshkol to a degree which the latter resented.[25] On one occasion (see below), Eshkol reprimanded Rabin for exceeding his authority, and, some sources claim, even contemplated deposing him.[26]

As Minister of Defence, Eshkol played the major role in drawing up the security budget, and was involved in all decisions regarding security policy and the security establishment, arms purchases and weapon developments. His greatest achievement was gaining access to the American arms market. 'If he had done this one thing alone, it would have sufficed to record his name in golden letters in the pages of Israel's history', wrote Rabin.[27] He was particularly concerned with the army's need for equipment, spare parts and ammunition reserves.[28] He was also involved in professional military matters. Rabin always reported to him in minute detail, and Eshkol questioned him closely and on occasion rejected his recommendations. No military operation was ever carried out without his knowledge and approval. Rabin, despite the special status he enjoyed, did not act independently.

However, it is questionable whether Eshkol in fact was endowed with independent judgement and a comprehensive view of the military setup and the doctrine and objectives of warfare. As far as the strategic dimension, tactical calculations and operative issues were concerned, he acted on the basis of intuition and common sense but, since he lacked professional know-how and advisers, he was dependent on Rabin.

This dependence, coupled with Eshkol's easygoing nature, predilection for compromise and his apologetic admission of his lack of military know-how, left Rabin a wide scope for expressing his views. He enjoyed a high-profile media presence and was 'amazingly popular', evoking Eshkol's envy. His evident authority undermined Eshkol's standing and created the impression of weakness.[29] Nadav Safran believes that the crisis of confidence in Eshkol stemmed in part from his collaboration with the army, which was so close that several of his ministers began to think that he had waived his own independent judgement on security matters.[30]

Viewing matters from within, Israel Tal claims that the standing of the Minister of Defence weakened after Ben-Gurion's departure not only because his forceful personality was lacking, but also due to basic structural changes. Ben-Gurion, writes Tal, 'commanded the IDF in the name of the Government', the Chief of Staff of the IDF functioned as the head of his staff, and the entire General Staff was at the disposal of the minister. After Ben-Gurion's departure, the division heads (with the exception of the Intelligence chief) ceased to play this role and the minister was neutralized and became dependent on the Chief of Staff, lacking his own professional instruments for decision-making.[31]

Eshkol was also weakened by his gradually evolving rancorous dispute with Ben-Gurion, who hurled serious accusations at him, claiming he was totally unfit for his position. The rivalry between them, in which the press played an active and enthusiastic part, also had a detrimental effect on Ben-Gurion's standing,[32] and in 1965 led to a split in Mapai and the establishment of the Rafi (Israel's Workers List) Party, headed by Ben-Gurion. The continuous censure of Eshkol by Ben-Gurion and his associates in Rafi, particularly Shimon Peres, focused mainly on security matters. The most damaging accusation levelled by Ben-Gurion was related vaguely to some mysterious 'security blunder'.[33] Safran claims that the verbal attacks impelled Eshkol to move to the other extreme and yield excessively to the demands of the military.[34]

The General Staff vs. the government

Under Major-Generals Zvi Zur (up until December 1963) and Yitzhak Rabin (up until the Six Day War), the General Staff focused on building up military might and preparing for war, evolving a strategic theory and planning. The government, on the other hand, was preoccupied with political, economic and social problems. Security was not necessarily the main priority, at least as long as calm prevailed.[35]

The crisis of confidence between the General Staff and the government reached its peak shortly before the Six Day War, but tensions existed between them throughout the period, as government policy appeared to the senior command to be increasingly restrictive.[36] Israel's main security problem was the guerrilla activity of Palestinian terror units, most of them affiliated to Fatah, which began to operate in January 1965. At first, the army denoted these activities 'harassment' and subsequently began to refer to them as 'hostile terrorist activity'. The IDF would have preferred to take the offensive while the government, fearing escalation, preferred to invest in defence. Senior officers abhorred the idea of defensive action, and tried to persuade the government that this strategy was ineffective. They believed, erroneously as it turned out, that offensive action would not necessarily lead to escalation.

There were considerable differences between the civil and military leaders, which help explain their disparate standpoints. The average age of Eshkol's government was sixty-four, of the senior command, forty-three. They differed, too, in background, origin, experience, mentality and language. Almost all the ministers had been born outside Israel and, although they had been living in the country for decades, their formative years had been passed abroad. As noted, only two of them – Yigal Allon (the only native-born Israeli) and Moshe Carmel – had military experience. The views they advocated on security accorded with their background. Most members of the government, with the exception of the Ahdut Haavoda ministers, were veteran politicians who had been engaged for many years in Zionist and party activity, remote from military experience.

Most of the General Staff, on the other hand, were native-born and veterans of the Palmach. They represented the second generation, the sons: the transition to a Zionism based on the realization that its aims could not be achieved without an armed struggle, and the transition from a defensive ethos to an offensive ethos.[37] Interestingly enough, at General Staff meetings the government ministers were often referred to collectively as 'the Jews'.

It is not surprising, therefore, that when the crisis worsened and tensions reached new heights, the generals viewed those ministers who opposed war as elderly, confused and timid nuisances (General Rehavam Ze'evi referred to them collectively as 'all kinds of Wahrhaftigs', after a particular timid minister[38]), whose inability to take decisions was endangering the country. And yet, although they brought heavy pressure to bear on the government, the generals did not force it to decide on war. It was rather the failure of political efforts, together with the aggravation of the objective threat and

Table 1 Composition of the Israeli government – 1967

Name	Party	Portfolio	Year of birth	Country of origin
Levi Eshkol*	Mapai	PM and Minister of Defence	1895	Ukraine
Pinhas Sapir*	Mapai	Finance	1909	Poland
Abba Eban*	Mapai	Foreign Affairs	1915	South Africa
Zalman Aranne*	Mapai	Education	1899	Russia
Yisrael Galili*	Ahdut ha-Avodah	Without portfolio	1911	Poland
Moshe Haim Shapira*	Nat. Religious Party	Interior	1902	Poland
Yaakov Shimshon Shapira*	Mapai	Justice	1902	Russia
Yigal Allon*+	Ahdut ha-Avodah	Labour	1918	Native born
Zerah Wahrhaftig*	Nat. Religious Party	Religious Affairs	1896	Poland
Moshe Kol*	Indep. Liberals	Tourism	1911	Poland
Yisrael Barzilai*	Mapam	Health	1913	Poland
Eliyahu Sasson*	Mapai	Police	1902	Syria
Haim Gvati	Mapai	Agriculture	1901	Poland
Yisrael Yeshayahu	Mapai	Postal Communications	1910	Yemen
Moshe Carmel	Ahdut ha-Avodah	Transport	1911	Poland
Yosef Burg	Nat. Religious Party	Welfare	1909	Germany
Mordechai Bentov	Mapam	Development	1900	Poland
Zeev Sherf	Mapai	Trade and Industry	1906	Poland

Notes
* Member Ministerial Committee on Security
+ Ex-Palmach
Average age: 63.9
Native born: 1
Born abroad: 17

Table 2 Composition of the IDF General Staff – 1967

Yitzhak Rabin+	Chief of Staff	1922	Native born
Haim Barlev+	Deputy Chief of Staff	1924	Austria
Ezer Weizman	Chief Operations Branch	1924	Native born
Aharon Yariv	Chief Intelligence Branch	1920	Russia
Shmuel Eyal	Chief Manpower Branch	1922	Russia
Mattatyahu Peled+	Chief Q Branch	1923	Native born
David Elazar+	CO Northern Command	1925	Yugoslavia
Uzi Narkis+	CO Central Command	1925	Native born
Yeshayahu Gavish+	CO Northern Command	1925	Native born
Yisrael Tal	CO Armoured Corps	1924	Native born
Ariel Sharon	Head Training Dept	1928	Native born
Rehavam Ze'evi+	Asst. Chief Operations	1926	Native born
Mordechai Hod+	CO IAF	1926	Native born
Shlomo Erel	CO Navy	1920	Poland
Elad Peled+	CO National Defence College	1927	Native born
Yitzhak Hofi+	Head Operations Dept	1927	Native born
Yaakov Hefetz+	Financial adviser	1923	Native born
Amos Horev	Deputy Chief Scientist, Ministry of Defence	1924	Native born

Notes
+ Ex-Palmach
Average age: 42.8
Native born: 13
Born abroad: 5

the subjective dread of that threat, which tipped the balance and left the government no alternative but to place its trust in the army.[39]

Paradoxically, the army's prestige was undermined by the crisis and its pressure on the government became less effective. Not only were most of the ministers anxious to avoid war at any cost, but the senior command had lost face in the eyes of the ministers due to the brewing crisis. Hence, at this critical time, a degree of equilibrium was restored to IDF–government relations.

A note on Minister of Defence Moshe Dayan

Four days before war broke out, Eshkol gave up the defence portfolio and handed it over to Moshe Dayan, whose military background transformed the pattern of civilian supervision and control of the army which had existed under Eshkol. Dayan, like Allon, was a sabra, member of the second generation, and a standard-bearer of the offensive 'ethos of the fighter' as Anita Shapira calls it. His appointment on 1 June 1967 (under circumstances which will be detailed below), which received massive public backing, was not a simple administrative move, but rather the victory of the military concept over the civilian. Only a day after Dayan's appointment, it was clear to Eshkol that Israel was going to war.[40]

Another interesting point: three days before the crisis erupted, *Maariv*, the Israeli newspaper with the widest circulation, published a lengthy article by Yosef Lapid under the heading: 'Is there a danger that the IDF will seize power?' Lapid listed a number of important arguments against such an eventuality, which together constituted a guarantee that democratic rule would endure. He noted, however, several undesirable phenomena: the senior officer level functioned like an exclusive 'sect'; Ben-Gurion had endowed the IDF with an 'aura of sanctity'; there was insufficient public criticism of the army. A very senior officer, when asked by Lapid whether the IDF might in fact attempt to take over, replied that any fool who tried would not find anyone to follow him. Lapid's article was a protest against the idealized image of the IDF in contrast to the impotent and ineffectual image attributed to the government and the Knesset. He feared that the absence of criticism could endanger democracy.[41]

A few days later the senior command, the apple of Israel's eye, found itself in direct conflict with a confused government which seemed to have lost the confidence of the public, facing what appeared to be a threat to national survival. The army, nonetheless, did not adopt undemocratic measures and it was the government which eventually took the decision to go to war. In hindsight it was evident that the hesitations and manoeuvres of the government at the time were grounded on greater political wisdom than the decisive approach of the military command.

Chapter 1

Personnel changes in the defence establishment

David Ben-Gurion's last government, in which he again served as Prime Minister and Minister of Defence, was presented to the Knesset and given a vote of confidence on 2 November 1961. It remained in power for less than twenty months until his resignation on 16 June 1963.[1]

Ben-Gurion's final term of office in the Ministry of Defence was a period of relative calm where current security was concerned, but which towards its end was marked by three affairs related to basic security issues, which were apparently among the reasons for his decision to resign.

The first was the affair of the Egyptian missiles developed with the aid of German scientists. Ben-Gurion's advocacy of a policy of restraint, which stemmed from his fear of a rift in Israeli–German relations, was fiercely opposed by Isser Harel, who headed the Mossad. Harel resigned, evoking public and political uproar.[2]

The second affair was the short-lived tripartite Union, which was proclaimed in April 1963 but was never really formed, between Egypt, Iraq and Syria.[3] It shocked Ben-Gurion, who subsequently launched a wide-ranging and somewhat embarrassing correspondence with a large number of international leaders on this matter.[4]

The third affair was President John Kennedy's emphatic demand for regular supervision and control of the atomic reactor at Dimona.[5] Relations with the United States were strained further by initiatives of the US administration aimed at finding a solution to the Palestinian refugee problem.[6] In addition, Ben-Gurion attempted, without success, to schedule a meeting with Egyptian President Gamal Abdel Nasser, in the hope of arriving at a political settlement.[7]

Ben-Gurion resigns and is succeeded by Eshkol

In spring 1963, in light of the upheavals in the Kingdom of Jordan in favour of joining the tripartite Arab Union, and the fear of a pro-Nasserite coup there, the IDF began to ready itself for the eventuality of intervention.[8] Ben-Gurion was apprehensive at the possibility, which conflicted with his desire to stabilize Israel's security on the basis of the status quo, and to suspend the conflict with the Arabs, as long as it seemed insoluble, through conventional and non-conventional deterrent measures. The threat to the Jordanian regime was the central theme in Ben-Gurion's letters to President Kennedy and other world leaders. The stabilization of the Jordanian situation and the disintegration of the Egyptian–Syrian–Iraqi Union restored relative calm at the beginning of the summer, and fears of an imminent unification of the Arab world under Nasserist hegemony were dispelled. However, the affair of the German scientists continued to evoke anxiety in Israel and behind the scenes it was estimated that a very serious crisis was brewing in relations with the United States due to US opposition to the dissemination of nuclear weapons and Kennedy's demand for effective supervision of the Dimona reactor. Ben-Gurion's counter-demand for formal and not merely declarative American guarantees of Israel's security – to include joint operative planning and supply of weapons systems – was rejected by the US administration.[9] It was under these circumstances that Ben-Gurion tendered his resignation.

Levi Eshkol, Finance Minister and one of the most prominent figures in the ruling Mapai Party, was a natural and undisputed choice as Ben-Gurion's successor as Prime Minister, but this was not the case where the Ministry of Defence was concerned. Although he had served as Deputy Minister of Defence responsible for financial matters, equipment and weapons purchase, Eshkol was regarded by Ben-Gurion's 'young guard' as unfitted for the task. They preferred to separate the two posts and entrust the defence portfolio to someone of more suitable background from the Ben-Gurionist school of thought, such as Moshe Dayan or Shimon Peres. Their criticism of Eshkol's appointment was scathing and offensive.[10]

Eshkol described his government as 'a continuing Government' and in his first few months in office he proceeded with circumspection under the long shadow of his predecessor. Changes were introduced later and gradually as Eshkol increasingly consolidated his position. In 1964, his independent political moves led to a confrontation with Ben-Gurion, which culminated a year later in a split within Mapai and the establishment of the Rafi Party. In the defence sphere as well, Eshkol succeeded in freeing himself from the shadow of the 'old man'. His 'declaration of independence' was his successful visit to the United States in 1964 and his achievements there, his decision to abandon Ben-Gurion's strategy and utilize the IAF in routine operations, and the success of his defence policy during the 1965 water dispute (see below). Ben-Gurion's 'young guard', Minister of Agriculture Moshe Dayan and Deputy Minister of Defence Shimon Peres, resigned in November 1964 and May 1965 respectively. Peres' resignation and the appointment of Zvi Dinstein as his successor led to organizational changes in the defence establishment.[11]

The impact of all these changes was gradually felt by the IDF as well. Eshkol, as noted above, was an easygoing minister, more responsive than his predecessor to military initiatives. The Chief of Staff Zvi Zur did not alter his mode of operation towards the political establishment. His successor (from January 1964), Yitzhak Rabin, soon found that Eshkol was giving him unprecedented free rein.

Eshkol and the General Staff – first encounters

On 24 June 1963, eight days after Ben-Gurion's resignation, Eshkol presented his government to the Knesset. In his address to the plenum, he assured them that the new government would strive for peace and respect the independence and territorial integrity of all the countries of the region. The Arab states, their internal disputes notwithstanding, he declared, were united in their hostility towards Israel and desire to annihilate it. He demanded that the Great Powers provide assurances that the armament balance would not be disturbed to Israel's detriment, and added: 'We will act for constant improvement of the professional, pioneering and moral standards of the IDF.... We will preserve the democratic nature of the IDF.'[12]

In July 1963 the General Staff invited Eshkol to a series of three comprehensive and illuminating staff meetings,[13] at which the Chief of Staff and several generals not only surveyed the overall military picture but also expounded their views on issues beyond the military sphere, and in particular the question of Israel's borders. The discrepancy between the civil approach, based on preservation of the status quo, and the military approach, was immediately evident. The generals believed that a unique opportunity had opened up, which had not existed in Ben-Gurion's day,[14] namely to realize their secret territorial aspirations. It was a clear attempt to influence the security policies of the new premier, so as to gain more freedom for the achievement of military objectives. Eshkol, for his part, showed no enthusiasm for border adjustments, apart from the desire to include the Lebanese Litani River waters within Israeli territory.[15]

Rabin, the Deputy Chief of Staff, who opened the proceedings, apologized for 'invading' the political sphere. He explained that he and his fellow officers were merely voicing their 'thoughts' and that the final decision naturally rested with the elected civil representatives. He declared that when it came to the conventional arms race – both qualitatively and quantitatively – Israel would, in the final analysis, be the loser, but overall, when non-conventional measures were also taken into account, time was on Israel's side. His conclusion was that 'there is no need to expedite matters [and initiate hostilities which will change the strategic balance] due to the assumption that time is against us'. On the other hand,

If we were to conclude that time is not in our favour, we might then decide that it would be to our advantage to bring about such geopolitical changes as would alter the balance of power, which is influenced not only by military, economic and political might but also by borders.

However, Rabin's formula was not as simple as it sounded; it transpired that he did not rule out Israeli military action to adjust the borders, and even considered it desirable, though not essential. He defined the ideal borders as follows: 'The Jordan line, the [Suez] Canal line and the Litani line.' But if Israel has no territorial goals, it would be advisable to build up deterrent power in order to prevent armed hostilities. The IDF, in any event, did not perceive itself merely as a defensive and deterrent force. It was also 'a violent instrument for the achievement of political objectives initiated by the political level, whether destruction of enemy forces or conquest of territory'.

Rabin's phrasing was tortuous but his intention was clear. The IDF did not intend to exert pressure for military action to improve borders, but in the event that such action proved possible – it would be beneficial. In any event, the government should be aware that the army also regarded itself as an instrument for achieving political goals.

The commander of the IAF Ezer Weizman was blunter. 'Whether it fits in with the political approach or not, the IDF should aim to expand the country's borders, for security reasons.' Weizman went on to expound his vision of peace in the region, but added that, if Israel's goal was

a state [within the divinely promised borders] as our forefathers saw it – then it may well be that between the present day and the peace we are all yearning for, there are a few things to be done [in order to expand the borders] because afterwards, when we have peace, we won't be able to do them.[16]

Shimon Peres: 'Today technology has replaced geography'

Deputy Defence Minister Shimon Peres represented a different viewpoint. 'Today technology ... has replaced geography and military thinking,' he said. 'The forces dealing with the atom, electronics, etc. are vehicles which cannot be halted. ... If Israel does not follow this path it will be abandoning its destiny to the unknown.' Peres shared the view expressed by Rabin that in a conventional arms race, Israel would not have the upper hand in the long run. But whereas Rabin considered border changes to be a possible means of maintaining the balance of power, Peres was convinced that it was incumbent on Israel to ground its security on its independent and non-conventional deterrent capacity and to pursue a political path which would facilitate this policy.[17]

Summing up the discussion, Eshkol rejected the views that it was necessary to seize considerable areas of the neighbouring countries. He warned explicitly against 'The thought of a preventive war and border modifications. . . . I don't want to swear that we will never [launch a preventive attack],' he said. 'It may well be that you arrive at such a situation when there is a sword at your throat.' But even so, he argued, they should not rely on the possibility of adjusting borders. Because of his close association with agriculture and the water issue, Eshkol coveted the Litani waters. As for peace, he hinted that it was not the task of the army but the exclusive responsibility of the government 'to turn the world upside down', although 'it may sound quixotic today'.

The General Staff as lobbyists for border expansion

On the face of it, the views expressed by the generals in their meeting with Eshkol bear out the claim that the General Staff functioned as a territorial lobby and that several of the senior officers, who advocated war from the outset, urged the government in May to June 1967 to launch a pre-emptive strike with the intention of expanding Israel's borders.[18]

As we shall see below, the General Staff under the Eshkol government and under Rabin adhered to its offensive doctrine and adopted a more activist stance than the government, the majority of whom favoured a cautious defensive policy. At General Staff meetings, some of the generals supported occupation of the West Bank or part of the Golan Heights and the water sources. This view, however, met with a sober and realistic response, born out of the lesson of the forced withdrawal from all the territory occupied during the 1956 Sinai campaign. 'The problem,' it was argued, 'is not the IDF's ability to conquer territory but the state's ability to hold on to it.'[19] The generals, remembering the trauma of withdrawal in 1957, were well aware that it would be pointless to spill blood for the sake of short-lived territorial gains. For the same reasons, operative planning placed greater emphasis on the need to destroy enemy forces than on the occupation of territory.

Some of the General Staff officers thought that crisis situations should be exploited in order to achieve border adjustments, particularly on the Jordanian front. However, they voiced these views in closed forums, and there was certainly no consensus within the General Staff on this issue; nor was there a 'lobby'. While such aspirations did exist,[20] Rabin, as Chief of Staff, apparently never voiced a demand for territorial modifications. The only occasion on record was the above-mentioned meeting of the General Staff with Eshkol, on 6 July 1963, when Rabin, then Deputy Chief of

Staff, expressed his (qualified) support on principle for the expansion of borders. The General Staff unreservedly accepted the authority of the political level in this period, and there is no indication of pressure on their part for operations aimed at conquering territory.

Notwithstanding, it is a fact that the General Staff chose to raise the question of borders in their first meetings with the new Prime Minister and Minister of Defence. This was not 'lobbying' on their part but rather a clear expression of the army's offensive and activist predilections.

The new Chief of Staff: Rabin's credo

In Ben Gurion's day, no ex-Palmachnik was appointed Chief of Staff, because the Palmach had been associated with the radical Zionist Left. The delay in Rabin's promotion to the highest position in the army was generally attributed to his past in the Palmach and to the well-known incident when he disobeyed an order from his superiors and participated in the Palmach get-together of 1949, rousing Ben-Gurion's fierce disapproval.[21] However, it was Ben-Gurion who appointed Rabin in 1960 as deputy Chief of Staff, thereby essentially guaranteeing that he would be the next Chief of Staff.[22] On the other hand, Ben-Gurion was of the opinion that it was not a good idea for 'Yitzhak, who will certainly make a good Chief of Staff, to have [another ex-Palmachnik, Haim] Barlev as his deputy',[23] and hence he supported the candidacy of Ezer Weizman for the post of deputy, although he was known to be close in views to the right-wing opposition Herut Party.

The affair was complicated by Weizman's insistence on handing on the command of the IAF to Colonel Motti Fein (Hod), rather than to Gideon Elrom, the veteran candidate, who was Rabin's choice. Haim Barlev, who regarded himself as a worthy candidate for the post of deputy Chief of Staff, was offered Northern Command but turned it down. Eshkol consulted Ben-Gurion, who considered Rabin to be 'an honest and intelligent fellow' who could be relied on, but 'slightly too cautious', so that it was preferable to appoint Weizman as his deputy.

Ben-Gurion advised Eshkol to impose his decision on Rabin and to appoint Fein as CO of the IAF: 'The Minister of Defence,' he argued, 'is not obliged to accept the opinion of the Chief of Staff vis-à-vis appointments.'[24] Eshkol, however, refrained from imposing his views on Rabin and, in the end, Weizman's insistence cleared the way for Barlev, who was appointed Chief of Operations, though without the title of deputy Chief of Staff. Weizman remained in the IAF for another three years.[25]

On 1 January 1964, Yitzhak Rabin became Chief of Staff and on the same day he convened his fellow members of the General Staff forum and explained his credo in his new position. There were two underlying motives for the Arab desire to annihilate Israel, he said: hostility towards Israel, shared by most Arabs, because Israel was an alien factor in the region, whose very existence was an affront to Arab pride and nationalist sentiment. The second motive was the fact that Israel constituted a geographical obstacle to Egyptian ambition to unite the Arab world and dominate it.

Turning to the role of the army in promoting peace, he said: 'The IDF can bring peace closer by readying itself for war.' And he added a comment which hinted at a more activist approach. Greater preparedness and 'a greater momentum for operational activity' would help to bring peace. Referring to the danger of an Arab attack, Rabin pointed to Egypt as the main adversary, without which there would be no hostilities. The present balance of power, he added, precluded war and it could be maintained in the future. Time was on Israel's side and not on that of Arab union under Egyptian hegemony. Israel was becoming an established fact, even in the consciousness of the Arab world, and was capable of preserving its qualitative edge in conventional warfare for the coming ten to fifteen years. In the more distant future, the answer lay in non-conventional measures, a sphere in which Israel was considerably ahead of Egypt and the other Arab states, but 'this is not a subject for the present forum'.

Rabin discussed the possibility of an Israeli pre-emptive strike with a twofold aim:

1   *To destroy the enemy force.* This step should be considered if it was known that the enemy was planning an attack in the near future. He went on: 'It seems to me that if these circumstances arise, it will be the task of the IDF to explain [to the civil level] the meaning of failure to act in order to forestall an Arab attack.'
2   *Occupation of territory.* He saw 'no moral flaw in thinking that the State of Israel must be large. I would say that the reverse is true. But I think that the problem today is not the ability of the IDF to conquer territory but the State's ability to hold on to it.' The Chief of Staff recalled the pressure which had forced Israel to retreat from Sinai and Lebanon in the 1948 war, while 'all the territory we captured within Palestine-Eretz Israel remained within Israel's borders'. In this respect, withdrawal from the Gaza Strip after the Sinai Campaign had created a grave political precedent. This did not necessarily have implications for the future, but under certain conditions a pre-emptive strike might occur on the Jordanian front to conquer territory 'for temporary occupation'. Israeli military intervention on the West Bank would not necessarily be aimed, therefore, so he argued, at improving the border lines, but rather would be exploited as a lever for political gain.

He concluded by assuring the General Staff forum that they would take part in future in formulating the IDF's basic stances before presenting them to the politicians.[26] In practice this did not always happen. Rabin felt free to represent the IDF's viewpoint when he saw fit, even when his views were not in accord with the mood of the General Staff. This tendency was particularly evident during the May 1967 crisis.

Chapter 2

Basic security issues

The underlying cause of the escalation which led up to the Six Day War, in contrast to the 1956 Sinai Campaign, was not disturbance of the balance of conventional armament between Israel and its neighbours. In the period under study, the arming of the Egyptian and Syrian armies by the Soviet Union[1] was counterbalanced by Western supply of weapons to Israel, and, above all – for the first time in Israel's history – US-made weapons systems: ground-to-air missiles followed by tanks and fighter planes.[2] The objective of the buildup of the IDF was to enhance Israel's deterrent capability, and emphasis was placed on upgrading the skills of the fighting units in accordance with the army's offensive doctrine.

Israel's political effort to gain access to the US arms market began in the early years of statehood, but the United States adhered to its traditional reluctance to become the main arms supplier to the region. However, at the beginning of the period under discussion, there were conflicting views in Israel as to which source was preferable, the United States or Europe, due to fears that the former could impose restrictions on Israel's freedom of military and technological capability. When Israel constructed a large nuclear reactor at Dimona (in addition to a smaller reactor at Nahal Soreq, supplied to Israel through President Dwight Eisenhower's scheme 'Atoms for Peace'), it was suspected in the United States and the Arab states that it was planning to manufacture atomic weapons. Israel denied this. At the time, Egypt was investing effort in developing ground-to-ground missiles and also attempting to establish a nuclear infrastructure, but it failed where Israel succeeded. This is one of the reasons cited for the outbreak of war in 1967.[3]

The doctrine

From the military viewpoint, the fact that Israel launched a pre-emptive strike on 5 June 1967 was the direct outcome of the IDF's offensive doctrine, crystallized in the early 1950s. After the War of Independence, Israel, having achieved almost all its strategic goals,[4] was anxious to maintain the status quo stipulated in the armistice agreements. Since the two sides had absolutely conflicting views – Israel refused to take back Palestinian refugees or to return captured territory lying beyond the borders of the 1947 UN partition plan while the Arab states demanded the opposite – the conference of the Palestine Conciliation Commission, held at Lausanne in 1949, ended in an impasse.[5] In addition, separate and clandestine contacts between Israel and Egypt, as well as with Jordan and Syria, produced no results. Hence the nature of the Arab–Israeli conflict was fixed and peace was no longer at hand.[6] The Arab states constantly reiterated their intention to initiate a 'second round' in order to alter the status quo by force and liberate Palestine.

The facts demonstrate that the disparity between Arab declarations and actions was great. Their belligerent pronouncements notwithstanding, the divided leaders of the post-1948 Arab world never managed to formulate a coordinated plan for an all-out onslaught on Israel, with one exception: the third summit conference in Casablanca in 1965 (see below), but then, too, the inter-Arab harmony soon disintegrated due to bitter internal rivalries. Nonetheless, fear that the Arab world might unite and launch a coordinated attack haunted Ben-Gurion throughout his terms of office as Prime Minister and Minister of Defence.[7] The IDF was called on to supply the operative answer for defence of the country in the event of the worst scenario. This scenario – referred to in the IDF as the 'all-out event' – did not appear a likely eventuality until the eve of the Six Day War.

In the first few years of statehood, the basic premise of the General Staff was that Israel would never initiate hostilities, a premise which dictated the 'defensive-offensive' doctrine; initially, the IDF would be deployed in a defence layout in order to block the enemy, and in the second stage it would launch a counter-attack and transfer the fighting to enemy territory. The first stage was to be grounded on the regular army and a highly developed system of regional defence, and from then on, on the reserve forces. This conception was, to a large extent, the continuation of the underlying concept of the War of Independence strategy.[8]

The transition within the Israel Defence Forces to an alternative 'offensive-defensive' doctrine occurred at a very early stage and stemmed from the conviction of the IDF's planning echelon that there was no certainty that the IDF could hold fast if faced with the 'all-out' scenario. An all-out, coordinated Arab attack might inflict irreversible damage in the first stage due to the proximity of the border to population concentrations and to the difficulty in deploying the armed forces for defence on all fronts simultaneously. It was feared that the outcome would be resolved in the critical arenas before the reserve forces could be mobilized in full.

This outcome would be achieved through infliction of severe damage on population centres and infrastructures and on Israel's few air force bases, the cutting off of the southern Negev, occupation of the Galilee panhandle, the cutting off of the Jerusalem corridor or splitting the country into two at its narrowest point on the coastal plain. In October 1952, before his retirement from the armed forces, the Head of the IDF's Planning Department Colonel Shalom Eshet, at Ben-Gurion's request, prepared a comprehensive report on the existing balance of forces and on the IDF's ability to fulfil its mission and to safeguard Israel's existence and territorial integrity in the face of an Arab onslaught. Eshet recommended replacing the basic premise of the security doctrine:

> Only one premise of ... the security doctrine needs to be changed, as I see it, namely the assumption that the initiative for initiating hostilities lies with the enemy. Comparison of the balance of forces and of time and spatial factors does not indicate the possibility [that the IDF can carry out its mission] if the enemy takes the initiative.[9]

Eshet's successor, Lt. Colonel Yuval Neeman, collected extensive data which was summed up in August 1953 in a document entitled: 'Order of battle in wartime: evaluation 1953–1960', which confirmed the changeover to an 'offensive-defensive' doctrine.[10]

Ben-Gurion, who held a pessimistic, almost deterministic, view of the Arab–Israel conflict, was easily convinced. In December 1953, when he first retired to Sdeh Boqer, Ben-Gurion appointed Moshe Dayan as Chief of Staff. Dayan was the man who implanted the new doctrine in the IDF, serving as the agent of change for the political echelon.[11]

The practical implication of the new doctrine was that Israel must not leave the initiative in enemy hands. This was a revolutionary and not uncontroversial conclusion,[12] and was certainly unacceptable to Foreign Minister Moshe Sharett. But once adopted, the new doctrine was almost irreversible. The IDF now refrained from large-scale investment in border fortification, the regional defence layout was weakened, and military purchases were earmarked mainly for the assault forces. The offensive doctrine engendered two terms which represented two separate approaches: preventive war and pre-emptive attack. The former, more radical concept was identified with Moshe Dayan, and the second with ex-Palmach commander Yigal Allon.

Before the 1956 Sinai Campaign, Chief of Staff Dayan, convinced that another war was inevitable, argued that Israel could not wait idly for the Arabs to achieve their proclaimed aim of launching a 'second round' for the annihilation of Israel under conditions and timing convenient to them; the IDF should choose the conditions and timing and initiate the fighting, thereby dictating the operative framework and the objectives. Allon, too, thought that Israel could not permit itself to fight a war launched on pan-Arab initiative, but should commence hostilities only if an imminent threat of Arab attack loomed or if Israel's security 'red lines' were crossed.[13]

The concept of a preventive war, originating in a more pessimistic view of the dispute and of the gravity of the threat, essentially evaporated after being put to the test in 1956. The subsequent bolstering of Israel's confidence and the lesson of the post-war political efforts left the pre-emptive strike theory as the ruling concept. The Sinai Campaign had demonstrated the tremendous military advantages to Israel of being the initiator, and at the same time had allayed fears of a military confrontation. The calm which now prevailed on the borders eliminated the immediate pretext for a preventive war.

Now all Israel wanted was to preserve the status quo and to maintain effective deterrence, pointing to war prevention as the goal of Israel's security policy. Only if deterrence failed and Israel was confronted with the real and imminent danger of Arab aggression or the undermining of its vital interests (through diversion of water sources, or the blocking of the Tiran Straits) would it feel entitled to deal the first blow. The theory of the pre-emptive strike, although never officially sanctioned, was from now on the cornerstone of the security doctrine.[14] During the May to June 1967 crisis it was the basis for the army's eagerness to deliver the first blow and for the government's decision to approve this move.

Orientation – Europe or the United States?

As noted, when Levi Eshkol took over, there was controversy as to which source of weapons supply was preferable – Europe or the United States. In light of President Kennedy's 1962 decision to accede to Israel's request to the previous administration to purchase anti-aircraft Hawk missiles[15] – which were clearly defensive weapons – it was hoped that the United States would now be willing to supply other weapons. The most urgent need was to update and expand the IDF Armoured Corps.[16] The dispute related to Israel's political orientation, and Deputy Minister of Defence Shimon Peres, architect of the security ties with France and Germany, was isolated in his efforts to foster the pro-European orientation. His viewpoint reflected the desire to bring Israel into Europe. He argued that because of the great distance between them, the United States could not comprehend the Middle Eastern situation. He predicted the establishment of a European union, directly involved in the Middle East, to which Israel's future would be linked.[17]

At the same time, Peres was mainly motivated by considerations connected to the Dimona reactor, the apple of his eye and his major achievement. The pressure exerted by the Kennedy administration on this issue stirred his anxiety. The willingness of the United States to guarantee Israel's security, its readiness to sell Israel weapons' systems or the idea of basing Israel's security on a defence treaty with the United States could not counterbalance that pressure so far as he was concerned.[18] He claimed that the world in general, and the region in particular, were on the brink of a technological revolution, and Israel could not permit itself to lag behind in this race and to remain dependent on others. This situation called for a total rethink of the situation. The weapons of the new era would erase Israel's qualitative advantage in manpower; the new formula would be technology versus technology. The development of missiles and nuclear weapons had rendered anachronistic all the classic strategic theories based on time, space and quantity.[19]

Peres endeavoured to recruit public and parliamentary support for his advocacy of the European orientation.[20] On 24 June 1963, the day Eshkol presented his new government to the Knesset, Peres, the Deputy Minister of Defence,[21] attended a General Staff meeting and delivered a political and defence survey. Peres tried to recruit support among the military for his standpoint, which was not shared by Eshkol. The generals listened, asked several questions but did not voice opinions. Chief of Staff Zur, who was a close associate of Peres, was about to end his term of office, and his successor, Rabin, had reservations about the deputy minister, but tended to be pragmatic rather than ideological.

Peres explained that, while France had proved its reliability in supplying arms to Israel, the support of the United States was conditional. He added that Kennedy was liable to step up pressure on issues vital to Israel. A new focus of power was emerging in Europe in competition with the United States, headed by France and Germany, and both were supportive of Israel. Hence Israel should give priority to its ties with them. Relations with Europe would enable Israel to develop its independent deterrent nuclear capability. On this issue not only did the United States have nothing to offer Israel, but it was acting against Israeli interests.[22]

Eshkol: 'I doubt whether a rift with the United States would strengthen us'

A week later, in the presence of the generals, Eshkol took issue with Peres on the weapons supply issue, and voiced his skepticism as to the advantage of security links with Europe. The importance of the large Jewish community in the United States and of US aid dictated consideration for the views of the United States. Eshkol emphasized that he had no intention of conceding to Kennedy on vital issues (such as Israel's nuclear programme), but, he added, 'I simply want you to know: there are limits ... in disputes with the West.' Israel, he admitted, was 'in a certain bind'. Not only were $150 million of US aid in danger, but the Americans 'have many whips to wield against us', and the situation could lead to alienation of the West, including Germany, from Israel. Israel had the moral right to do everything in its power to safeguard its existence in light of Arab schemes to destroy it, but 'I doubt if a rift with the United States would strengthen us. I would not hesitate to assert that it would weaken us.'

Eshkol added that despite his analysis, he had

> doubts about the Christian world. I am not in the habit of seeing anti-Semitism everywhere but I am acquainted with the fear that perhaps on a day of wrath, the Arabs might, Heaven forbid, exterminate us and then the Christian world will breathe a sigh of relief. We are a thorn in the side of the West as well.[23]

The General Staff were to a large extent bystanders while this polemic was being conducted. The generals were not preoccupied with this issue and if Peres had expected support, he was disappointed. Rabin's view was that Israel should not place its trust in any country but should use any contact with or willingness of any country whatsoever to strengthen the State of Israel and its army.[24] This detached attitude was rooted in the fact that the IDF was not in a position of influence on this matter. Eshkol encountered no obstacles from the army when he decided to opt for the US weapons supply and to invest political effort in acquiring tanks and aircraft from the United States.[25] The reverse was true.

The Dimona reactor and Israeli–US relations

The objectives and essence of Israel's nuclear programme are beyond the scope of the present context. Numerous studies have been devoted to the relevance of this subject in the pre-Six Day War period, and its possible impact on the developments which led to war.[26] Aronson offers a theory which perceives the nuclear issue as the core of the considerations and decision-making which preceded the 1967 war (as it was in 1956).[27] But the documents do not validate his theory.

The basic facts are as follows. In Autumn 1957, in the wake of the Sinai Campaign, when relations between Israel and France were at their best, the two countries signed an agreement for the construction of a nuclear reactor. The reactor, of some 40-megawatt capacity, was constructed under secrecy in the Negev near the town of Dimona and its exposure in late 1960 evoked an emphatic US demand that Israel clarify its intentions. On 21 December 1960, Prime Minister Ben-Gurion delivered a statement in the Knesset, denying any plan to manufacture nuclear weapons and asserting that the nuclear power was to be used for research purposes and for development of the Negev, as well as for the training of scientists for the future construction of an atomic power-station.[28]

Ben-Gurion's announcement and the change of administrations in Washington calmed the atmosphere and a visit to Dimona by two scientists from the US Atomic Commission yielded no evidence of military intentions. On 30 May 1961, some two weeks after the visit, Ben-Gurion met with Kennedy in New York and assured him that the reactor would be used solely for peaceful purposes. He had no objections, he said, to the Arabs being briefed on the conclusions drawn by the two scientists. At the same time, he pointed out that Israel would follow developments in the Middle East, particularly in Egypt, and that there was no knowing what the future would bring.[29]

For more than two years, the reactor was not a major issue in Israel–US relations, and was unconnected to the Kennedy administration's decision in 1962 to supply Israel with Hawk ground-to-air missiles. But Kennedy regarded the non-proliferation of nuclear weapons as a personal mission and a vital element of his global policy, and several months after the resolution of the missile crisis in Cuba, he stepped up his pressure on Ben-Gurion to permit regular effective supervision of the Dimona reactor. At the height of this pressure, on 16 June 1963, Ben-Gurion tendered his final resignation from the premiership and handed over responsibility to Levi Eshkol.[30]

In his missives to Kennedy, Eshkol displayed willingness, however vaguely phrased, to accede to the US demand. Kennedy responded by reiterating his country's informal commitment to Israel's security and readiness to discuss Israel's defence needs and launched a strategic dialogue between the two countries. Israel's political and military leadership vacillated between advocacy of a defence treaty (though it was universally agreed that there was no prospect of gaining US consent) and various financial, political and security demands, and in particular weapons supply.[31] In mid-November 1963, an Israeli military deputation, headed by Rabin and the Deputy Chief of Intelligence Aharon Yariv, set out for the first strategic dialogue in Washington, at which Israel's security needs were discussed. The Dimona reactor was not mentioned.[32]

Kennedy's assassination did not remove the Dimona issue from the agenda, but the views of his successor, Lyndon Johnson, were much less emphatic. American scientists visited the Israeli atomic reactor in January 1964, and again in January 1965, April 1966 and April 1967, and found no evidence of arms manufacture. In June 1964, when Eshkol paid the first official visit by an Israeli premier to the United States, he assured the President that 'Israel will not be the first to introduce nuclear weapons into the Middle East'. This slogan, apparently first voiced by Ben-Gurion in 1962 in a discussion with the committee of Israeli newspaper editors, and reiterated by Peres in an unplanned meeting with Kennedy in 1963,[33] now became the cornerstone of Israel's proclaimed nuclear policy. This promise more or less reassured Johnson. The Secretary of State Dean Rusk did not withdraw the demand that Israel consent to supervision by the International Atomic Energy Commission, but the President no longer brought his full weight to bear on this matter.[34] Eshkol's requests from the United States for conventional weaponry – at this stage mainly tanks – met with a sympathetic response. Israel's refusal to accept international control and the delaying tactics employed with regard to the visits of US scientists in Dimona did not have a negative impact on this response.

Talks on weapons supply: the visit of Harriman and Comer

The US vacillated for some time before agreeing to supply Israel with US-manufactured tanks and they were eventually supplied indirectly: the US sent Germany 150 state-of-the-art Patton M48A3 tanks in return for dispatching the older model M48A1 to Israel. The implementation began in early 1965 and encountered problems after one of the tanks broke down on its way to an Italian port. Publicity on this incident led to German withdrawal from the deal. The US administration then decided to supply the tanks directly and it was with this in mind that Under-secretary of State Averell Harriman was dispatched to Israel at the end of February together with National Security Council member Robert Comer.

Encouragement for direct supply of US arms was provided meanwhile by an unexpected source: the Arab summit conferences, held in Cairo and Alexandria in January and September 1964, decided to thwart Israel's water development schemes by diverting the sources of the Jordan River and reinforcing the armies of the countries involved in the diversion. The United Arab Command, established after the conference, allotted Jordan, Syria and Lebanon the sum of £154 million for military purchases.[35] Jordan was pressured to purchase Soviet arms and King Hussein appealed to the United States for weapons so that he would not be forced to turn to the USSR. The US agreement to sell arms to Jordan prepared the ground for direct sale of arms to Israel.

The mission of Harriman and Comer was aimed, among other things, at softening Israel's resistance to the supply of 100 American tanks to Jordan. It was agreed that: Israel would not conduct a diplomatic campaign against the sale of tanks to Jordan; Jordan, for its part, would guarantee to position the tanks on the East Bank alone; the tanks would be of an inferior type (M48A1) to those sold to Israel (M48A2); the United States would finalize the tank deal with Israel and add 100 tanks and upgrading systems. The question of supply of fighter aircraft to Israel and Jordan was also discussed but no decision was taken at this stage.

Yitzhak Rabin wrote in his book *Service Notebook* that the US emissaries demanded three guarantees: that Israel was committed not to launch a preventive war; that it would try to solve the Jordan water crisis by peaceful means; and that it would not equip itself with nuclear weapons. Israel rejected the first demand; on the water issue, it agreed to explore all other avenues before resorting to military intervention, and on the question of nuclear weapons, its response remained vague and unaltered.[36] Harriman and Comer's objective, therefore, was to finalize a package deal to include an Israeli promise to exercise restraint in reaction to security challenges, silent consent to the supply of US arms to Jordan and abandonment of the nuclear path.

In return, the US administration offered guarantees of Israel's security in the event of an Arab attack and reinforcement of Israel's conventional arsenal by supply of US weapons. Israel's reply to the US demands was generally intractable and the Americans threatened to torpedo the talks.[37] The Israelis were eager to derive the maximum advantage from the change in US policy and from the desire of the United States to sell weapons to Jordan. However, on the nuclear issue, Eshkol remained adamant and his standpoint was in fact accepted with tacit understanding by President Johnson.

Israel's obduracy in the course of the talks was ostensibly surprising. US arms supply to Jordan was, in the final analysis, commensurate with Israeli interests, and its readiness to become Israel's main arms supplier represented a fundamental, even historic, change of direction. Israel was naturally eager to acquire US weapons, but was apprehensive and even suspicious of US intentions and of its global and regional interests, which dictated restriction of Israel's freedom of military action. The conditions stipulated by the United States bore this out. Consequently, Israel rejected most of the demands. It waived its objections to the US–Jordanian arms deal, but refused to provide assurance that it would not launch a pre-emptive strike if a critical threat arose, and refused to consent to avoid, under any circumstances, the use of force to frustrate attempts to divert the Jordan river sources.

The Harriman–Comer talks with Israel lasted almost a month. Their reports to Washington indicate that the negotiations were tough and wide-ranging and that the US tried to extract far-reaching Israeli guarantees, particularly with regard to supervision of nuclear installations and a restrained Israeli response to Arab water diversion schemes. In the end, the Americans were obliged to make do with a limited memorandum of understanding, which included only implicit Israeli consent to the sale of tanks to Jordan and a US guarantee to sell tanks and a small quantity of aircraft to Israel.[38]

On 10 March 1965, the memorandum of understanding was signed between Eshkol and Comer (Harriman had left for India). It included a US commitment to Israel's security and territorial integrity, and Israel's assurance – for the first time in writing – that it would not be the first to introduce nuclear weapons into the Middle East.

As regards the request for fighter planes, the Americans demanded that Israel first exhaust the possibilities of acquiring aircraft from European sources. Israel, however, wanted US-manufactured aircraft, particularly Phantoms, and announced that it had not succeeded in finding suitable aircraft in Europe. In October 1965, IAF Commander Ezer Weizman visited

Washington and presented a very ambitious shopping list which included forty-five Phantoms and 165 Skyhawks, far beyond what the administration was willing to consider. In February 1966, the Americans approved the dispatch of twenty-four Skyhawks and the option for purchase of an additional twenty-four aircraft. This decision was indirectly linked to Israel's reiterated guarantee not to introduce nuclear weapons into the region and to permit US scientists to inspect the reactor. Shortly afterwards Israel signed an agreement for the purchase of fifty Mirage M5 aircraft from France.[39]

Missiles

On 21 July 1962, on the eve of the tenth anniversary of the Free Officers' revolt in Egypt, four ground-to-ground missiles of two different types were launched in the Egyptian Western Desert – *el-Kahr* (The Conqueror), with a range of 560 kilometres, and *el-Zaf'r* (The Winner), with a range of 280 kilometres. President Nasser announced that the Egyptian missiles were capable of reaching any target 'south of Beirut'.[40] Israel, which had dispatched the Shavit 2 into the atmosphere for 'meteorological research purposes' a year previously,[41] was taken by surprise by the launching of the Egyptian missiles. The fact that they had been developed with the aid of German scientists working in Egypt sparked off political and public hysteria in Israel, and Ben-Gurion's pro-German policy was sharply attacked by both the right- and left-wing opposition, and even within his own party. The furore aroused by the 'German scientists' affair' lasted up until Ben-Gurion's resignation in June 1963 and only gradually died down subsequently. A French source reveals that, in parallel and clandestinely, Israel arrived at an agreement with the Dassault concern in France for the accelerated development of ground-to-ground missiles of type MD620.[42]

The missiles race between Egypt and Israel was of great concern to the United States. The Americans did not attribute great significance or logic to the manufacture of missiles with conventional warheads, but regarded the combination of missile development and nuclear capability as a new and dangerous stage in the Middle Eastern arms race.[43]

Fear of the Egyptian missiles haunted the IDF General Staff at the beginning of the period under discussion, and this fear found expression in frequent Intelligence reports, evaluations and assessments. Although they were equipped with conventional warheads, these missiles rendered Israel's urban hinterland vulnerable and indefensible. High-level Egyptian ballistic capability was also liable to hamper Israeli ability to react to unilateral moves (such as the blocking of the Tiran Straits) for fear of reprisals against civilian populations and infrastructures.[44] It gradually became clear, however, that Egypt's ambitious project was encountering obstacles, and it received less frequent mention at General Staff meetings. Ground-to-ground missiles played no part whatsoever in the Six Day War.

Abortive American initiatives

Israel's shocked response to the launching of Egyptian missiles apparently impelled the Kennedy administration to take steps to pacify and reassure the Israelis. In August 1962, Kennedy's adviser on Israeli and Jewish affairs, Meyer Feldman, was sent to Israel to inform the government of the President's decision to respond to Israel's request for Hawk ground-to-air missiles, which had been submitted in 1961 by Ben-Gurion to Eisenhower. It is noteworthy that the IDF senior command was divided on the issue of missile purchase. Weizman was strongly opposed for fear it would subvert the offensive doctrine. One of the important reasons why missiles were necessary was defence of the Dimona reactor.[45]

The official announcement of the sale of Hawk missiles was published on 27 September 1962, and the missiles were introduced into the IAF (after a dispute with the Artillery Corps) in April 1965. The Kennedy administration failed in its attempt to render the agreement to supply Israel with missiles conditional on Israeli consent for a proposal that Israel would absorb 10 per cent of the refugees and the remainder would be absorbed by the Arab countries in a ten-year-long process funded by the Americans. The plan did not include Arab recognition of Israel or a peace settlement and Ben-Gurion opposed it, but was pressured by the United States into agreeing to negotiations. Events in the region and the assassination of Kennedy put an end to the plan.[46]

Another abortive US initiative was the attempt to base an indirect deal with Egypt and Israel on the missiles and the reactor. The Kennedy administration realized that its pressure on Israel must be accompanied by some form of compensation in the defence sphere. It was decided to attempt to formulate bilateral US–Egypt and US–Israel agreements. In return for Israel's consent to halt all nuclear development and missile purchase and to accept international control of the reactor, the United States would try to persuade Egypt to abandon its missile development programme and to permit supervision of its installations by the International Atomic Energy Commission. While stepping up the pressure on Israel, Kennedy also dispatched his personal emissary John McCloy to Egypt in June 1963. McCloy, who had negotiated with Nasser several years earlier on the shipping of goods to Israel through the Suez Canal,[47] was authorized to arrange the deal.

Johnson, too, tried to concoct a deal through his emissaries to Nasser – Philip Talbot (March 1964) and McCloy again (September 1964) – for the same purpose. Nasser, however, was suspicious of US intentions and voiced his objections to an indirect deal with Israel, totally rejecting any form of foreign supervision of the missile project as a violation of Egypt's sovereignty.[48] The US administration was thus forced to abandon its original scheme and to pay Israel in US rather than Egyptian currency, in return for consent to US inspection of the reactor.

Due to global calculations, the United States was reluctant to enter into a defence treaty with Israel and hence was forced to make do with Israel's guarantee not to be the first to introduce nuclear weaponry into the region and to consent to US periodic inspection of the reactor. In practice, due to Israeli delaying tactics, inspections took place at twelve- to eighteen-month intervals and were discontinued entirely in 1969. Israel's consent was based on US agreement to supply arms, maintain the strategic dialogue, and the continued informal commitment of the United States to Israel's security. In essence, Israel benefited from Egypt's inflexibility: it received payment in 'hard' currency – tanks and aircraft – and paid out 'soft' currency' – ambivalent consent on the nuclear issue. The Egyptian missile project, on the other hand, died a natural death due to technological problems and budgetary restrictions.

Israel's nuclear image in Arab eyes

The nuclear issue as such did not greatly preoccupy the IDF General Staff. The Intelligence Branch closely followed Egyptian efforts to develop non-conventional weapons, and the head of Intelligence and his deputy reported from time to time on current developments to the General Staff meetings, but the senior command was more concerned with the implications of Israel's nuclear image in Arab eyes and its impact on the short-term conventional threat. What they feared was an Egyptian surprise attack on the Dimona reactor aimed at obliterating what the Arabs perceived to be the Israeli atomic menace.

Public references by the Arab countries, particularly Egypt, to the purported development of Israel's nuclear capacity were not frequent in this period, but the subject was always on the agenda. The Egyptian statements were usually blunter and more threatening than those of Syria, which played down the issue. The Palestinian organizations favoured expediting the Arab confrontation with Israel before the latter's nuclear power became an established fact.[49]

The IDF senior command and the political echelon estimated that the Dimona reactor constituted a prime target for an Arab attack, whether through a concentrated air strike or in the framework of an overall military confrontation. At the strategic level, the answer lay in effective conventional deterrence and decisive capability. The construction of the reactor, therefore, provided an additional reason for reinforcing the conventional capability of the armed forces. At the tactical and operative level, this entailed establishment of a strong defensive disposition around the reactor consisting of ground and artillery forces, including Hawk missiles, and efforts to ensure that, at any cost, Israel would be the first to inflict a crushing blow on the Arab air forces in the event that hostilities began.

Despite Israel's assurances that it would not be the first to employ nuclear weapons in the Middle East, its unsupervised nuclear development never received international recognition and consequently the Israelis feared that an Arab attack on the reactor would be sanctioned. Rabin declared: 'If the Egyptians bomb Dimona and we want to go to war, we will receive an ultimatum from the whole world.'[50] Israel had no corresponding response to offer to the destruction of the reactor. It could react by launching an all-out war, destroying air forces or conquering territory, but it was questionable whether it had anything to gain thereof. Destroyed aircraft could be replaced, and all-out warfare and conquest could prove very costly. Moreover, the fruits of victory could be negated by international pressure, as had occurred after the Sinai Campaign. The loss of the reactor, on the other hand, would be irretrievable.

Israel's defence establishment was greatly concerned, therefore, by the prospect of a sudden Arab attack on the reactor. Egypt's threats to launch a preventive war because of the reactor did not seem likely to be implemented in light of the circumstances and the balance of power, but a concentrated air strike on the reactor was considered a feasible possibility. This was also the view of the Chief of Staff. Hence the government's hesitation to approve reprisal operations against Syria as demanded by the IDF (see below). Rabin explained to his fellow officers:

> There is an object in the south of the country, the ideal object for limited reaction [on the part of Egypt] for which it would receive the total support of the whole world. Dimona. [Ministers] claim that Egypt can refrain from transferring forces to Sinai or Syria but to deal with Dimona, that's not considered war. It is a limited operation.[51]

Fears of this eventuality increased during the crisis on the eve of the Six Day War and served as an important (though not decisive) motive for the Israeli pre-emptive strike.

The nuclear issue and the Six Day War

To what extent, if at all, was the nuclear issue the *casus belli* of the Six Day War? The Dimona reactor was, at most, a secondary factor which emerged in the final act.

Israel's nuclear developments greatly concerned the Arabs, and particularly Egypt, and the reactor was undoubtedly marked out by the Egyptians as a prime target. Egyptian reconnaissance flights over the reactor on 17 and 26 May 1967 were signs of this.[52] However, Nasser's conduct was curious: first, if he precipitated the crisis initially in order to destroy the reactor, or to neutralize it before Israel could consolidate its nuclear military capacity, why did he try to deter Israel from attacking Syria? He was depriving himself thereby of the pretext for reacting to such an attack by destroying the reactor.

Second, if the target was indeed the reactor, and such an attack would have been greeted with understanding, if not sanctioned, by world opinion, why did he entangle himself in an international imbroglio because of the Straits? Third, after blocking the straits, why did he expose himself to the danger of a confrontation with the United States instead of rendering the reopening of the Straits conditional on supervision of the Israeli reactor by the International Atomic Energy Agency, a demand which the United States would have found it hard to oppose?

It may never be known what role the nuclear issue played in the calculations of the Egyptian President, and whether the crisis and the way it was tackled were premeditated. In any event, in the course of the crisis the reactor issue did not apparently surface in diplomatic contacts, and certainly not in the public statements of the parties involved. Even after the war, no Egyptian source ever claimed that the reactor was the reason for the Egyptian-initiated crisis.

In feverish deliberations in the government and the Ministerial Committee on Security in the three weeks preceding 5 June 1967, fear of Egyptian attack on the reactor was constantly voiced, mainly by the hawkish ministers, who supported the army's demand for a pre-emptive strike. Several of the doves, on the other hand, argued that even an attaching on the reactor did not necessarily mean that Israel must respond in warlike fashion. In the end, the government decision to permit the IDF to launch an onslaught was inspired, not by the looming threat to Dimona, but by important considerations (to be detailed below), and the safety of the reactor was not in itself the major reason.

Peres' fears for the reactor, the pinnacle of his achievements, and for the future of Israel's nuclear effort, may explain his hectic efforts to persuade the decision-makers during the May to June 1967 crisis to refrain from war. Peres went so far as to claim that the IDF was not ready for war, thereby heightening the anxieties and doubts of ministers and party leaders and arousing the resistance of Eshkol and other ministers. Warfare was liable to void the strategy championed by Peres aimed at deterring the Arabs from launching a decisive battle against Israel. Not only would such a war be costly and superfluous since Israel had nothing to gain thereby, but it would place the Dimona reactor in danger, since it was undoubtedly an operative target for the Egyptian air force.

The Director of Rafael (The Israel Armament Development Authority), Monia Mardor, described in his memoirs Rafael's intensive efforts on the eve of the Six Day War to complete a weapons system, whose nature he did not specify. He described it, however, as of 'perhaps critical value'.[53]

Peres himself wrote that 'after Dayan became Minister of Defence [1 June 1967] I put a certain proposal to him which would have deterred the Arabs and prevented war'.[54] Is there any connection between the two facts? Was Peres' proposal connected in any way to the nuclear issue? If so, then Eshkol and Dayan, very wisely, chose to reject it.

Arms purchase and strategic buildup

The buildup of the IDF in the period under discussion was linked, as we have shown, to the dialogue with Washington on the reactor, which for the first time had placed Israel in a bargaining position vis-à-vis America. The dialogue conducted with the Johnson administration, Israel's guarantee not to introduce nuclear weapons into the region, and US pressure for more frequent inspection of the reactor, produced concrete results, which culminated in US consent to supply Israel with tanks and later also aircraft. The US commitment to Israel's security was now more emphatic. And yet, most of the arms purchase deals signed with the United States had not been implemented in the early summer of 1967.

The IDF fought the Six Day War with weapons purchased mostly from France. The Armoured Corps had only one operative Patton battalion (the 79th). In 1966 contracts were signed for the purchase of 100 French- and US-manufactured front-line aircraft, which were due to transform the IAF, but these Skyhawks and Mirage 5s were still on paper at that stage. This period also witnessed a new scheme for updating the navy with small, rapid, missile boats. However, the plan for reorganization had not reached the implementation stage before the Six Day War and the navy was still in poor shape, which was reflected in its performance during the war.

Naturally enough, the turnaround in US policy on the sale of weapons' systems to Israel was not only motivated by the nuclear issue. It also stemmed from the altering of circumstances in the Middle East: the increasing Soviet infiltration of the region after Nikita Khrushchev's visit to Egypt in May 1964; the growing rift in the Arab world between the conservative pro-Western, and the revolutionary countries; the deterioration of US-Egyptian relations due to Egypt's intervention in the war in Yemen and other reasons noted above. To all these was added the Arab summit decision to allocate funds for the arming of Jordan, and the subsequent US decision to sell Jordan US weapons. In the background was the involvement of the United States in Vietnam. The Johnson administration chose to equip Israel and leave it to fend for itself and thus avoid a scenario where it would be forced to make good its commitment to Israel's security in the event of an all-out Arab onslaught. This was also the case in May to June 1967.[55]

It should be emphasized that the buildup of the IDF, which did not lag behind the Arab armies, played a vital role in bolstering the IDF's confidence and deterrent capability. The priorities in allocation of resources for weapons purchase were based on the needs of the forces required for implementation of the offensive doctrine. The first priority was the air force, followed by the armoured units and paratroop units. Efforts to develop the navy were considered of secondary importance. Due to budgetary limitations, the air force and armoured units could not be developed concomitantly. Under Chief of Staff Zur (and Rabin as Chief of the Operations Branch), emphasis was placed on aircraft. Later, as Chief of Staff, Rabin initially accorded priority to the purchase of tanks, and only at a later stage to the purchase of new aircraft.

In 1964 to 1967, some 140 aircraft were purchased (including forty-eight Skyhawks from the United States and fifty Mirages, twenty-five Ouragan and twelve Super Frelon helicopters from France as well as some 500 US tanks and a dozen missile boats from France. The Artillery Corps capability was greatly improved after it absorbed 155 mm mobile guns and the introduction of heavy mortars. The equipping was carried out in accordance with the 1963 Bnei Or programme which was based on the assumption that war was unlikely in the foreseeable future. The most dramatic increase was in the armoured power and its quality, and by the end of 1966 the IDF had 1,300 tanks.

Comparison of the IDF's buildup and that of the Arab armed forces in 1964 to 1967[56] helps to explain the confidence prevailing in the Israeli General Staff at the time. It was mainly due to the military might of the IDF that Nasser (up until mid-May 1967) consistently asserted that the all-out war on Israel should be postponed until the Arab armies were ready and there was no danger of another defeat. This was also the reason for the assessment of US Intelligence bodies on the eve of the war that the IDF could defeat any Arab military coalition.

Conclusion

The central issues of the period – the arms race, the reactor, the missiles – do not appear to have been the underlying factors leading to the Six Day War. It was the current security problems which led to escalation. However, Israel's basic decisions on national security were connected to fundamental security issues. The reliance of the IDF on US supply of its main weapons systems began during this period, and entailed signing memoranda of understanding with the United States and Israeli guarantees not to cross the nuclear threshold. The accompanying strategic dialogue and the change of direction in US policy under Johnson enhanced the US commitment to Israel's security. As a consequence, when the crisis broke out in May 1967, Israel turned to Washington. The US administration did not deny its commitment but tried initially to stop the crisis and check it. When it failed, it essentially gave its tacit consent to an independent Israeli

Table 3 Border incidents by sector – 1 January 1964 to 5 June 1967

Period	Total	Sector			
		Syria	Jordan	Egypt	Lebanon
Total	288	182	100	3	3
1 January to 30 April 1964	7	3	4	–	–
1964/1965	88	62	26	–	–
1965/1996	64	31	31	2	–
1966/1967	123	81	39	1	2
1 April to 5 June 1967	6	5	–	–	1

Table 4 Terrorist attacks by sector – 1 January 1964 to 5 June 1967

Period	Total	Sector			
		Syria	Jordan	Egypt	Lebanon
Total	125	26	69	5	25
1 January to 30 April 1964	–	–	–	–	–
1964/1965	7	1	6	–	–
1965/1996	37	4	27	3	–
1966/1967	64	18	30	1	15
1 April to 5 June 1967	17	3	6	1	7

Table 5 Reprisal raids by sector – 1 January 1964 to 5 June 1967

Period	Total	Sector			
		Syria	Jordan	Egypt	Lebanon
Total	12	4	7	–	1
1 January to 30 April 1964	–	–	–	–	–
1964/1965	1	1	–	–	–
1965/1996	7	2	4	–	1
1966/1967	4	1	3	–	–
1 April to 5 June 1967	–	–	–	–	–

Source: *Periodic Survey* – Major-General Yitzhak Rabin (1 January 1964 to 31 December 1967)

pre-emptive attack, and after the war supplied Israel with firm political support.

Israel's pro-US security and political orientation was consolidated in this period, but was, to some extent, the paradoxical outcome of the prior orientation towards Europe. The Dimona reactor, built with the help of France, provided Israel with a bargaining card in its relations with the United States, for whom the restriction of nuclear weapons development was of supreme interest. The Americans could not sign a defence pact with

Israel in return for the latter's total abandonment of development of nuclear capability, but did something similar: it agreed for the first time to sell Israel weapons' systems and to reinforce its commitment to the security of the Jewish state in return for a vague promise by Israel not to go nuclear.

Chapter 3

Escalation – Stage I

From skirmishes in the demilitarized zones to aerial sorties

The Six Day War broke out ostensibly as a direct result of the growing tension between Israel and Syria, which reached its height in spring 1967, but the border dispute between them was not new. It was a protracted local skirmish. The traditional Syrian commitment to the Arab struggle against Israel had become increasingly radical, advocating and backing a 'popular war of liberation'. Israel for its part responded by launching massive aerial operations.

One fact is clear: the army promoted a forceful approach to the Syrians and later also recommended stepping up the confrontation to the point where a 'frontal clash' with Syria would take place. The government was opposed to escalation but the deterioration of the security situation forced it to seek answers which only the army could supply. As a rule, the IDF operated only within the framework dictated to it, but in several cases it permitted itself to interpret the intentions of the civil echelon in a wider fashion. This was particularly true of the IAF.

The demilitarized zones

Chronic instability prevailed along the Israel–Syria border up until 1967. The roots of the problems lay in the armistice agreement between the two countries signed on 20 July 1949, which designated certain areas west of the international border between Mandatory Palestine and Syria, a total area of some 65,000 dunams (a dunam = a quarter of an acre), as demilitarized zones. Sovereignty over these zones was not explicitly defined, military presence was banned, citizens who had fled due to the fighting were permitted to return and the employment of a limited number of Israeli and Arab police was allowed. A Mixed Armistice Commission was established, headed by the Chief of Staff of the UN Truce Supervision Organization.[1]

The basic dispute between Israel and Syria related to the question of sovereignty. The Israeli position, which was not sanctioned by the UN, was that the entire area west of the international border was under Israeli sovereignty. This claim was made during the negotiations on the armistice

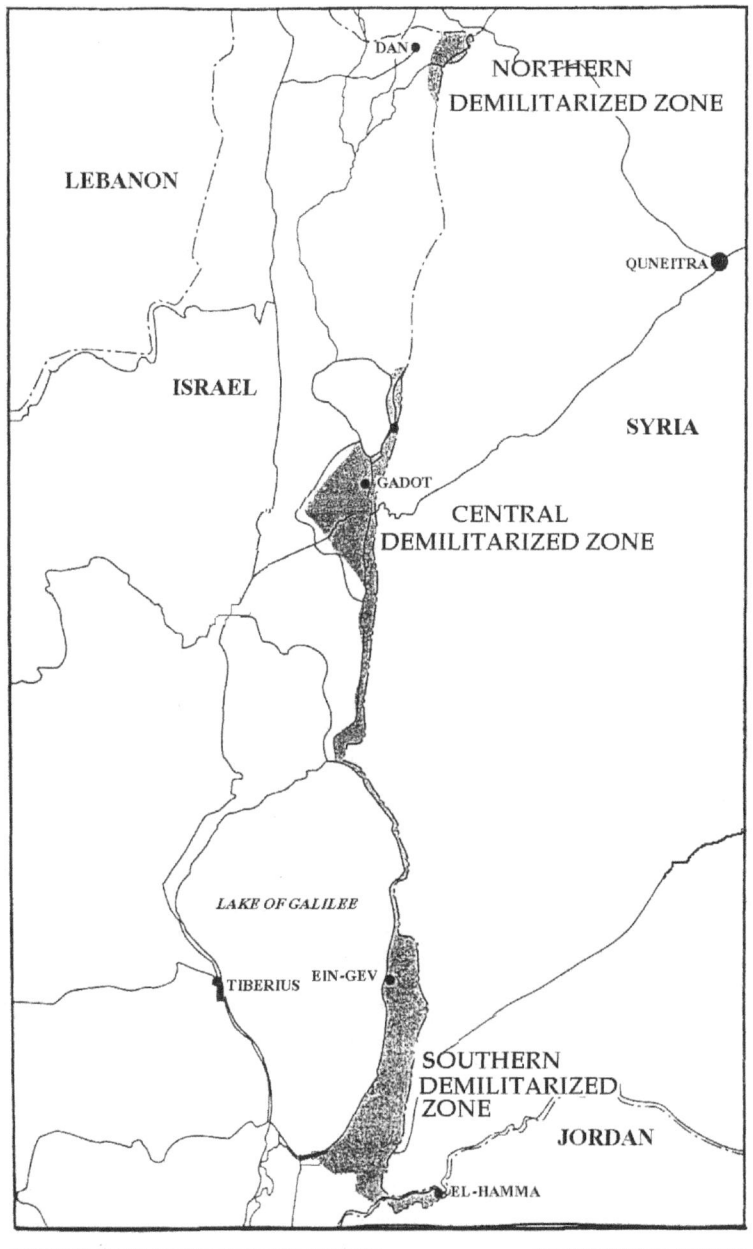

Map 2 The demilitarized zones along Israel–Syria border.

agreement, but Israel finally consented to downplay the demand in order to achieve an agreement. When the Israelis began the development of the area, the sovereignty claim was raised again more emphatically, and Israel now demanded that the Syrians be denied any authority in the area, particularly where Israeli water and settlement projects were concerned. The demilitarized zones thus became the focus of incessant disputes between Israel and Syria over water issues, land cultivation, pasture and fishing rights in Lake Galilee.

This was the situation at the beginning of the period under discussion. The problem was now chronic, and although there were no indications of escalation, there was also no solution in sight in the foreseeable future. If the problem had not been compounded in 1964 to 1967 by the 'War over Water', the 'Popular War', the radical nature of the Syrian regime and Israel's determination, it is questionable whether the tension around the demilitarized zones would have constituted a pretext for a military flare-up.

Prime Minister and Minister of Defence Levi Eshkol was deeply involved in and knowledgeable about the details of agricultural and military activity in the demilitarized zones. Eshkol relied on Rabin, who displayed discretion and understanding towards both political problems and political sensitivities, and whose approach, as reflected in the documents, was measured and reasoned. At the same time, Eshkol lacked military expertise and relied on data submitted to him by the Chief of Staff, having no Intelligence sources of his own. Even when a military secretary to the Prime Minister was selected, the appointee, Colonel Yisrael Lior, was – and apparently this was no accident – of a rank and authority which could not counterbalance that of the Chief of Staff.[2] Hence, Eshkol could rely only on his own judgement and political acumen for day-to-day supervision of military activities.

On the other hand, basic issues and important decisions which were pending were brought before the Ministerial Committee on Security, which in the two and a half years before the war could boast only one member – Yigal Allon – with a military background. However, Allon, unlike most of his fellow committee members, was a sworn activist, and served more as a catalyst than a brake on the army's offensive trends.[3] In practice, therefore, it was the army to a large extent which determined policy.[4]

With time, as tension mounted on the border with Syria and the IDF took the opportunities offered to hit out at the Syrians, Eshkol became uneasy about the IDF's initiatives. He knew that cultivation of the disputed areas in the demilitarized zones was not profitable and apparently favoured suspending cultivation in order to prevent incidents and save lives, but he yielded to the military.[5] Eshkol maintained direct contact with the head of the Truce Supervision Organization, General Odd Bull, with the aim of achieving an agreement on the demilitarized zones.[6] The Syrians indicated some willingness for a settlement when they introduced an unconditional ceasefire and even agreed in practice to hold direct negotiations with Israel under the aegis of the UN (see below).

However, Syria's policies were fraught with contradictions: its willingness to formulate a practical solution to the problems of the demilitarized zones was at odds with its ideological nationalistic stance and demand for immediate war for the annihilation of Israel, its efforts to implement the scheme for diversion of the Jordan waters, and in particular its support for the popular war of the Palestinians against Israel. Under these conditions there was no likelihood that Eshkol's approach would prevail and the tough military approach won the day. If the public atmosphere in Israel was blatantly anti-Syrian it seemed that Syria was supplying good reasons.

Perusal of the Israeli press in the pre-war period reveals endless news items on shooting incidents on the Syrian border, in which Syrians opened fire on IDF patrols or on Israelis working in the fields, and sometimes also inflicted damage on settlements. These news items, in addition to militant Syrian pronouncements, the diversion activities and the guerrilla raids, had a cumulative effect on Israeli public opinion, evoking anger, hostility and the desire for revenge. The IDF version of the incidents was accepted without question, until Moshe Dayan, years later, cast new light on it, asserting that at least 80 per cent of the incidents were initiated by the IDF.

In a 1976 interview, only published twelve years later, Dayan stated:

> We [the IDF] used to send a tractor to plough some land where nothing could be grown, in the demilitarized zone, knowing in advance that the Syrians would start shooting. If they didn't fire, we would order the tractor to advance until the Syrians finally got angry and fired on it. And then we brought in artillery and later the air force as well.[7]

The skirmishes in the demilitarized zones arose from an issue which, given minimal conditions of dialogue and trust, could have been solved in a pragmatic fashion. Israel staged incidents to undermine Syrian efforts to divert the Jordan waters so that they could not be used by Israel. The IDF also fired at Syrian farmers and shepherds who infiltrated the demilitarized zones, and there can be no doubt that in most cases the IDF was the first to open fire.

As noted above, the problem of the demilitarized zone in itself was not sufficiently grave to lead to the outbreak of war. It was the combination of circumstances which worsened the situation. The turning point which elevated a local dispute to new heights was Israel's decision to bring the air force into its border conflict with Syria.

A new stage: the IAF goes into action

Only once in the 1950s were aerial forces employed to attack Syrian targets during incidents connected to the demilitarized zones – during the al-Hama incident of 5 April 1951.[8] The sharply-worded condemnation of the incident by the Security Council and the negative international reaction, particularly on the part of the United States, ruled out, for all practical purposes, further aerial operations.[9]

The topographical facts which gave the Syrians the tactical advantage, and the vulnerability of the population centres in the Huleh Valley and east of Lake Galilee, led the senior command to the conclusion that only the IAF could provide an effective and deterrent response to Syrian gunfire. This was their regular recommendation to the political echelon, but so long as Ben-Gurion was in office he rejected it for fear of undesirable escalation and entanglement in a war. In March 1962 Ben-Gurion nevertheless put through a resolution authorizing him to deploy the IAF in the event of bombardment of civilian settlements; this resolution was not implemented until action was approved two years later by his successor, Eshkol.

The decision to employ the IAF was preceded by a series of discussions at the General Staff and the Ministerial Committee on Security inspired by the deteriorating situation on the Israeli–Syrian border. On 10 June 1964, Israel's National Water Carrier, a proclaimed Arab *casus belli*, was inaugurated with relative discretion.[10] However, it exposed Arab impotence to prevent the consolidation of the Jewish state and was interpreted as an additional defiant challenge to the Arab world. At the Cairo summit conference in January of that year, where Arab leaders resolved to divert the Jordan sources, Syria had adopted the most militant stance and demanded immediate war. A second summit conference in September approved the diversion schemes for immediate implementation. Chief of Staff Rabin proposed the restoration of a patrol path leading to the Dan spring inside Israel, the most important tributary of the Jordan. Rabin explained at a government meeting that the Syrians had expressed reservations as to the exact location of the border line, claiming that a section of the patrol path passed through their territory. Any adjustment might bring the Dan into joint Israeli–Syrian sovereignty.[11]

The question of whether it was essential to engineer a clash with the Syrians over the Dan is still open. Experience had shown that the Syrians would resort to force to halt work on the path which, so they asserted, passed through their territory. The Dan waters were flowing into the Jordan without disturbance; the Arab diversion schemes did not, in any case, include the Dan tributary, and effective control of its sources was in Israeli hands. Nor was there any information at the time about unusual Syrian activity which might threaten the status quo.

The explanation lies in the change in the psychological climate due to the diversion challenge, which set the Jordan river at the core of the Arab–Israel conflict. The senior command wanted a display of strength which would reflect Israel's determination to defend its water interests, and they felt that there was a prospect of obtaining a green light for employment of the IAF, which could provide a resounding counter-response to the tactical advantage of the Syrian army in most of the sectors of the border. Levi Eshkol, who was strongly committed to the water issue (he had founded the national water corporation Mekorot many years before), gave the army the necessary backing.

On 2 November 1964, David Elazar (Dado), a young, energetic, offensive-oriented officer, took up the post of CO Northern Command. His personal impact on events was not insignificant. His deputy in the early days was an officer whose personality was no less tempestuous – Colonel Ariel Sharon.[12]

Elazar's biography describes the incident which occurred on 3 November 1964 as the fruit of his decision on his first day as Commander to ensure Israeli sovereignty over the Dan sources. 'We'll take this path tomorrow', he ordered. One officer at headquarters questioned the decision to assert control over an area with such poor agricultural potential. Said Lt. Col. Pinhas Lahav, 'Why are we doing it again and again? It would be cheaper to fly grains of wheat wrapped in cotton wool and packed in cellophane from California, and it would not cost lives.'[13]

Friday the 13th – escalation

On 3 November 1964, after forces had been deployed in the sector on both sides of the border, work began on the controversial section of the path leading to the Dan. In the course of the (anticipated) incident which ensued, the IDF tanks, despite their tactical advantage, failed in their mission to destroy the Syrian tanks at Nuheila; this failure was regarded as a 'fiasco'.[14] Within a day, though, the path was completed and the IDF sent patrols along it for several days, reinforcing the units and preparing for further action. The patrols proceeded for a week without Syrian reaction, but at noon on Friday, 13 November 1964, the Syrians opened fire on a patrol descending from Tel Dan to the patrol path, and then opened fire from mortars, recoilless guns and tanks from positions at Nuheila, Tel Hamra, Tel Azaziat and the Banias Heights on Tel Dan and Kibbutz Dan. This time Israeli armour succeeded in hitting several Syrian tanks, but it was the shelling of the Kibbutz which led to bringing in the IAF.

Rabin telephoned Eshkol, reported on the Syrian bombardment and requested permission to launch an aerial attack on Syrian targets. Eshkol consented at once. The Chief of Staff ordered IAF commander Ezer Weizman to carry out the mission, but to avoid harming civilians. Weizman sent up fifty fighter planes of various types, nineteen of which participated in the assault on Syrian positions and artillery emplacements.[15]

It is hard to believe that Eshkol would have approved the unprecedented employment of dozens of aircraft in so casual a fashion. It seems more feasible that Eshkol envisaged a more limited attack. It appears that Rabin himself, giving the order by telephone to Weizman, did not go into detail, and he too did not set limits to the number of aircraft or the types of ammunition. The Head of the Operations Department of the General Staff, Colonel Mota Gur, explicitly attested to this during the investigation of the incident: 'There was no limitation as regards the type and volume of the aircraft fire, whether bombs, napalm or sniping, etc. It was left to the discretion of the CO of the Air Force.'[16] Hence Weizman decided for himself what the scope would be.

In this fashion, Israel raised the stakes in its confrontation with the Syrians. The operation was successful and for a time there was calm along the sector, but the situation had repercussions whose culmination occurred two and a half years later, on 7 April 1967 (see below).

Political calculation or lack of control?

At the government meeting of Sunday, November 15 1964, Eshkol, faced with criticism, defended his decision to approve an aerial operation. He described his conversation with Rabin as follows: 'I asked: don't we have any other means of halting them? His reply was: none. I agreed to approve the use of the Air Force.'[17]

At the Ministerial Committee on Security, the Minister of Religious Affairs Zerah Wahrhaftig claimed that the Prime Minister should have convened the Committee and wondered if the employment of aircraft had been justified. Eshkol replied that the shelling of the Kibbutz did not permit him to wait for the committee meeting, and if the IAF had not intervened immediately 'we would have had crushed settlements'. The Minister of Education, Zalman Aranne, asked why it had been necessary to employ so many aircraft and if it had been essential to employ napalm. Rabin explained that it had been necessary to silence four targets and to exploit the advantage of napalm to cover a wide area.[18]

The criticism within the government was engulfed in the waves of praise in the press and public opinion. Eshkol, whose relations with Ben-Gurion were at breaking-point, found that his decision had enhanced his political image as a leader who did not hesitate to employ force. There is no proof that Eshkol's decision was motivated by internal political calculations but he was a man with sharp political instincts and certainly never missed an opportunity to gain points with his party and with the general public. Only nine days previously, Dayan had resigned from Eshkol's government, calling for an end 'to the deBen-Gurionization of our security doctrine'.

Two days before the incident, the Mapai Central Committee held a stormy meeting at which Ben-Gurion furiously attacked Eshkol, charging that the party was on the verge of collapse. Two days after the incident, Eshkol again found himself in direct confrontation with Ben-Gurion at the same venue, where the agreement for the establishment of the Alignment Party with Ahdut ha-Avoda was to be approved. It was convenient timing for Eshkol to display resolve and activism, and thereby to neutralize the criticism of the Ben-Gurionites.

It would not be true to claim that Eshkol wanted to escalate the dispute with Syria. While his positive response to Rabin was based on resolutions passed by the government under Ben-Gurion, the fact is that Ben-Gurion never approved the implementation while Eshkol did so, almost casually, and without restrictions.[19] Ben-Gurion displayed great caution in employing the IAF, and the government was well aware that to bring in aircraft was 'a warlike act'.[20] The lengthy debates in the government on this issue dealt, and rightly so, with the basic question of whether and under what circumstances a Minister of Defence and a Chief of Staff would be empowered to employ the IAF during border incidents rather than with the scope and nature of the operation. This was left to the professional consideration of the army[21] and the supervision of the Minister of Defence. However, this indecision and the reluctance of the government to involve the IAF in border incidents indicate a clear intention, though not necessarily explicitly stated, to use it only in extreme cases and in minimal fashion. It seems that on 13 November, under pressure of time and circumstances, Eshkol and Rabin failed to exercise sufficient control over the officer commanding the IAF.

The incidents on 3 and 13 November 1964, stemming from the preparation of the patrol path, were essentially border incidents which took place outside the demilitarized zones. In any event, from this stage on up until the Six Day War, the question of the demilitarized zones was interwoven with the struggle for water and the problems of Palestinian guerrilla warfare against Israel.

Chapter 4

Escalation – Stage 2

Diversion

Israel's water shortage and the disproportional distribution of its limited sources between the country's north and south generated various schemes for development. In the early 1950s, Israel began to establish large-scale water projects, among them the reclamation of the Huleh Lake and the planning and building of the National Water Carrier to convey water southward.[1] On 19 June 1964, for the first time, water flowed continuously from Tabha in the north to Rosh ha-Ayin in central Israel, the linkage point to the Yarkon–Negev pipeline.

The dispute between Israel and Syria over utilization of the Jordan waters sparked serious clashes in the early 1950s after which relative, and temporary, calm prevailed. The two sides maintained regular dialogue both within the Armistice Commission and through direct, high-level contacts between the CO Northern Command Moshe Dayan and senior Syrian officers in attempts, albeit unsuccessful, to resolve border disputes.

In 1953, when Israel began work in the demilitarized zone in order to divert some of the Jordan water as part of the first stage of the National Water Carrier project, Syria complained to the UN Security Council. The US responded by appointing a special envoy, Ambassador Eric Johnston, to deal with the Jordan water issue.[2] Johnston conducted shuttle diplomacy among the countries of the region and, in 1955, he submitted a plan which allotted to Israel some 38 per cent of the Jordan water, the remainder to go to Syria, Lebanon and Jordan. Israel had to halt the pumping of water from the upper Jordan and adopted an alternative, more expensive plan to pump water for the Carrier from Lake Galilee.

This water dispute marked the beginning of the deterioration in Israel–Syrian relations. Ten years later the situation had changed radically: the Israel–Syria Armistice Commission had been suspended, the avenues of dialogue were blocked and the United States was no longer the mediator. Whereas in 1953 to 1954, Israel had the option of pumping from Lake Galilee, in 1964 to 1965 the choice lay between foiling the Arab diversion plan by force or giving up the water project entirely. Whereas in 1953 to 1954 the Water Carrier scheme was in its infancy, in 1964 to 1965 it had been completed and put into operation. Israel agreed to exploit only the water quota allocated to it by the Johnston Plan, and Eshkol announced that water was as vital for Israel 'as the blood in our veins'.[3] In return, Syrian President Amin Hafez threatened a 'suicide war'.[4] A clash was inevitable.

But Israel was clearly the victor in the struggle over water. The construction of the Water Carrier and its uninterrupted operation was a resounding success in the face of militant Arab rhetoric.[5]

The Cairo summit conference

Syria's secession from the United Arab Republic (UAR) in 1961 led to a deep and protracted rift in its relations with Egypt despite a brief apparent *rapprochement* with a 'revolutionary' Syria after the coups of February and March 1963 which brought the Baath to power in Baghdad and Damascus.[6] The negotiations between Baathist Syria and Iraq with Nasserist Egypt culminated in the Tripartite Agreement of 17 April 1963, which evoked great enthusiasm in the Arab world and upheaval in Jordan.

The agreement was essentially a cover for profound differences of opinion, but outwardly it seemed that a consensus prevailed, at least with regard to the conflict with Israel. Ben-Gurion saw this move as an existential threat to Israel. By the summer, however, the atmosphere of unity had been completely dispelled, and President Nasser fiercely attacked the 'fascist' Baath regime, which had massacred Nasserists in Syria, and broke off all relations with that country.[7] The bitter rivalries within the 'revolutionary' camp in the Arab world, and between that camp and the 'conservatives', further exacerbated relations between Egypt and Syria.

Towards the end of the year, unexpectedly, Nasser took a step which surprised both the Arab world and Israeli Intelligence services, calling for a summit conference of all Arab heads of state in Cairo. The background was the imminent completion of Israel's national water project, which the Arabs had repeatedly declared an act of aggression to which they would react with force. Nasser wanted to avoid a situation whereby Syria would drag him into a war against Israel whose timing would not be under his control, while much of his military force was bogged down in the Yemen civil war.[8]

In Israel Nasser's initiative was interpreted, rightly, as a transparent stratagem to disguise Arab helplessness. Israeli Intelligence, however, erred in evaluating the conference's long-term outcome and two of its main resolutions: to divert Jordan river tributaries originating in Lebanon and Syria and to organize the Palestinians, a decision which led to creating the Palestine Liberation Organization (PLO). A third resolution set up a joint Arab military command.[9]

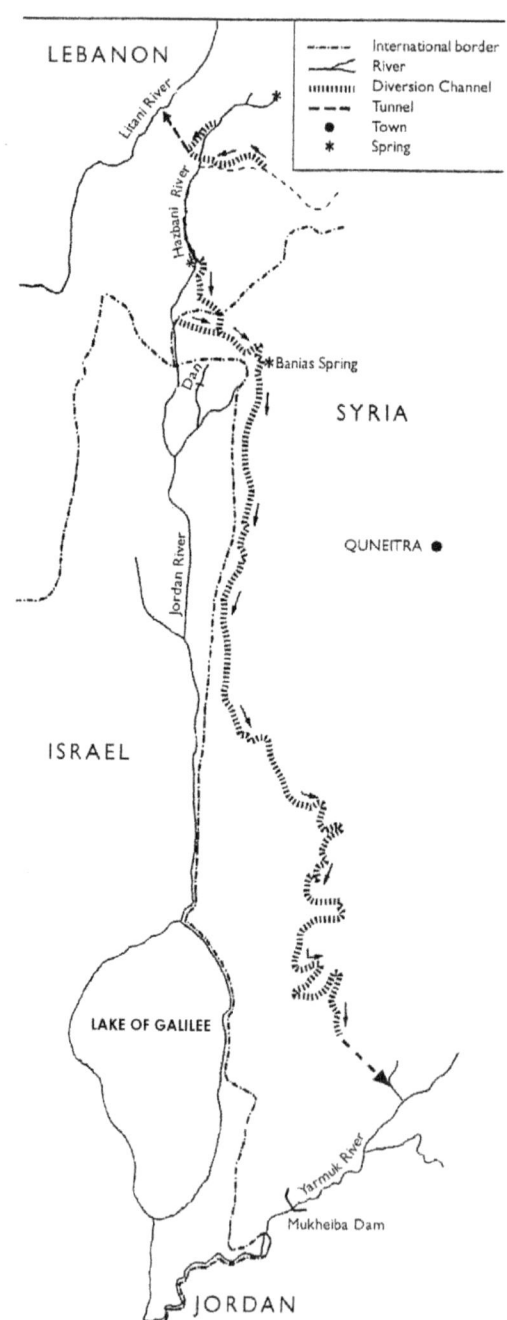

Map 3 The Arab diversion plan.

Deployment for war

Towards the end of 1964 it became evident that the diversion scheme was more serious than had previously been estimated, and that work on it had begun. Rabin believed that the IDF would recommend to the political echelon that Israel deal the first blow while Egypt was still occupied in Yemen. He realized that military action called for political preparation and a decision on the part of the political echelon, but thought that the army should exert pressure to act before the Arabs established facts.[10] The Chief of Staff expressed his fear that the Lebanese would first carry out a small-scale diversion, which would not constitute a sufficient pretext for Israeli action, and that the United States would then persuade Israel to exercise restraint.[11] He proposed a tough Israeli stance based on refusal to accept the diversion or to rely on Lebanon's ability to withstand Egyptian, Syrian and Iraqi pressures.[12] Rabin proposed increasing pressure on the Syrians and assaults on personnel carrying out the diversion work. Even when the political circumstances were not conducive to immediate response, Rabin believed that the IDF should provoke shooting incidents until the politicians were obliged to sanction military action.[13]

At the end of January 1965 Knesset Member Moshe Dayan published an article in *Haaretz* in which he declared that if Israel's deterrent capability proved insufficient to halt the diversion work, military action would be required. To concede on this issue, Dayan argued, would be a double mistake: on the one hand, the Arab project would deprive Israel of more than a hundred million cubic metres of water annually, salinate Lake Galilee and threaten the water project; on the other hand, the disturbance of the status quo would aggravate the situation and lead to a resumption of acts of hostility against Israel, which had ceased since the Sinai Campaign.[14]

At this stage the Chief of Staff was speaking specifically of the need to prepare the Israeli public (and the government) for the possibility of hostilities initiated by Israel, and to foster awareness that there was 'no alternative'. To his fellow officers on the General Staff, Rabin said:

> 'The question is what is the correct path to pursue ... to involve the [government ministers] in a small- or large-scale war ... any one thinking seriously about a clash must give the Jews the feeling that it is inevitable. The [government] will not choose a clash if there is some way out of it ... the only way ... is to present the thesis of "no alternative".'[15]

The task of the army, according to Rabin, was to guarantee operational capabilities and maximal readiness in order to grant the government the freedom to take decisions.[16] But Rabin went further: the army should 'try to expedite' action. This was, therefore, an additional expression of the typical General Staff conviction that its role was not restricted to preparing the armed forces for war and providing backing and room for government policy, but to serve as the catalyst for offensive military action.

The General Staff prepared four possible scenarios for thwarting the diversion scheme, which were presented by the Chief of the Operations Branch Haim Barlev:

1   Limited military action for deterrent purposes, namely a raid or fire directed at mechanical and engineering equipment.
2   A large-scale attack on the weak points of the diversion project (pumps, dams, etc.).
3   Occupation of demilitarized zones controlling the diversion areas, particularly the Banias Heights and Tel Azaziat.
4   Occupation of demilitarized areas and areas under Syrian sovereignty overlooking the diversion areas – Tel Hamra, Tel Azaziat and the Banias Heights as far as the Ram pool.[17]

It transpires from Barlev's remarks that the army regarded the first alternative, which was later preferred by the government, as the minimal choice, marred by numerous drawbacks and dubious effectiveness, which was unlikely to solve the problem but could serve as the introduction to a wider scale operation. This may explain the General Staff's subsequent amazement when this minimal method succeeded in foiling the diversion.

The standpoint represented by the American negotiators Harriman and Komer, said Rabin, was a serious obstacle to any Israeli plans for a military operation. The Americans claimed that there was as yet no proof that the Arabs would take more than had been allotted to them by the Johnston plan and, even if they did, this was not a *casus belli*. Diplomatic efforts, the Chief of Staff clarified, were aimed at arriving at an agreement with the United States as to the 'red line'; for example, the conveyance of water from Lebanon to Syria would constitute justification for an Israeli preventive strike. Hence military action would be subject to political constraints, unless the government decided that the IDF could act without prior coordination with the United States.[18] The Chief of Staff's remarks undoubtedly reflected the controversy within the government between supporters of independent military action against diversion and those who insisted on prior coordination with the US. The official version conveyed to the US administration was that if no peaceful means could be found of preventing implementation of the Arab diversion scheme, Israel would resort to force.[19]

A reconnaissance flight over the diversion area which the Chief of Staff conducted with the two US emissaries was intended to make it clear to them that Israel could damage heavy diversion equipment without crossing the border. The two, Rabin reported to Eshkol, listened to what he had to say but did not react. Rabin's interpretation was that a small-scale military action to disrupt the diversion works in Syria would not be disapproved by Washington. Eshkol agreed to submit Rabin's proposal to the Ministerial Committee on Security for approval.[20]

Plan (A) is put into action

The Israeli decision to use force to prevent the diversion was immediately put into action, surprisingly soon after the end of the talks with the US emissaries. The pretext was an incident which occurred on 16 March 1965, when the Syrians opened fire on Israeli farmers cultivating a plot of land at Hirbet Kara, near Korazim in the central demilitarized zone, killing an Israeli tractor driver. The land had not been under cultivation since May 1951 and it was only to be expected that the Syrians, anxious to prevent any change for the worse in the status quo, would react.

By that stage, the Syrians had already prepared 5 kilometres of the route of the diversion channel west and south of the village of Banias. On the following day, the IDF engineered another incident, by sending out a patrol on the controversial patrol path alongside Tel Dan. Two platoons of tanks were placed on alert, as was the IAF. When the Syrians opened fire from Nuheila, the tanks returned fire, aimed at the source of the gunfire and at the heavy construction equipment, damaging eight tractors. The Syrians were taken by surprise and did not respond, and the IAF was not sent into action.[21]

In the wake of this first action, the Chief of Staff made clear the intention to initiate additional military actions in order to disrupt the diversion project. Inside Syria, said Rabin, 'wherever we see tractors we will immediately go into action ... if the conditions are right'.[22] The original objective was to take action against equipment inside Lebanon as well, where the work was continuing, but for political reasons, in light of the imminent visit to France of the Lebanese President Charles Helou, it was decided to postpone the operation.[23]

Secret negotiations were being held concomitantly between Israel and Lebanon at which Israel made it clear that the water issue was a *casus belli*. The Lebanese proposed a secret settlement based on the principle that 'not a drop of Lebanese water would go either to an Arab country or to Israel', a principle which reflected Lebanese suspicion that Israel coveted the Litani waters. In light of the Arab pressure on Lebanon to fulfil its part in the diversion plan, Eshkol was sceptical as to the possibility of arriving at a settlement.[24]

On 13 May 1965, the IDF staged an additional incident with the aim of damaging equipment working on the diversion track, since the Syrians had renewed work in the central sector of the Golan Heights. Several hours before the operation, the Chief of Staff submitted the plan to the Minister of Defence: the intention was to send out a patrol south of Mishmar ha-Yarden, which would open fire at a spot which was not visible to the UN Observers, thereby provoking the Syrians to return fire. Subsequently the Israeli tanks positioned at the firing positions would destroy the equipment.[25]

The operation was prepared well in advance. Tank and artillery forces were lined up, the settlements were alerted to take shelter, traffic east of Lake Galilee was halted on the pretext of road repairs, and during the incident aircraft were launched to deter the Syrians from shelling settlements. The Syrians did not in fact react, but the tank fire missed the diversion equipment and after half an hour of gunfire only one or two tractors had been hit. 'The operation ended in a miracle,' the Chief of Staff summed up. 'If we had not hit that tractor we would have been in the worst position a Chief of Staff can be in vis-à-vis his Government, with all the implications for the future and for similar operations.'[26] Rabin, who had worked hard to gain approval for the operation, was afraid of losing face, which would cause difficulties in gaining the approval of the political echelon for future action.[27]

Buffer fire

Another mode of operation now adopted by the IDF, after the 16 March incident in the Korazim sector which exacerbated tension on the border with Syria, was the use of light weapons with the aim not of causing damage but of driving Syrian shepherds and fellahin out of the cultivated and grazing areas in the demilitarized zone. The method was simple and effective, and did not usually require more than a few rounds of ammunition. Hence, the objective was achieved easily and 'cheaply', but it altered the status quo and aggravated the Syrians. This was Israel's way of taking a forceful stance in the face of Syrian militancy: Syria's determination to continue the diversion work and its links with guerrilla activity which was now a source of harassment for Israel.

The employment of buffer fire was not a new method,[28] but henceforth it was employed by the IDF systematically and along a wide front. For ten days the Syrians refrained from reaction, apparently in the hope that the IDF would desist, but they then returned fire from light weapons.[29] However, they did not actually possess the suitable means of response, apart from retaliatory disruption of Israeli farming in the demilitarized zones. The buffer fire ceased in June 1966 in light of Syrian initiative for an 'unconditional ceasefire' under UN mediation (see below).

Egypt withdraws

Israel's move constituted a challenge to the Arabs. The Chief of the Intelligence Aharon Yariv assessed that Egypt might feel obliged to respond in some way in order to maintain its prestige but that it was not ready for war against Israel and would act to restrain the Syrians. The Syrians, for their part, complained that the United Arab Command, established by the Cairo summit, had left them to struggle alone against Israel, and argued again that a solution to the Palestinian problem would not be achieved through diversion but only through all-out warfare.

Yariv described the struggle over water and the consequent Arab dilemmas as a three-round boxing match. In the first, Israel scored a technical knock-out by opening the National Water Carrier. In the second, the Syrians scored with their diversion. But in the third, Israel disrupted the Syrian work. In response, Syria turned the issue into an all-Arab issue in order to 'enhance their prestige', demonstrate their nationalist credentials, 'and to be absolved of exclusive responsibility'. This, in turn, created a dilemma for the Egyptians who do not wish to become embroiled in a war with Israel but cannot escape their need to prove devotion to the Arab cause. Their problem, then, 'is how to double-cross the Syrians' by not becoming bogged down in the diversion effort while not giving away too much to the Syrians in exchange for this escape.[30]

Rabin understood that the noose should not be pulled too tightly. The Israeli move had led to temporary cessation of the diversion work and to frantic Arab activity, but it had also evoked protest on the part of the United States, which said that the Israeli action contravened the agreement underlying US readiness to supply Israel with weapons.[31] Rabin therefore ordered a policy of 'pacification and not exacerbation' on the Syrian front, aware that Israel must not cross the narrow line that would force the Arabs into providing united backing for Syria and disrupt the sensitive negotiations for purchase of weapons from the United States.

Nasser clarified his position on the diversion scheme: namely, as long as his army was occupied in Yemen, he had no intention of being lured into a premature war with Israel because of 'a Syrian tractor'. In a speech to the second conference of the PLO in Cairo on 31 May 1965, he declared: 'Fifty thousand of our soldiers are now in Yemen. How am I to attack Israel? First I must bring those fifty thousand back. We don't want a repetition of 1948. If we can't carry out the diversion today, let's postpone the diversion works until we can defend them.' Nasser claimed that an immediate assault on Israel would mean doing what Israel wanted: 'They say to us, expel the UN Emergency Force [from the Egypt–Israel border] ... and what then? If Syria is attacked, then I have to attack Israel. This means, therefore, that Israel can dictate to me when to attack it. They will destroy a tractor in Syria and then I will be forced to attack. ... Only we ourselves should decide the timing.' Nasser dismissed Syrian criticism and informed the Syrians that they should not expect Egyptian aid and should refrain from diversion work on dangerous sites.[32]

The immediate conclusion of Nasser's startling statement was that the IDF had gained a surprisingly easy victory without cost to itself, and had succeeded in disrupting the Arab diversion scheme by a simple, cheap and effective method of inflicting local damage without risking an all-out military confrontation. The conviction which had prevailed among the Israeli General Staff several months previously, to the effect that Israel should brace itself for the possibility of war in autumn 1965 or summer 1966 and prepare the public for this, now evaporated. It was evident that Nasser had no plans for war in the near future. The diversion problem was still on the agenda but Israel had discovered a simple and effective solution. Declared the Chief of Staff, sounding surprised at the fact: 'There is a real disproportion between what we did and what is happening ... after two such [minor] actions, Nasser stands up and talks in that way!? I would never have believed it!'[33]

Nasser's unexpected statement provided firm confirmation for the Israeli Intelligence assessment that he would not permit himself to be dragged into a confrontation with Israel if the time and circumstances were not under his control. Rabin's remarks indicate how amazed the senior command was at the fact that two small-scale local actions against a few tractors had resulted in what seemed to be Nasser's sweeping repudiation of the entire diversion project.

The fading of the diversion scheme

Nasser's proclamations notwithstanding, the liquidation of the diversion plan was not yet complete. Continuation of work in Lebanon confronted Israel with a challenge, but its hands were tied due to international diplomatic pressure. Rabin reported that the United States, France and Britain had made it clear 'that a military operation against Lebanon would be a catastrophe for Israel and [its relations with] the three Powers'. Simultaneously, pressure was brought on Lebanon, which suspended work.[34] In October 1965, after a wave of sabotage infiltrations from Lebanon, the IDF blew up the home of the mukhtar in the village of Huleh and damaged water installations in Mis el-Jabal.[35] These actions also deterred Lebanon from continuing diversion work.

Syria, in contrast, continued the diversion work, but shifted the focus to sites deep within its territory. Northern Command readied itself to damage mechanical engineering equipment at the work site east of Gamla, about 7 kilometres from the border. To this end, Israel resumed cultivation of the disputed area of land at Hirbet Kara in the central demilitarized zone, in the Korazim sector. The Head of the Operations Branch reported: 'We have resumed work in the Hirbet Kara area, where it may be assumed that there will be an incident when the Syrians open fire, which we can expand in order to damage tractors working on Syrian diversion further in.'[36] The incident took place on 12 August.[37] The Syrians, however, apparently apprehensive of Israeli provocation, acted with restraint. IDF tanks, which had been deployed earlier in firing positions, opened fire on Syrian tanks in the sector and scored hits on three of them. This developed into an exchange of artillery fire, with Israel hitting two tractors. Although the incident did not proceed according to the scenario Rabin had anticipated, he reported with satisfaction that the main objective had been achieved, providing 'further proof that we are ready to screw up the diversion work'.[38]

All in all, in this period there were four Israeli actions against the diversion scheme, in all of which the aim was to destroy heavy mechanical equipment: three tank raids on 17 March 1965 in the northern sector, on 13 May 1965 in the central sector and on 12 August 1965 in the southern sector, and one aerial attack on 14 July 1966 in the central sector.[39]

The Israeli initiatives led to the gradual abandonment of the diversion project, and the problem eventually disappeared from the IDF agenda. In the autumn, Rabin claimed that the diversion would not advance much for many years.[40] In spring 1966 the Chief of Intelligence described the slow pace of work. 'The Arabs are not treating it very seriously', he said, and the United Arab Command was incapable of providing military protection for the project.[41] From time to time there were Intelligence reports that work in Syria had been accelerated,[42] but the issue was no longer of great concern to the General Staff.

Was the war in June 1967 the continuation of the War over Water? Not necessarily. The struggle over water in 1965 to 1966 may have aggravated the Arab–Israel conflict but it was not the direct cause of the war. At most, it was a background factor.

The surprising Israeli success in thwarting the diversion scheme by simple measures and without military or political embroilment, along with a resounding triumph in the battle for water bolstered the confidence of the General Staff in its ability to solve Israel's security problems by launching military initiatives without necessarily escalating the situation. The success also reinforced the Intelligence Branch's evaluation that Nasser was clinging to his security doctrine, namely avoidance of entanglement in another war with Israel at a time when the conditions were not favourable for Egypt. This meant that Israel had considerable freedom of manoeuvre for offensive action. And above all: the government now increasingly put its trust in the Chief of Staff, and his operative proposals.

It should be pointed out that Nasser's unexpected moderation may also be explained in light of his attempt at that time to improve his relations with the United States. Egypt needed continued US economic aid, and particularly consignments of food, but encountered a cool response. The administration and Congress contemplated sanctions against Egypt because of its intervention in the war in Yemen, Nasser's support for the rebels in Congo, his anti-Western policy and his refusal to cooperate with Washington's initiative to check the missile and nuclear race in the Middle East.[43] At that time (May 1965) Nasser still hoped for American consent to Egypt's requests for aid, and consequently displayed moderation in his attitude to Israel. Two years later (May 1967) when he had despaired of the United States, he permitted himself a more aggressive stance.

Chapter 5

The dispute with Syria worsens

Syria was the last of the Arab states to sign an armistice agreement with Israel after the 1948 war, and the first in which the civil regime was replaced by the military in the wake of the war. The coup in March 1949, whereby Colonel Husni al-Zaim seized power, was the first in a long series of frequent changes of government in Damascus, the great majority of them military coups.[1]

The connection between the chronic instability of the Syrian regime and its relations with Israel and border disputes is not straightforward. The regimes of Colonel al-Zaim (March–August 1949), Colonel Sami al-Hinawi (August–December 1949) and Adib al-Shishakli (December 1949–February 1954) were not characterized by strong hostility towards Israel. Al-Zaim even put out feelers regarding a peace settlement with Israel, and al-Shishakli conducted lengthy negotiations with Israel for allotment of the demilitarized zones and exploitation of the Jordan waters. Arye Shalev divides the period between the signing of the armistice agreement (20 July 1949) and the Six Day War into three periods: up until March 1951 – the quiet period; March 1951 to September 1953 – the period of struggle and settlement; from early 1954 to June 1967 – the period of violent clashes. The reasons for the escalation from 1954 on were: (1) exhaustion of the possibilities for diplomatic negotiations for division of the demilitarized zones; (2) deterioration of the situation along Israel's borders with Jordan and Egypt, leading to acts of terror and reprisal raids; (3) the deposing (in February 1954) of Shishakli from the Syrian leadership, spelling the end of the pragmatic policy.[2]

It seems that the main reason for the deterioration in Syrian–Israeli relations should not necessarily be sought in the frequent coups in Damascus, but rather in the change in Syria's orientation after the downfall of Shishakli and its open alignment with Egypt and neutralist stand in the controversy on the West's defence schemes for the Middle East in 1954 to 1955. The dramatic rise of the Baath Party in the autumn 1954 elections and its subsequent representation in the government also marked a radicalization of Syria's policy trends.[3] After details of the Egyptian–Czech arms deal became known, Syria and Egypt signed a defence pact in October 1955. The IDF action in December 1955 against Syrian positions in the north-east sector of Lake Galilee, which had not been preceded by any particular Syrian provocation, again focused Syrian hostility on Israel. The 1956 Sinai Campaign greatly exacerbated the Arab–Israel conflict, and in the period of unity with Egypt (1958–1961) the Syrian members of the United Arab Republic urged adoption of a militant approach towards Israel compared to Nasser's cautious policy. After seceding from the UAR, Syria continued to brandish the banner of confrontation with Israel in order to score points against Egypt. The coups in Damascus in March 1963 and February 1966, which brought the Baath to power, strengthened this trend.

The third summit

The third Arab summit conference was convened in Casablanca (13–17 September 1965). Shortly afterwards, on 24 August, an agreement was signed in Jedda between President Nasser of Egypt and the Saudi monarch Feisal for solution of the Yemen problem and evacuation by stages of Egyptian forces from that country. This agreement, which neither endured nor was ever implemented, could not disguise the widening rift in the Arab world.

The failure of the diversion scheme in light of armed Israeli resistance, and the accusations which the Syrians hurled at Egypt in this respect, overshadowed the summit. Bitter disputes raged around the Egyptian demand that the other Arab states break off diplomatic ties with West Germany and impose an economic boycott because of its decision to establish full diplomatic relations with Israel.[4]

An additional affair which saw the Arab world in an uproar in the months preceding the Casablanca conference was connected to the public declarations of the Tunisian President Habib Bourguiba, who suggested that the Arabs reconcile themselves to Israel's existence and accept the UN partition resolution and the resolution on the return of the refugees as a means of solving the Palestinian problem in stages. The polemics led to fierce verbal clashes between Bourguiba and Nasser, and the former decided to boycott the Arab summit.[5]

In essence, the resolutions of the summit conference sanctioned the suspension of the diversion work, at least in places which were vulnerable to Israeli attack. The resolution calling for strengthening of the United Arab Command essentially implied that all military confrontation with Israel was to be postponed until military preparations were completed.[6] However, Israeli Intelligence learned that the leaders of the Arab states convened at Casablanca had also discussed a secret plan for the annihilation of Israel.[7] The conference also decided to shorten the period of preparations for war from five to three years.[8] It seems that acknowledgement of the failure of the diversion scheme, their sense of impotence and Syrian pressure persuaded the participants to accelerate their preparations for the all-out confrontation with Israel.

Several months after the Casablanca summit, a change occurred across the Syrian border, whose outcome was to have a far-reaching impact on acceleration of the processes leading the region to war.

The Damascus coup

On 23 February 1966 a violent military coup took place in Damascus, the thirteenth since 1949, deposing General Amin al-Hafez. The coup was executed by young officers from the Baath 'military committee' headed by Salah Jadid, a forty-year-old army officer of radical socialist orientation from the Alawite minority in Syria. Jadid appointed to key positions in the administration three physicians who held similar views, who had served as volunteers in the FLN guerrilla war against the French occupation of Algeria: Dr Nur a-din al-Atassi was appointed President, Dr Yusuf Zueyn as Premier, and Dr Ibrahim Makhous as Foreign Minister. An additional prominent member of the military committee, the Commander of the air force Hafez al-Assad, a thirty-five-year-old Alawite, was appointed Minister of Defence. As Chief of Staff, Jadid chose Ahmad al-Suidani, a Sunni Muslim, who had served previously as military attaché in Peking and had been influenced by Maoist theory regarding guerrilla warfare struggles.[9]

Israeli Intelligence at first concluded that the Syrian coup would have no impact on Israel. The Chief of the Intelligence Branch defined the new rulers as a more extreme group with a more aggressive approach to Israel, but surmised that coming to power would have a moderating effect on them.[10]

It soon became clear that the new regime in Damascus was not the direct continuation of its predecessor, but had characteristics of its own which would have a detrimental effect on the conflict with Israel. The main problem, so far as Israel was concerned, was not necessarily the border clashes in the demilitarized zones or the struggle for water, but the backing for, organization and operation of the 'popular struggle' against Israel which Syria now undertook.

In the inter-Arab arena, the ruling junta in Syria was regarded as an irresponsible and provocative element,[11] eager to foment 'revolution now' in the Arab world and to expedite its unification and struggle against imperialism and Israel. The concept of an immediate popular struggle was the strategic antithesis of Nasser's policy, namely to postpone the clash with Israel until the armies were ready and conditions were ripe for Arab victory.[12] It was the implementation of this alternative strategy which eventually expedited the military clash in 1967.

Between Damascus and Moscow

The regime of Jadid, Assad and Suidani might have been a fleeting episode, one of many, in the series of incessant military coups in Syria, but for the fact that this regime received Great Power backing which no previous Syrian regime had enjoyed. The Israeli Chief of Intelligence perceived the increasingly close links between Moscow and Damascus as the result of the Soviet decision to stabilize its standpoint in the region, in the face of what seemed to the Russians to be a US-led offensive against the revolutionary regimes in Afro-Asian countries. Coups and attempted coups in Ghana and Nigeria, Indonesia and Congo, and the Saudi initiative for the establishment of an 'Islamic alliance', roused the Soviets, who feared that the CIA was behind all these developments, to adopt countermeasures to defend their strongholds in the Middle East.

Israel was perceived as the spearhead of imperialism in the region and the US arms deals with Israel and Jordan were assumed to be part of a general scheme, endangering the Soviet hold on Syria. Syria's value was enhanced after the Communist Party began to be represented in the government.[13] Yariv feared therefore that closer relations between Syria and the Soviet Union would hamper Israel's freedom of movement, both political and military, on the Syrian border. At the same time, the Chief of Intelligence reported that the Soviet–Egyptian arms deal, signed in September 1965, was of 'giant' proportions, and would involve the dispatch of 1,500 Soviet experts to Egypt.[14] In other words, Soviet involvement in the region had taken on a new dimension.

The deep Soviet involvement and the backing it gave the Syrians in the international arena enabled the radical regime in Damascus to conduct an activist policy and to give practical expression to its ideological commitment to the idea of a 'popular struggle'. The Soviets did not spur the Syrians on to more extreme action; in fact they even tried to moderate their reactions, but in any event they rallied to their support and provided them with diplomatic backing, arms and training. Soviet patronage restricted Israel's freedom of action. From then up until the Six Day War the government did not permit the IDF, despite the accumulating reasons and the increasing pressure on the part of the General Staff, to launch a ground operation against Syria. However, in the final analysis, Soviet involvement was, without deliberate intent, apparently the direct cause of the development which led to war.

An 'unconditional ceasefire'

For a time it seemed that the moderating influence of the Soviet Union was having an impact not only on Israel but also on Syria. The Syrian Chief of Staff Ahmad al-Suidani met with the commander of the UN forces General

Odd Bull, and informed him that his country was interested in easing the tension. He proposed an 'unconditional ceasefire' and joint supervision of the border as the first stage in problem resolution, particularly in the Almagor sector. Bull conveyed the message to Israel, which responded positively. Rabin deduced that the initiative had stemmed from the Soviet Union. While he did not trust the Russians and the Syrians, the government had hopes of the new trend.[15]

It soon became clear that the formula promising an unconditional ceasefire had not eliminated the misunderstandings. Syrian peasants infiltrated the disputed area and the IDF refrained from 'buffer fire' on orders from the political echelon. Rabin defined the situation as a trap from which the army must extricate itself. He urged the politicians to test Syria's intentions by instigating cultivation of controversial plots of land in the demilitarized zones, thus forcing the Syrians to either exercise restraint or violate the ceasefire. The moderate policy vis-à-vis the Syrian border was seen in the IDF as a move intended to tie Israel's hands and prevent it from employing buffer fire, and, on the other hand, to enable the Syrians to back the 'popular struggle' against Israel from inside Jordan and Lebanon.

At the beginning of July 1966, the Deputy UN Secretary-General Dr Ralph Bunche visited the region and met with Prime Minister Eshkol and Foreign Minister Eban.[16] Bunche wanted to reduce the UN Emergency Force in Sinai, and in particular at Sharm al-Sheikh, for budgetary reasons. Rabin favoured retaining the existing deployment, but with fewer UN troops, although some support was also voiced for removal of the UN altogether.[17]

Operation 'Wind': the air force goes into action again

On 13 July 1966, an Israeli command car hit a mine south-east of Almagor, very close to the spot where, two months previously, two employees of the Jewish National Fund had been killed in a terrorist attack. This time the mine killed two soldiers and a civilian. On the same day the Ministerial Committee on Security was convened again, and the Chief of Staff declared that Israel could not remain silent. He tried to dispel the ministers' fears of entanglement. He stressed the lack of unity in the Arab world, and dismissed the possibility of Soviet intervention. On the contrary, an IDF operation could, he said, strengthen the 'Russian argument that it is not worth becoming involved with Israel unnecessarily and at the wrong time'. He proposed that the air force be dispatched to damage heavy equipment at Ain Sufira, south-east of Almagor. After a debate in which, as usual, the Minister of the Interior Moshe Haim Shapira and the Minister of Labour Yigal Allon represented opposite opinions, the Committee decided to approve an immediate reprisal raid against

Syria, and to empower the Minister of Defence to decide on the form the reprisal would take. The decision enabled the Minister, if no other form of reaction was possible, to employ aircraft against the equipment. On the following day (14 July) Israeli French-made Mystere and Vautour planes destroyed eight pieces of heavy engineering equipment working on the diversion route at Ain Sufira and the anti-aircraft unit defending them (Operation 'Wind'). The Syrians launched Mig 21s, and one of the Mirages patrolling the air space scored a hit on a Mig and brought it down. It was the first ever downing of a Mig 21 by a Mirage.[18]

At the government meeting of 17 July, Eban described the international reaction to the Israeli operation as 'balanced. . . . They all emphasized the Syrian provocations as leading to this attack.' Eshkol explained: 'Perhaps the world is accepting our claims this time, namely that the topographical situation is such that if we do not respond, we are the victims.' He added: 'An aircraft is now considered less than a cannon two years ago. . . . The United States is occupied with its war in Vietnam and is not in a position to preach to others.'[19] And indeed, even at the Security Council, Israel escaped condemnation, while the discussion of Syria's complaint turned into a Soviet–US verbal clash on Vietnam, and the Americans thwarted the Arab proposal.

At the General Staff debriefing on the IAF operation conducted three days later, the Chief of Staff explained that the intention was to restore to the IDF the freedom of action which had been gained as a result of employment of the IAF on 13 November 1964, and had been restricted again when the Syrians adopted the rules of the game according to which civilian settlements were not to be shelled. As Rabin saw it, the attack on the diversion work in the hinterland carried out by the IAF also had a deterrent effect on other countries which were seeking an 'alibi' in order to refrain from implementing the diversion work, according to Rabin's estimation. He admitted that the demonstrative employment of the IAF could have 'aggravated the escalation'. It was difficult to explain this to the political echelon, he said, but the action had been essential in order to confront the Syrians with the threat of a wide-scale clash and induce them thereby to stop provoking Israel. As for the downing of the Mig, the Chief of Staff's remarks indicate that this act exceeded the aims of the operation, and hence was criticized by the government, which feared a breach in relations with the Soviet Union.

Together with the praise he lavished on the Israeli pilots, Rabin commented:

> 'I know that fighter pilots are trained like paratroopers, tank crews, to sink in their teeth and not let go, like a bulldog with its prey. But, gentlemen, we operate according to rules and laws and must observe them without question. Because it is an order and we are an army. I know

that everyone is enthusiastic and it was a historic opportunity to down a Mig. . . . There were incidents here which I would not like to describe as failure to carry out orders, but I would not like them to be repeated in the future.'[20]

It appears that once again the IAF had exceeded its approved brief and escalated the dispute with Syria.

The IAF operation of 14 July 1966 should be regarded as an additional milestone, more important even than the Tel Dan incident of 13 November 1964. It would seem that the military and diplomatic success this time freed up the government and the IDF from constraints on the employment of aerial forces in border incidents. The rule, that Israel would only react with aerial bombardment to the shelling of settlements, was broken. From now on, Israel dared to employ the IAF with greater frequency, and US backing at the United Nations became a commonplace.

The border dispute between Syria and Israel was therefore growing increasingly complex. Syrian readiness to maintain calm in the demilitarized zones was tactical. The chosen strategy was to conduct a guerrilla struggle against Israel, and this goal was accorded priority. Soviet diplomatic backing extended Syria's space for manoeuvre. Rabin was concerned at Syria's calculated moves, which combined moderate policy on the borders with support for guerrilla warfare against Israel, based in Syria and carried out through 'two wings': Lebanon and Jordan.[21]

As a result of the new Syrian strategy, the main problem which preoccupied Israel from now on was no longer connected to the diversion work or to incidents in the demilitarized zones, but rather to Palestinian guerrilla activity.

Chapter 6

Escalation – Stage 3

'Harassment'

If there is one factor which seemingly may be isolated and regarded as the main catalyst for the escalation which led to the Six Day War, it is the guerrilla activities of the Palestinian organizations, and in particular the Fatah, against Israel. This form of warfare, which found expression primarily in acts of sabotage and mine-laying, began in early 1965, and gained momentum until it became – from Israel's viewpoint – intolerable.[1] It confronted the IDF senior command with a serious challenge, and despite endless discussions and indecision among the General Staff, they did not succeed in formulating an effective response which would end the incidents. Israel's pre-war borders, and in particular the Jordanian border, were easily penetrable and difficult to block. In the absence of a direct way of tackling the problem, Israel cast responsibility on any country through whose borders the terrorists infiltrated. Jordan and Lebanon, from which most of the saboteurs came, tried to prevent the infiltrations, while Syria, which supported the Fatah, was generally careful to ensure that the attacks did not stem directly from its territory, and tried to implicate Jordan.

Israel felt the need from time to time to provide Jordan with 'incentives' for fighting the Fatah by means of acts of reprisal, but was also anxious to preserve the stability of King Hussein's regime in Jordan and of the Lebanese government, and the fact that those two countries enjoyed firm Western backing restricted Israel's freedom of action. Syria, on the other hand, as noted above, strengthened its links with the USSR from 1966 on, and enjoyed Soviet diplomatic support and military supply. In the background was Egypt, which opposed the Fatah's mode of action for most of this period for fear of hostile involvement with Israel before the time was ripe. At the same time, in light of its widening rift with Saudi Arabia and Jordan, Egypt was in favour of undermining the Hashemite regime in Jordan, and eventually also gave its silent consent to the launching of attacks on Israel from inside Jordan.

The Israeli General Staff and political echelon were divided in their views on this intricate situation. Both bodies took a severe view of the escalation in terrorist attacks and concurred on the need to halt them before they disrupted everyday life in Israel. However, whereas the army emphasized offensive solutions, the government wanted the military to focus more on defensive and preventive activities, a policy which was anathema to senior officers. Because of political constraints and fear of deterioration into war, the government was reluctant to sanction operations across the border, and gave its approval only in isolated cases. It imposed stringent restrictions on the scope and objectives of such actions. On the only occasion when the government approved a large-scale operation inside Jordan in November 1966, the operation extended beyond its original aims, and the outcome almost caused the collapse of Hussein's regime.

The PLO

The initiative for the reorganization of the 'Palestinian entity', its evolvement from a mere refugee problem into a national body with representative institutions, had stemmed from Egypt as early as 1959, at a time when the prestige of Nasserism in the Arab world was at an all-time high. The intiative did not reach maturity until 1964, and it was only the resolution of the Cairo Arab summit which provided the impetus. In the wake of that resolution, the first Palestinian congress was convened in May 1964 in East Jerusalem. It culminated in the declaration of the establishment of the Palestine Liberation Organization (PLO), to be headed by the Palestinian representative on the Arab League Ahmad Shukeiri. The second Arab summit welcomed the establishment of the PLO and also ratified the organization's decision to set up the Palestine Liberation Army.[2]

Until the Six Day War, the PLO was closely linked to Egypt, although it had been founded on Jordanian soil and with the ostensible cooperation of the regime. King Hussein, who, as a result of the 'summit atmosphere', did not see any possibility of objecting to the establishment of the PLO, tried to control the inevitable process through supervision of the election of members of the Palestinian National Congress. However, as time passed and the atmosphere was dissipated and the gap between the 'revolutionary' and 'conservative' Arab camps widened, the anticipated rift between the PLO and Jordan materialized, and fierce, open hostility ensued. Only on the very eve of the Six Day War was a constrained conciliation achieved between the two camps. On 30 June 1967, when King Hussein 'went to Canossa' and signed the defence pact with Egypt in Cairo (see below), Nasser forced him to take his sworn enemy, the head of the PLO, Ahmad Shukeiri, back with him on his flight to Amman.

Until June 1967, the PLO followed the Egyptian line, and, in accord with Egypt's policies, did not perpetrate acts of sabotage against Israel. Its main activity was intra-Palestinian organization and institutionalization of the Palestinian presence at pan-Arab and international forums.

The 'Palestine Liberation Army' also took shape, in particular thanks to Egyptian support, and in spring 1967 it comprised three infantry brigades. At the same time, from 1966, in light of the *rapprochement* between Egypt and Syria and the rift with Jordan, the PLO too began to back terrorist activity against Israel emanating from Jordan. An important reason for this was the growing popularity of a rival Palestinian organization, the Fatah, whose guerrilla warfare against Israel gained wide support and won it considerable prestige among the Palestinian public.

Fatah

Unlike the PLO, which was to a large extent the product of inter-Arab politics, Fatah (initials in reverse of Harakat al-Tahrir al-Watani al-Filastini – Palestinian National Liberation Movement) was an authentic outshoot of the Palestinian diaspora in camps, universities and refugee concentrations. It represented a new and militant Palestinian generation, who had experienced the trauma of uprooting at an early age in 1948 and had undertaken the mission of repairing the injustice by annihilating the State of Israel and by achieving the 'return' (al-'Awda') to Palestine. The strategy which evolved, to no small extent inspired by the successful struggle of the FLN in Algeria and the spirit of the times, was a 'popular war', its objective to undermine Israel's security, restore the pride of the Palestinian people and recruit the young generation into the ranks, and accelerate the all-out confrontation between the Arabs and Israel, which would lead to achievement of their goals. The organizational efforts began in the second half of the 1950s, among members of the Association of Palestinian Students headed by Yasser Arafat, Isa Hamud and Halil al-Wazir, in Egypt and in Kuwait. Their organ, 'Filastinuna' (Our Palestine), advocated the establishment of an independent movement of Palestinian 'fidaiyyun' ('those who sacrifice themselves') movement, which would dedicate itself to the armed struggle, and no longer rely on the Arab states.[3]

The operational activity of the Fatah against Israel did not commence until the beginning of 1965. The total surprise evinced by the IDF at its emergence and early activities testified to the hithertoo over-casual attitude of the Intelligence Branch towards the Palestinian entity in general.[4]

Fatah activities were initially independent and relatively amateurish, and made an impact mainly in the propaganda sphere and on Palestinian morale. However, with time, Syria, loyal to the 'popular struggle' ideology, extended its patronage to the organization, and the methods of operation and implementation gradually improved and became more professional and daring. The Fatah successes[5] led to the emergence of additional small Palestinian guerrilla organizations, but until the Six Day War Fatah remained the dominant organization and a central factor in the escalation process which led to war.[6]

The primary objectives of the Fatah were initially related to Israel's water installations[7] and at first it seemed that this was a new type of operation as part of the 'War for Water'. It soon transpired that the Fatah was not restricting its objectives to water installations. From then on, almost unconsciously, the IDF launched a new stage in its methods of tackling routine security problems. After more than eight years of calm in the sphere of border infiltration and terror activities, the IDF was again required to find solutions to the problem, which was now referred to as 'harassment' and later as 'hostile sabotage activity'.

It is noteworthy that the term 'terror' or 'terrorists' hardly ever appears in references by the Israeli military at the time to Fatah activities. More commonly used are the terms 'guerrilla' or 'guerrilla warfare' and sometimes even the loaded term used by the other side: 'popular struggle'. But the most common phrase was the neutral definition – 'harassment activity', or, in brief: 'harassment'. This definition possibly implied a certain contempt for the phenomenon and its depiction as a nuisance and a minor problem which the army was forced to deal with, rather than a true military challenge. However, this 'nuisance' soon became a major issue which preoccupied the IDF increasingly and proved insoluble.

By March 1965 the Intelligence Branch already regarded the Fatah as an important factor, which was operating independently and complicating the situation. The Chief of Intelligence depicted Fatah's objectives as follows: 'They have an approach which claims that since the State of Israel will have an atom bomb in the nineteen seventies, the final test must occur before then. Since the Arab Governments cannot be relied on [to solve the Palestinian problem on their own initiative], we must create provocation and drag them into war.'[8] In hindsight it seems that the Fatah achieved their aim of instigating warfare between the Arab states and Israel, although the outcome of the war did not come up to its expectations.

Operation Cliff

After five months of consecutive, though ineffective activity on the part of the Fatah, mainly across the Jordanian border, the political echelon finally approved an IDF reprisal operation against Jordan, for the first time since October 1956. The restrictions imposed on the operation were stringent. It was intended to serve as a caution and incentive to the Jordanian authorities to utilize more effective methods of deterring the population from collaborating with the Fatah. The immediate pretext for the IDF operation was the laying of demolition charges in two buildings in kibbutz Ramat ha-Kovesh in the Sharon Valley on the night of 25/26 May 1965, and in a house in Afula on the following night, incidents in which seven Israeli civilians were injured. The IDF reacted immediately and in close proximity to the sites of the incidents. On the night of 27/28 May, infantry and paratroop forces operated against inanimate objectives: they blew up water pumps and a building in Qalqiliya, a flour mill and ice factory in Jenin and three buildings in a Fatah training camp at Hirbet Shuna. The army was far from happy at the restrictions imposed on it. Some members of the General Staff believed that so limited an operation would not only fail to deter but even encourage the Fatah.[9]

The General Staff vacillates

In July 1965 the General Staff devoted two consecutive meetings to a 'free debate', in the course of which the Chief of Intelligence surveyed the Intelligence picture, and the generals exchanged views and evaluations. The ideas ranged from drastic reprisal operations, occupation of territories on the West Bank and taking over the demilitarized zones on the Syrian border to counter-terror operations. At the time it was already evident that the diversion issue had decreased in importance and that terrorist activity was now becoming the central problem.

The 'free debate' was of particular importance, since it exposed for the first time views which later intensified and began to prevail among the senior command – namely that it was time to strike a severe blow at Syria and Jordan, as the preferred method of putting a stop to Fatah activity. Passive defence against infiltrations was costly, exhausting and ineffective, and above all at odds with the spirit of an army raised on the offensive doctrine. Experience had proved, so the senior officers believed, that there was only one effective measure for ending infiltration for sabotage purposes, and that was a wide-scale military operation such as the 1956 Sinai Campaign. This was the type of exercise that the army had learned and trained for and knew how to execute. The discussion was conducted against the background of the rising tension on the border with Syria because of the diversion work and the incidents in the demilitarized areas, but also in light of Nasser's retreat from his backing for the diversion, a fact which expanded Israel's freedom of action. The deliberations reflected the desire to exploit the Fatah attacks as a pretext for conducting a reckoning with Syria, with which Israel had a lengthy account. There also surfaced from time to time in the course of the discussions the territorial aspirations of some members of the General Staff, particularly towards Jordan.

Chief of Staff Rabin summed up the discussions by saying that he was not concerned about the balance of power between the IDF and the Arab armies, and that the IDF had devised a solution to the diversion problem which did not entail a serious clash. His main concern was the guerrilla warfare. He confessed that he had no satisfactory answer to propose, and 'if I were an Arab, I would choose this method'. The IDF had achievements to its credit in undermining Arab unity and in the 'water war', but the Fatah was endangering those achievements. Rabin saw no escape from the employment of diverse methods: on the one hand, to try to hit on Fatah members, despite the difficulty in locating them; on the other hand, to undertake various deterrent and punitive actions. To those who sought territorial gains, the Chief of Staff explained that the development of wide-scale actions against Syria, Lebanon and Jordan with the aim of occupation was a lengthy process which could endanger the IDF's arms purchases and modernization plans.[10]

The General Staff was therefore obliged against its will, by Fatah activity, to focus on routine security issues. The IDF was not accustomed to tackling guerrilla warfare, and Rabin defined its functioning against terror and infiltration as 'B minus', despite all the budgetary and operational investment.[11]

Operations 'Jewel' and 'Scales'

The continuing Fatah raids from Jordan[12] forced the government to approve an additional IDF operation, carried out on the night of 4/5 September 1965. Once again, severe restrictions were imposed on the operation, carried out by a battle team of the Parachute Brigade. The objectives, namely eleven wells in the Qalqiliya region, met with the disapproval of the Chief of Staff. The fact that it was a clean operation, with no casualties, brought him praise, but Rabin did not delude himself that it would put an end to Fatah operations. His remarks indicate that he did not believe in the efficacy of small-scale actions but was ready to try this method if he could obtain approval for a long series of them.[13] This method might have proved itself, but the government showed no intention to approve further reprisal actions of this kind.

An additional focused action conducted by the IDF in immediate response was directed against Lebanon. After a series of infiltrations for sabotage purposes into the village of Margaliyot and damage inflicted on the water pipe of Kibbutz Manara, the IDF, on the night of 27/28 October, blew up the house of the mukhtar of Hula village from which the saboteurs had come, and damaged three wells and water reservoirs in the village of Mis al-Jabal. As a consequence, the Lebanese Intelligence authorities and army stepped up their supervision of the concentrations of Palestinians in southern Lebanon and increased their own deterrent activity along the border.

A further serious discussion at the General Staff forum in October 1965 again exposed the misgivings of the IDF senior command as to ways of dealing with Fatah activities in general, and those stemming from Jordan in particular. Examination of the statements reveals that in practice there were two alternative plans of action which could be presented to the political echelon: the first plan was to react to sabotage from Jordan by a protracted consecutive series of local punitive small-scale actions, which would spur the Jordanian authorities to boost their struggle against the Fatah. The second alternative was to instigate a large-scale reprisal operation, to include, for example, occupation of a village and demolition of its houses, in a manner which would shock the Jordanian authorities into taking drastic steps to check the Fatah. The other proposals, which ranged from 'counter-terror' to occupation of the West Bank, were irrelevant, because they had no prospect of approval by the government.

On the face of it, the Israeli government, in light of its composition and moderate tendencies, should have chosen the first alternative. The paradox is that it was precisely the government's moderation which drove it in the second direction. The government was not eager to approve reprisal actions, and when it did so, this step was usually taken after vacillation and stringent constraints were imposed. And since it had refrained for a long period from approving small-scale operations, it was finally obliged, when the terrorist squads which had crossed the Jordanian border finally reached Jerusalem, to approve a wide-scale operation, which almost caused Hussein's downfall and was a source of serious political embarrassment to Israel's government. Eshkol's method, which he later defined succinctly as 'the book is open and it is all being recorded', created a lengthy reckoning, and in the end the government was forced to react on a large scale. As will be shown below, both in the IDF and outside it, the government was charged with having encouraged terrorist action by its very failure to react.

Operations 'Alpha' and 'Joseph'

At General Staff meetings held between October 1965 and January 1966 the Chief of Intelligence reported on the increasingly bitter struggle between Jordan and the PLO, and on the other hand noted information on the Fatah's intention to hit vital targets deep inside Israel.[14] In practice, however, there was a certain easing of Fatah activity during this period.[15] The relative calm lasted for some five months, and the Intelligence Branch attributed this to the firm line adopted by the Jordanian authorities against the Fatah.

In April 1966 Fatah squads which infiltrated from Jordan perpetrated a series of acts of sabotage, including an attack on Kibbutz Beit Yosef, which damaged three homes and injured two civilians, and the laying of a mine between Arad and Massada.[16] In reaction, on the night of 29/30 April, infantry and paratroop forces raided the village of Kal'at in the north of the eastern Jordan Valley and Hirbet Rafa in the southern Hebron mountains, and detonated twenty-eight houses. The pattern was still identical to that of previous operations, and the force was given strict instructions to avoid harming civilians. Notwithstanding, eleven Jordanian civilians lost their lives.[17] It was an omen for the future.

In the course of 1966, the new regime in Syria gradually took control of the Fatah and determined its policies. The organization, expelled from its bases in Jordan and Lebanon by action of the authorities there, required a base in Syria, and the regime there supplied ideological and practical backing. Syria's self-image as pioneer of the Arab struggle against Israel obliged it to grant backing and support to a Palestinian organization conducting guerrilla warfare in enemy territory. However, the Syrians exploited the Fatah in the inter-Arab struggle, in order to undermine the 'reactionary' Jordanian regime and embarrass the Egyptians. The change in Syria's attitude under the new radical Ba'ath regime was fundamental. Whereas in the past Syria had advocated an immediate pan-Arab frontal clash with Israel, from now on it preferred the longer path of a patient 'popular liberation war'. In response, the IDF senior command reached the conclusion that Syria must not be permitted to determine the rules of the game, and should be forced into a frontal confrontation which would lead to the downfall of the regime or its abandonment of support for a popular war. The political echelon, however, was still far from accepting this conclusion.

Chapter 7

The General Staff wants a 'frontal clash'

In summer 1966 the IDF General Staff arrived at the conclusion that the only way to halt terrorist activity was to inflict a resounding military blow on Syria. From the moment the Damascus regime had 'adopted' Fatah and began to activate it, there was a consensus among Israeli generals on the need to impose a 'frontal clash' on Syria which would shake the radical regime, perhaps even cause it to collapse and, in any event, force it to abandon the idea of a 'popular struggle'. The model which they envisaged was based on the 1956 Sinai Campaign which had put a stop to 'fidaiyyun' raids from the Gaza Strip. Egypt was now embroiled in Yemen, the Arab world was polarized and split, and Nasser was constantly proclaiming that he would not be lured into a war before the time was ripe. The situation appeared opportune for decisive action against Syria. While the close relations between Damascus and Moscow aroused some apprehension, it seemed reasonable to assume that if the Israeli blow was swiftly delivered, it would achieve its objectives without inducing the Soviet Union and Egypt to intervene.

The senior command of the IDF had long desired to 'teach the Syrians a lesson'.[1] This aspiration stemmed in part from the fact that the Syrian army was the only one of the forces that invaded the Jewish state in 1948 which was not defeated or driven back. The border skirmishes in the demilitarized areas and around Lake Galilee, the protracted obstinate battle over each plot of land, the shooting incidents which often claimed lives and caused severe damage to settlements, the diversion work which the Syrians continued doggedly even after suffering punishing blows, Syria's open militancy towards Israel in the inter-Arab arena – all these had evoked fury and frustration in the IDF command, which sought an outlet. The brutal treatment of Israeli prisoners at the hands of the Syrians, the 1955 suicide of the soldier Uri Ilan in Syrian captivity and the public hanging of the Israeli spy Eli Cohen in 1965 heightened hostility towards Syria. Yitzhak Rabin himself had bitter memories of his period as head of the Northern Command, and the current head, David Elazar, was also highly antagonistic towards Syria.[2]

The Israeli government did not see eye to eye with the army. It was ready to invest more and more resources in defensive and preventive measures, and insisted that the IDF do more in this sphere, its aversion to such measures notwithstanding. The IDF's efforts in this direction had scant success in checking terrorist activity, which was on the increase. In the end, the government had no choice but to accept the army's recommendations in one way or another. What the IDF did not take into consideration was the possibility that the Soviet Union and Egypt would intervene even before Israel and Syria clashed.

By summer 1966, the IDF Intelligence Branch was reporting on the consolidation of Fatah activity in Syria and the dispatch of squads to Lebanon and Jordan. However, the Syrians appeared to be outsmarting Israel: they moderated their border policy and even proposed an 'unconditional ceasefire' and negotiations on cultivation arrangements, a proposal which came as a pleasant surprise to Israel. The IDF was ordered to cease the 'buffer' fire, thus enabling Syrian fellahin and shepherds to return to the fields and pastures in the demilitarized areas. At the same time, the Syrians did not totally abandon diversion works, and continued to emphasize the need for a 'popular struggle' against Israel by means of organizing and dispatching Fatah squads through Jordan and Lebanon. This popular struggle was based, on Syria's part, on the indirect approach, which advocated neutralization of the focal points of frontal friction in order to deprive Israel of the pretext for direct attack on Syria. The Israeli General Staff, as noted above, regarded the situation as a snare from which Israel needed to free itself.[3]

At General Staff deliberations, the Chief of Intelligence dwelt on the difference between the Syrian approach, which favoured a popular struggle immediately and the Egyptian school of thought, which had no objections to guerrilla warfare but feared, out of experience, that Israel would react militantly before the Arabs were ready.[4] His conclusion was that the IDF had the option to initiate 'a large-scale clash' with Syria (Yariv later explained that he had been referring to 'seizing a significant area of land with large forces') and thereby undermine the regime in Damascus, without becoming involved in hostilities with Egypt. Egypt's reluctance to go to war with Israel before the conditions were ripe provided Israel with freedom of action against Syria, according to the Intelligence Branch. Israel's proclaimed aim of realizing this option would appear to have generated the May 1967 crisis, in the course of which the Intelligence conception fell apart.

The Chief of Staff noted to his fellow generals that the IDF could not evade preventive activities, such as guarding and ambushes, despite their dubious effectiveness, in order to ensure that settlements along the border were not abandoned by their residents. But defence was not enough, Rabin emphasized. The solution which could end Syrian backing for Fatah was 'to impose a frontal clash on Syria'.

Most of the participants expressed emphatic views as to the inefficacy of partial actions and the need for wide-scale measures. The Commander of the IAF, Motti Hod, argued that the Golan Heights should be occupied: the head of Northern Command, David Elazar, proposed a multi-stage operation, to culminate in occupation of the area inside Syria which served as a home base for the Fatah, but reminded his fellow officers that it was essential to operate against Lebanon and Jordan as well, since they must bear responsibility for raids originating in their countries. The Chief of the Training Department, Ariel Sharon, declared that the only solution was war, its objectives being to make territorial changes along the borders with Syria and Lebanon. He also favoured escalating the situation with Jordan in order to move the border back because 'in the long run we can't maintain the State of Israel as a fifteen kilometre-wide strip'; the head of the National Security College, Elad Peled, also advocated war with Syria and noted the lessons of the Sinai Campaign, which had ensured quiet along the Egyptian border for a decade and had convinced the Egyptians 'that it's not worth dealing with those Jews on a small scale [i.e., terrorist activity]'. None of the speakers rejected a frontal clash with Syria. The Director-General of Rafael, the Israeli Armament Development Authority, Monia Mardor, warned that Fatah activities could eventually be targeted against vital installations. Mardor was against linking the struggle against Fatah to border adjustments and said that the prospect that Egypt might exploit a clash with Syria to inflict a one-time aerial blow on Dimona should be taken into account.[5]

Rabin summed up the discussion and focused on the concrete objective, namely 'annihilation of Fatah'. He dismissed the proposals regarding occupation of territory inside Syria, because, he said, it would be costly in terms of casualties and the political reality would prevent Israel from holding on to its gains ('if we retreated from the Gaza Strip [after the Sinai Campaign], we will certainly retreat from Kuneitra [a town on the Golan Heights]', he explained). He was not spoiling for a fight, and if he thought it possible to end terrorist activity by technological means and passive defence, he would support such measures. But Rabin was convinced that 'through defence alone we will not eradicate the Fatah ... we have been dealing with this for a year and a half [with] a B minus record'. He, too, believed that, in light of the inter-Arab situation (and Egypt's hesitation to enter into a war), Syria had been left alone and was incapable of tackling Israel. The implied conclusion was therefore that there was no escape from a frontal clash with the Syrians and that the conditions were favourable. The main problem, according to the Chief of Staff, was to instil this conviction in the government.[6]

The Lake Galilee incident – August 1966

At 03:30 on 15 August 1966, a vessel of the Israeli navy, patrolling close to the north-eastern shore of Lake Galilee, was grounded on a shoal some eighty metres from shore, opposite Syrian positions. The mishap occurred due to an error on the part of a corporal who violated a standing order to maintain a distance of at least 250 metres from shore. At about 09:00, four Syrian Mig 17s strafed the stranded vessel. One of the aircraft was hit by anti-aircraft fire from the vessel and fell into the Lake.[7]

Word of the attack was immediately transmitted to the Chief of Staff, who ordered 'unrestricted pursuit' of the Syrian aircraft. A pair of Mirages, which had been launched previously, identified two Mig 21s approaching the sector. One of the Migs was downed by Mirage fire. The Chief of Staff then ordered the IAF to conduct a bombing flight against targets on the Syrian shore but to avoid damaging houses in the nearby village of Massadia. The bombardment, carried out by Vautour aircraft, missed the Syrian position, and several bombs fell on the village, causing casualties.

Attempts to rescue the patrol vessel were made under UN mediation on that day and the following one, but without success. The Syrian demand for permission to recover the aircraft and the body of the pilot was rejected by Israel, which claimed that since they were located in sovereign Israeli territory, Israel would recover them but would be ready subsequently to hand them over to the Syrians. Israel also responded negatively when asked by the Syrians if the recovery would be conducted in the presence of UN observers and if they would be handed over immediately on the eastern shore. The Syrians therefore announced that they would prevent the rescue of the Israeli boat.

As a result of a meeting between Prime Minister Eshkol and General Odd Bull, Chief of the UN Truce Supervisory Force, it was agreed that rescue of the vessel and recovery of the plane would be carried out simultaneously in the presence of UN observers. The IDF made preparations to renew rescue efforts on the morning of 17 August, but the Syrians, who meanwhile had concentrated a large force on the shore, announced that they would oppose the rescue until their conditions for recovery of the plane and corpse were met.

On the nights of 17/18 and of 19/20 August, Israeli navy divers attempting clandestinely to recover the corpse of the pilot and the plane succeeded in dragging sections of the aircraft to the shore. An abortive attempt to rescue the stranded boat was made by the navy on the night of 23/24 August. A further open attempt, also unsuccessful, was made on 25 August, after intensive mediation activity by the UN, and after Israel had consented to move navy patrol boats further back. The Chief of Staff denoted this move 'a slight lowering of the flag' which had been dictated by the Syrians as a result of the failure of the rescue effort. By this stage, the Chief of Staff and the head of Northern Command had lost confidence in the ability of the navy to carry out the task, and it was assigned to the Engineering Corps. The method they proposed appeared complicated and lengthy, and consequently Rabin acceded to the request of the Commander of the navy to make another attempt. A force under the command of Lt. Col. Bini Telem of the navy finally rescued the vessel on the evening of 26 August, and it was towed to a dock at Genossar after twelve days on the shoal.[8]

Entirely by chance, an additional drama, which attracted worldwide attention, took place at the height of the Lake Galilee incident. Protracted efforts on the part of the Mossad finally bore fruit, and on 16 August an Iraqi Mig 21, piloted by an Iraqi named Munir Radfa, landed in Israel. For the first time this advanced Soviet fighter plane was in the hands of a Western country. This acquisition provided the IAF with highly valuable information, which was reflected in the aerial fighting in the Six Day War. On the other hand, the pilot's desertion exacerbated the already fraught relations with the Soviet Union. The Mapam ministers in the government demanded that the plane be returned to the Russians. Eshkol yielded to US pressure and the Mig was handed over to the Americans for one month, after the Israelis had studied it thoroughly.[9]

The vessel incident, and the abortive rescue attempts, aroused rigorous self-criticism in the army. Investigation of the incident exposed many flaws and mishaps in the implementation methods and the chain of command. What are significant for our purpose are the conclusions Israel drew from the surprising audacity of the Syrians, evinced in the aerial attack on the Israeli vessel on Lake Galilee, and the undisturbed penetration by Syrian aircraft five kilometres inside Israel. It is almost certain that the Syrian aerial operation was conducted in response to the Israeli air attack a month previously against the diversion equipment at Ain al-Sufira.[10] Rabin himself defined the Syrian assault as a 'reprisal action', and regarded the very fact of penetration of Israel's air space for attack purposes as a dangerous precedent. The Chief of Staff noted that the possibility of extricating the vessel by military action, and occupation of the eastern shore of the Lake, had been examined and rejected, not for political reasons but because the area might have been shelled by high-trajectory fire. Rabin was undoubtedly aware that the government would not approve a military operation costly in human life in order to rescue the boat.

Rabin's gravest concern was the danger that the army's credibility would be undermined in the eyes of the politicians. It was he who had urged the ministers to permit the IDF to attempt clandestine rescue of the vessel without the aid of the UN. 'They gave us the chance and we failed,' said Rabin, 'and the failure had implications beyond the fact, because until now whenever I appeared before the political echelon and gave them my opinion that a certain plan should be executed, everyone knew that if the

IDF said "it can be done", it was in the bag, sealed and delivered. But this time it's as if we've lost the trust they showed in us when they said "go and do it", because we went and we didn't do it.' He placed the blame for the failure on the navy, which had given an unrealistic assessment on the prospects of rescue, which he had presented to the government.[11]

The General Staff meeting of 22 August was conducted under the impact of the Lake Galilee incident, which had begun a week previously and was ongoing. The IDF senior command had been particularly surprised by the fearlessness displayed by the Syrians, who for the first time dared to attack an Israeli target from the air. The Chief of Intelligence regarded this as a new stage in the confrontation with Syria, the outcome of the events of 14 July. 'We discussed the need for escalation with the Syrians,' he said, 'and here is the escalation, and it was the Syrians who initiated it.' Yariv tried to explain the Syrian 'philosophy' to his fellow officers. The Syrian Ba'ath, he noted, considered that it bore the main responsibility for warfare against Israel and claimed the crown of progressive, revolutionary, socialist Arab doctrine, deriving inspiration from Algiers and Hanoi. The regime regarded itself as the object of persecution and the target of international onslaught on the part of imperialism, spearheaded by Israel. It was precisely the weakness of the regime and its isolation which rendered its military reactions so extreme. Yariv did not rule out the possibility of an additional Syrian offensive. He commented that the Soviets avoided exerting too much pressure on Syria, and were ready to support it to the point where they would even break off relations with Israel in the event of a severe clash, but would avoid military involvement.

In theory, the IDF now had a golden opportunity to instigate the 'frontal clash' with Syria which the entire General Staff thought to be essential. However, not only was the political echelon not yet ready to agree, but even within the General Staff itself there were those who realized that the Syrians, too, were capable of inflicting a blow.

Weizman was worried: 'Now that we've had an air attack from the Syrians … there's no way of knowing how those idiots [will act], what they might do when they're angry.'[12] Rabin, too, was not interested at that particular moment in a wide-scale clash, but wanted to rescue the stranded vessel in the most discreet fashion possible. He regarded the affair as a test of the IDF's ability to implement Israeli sovereignty over Lake Galilee. An extensive aerial attack on targets inside Syria, after which the vessel would remain stranded and exposed to fire, would be interpreted, the Chief of Staff feared, as a Syrian victory. On the other hand, an attempt to conquer the north-eastern shore of the Lake could cost lives and invite heavy artillery fire against settlements. Apart from this, the United Nations was involved, and in theory there was still an 'unconditional ceasefire' in the demilitarized zones and ongoing negotiations on cultivation arrangements. And, in general, Rabin added, the circumstances had changed.

The discussion at the previous two General Staff meetings had been based on the assumption that the Syrians were not interested in a frontal clash, and the trend was to impose it on them in order to put an end to Fatah activity, which was the burning problem. Now it transpired that, in practice, the confrontation with the Syrians had been sparked off by the events of 14 July, and the Fatah problem was now secondary.[13]

Thus, the Lake Galilee incident had a twofold effect: it indubitably enhanced the IDF belief that the Syrians needed 'to be taught a lesson'. On the other hand, it reinforced the view within the military – and even more so among the politicians – that action against Syria could lead to painful reaction, including aerial and artillery bombing of Israeli targets near the border. The result was a temporary moderation of the tone of the General Staff demand to hit the Syrians, and the fading of the possibility that this option would be approved by the political echelon.

The Chief of Staff speaks out – and is reprimanded

The September 1966 (Jewish New Year) issue of *Bamahaneh*, the army magazine, included a special interview with the Chief of Staff. Rabin referred to the problem of hostile enemy activity and distinguished between Egypt, Jordan and Lebanon, which opposed terrorist action, and Syria, which supported it. He said:

> 'The components of the situation now prevailing between Israel and Syria are different, and call for a different mode of action on our part ... the reaction to Syrian activities – whether expressed in sabotage, diversion or aggression along the border – must be targeted against those who carry out the sabotage and against the regime which supports them ... the objective should be to change that regime's decisions and remove the motives for action. The problem with Syria is therefore essentially the clash with the regime.'[14]

This declaration was in accord with the assertions and charges of Moscow and Damascus that Israel was plotting to overthrow the revolutionary regime in Syria. However, it sorely embarrassed Israeli diplomats, who had always dismissed such accusations, explaining that the internal regimes of Arab countries were of no interest to Israel. The negative reverberations throughout the world, and the criticism in the Israeli press and political establishment, forced Eshkol to respond. He sent Rabin a private letter of severe reprimand.[15] Publicly, after the 18 September government meeting, the Prime Minister issued a delicately worded statement, which merely hinted at his reservations, but again cast responsibility for terrorist action on the Syrian government. Rabin ordered his generals to refrain from participating in any discussion or debate on this subject with the press.[16]

The Prime Minister's statement began as follows: 'A certain section of the interview with the Chief of Staff granted to Bamahaneh on the eve of the New Year was wrongly interpreted, and contravenes our intentions. I have talked to the Chief of Staff on this subject, and I feel it necessary to reiterate that the State of Israel does not interfere in the internal affairs and regimes of other countries.' Eshkol's military attaché, Yisrael Lior, notes in his memoirs that Eshkol's reprimand to Rabin was not free of other calculations. Eshkol envied Rabin's popularity and ordered him to submit all requests for interviews for his prior approval.[17]

It should be noted that this was not the first time that Eshkol had felt the need to put Rabin in his place. Two years previously, on 24 September 1964, in a 'private and personal' letter to Rabin, Eshkol wrote: 'Recently I have frequently encountered in the press and on the radio political pronouncements attributed to you. It seems to me that such pronouncements should be avoided, and if they are essential they should be coordinated with the relevant bodies.'[18]

After the Lake Galilee incident, there was a brief lull interrupted by a series of attacks. The two gravest incidents were the laying of three explosive devices on the night of 7/8 October in the Romema district of Jerusalem, which damaged two houses and injured four civilians, and the detonation of a mine in the plantations of Kibbutz Sha'ar ha-Golan on the night of 8/9 October, which killed four border policemen and injured two. Visiting the site of the Jerusalem attack, Eshkol made his famous announcement: 'The book is open and the pen is recording.'[19] The terrorist squads had infiltrated Jerusalem through Jordan, but the Intelligence Branch had no doubt that the Syrians were behind the attacks. Yariv offered a possible explanation, namely that in the absence of an Israeli reaction, the Syrians sensed that 'it was no big deal'.[20]

Rabin's remarks at the General Staff meeting reflected the difficulties he had encountered in persuading the government of the need for a wide-scale operation against Syria. Soviet backing of the Syrians was a cause of concern to the ministers. Not all of them were persuaded that the aerial operation on 14 July had produced the desired result, and the bravado displayed by Syria in attacking the naval vessel on Lake Galilee was an additional reason for fear among the ministers of Syrian reprisals.[21]

An additional concern of the government was the prospect of a focused, but highly damaging, Egyptian response to Israeli action against Syria. 'There is an object in the south of Israel which is the ideal object for a limited response which would win the total support of the whole world. Dimona. [Ministers] say, Egypt can refrain from moving forces but to deal with Dimona, that is not considered war, it's a limited action.' Rabin presented these facts as if he did not share the anxieties, but his remarks indicate clearly that he understood why the political echelon preferred diplomatic activity at that stage. He was convinced, at the same time, that the government was becoming increasingly aware that in the final analysis there would be no escape from a serious clash with the Syrians.[22]

The tracks of the mine-layers at Shaar ha-Golan led to the Syrian border. This fact seemingly again provided the occasion for acting against Syria, which the General Staff had been eager to do for some time. The government, however, did not consent to approve such an operation and decided, under US pressure, to act through diplomatic channels. Israel complained to the Security Council. Although proof of Syrian responsibility was clear-cut, the UN deliberations lasted for many weeks. The Soviet Union opposed any condemnation of Syria and finally imposed a veto, although the draft resolution had been very mildly worded.[23] Israel's restraint following the October attacks and its despair of the UN were among the underlying reasons for the reprisal operation at Samu on 13 November 1966 (see below).

At the General Staff meeting of 17 October, Yariv quoted a report on a meeting two days previously between Soviet Deputy Foreign Minister Vladimir Semyonov and the Syrian Ambassador to Moscow. Semyonov informed the Syrian of a meeting between the Soviet Ambassador to Israel Dimitri Chubakhin and Eshkol, and said that his government had no information about Israeli aggression. He advised the Syrians to maintain calm and to cool down their emotion. Such a tone, said Yariv, was incapable of curbing the Syrians. The fact that such information had reached Israeli Intelligence in 'real time' is, of course, testimony to the excellence of its sources. The IAF Commander, Motti Hod, asked Yariv a 'speculative question'. Could the Soviet Union actually be interested in an Israeli–Syrian clash in order to increase its hold in the region? Yariv replied that he believed 'that this is not a case of Russian Machiavellism'. He estimated that the Soviet Union was apprehensive at the prospect of serious deterioration of the Middle Eastern situation, which could lead to confrontation with the United States. The Soviets were not pressuring the Syrians because they were anxious 'not to rock the boat' for fear of a military coup against the regime in Damascus.

The continuing terrorist activity of Fatah and other Palestinian organizations[24] and the restraint ordered by the government evoked strong criticism among the general public and within the military. Rabin was uncomfortable at the restriction of the army, but was also afraid that the resentment voiced in army circles towards the government could have a negative impact on morale. He was convinced that, with time, the government would be won over and would permit the IDF to act, but he warned that in the interim 'we must bite our tongues and grit our teeth, but not give free rein to our mouths'.[25]

The Egyptian–Syrian defence pact

Israeli Intelligence received another surprise in November 1966. Egypt and Syria overcame their rivalries and unexpectedly signed a bilateral defence pact. The clauses of this pact were very explicit, and included the viewing of any 'armed aggression' against one of the two as aggressive action against both. There were, however, also qualifications: the defence policy of both sides must be the outcome of 'joint consultations', and in the event of a brief surprise onslaught on one of the two countries the response would be conditional on mutual consultations and consent.[26] The signing was preceded by indicators which were not correctly assessed by the IDF Intelligence Branch. But what was more important was that the implications of the agreement had little effect on the Intelligence perception of the Egyptian stance and of Egypt's commitment in the event of a 'frontal clash' between Israel and Syria. On the contrary, Intelligence perceived the signing as an Egyptian move aimed at curbing the Syrians and forcing them to coordinate moves with Egypt and avoid entanglement with Israel. With regard to Egypt's response if Israel acted against Syria, Intelligence sources continued to believe that avoidance of war before the time was ripe would remain the guiding principle for Egypt, the pact notwithstanding. It is possible that the direct impetus for signature of the pact was Rabin's imprudent statement, which was interpreted in Moscow and Cairo as the proclaimed intention of military circles in Israel to overthrow the 'revolutionary' regime in Damascus. The pact could have been a twofold move on Egypt's part, encouraged by the Soviet Union, an attempt to restrain Syria's conduct and simultaneously to deter Israel from acting against that country. Future events were to prove that the enhanced Egyptian commitment, anchored in the defence pact with Syria, was pregnant with consequences far beyond the assessment of Israeli Intelligence.

Chapter 8

Israel–Jordan

The Israeli dilemma, the Jordanian dilemma

The period under discussion witnessed the beginning of a direct diplomatic dialogue, at the highest level, between Israel and the Hashemite Kingdom of Hussein ibn Talal, which was to culminate thirty-one years later, in 1994, in the signing of a peace treaty between the two countries.[1] However, these years were also marked by rising tension along their long shared border and by two acute crises: the first was the IDF reprisal operation at Samu in the southern Hebron mountains on 13 November 1966 whose consequences threatened to destabilize Hussein's rule; the second was Hussein's decision to become part of the military alignment against Israel by signing a mutual defence pact with Nasser on 30 May 1967 and placing his armed forces under Egyptian command. This move accelerated the outbreak of hostilities, in the course of which Israel occupied the West Bank and Jordan reverted to its original dimensions as Transjordan.

The contacts between the Jewish agency and Israeli government on one side and the Amman monarchy on the other began in the 1930s, but the ties established and the intensive contacts with King Abdullah on the eve of the Arab invasion in May 1948 did not deter the Transjordanian 'Legion' from participating in the Arab invasion of Israel upon its birth.[2] The 1948 fighting and the 1949 armistice agreement left a long and highly problematic border between the two countries, and Jerusalem was criss-crossed by tactical positions, fortifications, mines and by barbed wire fences along the 'urban line'. The most sacred places to Jews – Temple Mount, the Western Wall and the Mount of Olives as well as the Jewish Quarter of the Old City – remained in Jordanian hands.[3] On the other hand, Mount Scopus – consisting mainly of the buildings of the Hebrew University and the Hadassah hospital – remained an Israeli enclave in the east of the city. A guard force of Israeli 'policemen' (in fact, soldiers) was assigned to the Mount and a supply convoy wended its way through the Mandelbaum Gate fortnightly, under UN supervision, to and from the Mount.[4]

At the end of the War of Independence, it seemed that the IDF was now in a position to occupy east Jerusalem and the West Bank and to shift the border back to the Jordan River. The Israeli government was dissuaded by political and demographic considerations from carrying this out. Contacts with King Abdullah, who annexed the West Bank to his kingdom, were intended to replace the armistice agreement by a peace settlement. These contacts were cut short by Abdullah's death in July 1951 in Jerusalem at the hands of a Palestinian assassin.

As far as Israel was concerned, and in light of the alternatives, the Kingdom of Jordan was a convenient neighbour, a 'status quo country' as regards the character of the regime. But Jordan had always, and particularly up until 1967, been marked by acute tension between the Western-oriented policies of the Hashemite rulers and the widespread popular sentiment of the Palestinian majority, who favoured Nasser and yearned for 'the liberation of Palestine'. Moreover, Jordan was also the undisguised target of 'revolutionary' elements encouraged by Syria, Iraq and Egypt. For all these reasons, Jordan was frequently in a state of upheaval. Israel, for its part, threatened that it would not sit idly by in the event of a coup or the movement of foreign forces into the West Bank. The Israeli stance undoubtedly had a restraining effect, which helped to prevent a coup in Jordan.

After the Sinai Campaign, David Ben-Gurion relinquished all territorial aspirations and limited the IDF's contingency plans for intervention in the event of a coup in Jordan, to safeguard the connection with Mount Scopus alone.[5] Up until 1958, Ben-Gurion had contemplated the possibility of a division of Jordan between Israel and Iraq, but following the military coup and the rise to power in Baghdad of the radical regime of Abdel Karim Qassem, he became convinced that preservation of the integrity and independence of Jordan were in Israel's strategic interest.[6]

As noted above, the riots in Jordan in spring 1963, following the proclamation of the Egyptian–Syrian–Iraqi 'Tripartate Union', shocked Ben-Gurion, and he urged US President Kennedy and the other Western leaders to guarantee the stability of the Hashemite regime and the integrity and independence of Jordan. This was apparently the background to the first Israeli–Jordanian diplomatic encounter, which took place in the autumn of that year between King Hussein and the Director-General of the PM's office, Dr Yaakov Herzog. A second meeting was held two years later with the participation of Foreign Minister Golda Meir and Herzog.[7] Concomitantly, meetings were held at senior military level between the sides, including the chiefs of Intelligence, and counter-terrorist information was transmitted.[8]

The delicate fabric of relations between Israel and King Hussein was severely damaged by the IDF operation at Samu in November 1966.[9] The King and the Jordanian establishment had always suspected that Israel coveted the West Bank and was plotting to occupy it.[10] The shattering of the fragile trust which had grown up between them may have had some effect on Hussein's decision in late May 1967 to jump on the Nasserite bandwagon.

Samu

Border relations between Israel and Jordan in this period were far from tranquil, despite the intention of both governments to maintain calm insofar as possible. Infiltration into Israel and locally initiated shooting incidents occurred from time to time and there was friction around various, often petty issues in Jerusalem, in the Latrun enclave and elsewhere.[11] The Israel–Jordan Armistice Commission was kept busy.[12] But the real problems commenced with the onset of Fatah activity in January 1965. Most of the infiltrators for sabotage purposes came through the long border with Jordan, beyond which lay a hostile Palestinian population. The Jordanian authorities attempted to check the Fatah organization in their area and stop the penetrations into Israel, but with only partial success, mainly due to the tense relations between the Amman government and the Palestinian population and the former's efforts to avoid the appearance of collaboration with Israel. The latter, for its part, cast blame for the penetrations on the countries from which the terrorist squads entered, usually Jordan. Syria, which had become the patron of the 'popular struggle' against Israel, was happy to involve Jordan in the confrontation. Israel felt it necessary to provide Jordan with 'incentives' from time to time in the form of limited reprisal raids. The army had reservations about the operations approved by the political echelon, considering them too small in scale, too few and of dubious effectiveness. In autumn 1965 the General Staff began demanding a demonstrative punitive action against Jordan, to be conducted in daylight and with a large force, in order to conquer a village and blow up its houses.[13]

The unusual decision of the Ministerial Committee on Security to approve a daylight large-scale operation by a combined armoured paratroopers force was influenced by the cumulative impact of the preceding events, in particular since the beginning of October 1966, and frustration at the Security Council's failure, due to the Soviet veto, to charge Syria with responsibility. In June 1966 a serious shooting incident on the Jordanian border at Beit Mirsim in the southern Hebron mountains claimed two Israeli lives,[14] but no Israeli reaction ensued. On the night of 7/8 October, as mentioned above, explosive devices were detonated in two houses in the Romema district of Jerusalem and four civilians were injured. On the following night, four members of the Border Police were killed and two injured by a mine in the plantations of Shaar ha-Golan. The government decided to exercise restraint and to try to achieve results on the diplomatic plane, an attempt which proved unsuccessful. On the night of 11/12 November, three paratroopers from the 890 Battalion were killed and six injured when their vehicle hit a mine in the southern Hebron mountains, where they were engaged in setting ambushes against terrorist activity. It was the subsequent public fury at these attacks, one of them in the heart of the capital, which persuaded the Ministerial Committee on Security to accept the recommendation of the Chief of Staff to permit an immediate large-scale operation in the Hebron mountains (Operation 'Crusher') in the village of Samu. The Prime Minister, however, ordered Rabin to restrict the size of the assault force, a restriction which the army did not observe.

At dawn on the following day, 13 November, a combined armoured paratrooper force set out to Samu. The main paratrooper force captured the village and blew up fifty of its houses, while the armoured force acted against secondary objectives: a police building and two Bedouin villages near the border. In contrast to prior assessments, Jordanian army units intervened and suffered heavy casualties: fourteen dead and thirty-seven wounded troops, and another four dead and seventeen wounded civilians. A Jordanian Hunter plane was downed. The Israelis had one fatality and four wounded. The operation was brief and effective. At 06:00 the forces crossed the border and at 10:00 crossed it on their way back, having completed the mission. However, the consequences were of a gravity far beyond the intentions of the political echelon.[15] There were strong repercussions in the Hashemite Kingdom which placed the future of the regime at risk for several weeks.[16] International criticism of Israel was widespread and very harsh.

That evening the Chief of Staff met with the Newspaper Editors' Committee, and found it difficult to explain why the operation had been targeted against Jordan. It was even harder to justify the scope of the operation to the political echelon. Rabin admitted that he had erred in his appraisals, particularly regarding the intervention of the Jordanian army and the quality of their fighting, which had included an aerial battle conducted with inferior aircraft.[17]

At the General Staff meeting the day after the Samu operation, there was evident embarrassment in light of the unanticipated dimensions of the action and the number of Jordanian casualties. The Chief of Intelligence apologized for not having cautioned against Jordanian military movements in the region, and for not having accompanied the Chief of Staff to Southern Command to oversee the operation.[18]

Rabin explained that the decision to act against Jordan was intended as a 'statement to the world' that things could not go on as they were. He blamed the Jordanian army for the complications in the course of the operation, but did not spare himself criticism for his erroneous assessment of the scope of Jordanian opposition. Rabin admitted that he should have contemplated an intimidation flight over the area by the Air Force in order to curb the Jordanians.[19]

Operation 'Stratum'

The fears of Jordanian military response to Samu waned as the days passed, but, after a two-week delay, the United Arab Command reacted by ordering the movement of forces in a display of strength. The IDF response was cautious but alert. The mustering of forces and preparations for mobilization in order to anticipate the threat was denoted 'Operation Stratum' and served as a kind of preliminary exercise in miniature for the May 1967 events. When it became clear at the end of November that the Egyptians were not moving forces into Sinai, the IDF force concentrated in the south was withdrawn on the night of 29/30 November, to prevent a 'chain reaction' of mobilization.[20]

The stunned reaction in the Hashemite Kingdom to the IDF raid on Samu was of considerable concern to the West. The Chief of Intelligence Aharon Yariv claimed that King Hussein was deliberately instilling 'panic' in the Americans in order to obtain financial aid and advanced weaponry, particularly aircraft. The US Ambassador to Israel, Walworth Barbour, met with the Chief of Staff on his own initiative on 20 November. The main question posed by the Americans was whether Israel intended to occupy the West Bank. Rabin hastened to reassure the ambassador.[21] The international denunciations and the criticism voiced inside Israel had placed the government in a difficult situation. Eshkol ordered that defensive activity on the borders be intensified in order to reduce the need for reprisal operations in the future.

The political echelon: Defence! The military echelon: Attack!

Three weeks after the Samu operation, Rabin felt that both public opinion and the politicians had calmed down. He was convinced that the operation would be remembered in hindsight 'as one of the better operations', and that its importance lay in the attention it had focused on the grave Fatah problem. He attributed the government's diplomatic predicament to the ineffectiveness of official information activity.[22] Rabin feared that from now on it would be even more difficult for the military to gain permission for offensive action and that he would be forced to resort to passive defence. 'We will struggle against the psychology which is beginning to gain ground ... which suggests that there is a [defensive] solution to the [terror] problems. They will construct electrified fences and set up another ghetto in the State of Israel ... we cannot turn the defensive method into the central axis of [our] doctrine.'[23] Rabin was also concerned at US eagerness to assist Israel in finding technological solutions for the prevention of border penetration lest this restrict Israel's freedom of action.

The Israeli military attaché in the United States, Brigadier-General

Yosef Geva, who conducted the negotiations in Washington for American technological aid to prevent border infiltration, represented the Chief of Staff's viewpoint faithfully, but not necessarily the wishes of the government. Static defence was unimportant, Geva said, and Israel must avoid creating the impression that it had waived its right to act in different ways. Excessive emphasis on technology could create a defensive and defeatist 'ghetto psychology' and encourage Arab attacks. US support for passive defence, Geva declared, encouraged the aggressor and at the same time demanded that the victim limit his own freedom of action.[24]

In the wake of Samu, the United States did in fact offer Israel defensive and warning systems against border infiltration, but the range offered was initially so disappointing that Rabin defined it as a 'mark of discredit to American technology'. A US expert, Alexander Rabinowitz, was subsequently dispatched to Israel. He toured the borders accompanied by the assistant to the Chief of the Operations Branch, and eventually 'pulled out of his hat several interesting devices for pinpointing border penetrations, night vision, and early warning'. The Americans, however, adopted delaying tactics. Rabin abhorred the appeal to a foreign country for the solution to a security problem and was afraid that it would extract a political price.[25]

On 12 December 1966, a month after Samu, Eshkol attended a meeting of the General Staff forum in order to discuss problems stemming from terrorist activity. The meeting illustrated the widening gap between the defensive and offensive approaches.

The Chief of the Operations Branch, Ezer Weizman, surveyed the army's deployment for defensive activity against terrorist infiltrators. The course of the discussion indicates that Eshkol's main objective was to press the military to intensify defensive activity and to forget about offensive action. Having been castigated both internally and internationally for the Samu operation, Eshkol was anxious to learn what the IDF was doing in order to guard and protect against terror. He was determined to invest increased resources and effort in defence and prevention, in order to preclude the need for severe reprisals, whose outcome could not be predicted. Weizman described the defensive deployment: fortified positions, patrols, guard rosters and ambushes, the assignment of forces and the scope of planned operational activity. He went on to list the various technical measures the army was employing for lighting, protection and early warning, and the fencing of border settlements.[26]

Summing up, Rabin emphasized that what the Prime Minister had heard touched only on the 'defensive aspect'. He wanted to explain how he perceived the problem as a whole.

Terrorism had confronted Israel with a grave problem, said Rabin. It was not just a question of 'a few bandits',[27] but a serious attempt on the part of the Arab states to harm the State of Israel by undermining its security. If this method proved successful, it could even change the approach of the 'responsible leadership' (namely Nasser). Rabin was of the view that Israel should not place too much faith in the assumption that Nasser would not become embroiled in a clash with Israel until the conditions were propitious, and therefore would refrain from licensing and initiating terrorist activity against Israel. Hence, the approach of the military was explicit: it was necessary to act in the international diplomatic arena and to invest in defensive activity, but these efforts alone could not suffice to root out terror. The solution was to grant the IDF the opportunity to take such action as would make it abundantly evident to the Arab states, and in particular Egypt, that if the terrorist acts continued they were liable to find themselves embroiled in a war with Israel against their will.

Rabin ostensibly acknowledged the need to step up defensive efforts on the Jordanian and Lebanese borders, and demanded generous funding for this purpose: 'I think that the cash faucet should be turned on.' 'Millions' were needed, he told Eshkol, but 'the question is if we build a Maginot line of fences, is that a sufficient solution?' His tone made it clear that he did not believe in defensive tactics and knew that the government could not allocate the 'millions' he was demanding at a time of economic recession. This was Rabin's way of telling Eshkol that the government would eventually have to accept the army's point of view.

Eshkol concluded the discussion with a brief statement, explaining why the army must increase its defensive and preventive efforts. He sympathized with their aversion to reliance on defence measures, he said, but this was essential in light of the situation and the political considerations. He regretted that in the past two years, not enough resources and efforts had been invested in this sphere. To appease his audience, he explained that more vigorous defensive activity could also serve as the background to future offensive action: 'It will be much easier to explain, if we again need to carry out serious acts, that we did this and that, but without success.' He requested that the army's demands be concentrated, so that the cost of all the 'instruments' needed for defence could be assessed, and gave his promise: 'If I receive the figures within the next few days, I will sit down with the Ministry of Finance people. I don't think that [we will save on] things we all regard as valuable, whether preventing killing or preventing undesirable complications – because we don't want war.' Eshkol pointed out ironically that reprisal operations were also very costly: 'I didn't ask but I can imagine how much the Samu battle cost.'

One sensitive issue worried Eshkol in particular, namely the vulnerability of Jerusalem to terror and sabotage, along both the 'urban line' and the exposed border to the north and south. The terrorist act perpetrated by the 'Heroes of the Return' in Romema in October disturbed him considerably. Eshkol asked himself whether there was a certain disproportion in the assignment of a small force to defend and protect Jerusalem, in comparison to other sectors. An act of terror in Jerusalem, 'in the heart of the country', was a 'disgrace' which 'makes one's blood boil', said Eshkol. His dialogue with the Chief of Staff on Jerusalem revealed not only the Prime Minister's sensitivity at the prospect of future attacks on the capital, but also Rabin's conviction that there was no way to close off the borders, so that only the solution put forward by the military could solve the problem.[28]

The Israeli operation at Samu was regarded by the political echelon as a grave mistake. It constituted a real threat to the survival of the Hashemite regime in Jordan, which the Israeli government had been anxious to preserve for the past decade, and caused a rift in the delicate fabric of relations with that country. It played into the hands of Syria and Egypt and the PLO, which were interested in the overthrow of the Amman regime and proved to them that Israel could be provoked into attacking Jordan in order to achieve their objective. It also exposed Israel to savage criticism on the part of the West, and spurred the United States to send Jordan additional military aid. On the other hand, there is logic in the assertion of the Intelligence Branch that the Samu operation expedited the inevitable clash between Hussein's regime and the PLO before the Palestinian organization was ready, the outcome of which, in the final analysis, was the bolstering of Hussein's standing.

One fact is clear: the government realized that it had erred in yielding to the military's demands, and the differences between the defensive predilections of the political echelon and the offensive doctrine of the military were intensified as a result. Until shortly before the Six Day War, the government refrained from approving any further offensive initiatives or reprisal operations, although hostile enemy activity continued. It was only the cumulative effect of the terrorist acts which eventually led even the politicians to the conclusion that there was no escape from acting against Syria.

Chapter 9

The clash with Syria approaches

Despite the proclamations of its leaders over the years, it is highly unlikely that Syria was really seeking a confrontation with Israel in 1967. On the contrary, the concept of a 'popular struggle' was grounded on patience, staying power and sustained action. The reverse of the Egyptian strategy, which entailed waiting for the right moment to arrive and meanwhile amassing military might and equipment and preparing the ground for victory, it advocated a constant and tenacious fight employing simple means and guerrilla methods. The Syrian Chief of Staff Suidani rejected the idea of a purposeless arms race: 'We must not pursue the path of conventional warfare with conventional armament, but rather that of a popular war of liberation, based primarily on the individual and his faith, and on the rifle, which is preferable to all heavy weapons.'[1] Syria's leaders had no ideological objections to attempts to achieve a practical settlement with Israel for the cultivation of the disputed land in the demilitarized zones, but their national pride and obstinacy barred them from summoning up the necessary flexibility. On the other hand, the Syrians had no alternative but to support the Palestinian guerrilla struggle against Israel, because it was a central tenet of their revolutionary ideological conception. It was by no means certain that any other country, not even Egypt, would hasten to their aid in the event of a war with Israel. The crisis and the war came as a total surprise to Syria and Nasser failed to coordinate his moves with the Damascus leaders, who were relegated to the sidelines in the role of 'anxious bystanders'.[2]

The border heats up

As the traumatic impact of the IDF operation at Samu faded due to the stabilization of the situation in Jordan, and Syrian-inspired terrorist activity was resumed, the IDF, backed by public opinion, resumed its pressure on the government to approve a punitive action against Syria. The pressure bore fruit. Despite strong misgivings in the government, the IAF was employed on a massive scale several weeks later, a decision which led to critical escalation.

At the end of December 1966 the IDF renewed its buffer fire in the demilitarized zones, after a six-month lull due to the 'unconditional cease-fire' initiated by the Syrians. The Chief of Staff persuaded the Minister of Defence that the prevailing situation served Syrian interests since it tied the hands of the Israeli military and facilitated uninterrupted infiltration by Syrian farmers and shepherds into the demilitarized zones, while Syria was continuing to back the 'popular struggle' against Israel. The Syrians reacted instantly to the renewal of buffer fire by firing across the border at Israeli tractors, and deploying tanks and heavy mortar, while at the same time dispatching terror squads directly from Syria into Israel.

The heating up of the border on IDF initiative, though approved by Eshkol, was fiercely criticized in government circles. Thus the Ministerial Committee on Security decided on 3 January 1967 that the IDF was to refrain in future from returning Syrian tank fire. The army was forced to obey this decision, even when Syrian tanks fired on Israeli workers in the vicinity of kibbutzim ha-On and Tel Katzir on 6 January. The Chief of Staff voiced his resentment on the following day at a meeting of the Committee, claiming that a dangerous precedent had been established, which would be interpreted as weakness. Rabin repeatedly proposed that aircraft be launched against Syrian tank positions. Among the Committee members, opinions were as usual sharply divided: the National Religious Party leader, Moshe Haim Shapira, vehemently opposed Rabin's proposal, while Yigal Allon of Ahdut ha-Avoda – a consistent champion of the military's standpoint – favoured employment of the IAF even in the event that Syrian fire was targeted at tractors and farmers rather than at settlements. 'We know that the employment of aircraft is an open invitation to a more serious clash, which is liable to lead to war', Shapira declared. The Minister of Health, Yisrael Barzilai of Mapam, was adamant in his opposition to changing the rule that the IAF be brought in only in response to the shelling of settlements. He warned that Egypt's commitment to Syria under their mutual defence pact 'could escalate the situation and nobody can foresee how it will end'.

Eshkol and several of the ministers thought it necessary to bring in the IAF, but the objections of the National Religious Party and Mapam were so emphatic that they bordered on an ultimatum and a threat to resign from the coalition. The Committee refrained therefore from deciding on involvement of the IAF. It approved the continuation of work only in undisputed areas, and decided that if the Syrians continued to fire on workers, the IDF would return fire, and if Syrian tanks were spotted at firing positions, the IDF armour could launch pre-emptive fire.[3]

Long-term provocation on the borders was not in Syria's interest, and consequently the Syrians – who wanted to enable uninterrupted access of fellahin and shepherds to their fields in the demilitarized zones – again proposed negotiations to restore calm on the border, and displayed uncommon willingness to meet Israeli representatives face to face under UN auspices. Their proposal was formulated by General Odd Bull and conveyed to Israel.

On 23 January 1967 Prime Minister and Minister of Defence Levi Eshkol and Deputy Minister of Defence Zvi Dinstein attended a meeting of the General Staff to continue the deliberations on routine security problems. The Chief of Staff and the generals insisted again that defensive strategy was not sufficient, and demanded planned escalation along the Syrian border and a 'smashing blow' even to the point of war, in order to force the Syrians to suspend their support for the 'popular struggle'. There was not a single case in history of the problem of guerrilla activity being solved by defensive methods, claimed the Assistant Chief of Operations Rehavam Ze'evi, and Israel lacked the capacity to withstand a lengthy 'popular struggle'. First, the IDF was small in proportion to the length of the borders, and was not built for this type of warfare. Second, the staying power of the immigrant villages along the border was not great, and the inhabitants were liable to flee. Third, the serious burden on the economy of increased reserve mobilization and the reduction in tourism due to the security situation must not be permitted to continue for long. The model to be emulated as he saw it was the 1956 Sinai Campaign which had forced the Egyptians to halt all fidaiyyun activity because they had realized that 'there is no such thing as a half-war'. A war with Syria, Ze'evi emphasized, would solve the three main problems between that country and Israel: the demilitarized zones, the diversion and, gravest of all, terror. He warned that the greatest danger of terrorist activity was the fact that it was 'contagious', and in the absence of an Israeli reaction, the other Arab states were liable to join in. Rabin expressed his full support for Ze'evi's outlook.

Levi Eshkol put a damper on the General Staff's proposal. He had come to discuss the improvement of defensive measures against terrorism, and the senior command had argued in return that only by inflicting a 'smashing blow' and occupying territory in Syria could the problem be solved, just as the Sinai Campaign had put an end to terror from Gaza, and the Samu operation had impelled the Jordanians to make a concentrated effort to check the Palestinian organizations on the West Bank. Eshkol rejected this analogy. As far as he was concerned, only defensive measures could yield definite results, even if they did not provide a complete solution. On the other hand, the military action which the army advocated could not only cause political complications but its outcome was by no means certain. It was not impossible, Eshkol argued, that the worst possible scenario would ensue in the wake of a severe blow to Syria, namely the 'all-out scenario', the rallying of all the Arab states, including Jordan, for the overall attack on Israel.[4]

Despite Eshkol's unequivocal remarks, the generals continued to present a united front in favour of offensive activity against Syria, their proposals ranging from war, 'massive reprisal', a forceful blow against the Syrian air force to a counter-terror attack. Following this discussion, and for an additional two and a half months, the army was not permitted to act as it wished, despite the continued attacks.[5] When the go-ahead was finally given to the IDF, on 7 April 1967, it did in fact act against the Syrian air force, but without the anticipated result, and the later repercussions bore out Eshkol's fears.

Futile talks with Syria

At the end of January and the beginning of February 1967, meetings took place between Israeli and Syrian representatives, under UN auspices, as part of what was denoted 'an extraordinary convening' of the Joint Armistice Commission.[6] The objective of the talks was to try to achieve a settlement in the demilitarized zones which would enable farming and grazing by both sides without harassment. However, the talks resembled a dialogue of the deaf and were totally futile.

Moshe Sasson, then Head of the Armistice Committee Department of the Israeli Ministry of Foreign Affairs, who headed the Israeli delegation to the talks with the Syrians, later related that the atmosphere was chilly. At a meeting on the Syrian side of the border, the hosts did not even serve water to their guests, and the Syrian representative addressed the Chairman without ever glancing in the direction of the Israeli delegation. When a meeting was held on the Israeli side, Sasson asked the IDF to erect three large tents: one for talks, a second for refreshments and the third for the Syrians, if they chose to isolate themselves. The Syrians did in fact keep to their separate tent during the intermissions in the talks and did not touch the refreshments.[7]

The first session was held on 25 January 1967 on the Syrian side in the customs house east of the Bnot Yaakov bridge. It was agreed that the Chairman, General Bull, with the consent of both parties, would read out a summary reconfirming the non-aggression clauses of the armistice agreement. Sasson, as head of the Israeli delegation, presented the Israeli stand regarding a practical settlement in the demilitarized areas, the crux of which was abstention from any aggressive action, including border crossing and terrorist activity, and arrangements to be based on the status quo in those areas. The Syrian representative accepted the agenda, but rejected the Israeli claim to sovereignty over the demilitarized areas. The second meeting was held on 29 January on the Israeli side, adjacent to the Mahanayim airfield, with the same participants. The Syrian representative read out a long speech about Israeli violations of the armistice agreement, rejected direct talks, and proclaimed Syria's commitment to the restoration of the Palestinians' rights to their stolen land. He demanded the removal of all forces and military positions from the demilitarized areas and a reversion to the 1949 ceasefire line, as well as the return of the Arab population and their property to these areas. He referred to the expulsion of the Arab villagers from the southern demilitarized area and to the UN resolutions calling for their return, which Israel had ignored. He went on to state that Syria had views of its own on the cultivation of land in the demilitarized zones, which he would present when the time came. General Bull's attempts to persuade the Syrians to adhere to the agenda proved fruitless.

The third session was held on 2 February on the Syrian side. General Bull again appealed to the sides to follow the agreed agenda. However, the Syrian representative reiterated the main points of his previous speech and claimed that they were in accord with the agenda. As a precondition for any settlement, the Chairman of the Syrian delegation Colonel Abdullah demanded that Israel obey the Security Council resolutions and withdraw to the ceasefire line. Before they discussed any particular area, he said, the Arab inhabitants must be allowed to return to their land. He also argued that Israel's demand for non-aggression was beyond the scope of the agenda.[8]

The talks reached an impasse and were on the verge of breaking up. After the third meeting, Bull decided to suspend the meetings in order to conduct quiet bilateral contacts and ensure that future contacts would be more productive. Rabin was of the opinion that the Syrians 'have manoeuvred themselves into a corner' and that the failure of the talks could provide a convenient background for Israeli military action. He referred to the large-scale clash with Syria as a certain prospect, for which the right pretext must be found.

Yariv: 'Until the Syrians are given a "good shake-up" they won't stop'

In the second half of January 1967 the Chief of Intelligence Aharon Yariv visited several Western European countries, including Great Britain, France and Germany. On his return, he reported to the General Staff his impression that the 'gentiles' were preoccupied with larger issues such as the Vietnam war, events in China – where the 'cultural revolution' was being waged – and the problems of Europe, and not with the Middle East. It transpired that one of the objectives Yariv had set himself on this trip was to prepare the background for an Israeli military strike against Syria. He had been criticized for the Samu operation, he said, but his audience had 'bought' the 'Syrian theory'. The main point of this theory was that 'until they [the Syrians] are given a good shake-up they won't stop [terrorist activity]'. The Europeans had merely asked that the 'shake-up' be carried out in such a manner that 'there won't be too much commotion'. Yariv predicted, therefore, that 'our swipe at the Syrians, if it's done properly with a suitable background, naturally won't win us compliments, but there won't be great excitement either'.[9]

The infiltrations from across the border for terror purposes continued in February, and Syria's handiwork was evident.[10] However, the differences of opinion between the military and the government on the required reaction endured. Yet, as time passed and more and more terror acts were perpetrated, the government weakened on this point. Its hopes that intensifying the defensive and preventive efforts would check terrorism were dashed. The talks with the Syrians had led nowhere, and in any event the Syrians were not willing to abandon their support for the 'popular struggle'. The government had no political alternatives and the IDF alone proposed a method which ostensibly guaranteed success. The conflagration was inevitable.

Chapter 10

Conflagration

On 27 February 1967, the senior command of the IDF (from the rank of colonel upwards) convened in Tel Aviv in the presence of the Prime Minister and Minister of Defence. As usual, the Chief of Intelligence and the Chief of Staff surveyed the security situation and the IDF's deployment. Underlying their remarks was the Intelligence appraisal that no war was to be anticipated until at least 1970. In his address to the senior officers, Eshkol deviated from his prepared text and questioned the categorical nature of this appraisal. He employed the Yiddish expresion 'Tomer efsher', in other words, 'Is it perhaps possible that you are wrong?'[1]

At the time, Eshkol was under considerable pressure: the negative psychological impact of the economic recession; the deterioration in the security situation; the unsparing criticism of the opposition – and in particular the Rafi Party and Ben-Gurion – which went so far as to imply that he was unfit to serve and to accuse him of a 'security blunder' – all these undermined Eshkol's standing in the eyes of the general public and of the military in particular.

As the terrorist incidents multiplied, the senior command's conviction that the sole solution was to launch a wide-scale punitive action – which would topple the Syrian government or at least force it to withdraw its support for the 'popular struggle' – gained validity. Its officials claimed that reliance on defensive measures alone could not solve the problem and that Eshkol's doctrine of 'the open notebook and the recording hand', which had been based on moderation and patience, could not prevail in the long run. The 'notebook' was rapidly filling up and the public mood in Israel in the first few months of 1967 was such that a military clash with Syria seemed only a matter of time. Suddenly, on 7 April, without prior official decisions or General Staff planning, a relatively routine incident on the Syrian border was inflated to unanticipated proportions, and the IAF was brought into play on a massive scale.

This uncalculated and unconsidered development proved to be an additional leap forward to the brink of war. This event did not deter the Syrians, who continued defiantly to back terrorist action and even increased their support. Israel, for its part, continued to caution Syria. The expectation was that Israel would launch an even more massive strike against Syria. The problem now was that on 7 April the hurdle had been set too high, and there was little room for manoeuvre between an operation of this kind and full-scale warfare. Under these circumstances, the Soviet Union intervened to halt the downward course of events and to deter Israel by activating the Egyptian–Syrian defence pact signed in November 1966 under Soviet pressure for this precise purpose.

However, as is well known, the deterioration continued and none of the aims were achieved. The IDF's actions produced the opposite result to what the Israeli government had intended and Israel found itself unwillingly embroiled in full warfare. Although Israel won a resounding military victory it failed to achieve the modest goal of the planned escalation with Syria – namely the end of hostile terrorist activity.

Rabin: 'We must never again divert attention from the source and focus of the problem – Syria'

Towards the end of the winter, infiltrations from Jordan for sabotage purposes were renewed,[2] and on 12 March there was a serious attempt at sabotage when a mine was laid on the Tel Aviv–Beersheba railway track near Kibbutz Lahav. It was discovered in time and dismantled. The Commanding Officer of Southern Command, Brigadier General Yeshayahu Gavish, demanded a reprisal raid against Jordan, but Rabin was firmly resolved not to divert attention from the core of the problem. He tried to persuade the political echelon that the only way to solve the problem of terror was to hit hard at Syria, and was apparently confident that Eshkol was close to being convinced. Rabin focused therefore at this stage on plans for a large-scale move against Syria, and was strongly opposed to marginal operations which might disrupt these plans. The public mood in Israel was ripe for a punitive action against Syria.[3]

The number of terror incidents increased in the spring. Most of the infiltrators came from Jordan and Lebanon, despite the efforts of those two countries to check them. The army, following instructions from the political echelon, invested greater effort in ambushes and passive defence measures. The United States proposed a collaboration agreement for research and development of defensive and preventive measures. The government, under pressure from the army, hesitated to sign such an agreement for fear that it would restrict its freedom of action.[4] Rabin feared that US interference would both reinforce the demand of the politicians that the military focus efforts on defensive measures, and undercut the army's demand for an offensive move for solution of the problem.

However, the Chief of Staff's fears proved to be in vain. Eshkol too came to the conclusion that what was required was a 'strong blow' which would inflict damage on the Syrian army and regime, but not on civilians, and would be conducted with great care to avoid loss of life. Rabin naturally agreed with Eshkol and declared that 'a few serious knocks' would indeed teach the Syrians a lesson. He proposed exploiting the opportunity the next time the Syrians heated up the border in order to hit back.[5] The opportunity soon arrived.

7 April 1967: The CO of the IAF starts a war

The events of 7 April 1967 had served, so it transpired, as the spark which five weeks later was to ignite a crisis which culminated in war. On that day the IDF struck at the Syrian army from the air, something the senior command had long been eager to do. This large-scale operation by most of Israel's fighter aircraft, in which six Syrian Migs were brought down and Israeli planes circled over Damascus, was neither planned in advance nor submitted for prior approval to the Ministerial Committee on Security. If such a plan had indeed been submitted, it is inconceivable that it would have been sanctioned.

The situation developed as follows: the air force was placed on alert in anticipation of the renewal of work on land in the southern demilitarized zone close to Kibbutz Ha-On.[6] It was to be expected that the Syrians, who since the beginning of January had been reacting to buffer fire, would respond this time as well. The Chief of Staff, discussing the renewal of work with the Minister of Defence, 'gave him to understand that it could lead to employment of the IAF', but Eshkol, according to the evidence of his military secretary, 'took it calmly' and gave the go-ahead for the work.[7]

Work began Friday morning, 7 April, and shortly afterward the Syrians opened fire at the tractors with light weapons from the position at Imarat Izz al-Din on the Golan Heights. The IDF responded with tank fire, and exchanges of artillery and mortar fire soon followed. When stray shells fell on Kibbutz Tel Katzir, Rabin informed Eshkol at noon that the choice lay between suspending work or continuing it and bringing in the IAF to silence the Syrians. Eshkol gave orders not to stop the work, and said that 'if there is no alternative then I approve the employment of the air force'.[8] The go-ahead to the IAF was conditional on the continuation of Syrian shelling of Tel Katzir. The shelling ceased, but since the Syrians continued to fire at tractors, permission was granted nonetheless for a sortie against the Syrian positions.[9]

The Syrian air force launched Mig 21 interceptor aircraft against the Israeli assault aircraft. As a result, the IAF Control Centre ordered that the attack be halted and sent up Mirages against the Syrian Migs. The dog fights commenced at 14:00 hours over Kuneitra and continued until two Migs had been downed to the west and east of Damascus. As a result calm was restored, and Israeli aircraft returned to base to be refuelled.

Suddenly, at 14:45, when there were no Israeli planes in the air, Syrian artillery launched a heavy bombardment on Kibbutz Gadot in the central demilitarized zone, at some distance from the previous arena. The IAF was summoned again, and from 15:25, for an hour, Israeli aircraft strafed Syrian artillery positions in the area. The shelling of Gadot lasted fifteen minutes, but the damage was great. Another aerial battle commenced, in which a third Mig 21 was downed. Additional Mirages, which were patrolling the area, pursued a foursome of Migs and brought down three of them inside Jordanian territory.[10]

This sequence of events indicates that, although the IDF had contemplated the possibility that the air force would be sent in, no plans had been formulated for inflicting the longed-for 'smashing blow' on that occasion. If the Syrians had not sent up aircraft, if they had not shelled Gadot, the event would have been limited to a local incident in the southern demilitarized zone, in the course of which the IAF would have been sent into action locally and on a small scale. However, at an early stage in the events Israel took aberrant action: for the first time the IAF was employed before an Israeli settlement had actually been shelled (with the exception of stray shells which fell in Tel Katzir) and Israeli planes penetrated as far as Damascus.

At noon that day, Eshkol visited the IAF Control Centre. Rabin was at Northern Command at the time. The IAF commander Motti Hod apparently exploited Eshkol's presence in order to obtain his direct permission to launch a large-scale air operation. According to Hod, Eshkol 'gave it the nod without other considerations apart from tactical considerations which had dictated my request at the time. He may have been influenced by the atmosphere, but the fact is – that there in the Control Centre there was no problem in obtaining approval'.[11] According to this testimony, Eshkol, under the impact of the exhilarated mood in the Centre, abandoned his 'other considerations' – political, diplomatic and strategic – in favour of the tactical considerations of the IAF commander.

Thus, Hod claimed to have received full 'cover' from the political echelon for the decisions he took in the course of the incident. But did Eshkol really grasp at the time the implications of a massive employment of aircraft? Had he thought it out? This seems most unlikely. Eshkol was undoubtedly aware that his government would never have approved so massive an air operation if a prior discussion had been held. Hod may have been right in claiming that Eshkol was swayed by the prevailing mood and hence decided not to put a damper on the proceedings. It seems more likely to assume that he did not realize the true scope of the operation and lacked the qualifications to gauge the full implications. He had nobody to consult at the time and, having no alternative, gave his passive backing with a nod of the head. Eshkol wanted Syria to receive a 'smashing blow' but left it to the discretion of the army to determine its scope.

It would be hard to overestimate the significance of this incident in pre-cipitating the events which were to lead five weeks later to the brink of war. The massive employment of the air force was unprecedented. All the IDF's fighter squadrons, and more than half of the frontline aircraft, took part in the operation. The IAF carried out 171 sorties (eighty-four for attack and fifty-two for interception and patrolling) and dropped sixty-five tons of bombs, apart from rockets, air-to-air missiles and sniping fire.[12] All of this occurred without prior discussion or decision on the part of the Israeli government or the Ministerial Committee on Security. At most, the operation was covered by previous decisions empowering the Minister of Defence to approve the employment of aircraft in extraordinary situations in order to silence artillery shelling of settlements. Under no circumstances did government forums contemplate the possibility of such extensive use of the air force, including in the skies over Damascus. The mood among the ministers was such that they would never have permitted such drastic aerial response, and this was reflected in the criticism voiced at the 11 April meeting of the Ministerial Committee.[13]

Thus the military ignored the restrictions defined and dictated by the political echelon, and acted on their own initiative. Moreover, it is doubt-ful whether the Chief of Staff exercised control over the scope of the IAF operation. What seems to have occurred was a repetition of the pattern of events of 13 November 1964, when the air force was summoned in the course of a shooting incident which got out of hand, and its commander alone decided on the scope and objectives of the action and the ammuni-tion to be employed, without the intervention of the Chief of Staff.

If this assumption is correct, as it appears to be, then Motti Hod fol-lowed in the footsteps of his predecessor Ezer Weizman, and acted on his own initiative and as he saw fit at the height of a border incident, without restrictions. What is relatively evident is that Hod did not request the Chief of Staff's approval as to how the IAF was to operate.[14] The actual decision to bring in aircraft was taken by Eshkol on Rabin's request,[15] but from that moment on, there is no indication that Rabin intervened in Hod's decision-making.[16]

Thus, almost casually and without prior discussion and consideration, a local border incident was upgraded into a move of strategic significance. Israel's readiness to employ the air force on such a scale was undoubtedly perceived in Moscow, Cairo and Damascus as an indication of a far-reaching Israeli decision to bring down the Syrian regime. Nobody could have con-ceived that the scope of the operation was determined by the ad hoc decision of an Israeli colonel (Hod's rank at the time), rather than being the outcome of a measured policy, of analysis, and of clearly defined polit-ical and military goals. It is no wild exaggeration, therefore, to state that Motti Hod was, to a large extent, the single individual who, on 7 April 1967, inadvertently led the State of Israel to the brink of war, while the political and military echelons above him did not exercise the necessary control over his actions.[17] This is not, of course, to denigrate the leadership qualities displayed by Hod, who brought the air force to the pinnacle of its achievements in its finest hour during the Six Day War.

If one can point to a failure of the political, military and Intelligence systems which drove the State of Israel, against its wishes, into the June 1967 war, it was most clearly manifested on 7 April. The IDF took a step which was neither discussed nor approved by the political echelon, nor were its implications analysed accurately either before the event or subsequently. The Intelligence Branch was fixated on its conviction that nothing had changed, and neither the Soviet response nor Nasser's moves were anticipated or evaluated correctly.

Rabin: 'The confrontation theory has received strong corroboration'

As a result of the clash with the Syrians on 7 April, euphoria reigned in the General Staff, but while the objective of the action had been to end terrorist attacks stemming from Syria, the immediate Syrian response was defiance. By 9 April sabotage squads had already been dispatched to Margaliyot and Maayan Barukh.[18]

The Chief of the Intelligence Branch briefed his colleagues on the reactions of the Arab world. Egypt had raised the military alert level, in particularly in aerial defence units, but this move was no more than a routine cautious measure. The Egyptian Prime Minister Sidki Suleiman and a high-level Egyptian air force delegation were about to leave for Damascus. Yariv emphasized the moderation of the Egyptian reaction. The Egyptians had sent congratulations to the Syrian army and people for their courageous stand, and this, according to Yariv, was meant to imply that if the Syrians had put up a good show, there was no need to come to their aid. In the international arena, Yariv noted the minor-key Soviet reaction, possibly due to embarrassment at the downing of the Migs, and the satisfied response of the West.[19] He thought that the Syrians and Egyptians possibly believed that the blow inflicted by the IDF was only the beginning, and that a larger scale onslaught should be expected. This could explain the delegation to Syria.[20]

The Chief of Staff summed up the situation. It would be a good thing, he said, if the Syrians gained the impression 'that this is not the end, but only a stage ... although I know that there are several Jews who are not happy at the idea', he added, hinting at the views held by several ministers. The main significance of the action, he believed, was in the changing of the rules of the game so far as the IAF was concerned. The rule that aircraft were only employed in response to the shelling of settlements had been broken this time. No longer would the Syrians be able to exploit the rules to their advantage, said the Chief of Staff. 'They must be kept worried and not know what our rules are. . . . It's none of their business when and why we employ the air force.' Rabin attributed great significance to the fact that the IAF had operated openly above Damascus, thereby revealing to one and all the impotence of the Syrian army and its inferiority in comparison to the IDF.

But above all, he believed, it had been important to prove to the political echelon that it was possible to act against Syria without activating the Egyptian–Syrian pact. He declared:

> 'I think that this action will gain us, as far as the consciousness of all sorts of [ministers] is concerned, the conviction that it is possible to act against the Syrians. Anyone who needed proof of this, and there were quite a few who did, have got it now.'

For the future, it was essential to adopt a tougher line with the Syrians, extend the buffer fire, increase the display of strength in the demilitarized areas, and initiate frontal clashes in order to put at end to terror. On this point, Rabin added: 'For me the confrontation theory has received strong corroboration.'[21]

Dayan: 'Have you gone crazy? You're leading the country into war!'

The aerial onslaught on Syria was accepted by the Israeli public with great satisfaction and even enthusiasm. But not everyone shared in the euphoria, and there were those who were apprehensive at the worsening of the security situation. The most stringent critic was the former Chief of Staff, Knesset member Moshe Dayan, who angrily asked the Operations Chief Ezer Weizman: 'Have you gone crazy? You're leading the country into war!'[22] Several weeks later, when Nasser moved his forces into Sinai in order to foil a planned Israeli attack on Syria, or so he claimed, the criticism resurfaced with greater force in political circles in Israel.

At the 11 April meeting of the Ministerial Committee on Security, the Chief of Staff recommended, in accordance with his customary approach, that the success be exploited in order to establish additional facts in the demilitarized areas. He proposed that work commence on the controversial Khirbet Kara lands and his proposal was accepted. In reaction, Minister of Health Yisrael Barzilai of Mapam demanded an urgent meeting of the government plenum, which was in fact convened. Barzilai was troubled at the possibility 'of considerable escalation, both embroilment in a minor war and international complications'. The government did in fact decide, against Rabin's recommendation, not to cultivate the Khirbet Kara land for the time being and to discuss policy with regard to employment of the air force on another occasion.[23]

The Intelligence evaluation is unchanged: Egypt will not become involved

The conviction of the Intelligence Branch with regard to Egypt's intentions did not waver even in light of the senior-level military-political dialogue between Egypt and Syria in the wake of the 7 April events. Israeli Intelligence had 'authentic' information on the talks in Damascus with the Commander of the Egyptian air force General Sidki and Prime Minister Sidki Suleiman. The Syrians claimed that the Israeli operation had been only the first stage, and the next would be an attack on the town of Kuneitra on the Golan Heights with the aid of 'imperialism'. However, they rejected the Egyptian offer to station two Egyptian fighter squadrons on Syrian soil under Egyptian command and to undertake responsibility for the entire aerial arena. Both the commander of the Egyptian air force and the Egyptian premier made it abundantly clear that Egypt would intervene 'only in the event of a total Israel onslaught'[24] against Syria. The Deputy Chief of Intelligence David Carmon, declared: 'The basic tenet in Egypt today is not to become involved in a war with Israel.'[25]

Towards the end of April and at the beginning of May, incidents of terror increased.[26] On 7 May the Ministerial Committee on Security decided that if Syria did not cease its attacks and its support for hostile action, the IDF would launch a limited reprisal attack. The political echelon, therefore, had now accepted the army's stand even if only partially: a limited operation, but no 'smashing blow' or 'frontal clash'.[27]

The efforts of General Odd Bull to renew the Israel–Syria talks at the Armistice Commission reached an impasse at the beginning of May. Bull announced that he no longer saw any possibility of convening the Commission.[28] A military clash between Israel and Syria now appeared inevitable.

In light of the rising tension, the Knesset's Foreign Affairs and Security Committee met on 9 May during the parliamentary recess for an extraordinary meeting attended by the Prime Minister and Minister of Defence and the Chief of Staff. There was unanimity of opinion on this occasion between the government and the opposition that it was essential to take action against Syria. Rabin surveyed the increase in sabotage incidents since 7 April.[29] Elimelech Rimalt of the Gahal-Liberal Party demanded an 'impressive' military action like that of 7 April. His colleague, Haim Landau (Gahal-Herut), warned that without a deterrent response the situation would deteriorate into classic guerrilla warfare which would also recruit 'local elements [i.e. the Israeli Arab minority]'. Even Moshe Dayan, who in the past had displayed restraint and underplayed the severity of the hostile action,[30] now took a firm stand and proposed occupying the demilitarized areas. Only Yaakov Hazan of Mapam expressed reservations and suggested that the government and the military first formulate their stand

and present it to the Committee. Eshkol summed up the general mood: 'We all admit that the day of retribution must arrive.'[31] It is only against this background that one can understand the evolvement of the crisis of mid-May 1967. The Soviet, Egyptian and Syrian Intelligence services had no difficulty pin-pointing Israel's intention to act against Syria in the near future. Moscow cautioned, Cairo responded and the situation went rapidly downhill.

Interim summary

In spring 1967 the State of Israel was on the brink of war without having wanted it. Its security policy, which was aimed at deterrence and the prevention of war, had produced the opposite effect, and the events described above explain how this came about.

In the period under discussion Israel could see no way of solving the conflict with the Arab world. Israel's objective in this period was to maintain the status quo. The proclaimed aim of the Arabs, on the other hand, was to alter it. Israel chose to defend the status quo by maintaining the weapons balance and fostering deterrent military capability, and to this end also made every effort to develop nuclear capacity. For the decade after the Sinai Campaign, Israel succeeded as regards the status quo, in part because this aim was in tune with the strategy of Nasser who was anxious to postpone the confrontation with Israel. The problem was that the Arab world was not united behind this strategy, and Syria and the Palestinians took steps to undermine the status quo. Israel's reactions to their activities helped to shatter it.

Did Israel have any other choice? As noted above, there was no promising diplomatic alternative, but there may have been a military alternative. The three security problems which aggravated the conflict in this period were the diversion of the Jordan sources, the dispute over the demilitarized areas and terrorist activity. The measures employed to deal with the diversion problem were low-key, focused and highly effective. In contrast, Israel's stand on the demilitarized zones was not imperative because this was not a vital issue; greater flexibility on Israel's part could have lowered the level of friction on the border.

The main problem, however, was Israel's conduct with regard to terrorist activity. Here in particular we can observe the tension between the defensive and offensive doctrines. Eshkol tried to find the middle way through his strategy of 'the open notebook' but it missed the mark and led to escalation. The alternative which was never tried, and which could perhaps have prevented escalation, was acceptance of the fact that there could be no rapid and total solution to this problem, and that Israel would have to live with it for some time and hence should reduce it to tolerable dimensions. In hindsight, a better path to avoid escalation and war could have been a combination of increased investment in sighting and prevention device, border systems and active defence measures, together with low-key, localized and continuous offensive action. The problem was that the political echelon denied the IDF permission to launch offensive retaliation until Eshkol's 'notebook' was full, and only then did it permit a large retaliatory action (such as on 13 November 1966 or 7 April 1967) which generated escalation.

Israel did not follow the alternative path, because the government was fixated on the defensive approach while the military were focused on offensive doctrine. The ministers, for the most part, had no stomach for offensive action. The General Staff, on the other hand, abhorred the idea of defensive measures alone and advocated a drastic solution similar to the Sinai Campaign.

In the absence of a coherent approach and agreement between the echelons on ways of combating terrorism, and because of the ineffective civil control of the army and the rigid Intelligence conception, the IDF often acted in ways which promoted escalation, and were at odds with the supreme objective of the security policy: prevention of war.

Chapter 11

The trigger

In early summer – suddenly, war! Although for three weeks before the out-break of hostilities the atmosphere had been growing increasingly ominous, the war itself was totally unexpected. Neither side had planned it for that particular time and none of those caught up in it had wanted it. And yet, as events occurred in rapid succession and at a dizzying pace, all the participants were swept helplessly into the vortex.

Conspiracy?

Was the situation the outcome of a conspiracy, a plot concocted by the Kremlin, the CIA, the Mossad or the IDF General Staff, as some researchers claim?[1] Or was the entire scenario dictated from the outset by covert considerations connected to the nuclear sphere?[2]

The known facts and the extant documentation do not appear to support a conspiracy theory, nor does the nuclear theory have a solid factual basis. Moreover, the numerous documents available to me, relating to the most senior levels of the military and political echelons, rebut the charge of a deliberate Israeli scheme to kindle the flames of war. On the contrary, the stunned shock and confusion displayed by some of the major figures both in the government and the army attest clearly the absence of such a plot.

On the twenty-fifth anniversary of the Six Day War, a fascinating meeting was convened at Roslyn, Virginia. It brought together people – from the United States, the Soviet Union, Egypt, Syria, Jordan, Israel and the United Nations – who played active and major roles in the events which led to war, together with prominent scholars in various related fields. The participants gave first-person testimony, compared various viewpoints and cross-checked sources. Among other subjects, the conflict-ing conspiracy theories were discussed, and no convincing evidence was revealed.[3]

Conspiracy theories are naturally intriguing and fire the imagination. Nonetheless, it is more feasible to postulate that what occurred was a chain of miscalculations on the part of all those involved: Egypt, Syria, Jordan, the Palestinians, the Soviet Union, the United States and the UN, and of course – Israel. If each and every one of these players had acted differently at the various stages, the chain reaction might have been interrupted and war prevented.[4]

On one issue, in any event, there is no controversy: the immediate crisis which kindled the flames began with a spurious Soviet report to Egypt to the effect that Israel was 'concentrating a large force' on the Syrian border in preparation for an imminent attack on Syria. The Soviet motive has never been satisfactorily clarified.[5]

Since the extensive literature on the origins of the Six Day War discusses the role of the various above-mentioned factors in great detail, it will not be dealt with here. But, to the best of our knowledge, none of them have examined whether an additional important country in the region, which seemed to have been uninvolved, played any part in activating the process which led to war. The country to which I am referring is Iran.[6]

The Iranian–Israeli connection

The close cooperation between Israel and Iran was reflected in visits to Iran by senior Israeli political figures and the army. The two countries maintained strong and intimate clandestine ties in the Intelligence sphere, in sharp contrast to the official diplomatic sphere, where relations were cool and reserved.

At the end of 1966 the Iranian Premier Abbas Hoveyda and Chief of Staff General Baharam Aryana visited Israel. Aryana invited Yitzhak Rabin to pay a return visit to his country. Rabin arrived in Teheran on 14 April 1967 accompanied by his wife Leah and his bureau chief, Lt. Col. Rafi Efrat, and two days later had an audience with the Shah. He also visited Persepolis, Shiraz and Isfahan. The meetings were coordinated by the IDF attaché in Teheran, Colonel Yaakov Nimrodi.[7]

Rabin's secret visit to Iran took place only four weeks before the outbreak of the crisis which led to the Six Day War. Rabin met with the senior military, toured military installations and held talks with leaders, including Hoveyda and the Shah. These talks were of a strategic nature, and on his return he reported to the General Staff forum.[8] It may be assumed that he also reported to Eshkol.

Rabin pointed out Israel's interests: first and foremost the supply of oil; 85 per cent of Israel's oil supplies came from Iran. Negotiations were being held at the time on the expansion of the oil pipeline from Eilat to Ashkelon, so that Persian oil could be exported through Israeli ports without having to pass through the Suez Canal. Iran was also a large potential market for Israeli industry and agriculture and a partner for joint economic enterprises. And finally – and this was the crux of the matter so far as Rabin was concerned – there were security and political interests. Since Iran was 'a Middle Eastern Moslem country with a strong anti-Nasserist stance ... by virtue of this shared anti-Nasserist interest, there is a basis for identity and for all kinds of joint enterprises between the two countries'.

According to Rabin, he had presented the following thesis in his talks with the Foreign Minister, the Prime Minister and the Shah:

> 'There is a bad troika in the Middle East, which is anxious to alter the status quo and is not content with the present situation. It is headed by Nasser's Egypt – and its other branches are Syria and Iraq. It is in the interest of both our countries to deal with this troika. The method must be containment of Nasser in the southern Arab peninsula [i.e. Yemen] (so as to create the conditions for bringing him down), the neutralization of Iraq and a strike against the Syrians.'

Rabin found the Iranians to be seriously concerned by Nasser's moves in the southern Arab peninsula. They regarded themselves as partners with Saudi Arabia and Pakistan in an axis aimed at blocking the spread of Nasserism towards the Persian Gulf. The Iranians acknowledged the shared interests with Israel, Rabin said, but demanded categorically that Israel play its part by pinning Nasser's forces to the Israeli border. 'That is their interest in us,' Rabin explained to the generals, 'and a deal which is not based on interests – is not serious.' He summed up the Iranian demands as follows:

> 'And where are you?! You want them [the Egyptians] to clash with us while you stand aside and lick your fingers? You are the ones who can hold them down and threaten them; you can restrict Nasser's freedom of action in the southern Arab peninsula [and you are not doing it].'

In contrast to their fear of Egypt, the Iranians were not concerned about Iraq. They believed that Aref's regime was weak, and that the great majority of Iraqis did not sympathize with Nasser. The Shah, Rabin said, 'knows how to play' the Kurdish card in order to exert pressure on Iraq and neutralize it. On the other hand, the Syrian regime 'is abhorred' by the Iranians. They were 'delighted' at the Syrian debacle on 7 April, and hoped that the skirmishes between Israel and Syria would continue, forcing Egypt to intervene, thereby easing the pressure in southern Arabia. This was the fervent hope of the Iranians 'which they would like more than anything'. If Egypt did not rush to Syria's aid against Israel, Nasser's prestige would be damaged, and this too would gratify the Iranians. Rabin's hosts 'almost all wondered how we see the significance of the Egyptian–Syrian [defence] pact and under what conditions Egypt will come to Syria's aid'.

Rabin concluded that there was no prospect of the Iranians dispatching military units to southern Arabia. They were not willing to take such action nor was their army prepared for it. The Shah and the Premier told Rabin: 'Our problem is that we prepared for a war [against the Soviet Union] which we did not fight, and found ourselves unprepared for the problems confronting us ... we have many partners against the Russians, but that should not be the main focus of our military preparations. Today we are not ready for a war against Nasser.' They told Rabin that the Saudis also lacked an effective military response to Nasser, and the bombing of the Saudi town of Najran by the Egyptians had deterred King Feisal, who had discovered that the British and Americans would not hurry to his aid. Iran and Saudi Arabia were building up military capability so that, within three or four years, they would no longer have to rely on the United States, which had disappointed them.

Rabin reminded the IDF generals of the various export deals between Israel and Iran, including the defence industries, and noted that the Iranians 'have faith in us like in God. It's incredible.' In the political sphere, Iran 'is the axis for contacts with the Arab [and] Moslem states', even though 'the hatred of Arabs is extraordinary' there. Iran, he added, 'is not a particularly enlightened country according to our concepts, but such is the Middle East, and we have to examine the matter from the aspect of interests, and less from other aspects.'

The visit to Iran, the meetings with the Shah and political and military leaders in Teheran, evidently left a strong impression on Yitzhak Rabin. During his visit he understood even more clearly that Israel's economic, political and strategic interests required the consolidation of ties with this large Muslim country. He did not say explicitly that Israel should respond to the Iranian demand to 'pin down' Nasser's forces and lure his army to Sinai, but neither did he state the reverse. He merely said: 'That is their interest in us, and a deal which is not built on interests is not serious', and left it to his audience to interpret his meaning. At the same time, his remarks suggest that the Iranian expectations called for some response if Israel wanted to maintain and strengthen the strategic connection between the two countries.

Only a month after Rabin's visit to Iran, his hosts' great wish was fulfilled: Israel's threats to inflict another blow on Syria forced Nasser to honour his commitment under the defence pact, move his army into Sinai and even transfer units from Yemen to the Israeli border. The ensuing military flare-up ended Nasser's five-year Yemenite escapade, which was regarded by the Gulf States as a far-reaching strategic threat. Israel's victory in the Six Day War was also the victory of the two monarchs, Reza Pahlevi and Feisal, owners of the oil reserves on the Gulf coast. Rabin had lived up in full to the expectations of his Iranian hosts.

The details of Rabin's visit to Iran in April 1967 may gratify the advocates of conspiracy theories, who can now argue that the key to the crisis which led to war lies therein. They can also interpret Israel's threats against Syria (see below) on the eve of Israeli Independence Day not as routine pronouncements characteristic of this period, but as deliberate moves. Perhaps the 'off-the-record' briefing of foreign correspondents by the Chief of Intelligence Aharon Yariv on 11 May (see below) was intended to exert pressure on Nasser (at which it succeeded).

One can also find additional confirmation of the hypothesis that Rabin merely wanted to repay his courteous hosts, on behalf of their joint interests and in order to reinforce their unwritten strategic alliance, and, unintentionally, 'found himself at war'. In the initial stages of Egypt's involvement in Yemen in 1963, Rabin, then still Deputy Chief of Staff, in an appearance before Prime Minister and Minister of Defence David Ben-Gurion, Minister of Finance Levi Eshkol and Foreign Minister Golda Meir at the General Staff forum, voiced his discontent at the fact that the IDF was not forcing the Egyptian army to remain in Sinai. He said then: 'I must admit that the present situation whereby Egypt can dispatch nine to ten brigades 1,000 miles from Egypt – it's as if we were to dispatch forces to Rome – while Israel is not a threat [causing him to] pin down his force. I don't feel good about that, I am even ashamed of it.' He had a concrete proposal to offer: to pin down Egyptian forces in Sinai 'not by action' but 'by threats', in order to foil a possible Nasserite victory in Yemen and to weaken Nasser's standing.[9]

The Iranians, therefore, did not have to work hard in April 1967 in order to persuade Rabin of the need to 'pin down' Nasser's force. They were preaching to the converted. All that was needed now was for him to implement the scheme 'by threats'. Syria's conduct and the Egyptian–Syrian pact provided the pretext. His statement in September 1966 about the regime in Damascus, which, as noted above, won him a reprimand from Eshkol, was proof that, in word if not in deed he allowed himself to go beyond the permitted bounds as a military man and beyond what was acceptable to the government. This assumption may perhaps explain Rabin's remorseful remark to the Head of Operations, Ezer Weizman, at a time of crisis (see below): 'I complicated things for Israel.'

The facts, as we know them, disprove the theory of an Israeli 'conspiracy'. Moreover, they offer no evidence to support the theory that Rabin, in the few days between his return from Teheran and the outbreak of the crisis, acted in any way under Iranian inspiration. The sequence of events, where Israel was concerned, may be explained without recourse to conspiracy theories. Rabin's character and patterns of behaviour were such that he would not have taken a provocative step against Egypt without the approval of the political echelon. It is inconceivable that the Ministerial Committee on Security would have sanctioned such a move. Israel's fear of an attack on Dimona and the closing of the Straits undoubtedly carried weight against such a move. Israel derived satisfaction from the Egyptian entanglement in Yemen (no longer fearing that Nasser might succeed in occupying the entire Persian Gulf area). There were even those who believed that Nasser was seeking a way of extricating himself from Yemen without losing face[10] and that it would be a foolish mistake on Israel's part to provide him with the excuse. The luring of Egyptian forces into Sinai was liable to create problems for Israel and hamper its freedom of action against Syria. And, in general, the above-mentioned declarations about 'pinning down' Egyptian forces in Sinai were too few and far between to enable one to draw far-reaching conclusions. This was not Rabin's 'line', and perusal of the documents reveals no discussion of or additional reference to this issue.

Israel did not want war. The aim of its security policy was to avoid war through deterrence and to maintain as calm a status quo as possible. The ongoing terrorist activity and the incidents on the Syrian border called for solution, but, as noted above, the intention was to inflict a blow on Syria without bringing in Egypt and subsequently fighting on two fronts. The reverse was true: in order to strike at the Syrians, Israel required calm on the Egyptian border and the deployment of the Egyptian forces in Yemen rather than Sinai. Moreover, in principle, in analysing conspiratorial theories, one should perhaps recall the Ockams Razor principle, namely that the best explanation for any puzzle or phenomenon is almost always the one involving the least complexity. I have seen fit, however, to raise the theoretical possibility which could be deduced from the few statements mentioned above, if only in order to refute it.

The Iranian–Soviet connection

Nonetheless, Rabin's remarks offer a broad hint which can help explain the conduct of the Soviets rather than the Israelis in precipitating the crisis. The prevailing view since 1967 has been that the warning dispatched to Egypt by the Soviet Union regarding a concentration of Israeli forces and an imminent Israeli attack on Syria stemmed from the Kremlin's anxiety about the future of the Damascus regime. This assumption has a sound logical basis: the events of 7 April severely damaged the prestige of the Syrian military establishment and undermined its stability. Shortly afterwards the Baath regime was shaken by the publication of an atheistic article in the army journal *Jaish el-Shaab* which sparked off widespread riots in Syria.[11] On 21 April a coup took place in Athens which toppled the socialist regime. On 25 April a conference of communist parties was convened at Karlovi Vari in Czechoslovakia to discuss the impact of a world 'imperialist' attack, headed by the CIA, against the 'progressive' regimes. On 21 and 25 April a harshly worded protest was conveyed to the Israeli ambassador in Moscow.[12] It was no secret that in Israel the prevailing conviction – not only among the General Staff – was that a strike against Syria was inevitable because terror attacks were continuing, and that the goal should be the downfall of the Syrian regime. Soviet Intelligence sources must have been aware of this fact, particularly after Israel's leaders uttered threats and declarations against Syria on the eve of Israeli Independence Day, and the Chief of Intelligence, in a briefing for foreign attachés, referred explicitly to a wide-scale Israeli strike against Syria (see below). Thus, in mid-May 1967, the Soviets had good reason to believe that if they wanted to save the Damacus regime, their protégé, they needed to act swiftly. They therefore called on Nasser to exert pressure on Israel from the south and thereby prevent Israel from operating in the north. This is the logical and acceptable explanation for the conduct of the Soviet Union, which did not envisage that events would spin out of control and deteriorate into war. While it is apparently correct, it is not necessarily the sole explanation. It transpires that the Soviet Union apparently had an additional, hitherto unknown motive, which is in fact linked to its relations with Iran.

In March 1967, Soviet Foreign Minister Andrei Gromyko paid a surprise visit to Cairo, the reason for which was not evident at the time. All the Israeli Chief of Intelligence could say was that it was connected mainly to the southern Yemen issue,[13] and that Gromyko's message to Nasser was: 'Go slow!'[14] On the agenda were not only the civil war in Yemen, which was then dying down, but also, and mainly, Britain's anticipated departure from Aden at the beginning of 1968 and the establishment of the shaky federation of South Yemen, which FLOSY, the Marxist Front for the Liberation of South Yemen, was threatening to take over, with Nasser's backing. The Gulf States feared the entry of Egyptian forces into Aden and the Federation as a vitally important strategic stronghold and a launching pad for Egyptian hegemony over the region.

The question arises: What was the underlying reason for the Soviet initiative aimed at restraining Egyptian involvement in southern Yemen and curbing Nasser's ambitions, at a time when the British were due to withdraw from Aden and the strategic stronghold of southern Yemen was about to fall into Nasser's hands like a ripe fruit? The answer may lie in what Rabin was told in Teheran by Shah Muhammad Reza Pahlevi.

Rabin reported their conversation as follows:

'On the Russian question, the Shah took an unusual step which surprised even the Americans. He signed extensive commercial agreements with them [with the Russians] for the sale of oil, gas, the construction of large Russian factories as well as commercial agreements. He says the following: I want to face the Russians with a dilemma concerning their relations with me as against their relations with Nasser – what do they have to gain from Nasser and what do they gain from me, and the calculation in the struggle between me and Nasser in Russian eyes will be – what reward will they receive from relations with us and what from their relations with the Egyptians?'[15]

The obvious conclusion is that the Shah, whose main concern was the possible expansion of Nasserism into the Gulf States, had decided that he could not rely on the United States, which was bogged down in the Vietnam mud, to check the Egyptian President's dangerous aspirations. He therefore turned to the Soviet Union, to the surprise and undoubtedly the displeasure of the Americans, and held out the offer of considerable economic benefits. His intention was to prove to the Soviets that their interest in Iran was as weighty as their interest in Egypt. In return he demanded that Nasser be stopped. The same consideration which prompted the Iranians to exert pressure on Rabin to pin Egyptian forces to Sinai in order to subvert Egypt's efforts in southern Yemen, impelled them to bind the Soviet Union to Iran with bonds of strong interests in order to curb Nasser. There are even indications that, during his surprise visit to Cairo, Gromyko discussed the evacuation of the UN Emergency Force from Sinai and the transfer of Egyptian forces from Yemen to Sinai.[16]

According to this view of events, it transpires that the Soviets had an additional strong motive which even justified use of disinformation in order to 'lure' Nasser out of southern Arabia and direct him against Israel. This is not to suggest that the Soviets deliberately fomented war. There can be little doubt that this was not their intention. However, if this interpretation is valid, it can cast new light on the actions of the Soviet Union which ignited the crisis.

Israel's threats

The Soviet message to Egypt referred to deployment of at least eleven brigades, a totally spurious and even absurd figure.[17] Almost certainly, the Soviets were aware that the information was false. A short tour of the Galilee panhandle would have sufficed in order to ascertain the facts. What led them to provide such blatantly false information? Was it for an 'Iranian reason' or out of sincere concern for the Damascus regime, or possibly for both reasons?

What is clear is that the Soviets acted in immediate response to the pronouncements by senior Israeli military and political leaders. They may have wanted at one and the same time to prevent Israel from attacking Syria and to sabotage the Egyptian effort in southern Arabia in order to appease the Iranians. To this end they were ready to feed Nasser exaggerated and implausible information. On the other hand, as noted above, there is no evidence that the USSR wanted war, and their conduct in the course of the crisis apparently indicates an attempt to prevent it. The Soviets were well aware of their strategic inferiority in the Mediterranean arena due to the permanent presence of the US Sixth Fleet, and hence were reluctant to intervene, since such a move could have led to a Superpower confrontation.[18]

What then was the nature of the Israeli declarations which disturbed the Soviets, or alternatively, provided them with the pretext to alert Nasser?

From the Israeli press in the spring of 1967 we learn that the Syrian leadership was panic-stricken at what it saw as an imperialist plot to bring down the Baath regime in Damascus, a plot which would culminate in an Israeli assault liable to occur at any moment. Before the regime had recovered from the blow it had suffered on 7 April, severe riots broke out, instigated by the Muslim Brothers (after the publication of an anti-religious attack in the army magazine on 25 April), and the ferment continued until the mid-May crisis broke out.[19] 'The situation in Syria is on the verge of explosion', cried the banner headlines.[20] Nor was Syria better off in the political arena. An Israeli diplomatic campaign against Syria proved unexpectedly successful. On 9 May Israel dispatched a missive to the UN Secretary General and the Security Council, listing the terror incidents originating in Syria or inspired by that country. The Ministry of Foreign Affairs conveyed a message to the members of the Security Council to the effect that Israel could no longer refrain from action if the sabotage continued. On 10 May Eshkol met with General Bull and cautioned that the Israeli government would regard itself as free to act against Syria in self-defence. The Israeli campaign was interpreted, and rightly so, as preparation for the military strike against Syria. In a preventive move, the UN Secretary General issued a statement on 11 May condemning Fatah activities and demanding that the governments take every possible step to end them.[21]

The most striking fact is that, despite the internal situation in Syria, the blow the regime had suffered on 7 April and the fear of a wide-scale Israeli action, the Damascus leadership did not put a stop to forays against Israel, and these even became more frequent.[22] For the Baath regime, defiance was a basic tenet and support for the 'popular struggle' a major principle. Representatives of the Security Council member states were summoned on 13 May to the Syrian Foreign Minister Ibrahim Makhous, who asserted that Syria was not responsible for fidaiyyun activity. They were warned that Israel was planning 'aggression on a wide scale' against Syria, and that in such an event, the Egyptian–Syrian defence pact would be put into motion.[23]

If the impact of the Israeli air force operation on 7 April had not sufficed, the ensuing provocative Israeli declarations[24] and diplomatic campaign, which was seen to be preparing the ground for a military action, and the Independence Day declarations of Israeli political and military leaders added fuel to the fire. There was certainly no deliberate plan to heighten the tension, but in the prevailing strained atmosphere, these declarations seemed to result from a dearth of wisdom and an excess of rashness, which was realized too late.[25]

The Israeli press traditionally publishes Independence Day interviews with the country's leaders, and it is the latter's habit of issuing headline-catching statements. Most of the statement this time were relatively routine. Eshkol declared: 'Quiet cannot prevail on only one side of the border';[26] 'If there is no escape, we will take action against the hubs of terror and those who encourage it';[27] 'If the Arab states try to stir up our border – their own border will be stirred up'.[28] However, it was an incautious statement by Eshkol at a party meeting which caught the headlines: 'We may be forced to adopt measures no less serious than those adopted on 7 April.'[29]

It seems, however, that the most extreme declarations came from the military, apparently without authorization. The Chief of Staff was saying nothing new when he declared that terrorist action could not be suppressed by defensive measures,[30] although his statement was not compatible with Eshkol's attitude. However, its implications were serious because he was reiterating an earlier statement (in an interview in the [Jewish] New Year issue of *Bamahaneh*), for which he had been reprimanded by Eshkol. Again he said that action such as was taken against Jordan and Lebanon was suited to countries which were not interested in encouraging terror. 'In Syria, there is a different problem because it is the regime that activates the terrorists. Hence, an operation against Syria has a different objective to operations against Jordan and Lebanon.'[31] In other words, quite explicitly and despite the reprimand he had received, Rabin was again advocating the overthrow of the Damascus regime.

Even more explicit was Chief of Intelligence Yariv, in his off-the-record briefing of foreign journalists and military attachés on 11 May. UPI reported on the following day that a senior Israeli source had claimed that 'Israel will take limited military action with the aim of overthrowing the military regime in Damascus, if Syrian terrorists continued to enter Israel for terror purposes. Military observers said that such an attack would not reach the proportions of general warfare but would teach the Syrian Government a lesson.' Elsewhere there is a partial direct quotation from the recording of the briefing: 'I can state that we are obliged to use force in order to compel the Egyptians to persuade the Syrians that it is not worthwhile [to permit the Palestinians to cross the border for terror purposes] ... I believe that the only secure answer to the problem is a military operation on a large decisive scale.' In reply to a question as to what such an operation would entail, the Chief of Intelligence said that 'there are various alternatives ranging from counter-guerrilla action to a widescale invasion of Syria and occupation of Damascus'. In a more detailed version, where the remarks are attributed to the 'army spokesman', it is stated that

Israel must act so as to make the Syrians understand that they are in danger of 'an immediate general military confrontation' with Israel.[32]

It is interesting that the Egyptians attributed to Rabin and Eshkol an explicit threat to invade Damascus and overthrow the regime.[33] I have found no evidence of this and they may have misunderstood, attributing Yariv's statement that 'there are alternatives ranging from counter-guerrilla action to a widescale invasion of Syria and occupation of Damascus' to Rabin. Yariv was thinking of something 'in between', as United Press reported. It is not impossible that the Soviets, fearing that it was the intention of 'military circles' in Israel to strike at Syria, conveyed an edited version of Yariv's remarks to the Egyptians, attributing them to Rabin, in order to spur Nasser to action. The Soviets also reported, as noted above, that Israel was concentrating between eleven and thirteen brigades near the Syrian border. Thus all the Soviet reports were disinformation for a specific purpose: to deter Israel from striking at Syria.[34]

Even more interesting is the fact that the Egyptians checked immediately and discovered that the information given by the Soviets was false. Egyptian Chief of Staff General Mahmoud Fawzi left for Syria on 14 May by order of Deputy President Abdel Hakim Amer to verify the information. Fawzi toured the border area, conducted observations, examined aerial photographs, and found no evidence to support the information. His visit was brief, only twenty-four hours, but his report arrived too late, after the wheels had begun to turn.[35]

The question is whether the pronouncements by the military were authorized by and coordinated with the political echelon. Rabin's remarks in an interview to *Lamerhav* were certainly not approved by Eshkol, who had already reprimanded him for a similar statement.[36] Yariv's briefing of foreign journalists may have been directed at Syria as a final warning. If he did indeed hint at the intention to overthrow the Syrian regime, as UPI reported, then he too was exceeding his authority.

The profusion of anti-Syrian declarations and threats prior to Independence Day may have added fuel to the blaze, but the fire had already been lit, the terrorist activity under Syrian auspices was continuing and the feeling in Israel was that military action against Syria was imminent.[37] While the flood of threats possibly acted as the catalyst and determined the timing of the crisis, under the circumstances, it had been due to erupt anyway. In any event it is clear that the Soviet assessment from mid-May 1967 that Israel was about to strike at Syria was correct and well founded, and was not merely based on the public threats issued by Eshkol, Rabin and Yariv.[38]

The 'mini-parade' in Jerusalem

The story of the 'mini-parade' in Jerusalem on Israel's nineteenth Independence Day (15 May 1967) deserves to be mentioned, although it is connected only tenuously to the events which led to war. Since the early years of statehood, a military parade had been the central happening on Independence Day, and it was held from time to time in different cities. To hold it in Jerusalem was problematic because the armistice agreement with Jordan restricted the size of the military forces and prohibited entry of certain types of weapons into the city, including aircraft and armoured military vehicles. The last parade had been held in Jerusalem in 1961 under Ben-Gurion's premiership, in contravention of the armistice agreement (Israel claimed that Jordan too had contravened the agreement by denying the Israelis free access to the Holy Places in the Old City, regular use of the institutions on Mount Scopus and passage along the Latrun road). At the time there were international objections to holding a parade in Jerusalem, reflected in Security Council resolution No. 162. Now, six years later, the atmosphere was fraught with tension, and the internal political mood had changed. It had long since been Jerusalem's 'turn' to host the parade, and in 1965 the government had even decided to allow the Chief of Staff to choose: a small-scale parade in Jerusalem under the restrictions of the armistice agreement, or a full parade in Tel Aviv. At the time, Rabin chose the latter.[39]

In late 1966 the government decided to hold the next parade in Jerusalem and to observe the armistice agreement restrictions. The IDF made preparations accordingly, but the government was inundated with external and internal pressures. The United States, Britain, France and other countries, as well as the UN Secretary General, urged Israel not to hold the parade in Jerusalem. When the government did not acquiesce, the entire diplomatic corps, with the exception of several military attachés, boycotted the parade.[40] On the domestic front the government was fiercely criticized, and the most furious onslaught came from Ben-Gurion, who even returned his invitation to the parade. He claimed that the government was undermining the standing of the capital and that a 'feeble and pathetic' parade was 'an insult to Jerusalem ... I don't care what the Superpowers say and whether or not ambassadors will come. The parade is held so that the nation and the neighbouring countries can see the might of the IDF.'[41] From the moment the government decided on Jerusalem, it was unable to retreat even in the face of heavy international pressure. However, the modest scope of the parade attested to the government's cautious approach and reluctance to heighten the tension. Under the conditions prevailing in April 1967, this was a balanced and feasible decision, and Ben-Gurion's criticism was unfair. In fact, he contradicted himself several days later when he accused the Eshkol government of irresponsible escalation of the security situation.

A final relevant point on this issue: at the dress rehearsal of the public rally at the Hebrew University stadium on Independence Day eve (an event introduced two years previously in order to 'compensate' the Jerusalemites for being deprived of the parade), the programme included recitation of a verse from a poem by the poet Natan Alterman: 'Arabia, Arabia, ponder your path in good time!/The thread is growing tauter, growing tauter/... Awake from your fanciful dreams/Perhaps this is the final hour!' Someone in the audience commented that the text sounded excessively threatening and it was replaced at the event itself by another verse: 'Arabia, Arabia, before the die is cast/Before the sun is darkened for us both/Hold back, and do not open/The latch on the gates of war!/And you will see the difference/Between a nameless malediction/And a peaceful greeting and blossoming era/Such as the sons of Shem have never known!'[42]

It cannot be claimed that the decision to hold the parade in Jerusalem had a tangible impact on the sequence of events, but it increased the existing tension. The Arabs were convinced that no heavy weapons had been displayed at the parade because the Israelis were concentrating forces along the border.[43] The parade itself took place several hours after Egyptian units began to move towards Sinai. The Chief of Staff received the first reliable information on the movement of Egyptian forces on the dais at the parade.[44]

Chapter 12

The start of the crisis

In the decade between the withdrawal from Sinai in 1957 and the Six Day War, border relations between Israel and Egypt were generally stable and uneventful. The organized infiltrations through the Egyptian border and the Gaza Strip for sabotage purposes ceased completely. The UN Emergency Force (UNEF), deployed at control points along the border and at Sharm al-Sheikh, was mostly idle, and in 1966 the UN Secretariat even contemplated reducing the force drastically. This was not carried out due to Israeli objections. The main role of UNEF, so far as Israel was concerned, was to ensure free shipping through the Straits of Tiran at the entrance to Eilat (Aqaba) Bay. Eilat was Israel's maritime gateway to Africa and Asia, and above all a vital port for the Iranian oil on which Israel was dependent.

The relative lull on the border did not reflect the depth of the basic conflict between the two countries, which became increasingly acute after the Sinai Campaign.[1] Nasser now had two defeats to revenge on Israel: 1948 and 1956. He had been occupied since then with other problems both internal and external, but he never forgot.

Towards the end of his term of office, Ben-Gurion pinned hopes on efforts to conduct a dialogue with Nasser through the editor of the *Sunday Times*, Charles Hamilton, but they proved unproductive.[2] However, in 1965 to 1966, a seemingly promising connection was established through the Mossad with General Mahmoud Khalil, former Deputy Head of Intelligence in the Egyptian air force. The head of the Mossad, Meir Amit, and Deputy Defence Minister Zvi Dinstein were invited by Khalil to pay a clandestine visit to Cairo for a possible meeting with Vice-President Abdel Hakim Amer.

Isser Harel, the Prime Minister's adviser on Intelligence affairs, who was Amit's bitter rival, pointed out Khalil's dubious character and claimed that the invitation might be a trap. He proposed that the meeting take place at a neutral location, and the Prime Minister accepted his advice. Amit regarded the frustrating of his plan to visit Cairo as a missed historic opportunity,[3] but Egypt's refusal to hold the meeting on neutral ground cast doubt on the whole matter.

Another aberrant event which occurred in February to March 1960 on the Egyptian front was a 'trial run' in miniature for May 1967. This event, which had a traumatic impact on the General Staff, was known as 'Rotem'. On 31 January/1 February 1960, after a series of shooting incidents on the Syrian border in the southern demilitarized area, a force from the Golani infantry brigade carried out the first reprisal mission since the Sinai Campaign. The force attacked the village of Khirbet Tawafik on the southern outskirts of the Golan Heights and the adjacent Syrian position. At the time, Syrian and Egypt were linked in the United Arab Republic. The Soviet Union fed the UAR false information on concentrations of Israeli forces on the Syrian border, and on 18 February Egyptian forces began to cross the Suez Canal secretly and to concentrate in northern Sinai.

It will be recalled that, under Ben-Gurion's premiership, the IAF rarely conducted reconnaissance sorties across the border. It was only six days later, after an American alert, that the IDF General Staff learned of the presence of the Egyptian force, which now numbered some 500 tanks, as against the thirty or so tanks in Israel's Southern Command. 'We were caught with our pants down,' wrote the Chief of Operations Yitzhak Rabin to the IAF commander Ezer Weizman. 'For the next 24 hours everything depends on the air force.' The IDF rallied hastily and launched Operation 'Rotem', concentrating large regular and reserve forces in the Negev. Ben-Gurion adopted a policy of pacification, announcing his forthcoming visit to Washington, and three weeks later Nasser withdrew his forces beyond the Suez Canal and announced that the objective – to deter Israel from attacking Syria – had been achieved.[4]

Initially, Gamal Abdul Nasser's decision of May 1967 to move his army into the Sinai Peninsula (this time, in contrast to 1960, it was done openly) was reminiscent of the Rotem situation. In hindsight it became evident that this was the first in a sequence of fateful decisions which were to change forever the face of the Middle East and the Arab–Israeli conflict. It created a new dynamics, and from then on nothing could turn back the clock.

The General Staff is alert and cautious

The Egyptian move took the IDF General Staff by surprise. None of the Intelligence evaluations had forecast it. At most, they had predicted the possibility of Egyptian intervention in the event of a 'total' Israeli onslaught against Syria. All the Intelligence Branch experts opined that Egypt would not permit Syria to drag it unwillingly into an untimely war with Israel, a view which had a firm basis. Even in the more unlikely case of Egyptian intervention after a major Israeli operation against Syria, the view was that the Egyptians would only intervene after the event as a reaction. The possibility of prior intervention in order to foil an Israeli scheme was never taken into account.

However, even more remarkable is the very fact that Israeli Intelligence bodies were taken by surprise. It had apparently known by the end of 1966 about Egyptian Vice-President Abdel Hakim Amer's message to Nasser, dispatched while he was en route to a visit to Pakistan, urging that the Egyptian army move into Sinai and block the Tiran Straits.[5] The underlying motive was probably the IDF operation at Samu and the strong criticism of Egypt's failure to act. The fact that Amer's recommendation was rejected may have reinforced the Intelligence estimation that Nasser would not risk war so long as his army was in Yemen.

In fact, the Egyptian move may also be viewed as a reaction, delayed by five weeks, to the IAF operation of 7 April. This pattern of delayed reaction was not new. It recalled the situations of February 1960 when the main Egyptian force was moved into Sinai two to three weeks after the IDF operation at Tawafik, and of November 1966 when the United Arab Command, headed by Egypt, reacted only two weeks after the Samu attack. The IDF Intelligence Branch should have assumed on the basis of experience that some form of Egyptian response to a significant Israeli attack on an Arab country was a feasible prospect. Instead, they clung to the concept that avoidance of entanglement with Israel was so basic an Egyptian principle that Israel was still free to act against Syria again on a large scale without much fear of Egyptian intervention.

At first, the IDF calculated, and this was also the general impression, that Egypt's intention was to deter Israel from taking action against Syria and also to bolster Nasser's standing as the leader of the Arab world and its shield against Israel.

The concentration of forces recalled the Rotem operation,[6] with one important difference: at that time, the movement of Egyptian forces into Sinai had been clandestine and discreet, while now it was carried out openly, in the light of day and in front of TV cameras, in a manner which evoked widespread popular enthusiasm in the Arab world. It was feared in the military that the Egyptian move might tie Israel's hands in its struggle against terrorist activity which would increase, thanks to the backing of the Egyptian force. In any event, the IDF's first move was to concentrate a regular armoured force in the south, and to conduct patrols, observations and mining of sensitive sectors. The day after Independence Day, due to the accelerated movement of forces into Sinai, it was decided to strengthen the IDF defensive deployment along the Egyptian border. All the Israeli moves were carried out cautiously in the first instance to avoid heating up the situation. The Chief of Staff believed that Israel's actions should be dictated not necessarily by evaluations of Egypt's intentions but by the possibilities inherent in the concentration of forces in Sinai.[7] For reasons of caution, Israel had to consider the possibility, however unlikely, of a more drastic Egyptian move: the blocking of the Straits of Tiran, the bombing of the Dimona reactor, and concentrating Egyptian forces in Sinai in defensive deployment in preparation for a possible Israeli attack.

The Operations Branch of the General Staff, headed by Colonel Yitzhak Hofi, was now to become the 'nerve junction' of the army, coordinating staff activity throughout the crisis. It ordered that IDF forces be moved to their destinations in the hours of darkness and that all field security rules be strictly observed. The objective was to maintain a low profile and a discreet defensive deployment without provoking the other side and causing a chain reaction. Due to the continuing flow of Egyptian troops into Sinai, Eshkol acceded to Rabin's request to mobilize a reserve brigade. On 16 May the Operations Branch issued a mobilization order for 520 Armoured Brigade.[8]

Inside the government: 5 per cent danger of escalation

The Israeli government convened on 16 May 1967, just after Independence Day, for a routine session. No military representatives were present, but Eshkol opened the meeting with a survey of the security situation. He made brief mention of five terrorist attacks perpetrated the previous week and then read out the Intelligence evaluation:

> It is estimated that, in light of Syrian reports and appeals to Egypt regarding Israel's intention to take major action against Syria; in light of declarations and warnings issued by Israel in the past few days; and Egypt's predicament since 7 April, Egypt has come to the decision that in the present circumstances it cannot sit by idly. It has therefore decided, in the face of the Israeli threat, to demonstrate readiness to come to Syria's aid within the framework of the mutual defence pact. At the same time, it may be assumed that the Egyptians hope that their actions and demonstration will achieve the practical effect of deterring Israel from implementing its threat. This Egyptian move is to a certain degree an achievement for Syria, which has succeeded in drawing Egypt unwillingly into openly backing it, and therefore providing indirect support for Damascus' extreme policy towards Israel.

At that stage according to this evaluation, the size of the Egyptian force and its activity attested to the buildup of a defensive deployment in Sinai. The transition to offensive would require an increase in the number of tanks and the movement of additional forces into northern Sinai, and of this 'there are no indications'. As for the intentions of the Egyptians, 'It seems feasible that they will intervene only in the event of a major [Israeli] attack [on Syria], to include the conquest and holding of territory.'[9] Hence the first evaluation submitted to the government was not a cause for alarm: Israel continued to hold the winning cards. The Egyptians would intervene only if Israel invaded Syria for purposes of conquering territory. The implication was that the government had no intention of ordering the army to occupy territory in Syria, and consequently Israel's freedom of action would not be restricted.

The government's discussion of the matter was brief, and the mood did not seem to be particularly anxious. Foreign Minister Abba Eban was praised for his diplomatic triumphs in the campaign against Syria: the US administration had asked Israel to refrain from taking action against Jordan, but 'as for Syria – they were purposely vague'. UN Secretary General U Thant had condemned the Fatah operations, although he was later forced by Arab pressure to clarify that he did not condone Israeli reprisals. 'There can be no doubt,' Eban summed up, 'that our proclamations and warnings were taken seriously ... and were on target.'[10] Only the Minister of Education, Zalman Aranne, was apprehensive, saying that wherever there were large concentrations of soldiers and weapons 'sooner or later something starts up', and asked if steps were being taken to anticipate 'even a 5 per cent threat of escalation'. Eshkol assured him that this was so, but hinted at the need to conciliate and to lower the tone: 'This week has been filled with warnings and threats on our part.' It was not necessary, he said, to react immediately to the latest terror attacks.[11]

The government's fears of escalation at this stage were therefore minimal – '5 per cent' according to Aranne. But there was a note of self-criticism in Eshkol's comment, suggesting that the numerous declarations and threats issued prior to Independence Day had heightened the tension, and indicating a desire to reduce it.

The crisis gathers momentum

Whereas a feeling of déjà vu, a conviction that the Rotem events were repeating themselves, had prevailed among the IDF senior command up until now, this feeling was swiftly dispelled at dawn on 17 May. Radio Cairo announced that Egypt was demanding the evacuation of UNEF forces from their positions along the border with Israel back to the Gaza Strip.[12] Rabin, however, assumed that the evacuation of the UNEF and the concentration of Egyptian forces in Sinai in themselves neither committed Israel to go to war nor enabled it to do so from the political aspect, so long as it had not been attacked and the Straits of Tiran had not been closed. The view at the time, according to Rabin, was that 'the Arabs have gone into a state of frenzy' which could lead to war.[13]

In the afternoon of 17 May, the Prime Minister and the Chief of Staff attended a meeting of the Knesset Foreign Affairs and Security Committee. The continuous flow of forces into Sinai and the Egyptian demand for the evacuation of the UNEF charged the atmosphere. At the beginning of the meeting, Rabin said that the Egyptians were not contemplating a confrontation with Israel and that their defensive deployment in Sinai was due to anticipation of a large-scale attack against Syria. But the remarks of the Committee members reflected their fear that Israel's hands would be tied in its struggle against Syrian-inspired terror because of the Egyptian deployment.

The severest critic was Moshe Dayan. He had not been surprised, he said, by the Egyptian move. The short-sighted policy of the government had led up to this situation. 'Anyone who sends up smoke signals must understand that the other side ... is liable to think that a fire has been lit.' The extension of compulsory military service (from twenty-six to thirty months as of November 1966 as a result of the worsening security situation), the deployment of 130 aircraft on 7 April, the penetration of the skies over Damascus and the downing of Migs had shocked the Syrians. Dayan did not underestimate the significance of the Egyptian move, which he regarded as a 'promissory note' on Nasser's part, liable to commit him to intervention if Israel retaliated against Syria. If Egypt had been firmly resolved not to be lured into military activity, it would have conducted its policies differently and told the Syrians to 'forget it'. The anticipated Egyptian action, Dayan suggested, would take the form of 'either bombing of Dimona [atomic reactor] or the closing of the Straits'. At the same time, he believed that Nasser's goal was diplomatic and that his order to evacuate the UN force was intended to exert international pressure on Israel to refrain from reprisals. It was his view, conflicting with Eban's, that the UNEF would leave if the Egyptians insisted. He himself would regard this as a blessing since the prospect of arriving at a settlement with the Egyptians would be greater without 'all the UN concoctions in the middle'.[14]

Eshkol disputed Dayan's evaluation, and reminded Dayan that he had once proposed at a Committee meeting that the IAF be employed against the Syrians. He explained the difficulty: 'If the Syrian border is swarming with 120–130 guns and mortars, our settlements are beneath them, and in 10–15 minutes they can "deal with" almost all the settlements then perhaps we should have employed 80 planes and not 130. In any event, you can't fix things with only 12 planes.' Dayan responded that when he had suggested using aircraft 'I was talking against the occupation of the Heights, about complete localization, local employment of aircraft ... throughout the Sinai Campaign we employed 130 aircraft. This is an act on a scale far in excess of the dispute.' Later, at the same meeting, Dayan repeated his criticism of the Samu action which, so he said, had led to the severance of direct ties with Jordan. Eshkol hinted in reply that the ties had not been completely severed, and yet 'that doesn't mean that I can rely on this, and I'm not sure, if there is war, whether he [King Hussein] will not join our enemies'.[15]

Other members of the Committee also criticized the scope of the 7 April action, but the main subject of concern was the intensification of terrorist activity, as was evident from the tone of all the participants. 'The Egyptian move was intended to render us passive with regard to terror in the north', said the Chairman David Hacohen, and expressed his fear that the terrorist incidents would increase and Israeli Arabs would join in.[16]

Eshkol summed up the situation by giving a not uncritical report on 'how we arrived at this situation with the Syrians'. At the same time, he lauded his 'open notebook' policy and defined it as 'supreme political wisdom'. His policy in the face of the present crisis, he said, was aimed at maintaining the status quo for 'fifty years', preventing war, and manoeuvring accordingly.[17]

Eshkol reiterated this view at a meeting of the Ministerial Committee on Security, which was convened immediately afterwards. The 'doves' on the Committee set the tone of the meeting. Eban proposed a policy of 'increasing security alertness and insofar as possible political de-escalation'. At the time, he still sounded unruffled. He distinguished between the security approach, which must be based on the gravest contingency, and the political assessment, according to which Egypt had not wavered from its 'deep-rooted policy of avoiding military confrontation with Israel'. He interpreted Egypt's conduct as the result of 'genuine panic' in Syria since the 7 April operation. Israel's warnings, said Eban, had achieved their aim and made clear to the Syrians that the continuation of terror would lead to an Israeli reaction 'of a high degree'.[18]

Within a day the mood had changed, particularly at the civilian echelon, from a certain degree of complacency to anxiety. It was fostered by the dramatically overt character of the movement of Egyptian forces, the militant proclamations from across the border, the press headlines, and the Arab radio and TV broadcasts.[19] Above all, the demand for the evacuation of the UNEF had created a new psychological climate of concern by exposing the border to a possible imminent clash.

Nonetheless, it should be noted that the views of both the military and the political echelons remained unchanged at this early stage: namely that Egypt was not interested in war with Israel right now and its moves were not directed at starting a war. The major security problem was Syrian-backed terror. The Intelligence Branch was still convinced that Egypt would intervene only in the event of a massive 'total' Israeli action against Syria. In other words, despite the movement of Egyptian forces into Sinai, Israeli Intelligence still had difficulty abandoning its conceptions. However, there were subtle indications of dispute between the army and the government: Rabin thought that the anticipated continuation of Syrian-based terror attacks called for an appropriate Israeli response, while Eshkol advocated restraint together with intensified defensive and deterrent measures. At most, in the event of a drastic terrorist incident, Eshkol was ready to consider a very limited response. The disparity between the views of the military and political echelons was evident again.

An Egyptian sortie over Dimona

At the above-mentioned meeting of the Foreign Affairs and Security Committee on 17 May, Rabin estimated that three possible paths of action were open to the Egyptians: to exert pressure on Israel; to close the Tiran Straits, and to strike at Dimona. While he was speaking, at 16:00 hours, he was handed a report from the IAF commander that a pair of Egyptian Mig 21s had penetrated Israeli air space from Jordan and flown over Dimona, and the air force had not succeeded in intercepting them. Rabin immediately informed Eshkol, who was present.[20]

After the meeting, the General Staff branch chiefs met in the Chief of Staff's office to analyse the significance of the sortie. Aharon Yariv believed that an operation directed solely against Dimona was unlikely.[21] He apparently thought that the Egyptians would prefer to launch simultaneous attacks on Dimona and on airfields in order to derive the maximum advantage. It was decided to proclaim a Level 3 alert in the IAF. The possibility of mobilizing an additional reserve armoured brigade for Southern Command was also discussed.

The question of the evacuation of UNEF became a vital issue at that stage, when Israel learned that the UN Secretary-General was of the opinion that if Egypt insisted on evacuation it should be full and permanent. U Thant's response to Egypt's demand to move UNEF from the border to the Gaza Strip, which was conveyed to the participants at the meeting, was unanimously interpreted as a further deterioration of the situation.

Immediately after the meeting, Rabin met with Eshkol to discuss the implications of the constant influx of Egyptian reinforcements into Sinai, the sorties by Egyptian aircraft and U Thant's reply. Eshkol approved the mobilization of IAF reserve units at the request of the IAF Commander, as well as the mobilization of Armoured Brigade 200.[22]

Thus, by the end of the third day of the crisis, 17 May, there was increasing awareness that the crisis was worsening. The Dimona reactor had always been perceived as a major target for Egyptian aerial attack, but the foolhardiness and skill demonstrated by Egypt in the flight over the reactor sharpened the sense of danger. The impact of the anticipated evacuation of the UN force, the inflamed emotions in the Arab world, the continuing Egyptian troop movements into Sinai and the propaganda war, were enhanced by the dramatic news that Dimona had been photographed from the air, which the Chief of Staff received at the height of the Knesset meeting.

The mood was now sombre, but the Intelligence Branch's basic tenet was unaltered: the Egyptians were not interested in a military clash with

Israel. They were preparing the option of a limited military move in response to a large-scale Israeli strike against Syria, but their main objective was to deter Israel and gain a diplomatic and propaganda victory. According to this theory, Israel was still in control of the situation.

At 23:30 a stage-two alert was declared throughout the IDF.[23]

On the morning of 18 May, a further meeting took place between the General Staff branch heads and the Chief of Staff. According to the summary: (1) if Dimona was attacked, IDF planes could chase the enemy aircraft across the border to intercept them; (2) the IAF would not automatically be granted permission to attack Egyptian airfields after an attack on Dimona; (3) if the Egyptians attacked airfields the IAF would immediately counter-attack Egyptian airfields.[24]

These instructions to the IAF require further explanation. Fear of an Egyptian air attack on the nuclear reactor always loomed in the background, but no decision had ever been taken at the political level as to how Israel should react to such an attack. On the face of it, any attack on a target inside Israel was a warlike act, and Israel had the right to respond. But this particular case was by no means simple. The development of nuclear military capability, of which Israel was suspected although it did not admit to it, was liable in the eyes of the world to justify a 'legitimate' Egyptian preventive strike. Even the United States, with its proclaimed stand on nuclear issues, would be obliged to display a modicum of understanding of such an Egyptian move. If Israel reacted automatically by launching hostilities, it would find itself isolated and engaged in a costly and bloody war, with no guarantee of a positive outcome.

If the reactor was destroyed by an Egyptian attack, the damage would be irremediable. On the other hand, it was unlikely that Israel would calmly accept an Egyptian attack and permit Nasser to bask in glory unscathed. Such a failure to act would have far-reaching implications for Israel's standing and deterrent capability. The dilemma was clear to the senior command, but it required a decision on the part of the political echelon, since the army had no authority to act without it. Hence, the order to the IAF was neither a 'yes' nor a 'no' with regard to attacking Egyptian airfields in retaliation for the bombing of the reactor. It merely established that the IAF did not have an automatic go-ahead for action. The government would decide the matter. If, however, the Egyptian air force attacked Israeli airfields simultaneously with its bombing of the reactor or without connection, Israel would have the legitimate right to launch a counter-attack.

During that day, the Chief of Staff's office received reports that the UNEF evacuation had begun. The aircraft carrying the UNEF Commander Indian General Indar Jit Rikhye penetrated Israeli air space. IAF planes, suspicious of its intentions and nervous in the wake of the Egyptian flight over Dimona, tried to intercept it and even fired warning shots at it.[25] In the evening word was received that Sharm al-Sheikh had been occupied by an Egyptian force, and UN positions there had been abandoned. The Intelligence Branch reported that an Egyptian brigade had been brought back from Yemen and that the Lebanese army was now deployed along the border with Israel. In light of this information, the Chief of Staff held a third meeting that night with Eshkol and the participation of Ministers Yisrael Galili and Moshe Haim Shapira. Rabin estimated that the Egyptians might close the Straits within two or three days, a challenge which could lead to war. He also said that the Egyptians intended to maintain their force in Sinai for a lengthy period, and this could create a new situation to which Israel was unaccustomed.[26]

Rabin's remarks attested to a change in the army's reading of the situation. At first, events had been perceived in the context of terrorist activity, continuing the pre-crisis line of thought. Now the Chief of Staff raised the problem which the army was subsequently to view as the main issue: the possibility of protracted, unlimited concentration of Egyptian forces along the border with Israel.

From Egypt's viewpoint, this was merely a logistic problem. For Israel, it was an existential question. The presence of a long-term direct and immediate threat on the border would require the IDF to mobilize its reserves and stand ready, thus severely disrupting normal life in Israel at intolerable economic cost. We shall see below that the army shifted its main focus to this issue of Egyptian troop concentrations in Sinai. This situation, together with Nasser's challenge to Israel and Israel's fear of the grave consequences of potential loss of deterrent capability, and above all the possibility that the Egyptians would anticipate the IDF and launch a pre-emptive strike, were to become the lever for military pressure on the political echelon.

That same night and on the following day, 19 May, the General Staff moved into emergency mode, and the supreme command post (or 'pit' in military slang), went into full action until the end of the war.

Plate 1 Ben-Gurion takes his leave of the Ministry of Defence – flanked by his successor Levi Eshkol and the Deputy Minister of Defence, Shimon Peres (28 June 1963).

Plate 2 Chief of Staff Zvi Zur welcoming the new CO of the UN Truce Supervision Organization, Norwegian General Odd Bull. Between them: Deputy Chief of Staff Yitzhak Rabin and Intelligence Chief Meir Amit (6 June 1963).

Plate 3 Prime Minister Eshkol announces the handover of command of the IDF from Zvi Zur to Yitzhak Rabin (31 December 1963).

Plate 4 Prime Minister Eshkol presents Deputy Defence Minister Shimon Peres to President Lyndon Johnson at a reception at the White House (1 June 1964).

Plate 5 The Eshkol government with President Zalman Shazar after taking the oath of office in the Knesset (12 January 1966).

Plate 6 Ezer Weizman handing over command of the IAF to Motti Hod (26 April 1966).

Plate 7 Eshkol and CO Northern Command David Elazar examining the damage inflicted by the heavy Syrian shelling of Kibbutz Gadot (8 April 1967).

Plate 8 Observers from the UNEF dismantling the Erez border point before their evacuation from Egypt (19 May 1967).

Plate 9 Israeli tank crews mounting tanks somewhere in the Negev during pre-war training (20 May 1967).

Plate 10 Eshkol addressing the Knesset several hours before Nasser's announcement of the blocking of the Tiran Straits. 'We have no plans to attack', he said (22 May 1967).

Plate 11 Prime Minister Levi Eshkol, Labour Minister Yigal Allon and Chief of Staff Yitzhak Rabin touring IDF divisions in the Negev (25 May 1967).

Plate 12 Deputy Chief of Staff Haim Barlev, CO Thirty-eighth Division Ariel Sharon and CO Southern Command Yeshayahu Gavish during the 'waiting period' (1 June 1967).

Plate 13 Chief of Staff Yitzhak Rabin, Deputy Chief of Staff Haim Barlev and Operations Chief Ezer Weizman (3 June 1967).

Plate 14 The new ministers in the National Unity government: (*l to r*) Defence Minister Moshe Dayan and Ministers without Portfolio Yosef Sapir and Menahem Begin. Beside Dayan, half hidden: Zerah Wahrhaftig (4 June 1967).

Chapter 13

The era of diplomacy

Diplomacy played a major role in the crisis, although it failed to avert war.[1] The Israeli government put its faith in diplomacy but the military, from a very early stage, displayed growing impatience with the diplomatic process, which appeared to be protracted and useless, merely playing into enemy hands. But while diplomatic efforts failed to prevent war, they were not without results. In retrospect, it is clear that the IDF and the State of Israel derived great advantages from them.

In the end, though not necessarily through prior intent, it transpired that Israel had managed the crisis sagaciously, thereby preparing the ground, from the diplomatic aspect, for military action. The army's 'noble steeds'[2] stamped their hooves restlessly but were forced to wait until the diplomatic carriage, with precise timing, had cleared the course for them.[3]

The American role

The key to understanding the developments which led to war should be sought, perhaps above all, outside the region in Washington. American involvement in the crisis has been investigated and well documented since most of the archival material was made available for study.[4] Egypt's relations with the United States were clouded during Johnson's administration due to Egypt's involvement in Yemen, Nasser's general anti-Western foreign policy, the Soviet Union's growing influence in the Middle East, and the cold personal relations between Nasser and Johnson.

Nasser tended to see an American conspiracy by the CIA in every move against him, and his suspicious attitude to the US was undoubtedly also fostered by the Kremlin's attitude to Johnson.[5] In light of the tension and mistrust between Egypt and the United States, US influence on Egypt's policies could be expected to lessen. Indeed, the Americans did not succeed in dissuading Nasser from blocking the Straits of Tiran or inducing him to accept a compromise which would prevent the flare-up.

On the other hand, it may have been precisely the fact that Nasser 'ventured to the brink' in closing the Straits, US efforts notwithstanding, which barred him from taking additional aggressive steps against Israel. When Israel informed the United States that a surprise Arab attack was anticipated (see below), the US administration saw fit, despite its doubts as to the reliability of the information, to issue a grave warning to Egypt. If Nasser harboured aggressive intentions – against the Dimona reactor, airfields or the southern Negev – he was forced to abandon them for the time being, for fear that the United States would take action.[6]

The bottom line is that the United States tried initially to pinpoint the crisis and prevent escalation by exerting pressure on Israel to refrain from unilateral moves, and on Egypt not to restrict freedom of shipping. When Egypt announced the blocking of the Straits, the US continued to urge Israel to abstain from military action, cautioned Egypt against attacking Israel, and concomitantly tried to recruit international support for action to guarantee free shipping through the Straits. When it became clear to Washington that international backing was not forthcoming, that the plan of action was complicated and impractical, and that the threat against Israel was growing, it relaxed the pressure on Israel. Thus there is a certain degree of truth in the Egyptian claim that the United States misled it, and that while putting clamps on Egypt, it released Israel for action. While there was no premeditated conspiracy, US assistance undoubtedly helped to create convenient conditions for an Israeli attack. In hindsight, this was the great success of Israeli diplomacy.

On 18 May Eshkol received, through US Ambassador Walworth Barbour, a message from President Lyndon Johnson. The President assured Eshkol that he was 'following very closely' developments and that his government had expressed its concern to Damascus and Cairo. But, he warned,

> I would like to emphasize in the strongest terms the need to avoid any action on your side which would add further to the violence and tension in your area. I urge the closest consultation between you and your principal friends. I am sure that you will understand that I cannot accept any responsibilities on behalf of the United States for situations which arise as the result of actions on which we are not consulted.[7]

This study does not focus on the diplomatic arena, but let it be noted briefly that from now on where Israel was concerned, there were two goals to the diplomatic efforts: one was to curb the crisis by bringing international pressure to bear on President Nasser, in particular in order to dissuade him from barring free shipping through the Straits of Tiran and – once he had blocked the Straits – wielding international pressure to compel him to open them. The second target was to guarantee freedom of action for Israel, with passive backing on the part of the US, so as to counteract Soviet backing of Syria and Egypt. The former effort failed, while the latter succeeded. However, US readiness to 'unleash Israel' (according to officials in Washington) was not immediately evident, but only emerged two weeks later, and then was implied ('yellow light', in the words of W.B. Quandt) rather than explicit ('green light').[8]

In his reply to Johnson, Eshkol emphasized that the source of the trouble was terrorist action stemming from Syria. He demanded that the UNEF should not be evacuated without the approval of the General Assembly, and requested an American declaration of support for Israel as a counterweight to the Soviet support for the Arabs.[9] The Americans did not hasten to respond.

The chosen option: quiet diplomacy

In the evening hours of 18 May, Eshkol convened the committee of editors of the Israeli press[10] for what was denoted an off-the-record 'background talk'. The emphasis was still on the problem of hostile terrorist action, but he also expressed concern at the possibility that the Straits would be blocked. Surveying terrorist action since 7 April, he placed the blame squarely on Syria.

Among other things, the Prime Minister referred to an incident which was not reported at the time. On 8 May a Palestinian infiltrator, fluent in Hebrew and a university graduate, had been apprehended south of Kiryat Shmona carrying twelve kilograms of explosives, a forged British passport and letters addressed to Eshkol, Ben-Gurion, Golda Meir and newspaper editors. His mission was to penetrate population centres and perpetrate a wide-scale terror attack around Independence Day.

Eshkol explained that Israel did not want war, but the continuation of terror could not go unanswered. He described the Egyptian deployment in Sinai as defensive, but capable of transition into offensive within a day or two. In answer to a query from the editor of *Haaretz*, Gershom Schocken, about the possibility that the UN force would be evacuated from Sharm al-Sheikh, the Prime Minister said: 'If they leave and we [i.e. Israeli shipping through the Straits] are not harassed – that's one thing. If they harass us, I am sorry to say, as they say in the army, there could be a lively situation – of all the issues, this is the decisive one ... if they disturb us from using that water [for shipping].' His remarks also implied concern at the unclear stand of the Soviet Union: 'It's not clear whether the Soviets have guaranteed to support Egypt and Syria in the event of a military clash.'[11]

On 19 May, at a meeting with Soviet Ambassador Dimitri Chubakhin, Foreign Minister Eban tried and failed to clarify the Soviet standpoint or to influence it. Eban told him: 'There will be no war unless our territory is attacked or our freedom of shipping affected.' Chubakhin was impervious to Eban's arguments, and cast full responsibility on Israel. 'It was Israel that attacked Syria. It was Israel's planes that flew over Damascus. Have

Syrian planes flown over Tel Aviv? ... We hear all the time about terrorists and mines ... but we have seen no evidence so far that the Syrians are responsible and not CIA agents', he retorted.[12]

Israel's dilemma was how to conduct the diplomatic campaign to safeguard its freedom of shipping. In retrospect it seemed apparent that Nasser had been more impressed by Israel's public silence than by clandestine efforts conducted through diplomatic channels.[13] But from the outset political sagacity seemed to indicate that the Egyptian President should not be provoked by threats, and that he be offered a dignified way out, namely to bow to international pressure rather than ostensibly to capitulate to Israeli threats. The government, 'once bitten, twice shy' after the excess of declarations on Independence Day eve which had sparked off the crisis, now tended to avoid public statements. The Prime Minister even asked the newspaper editors to cooperate by making no mention 'of mobilization, of freedom of shipping, or Dimona or of the mining question'. Minister Yisrael Galili praised the 'deliberate moderation' of official statements since Independence Day and emphasized that this policy had been instituted by the Prime Minister 'who was strongly backed by the Chief of Staff'.[14] Eshkol and Eban decided on 19 May to conduct a discreet diplomatic campaign. Eban stressed this decision at the Ministerial Committee on Security and warned against public pronouncements because 'life and death are now decided by the tongue'.[15]

The Americans, too, advised a low profile on the issue of free shipping.[16] Israel's UN Ambassador Gideon Raphael was instructed to convey a personal communication from Eban to U Thant in complete secrecy and was also instructed not to mention the shipping issue if asked by the media about the reason for his visit to the Secretary-General's office. In his message, Eban charged U Thant with heavy moral responsibility for the evolution of the crisis. It was vital, he wrote, that the Secretary-General, in his contacts with Cairo, be aware of the Israeli government's resolute stand to the effect that freedom of shipping was a supreme national interest, that Israel would defend it at any price and any sacrifice.[17] Through clandestine channels, Israel conveyed the information to Nasser that there were no Israeli army concentrations on the Syrian border and that Israel had no intention of overthrowing the Damascus regime; it did not warn specifically against the blocking of the Straits.[18]

Israel's political 'anchor' in its efforts to prevent any disruption of freedom of shipping through the Straits was a statement by then Foreign Minister Golda Meir at the UN Assembly on 1 March 1957, while announcing her government's decision to respond to the demand for withdrawal from Sinai and the Gaza Strip, to the effect that Israel would view disruption of free shipping through the Tiran Straits as an act of aggression and would reserve the right to react in accordance with Clause 51 of the UN Charter.

In Israel's eyes, this declaration, made after consultations with France in the wake of the understanding that the US would support freedom of shipping in the Bay,[19] provided the moral sanction for its two demands: first, support of the Western Powers for its demand for free shipping; second, their acknowledgement of Israel's right to act if shipping in the Bay of Eilat (Aqaba) was disrupted.

In a message to President Charles de Gaulle on 19 May, Eshkol cited Golda Meir's statement. He accused Egypt of violating the security balance by increasing its force in Sinai and evacuating the UNEF, but promised that Israel would not initiate hostilities and would not attack the Egyptian forces at Sharm al-Sheikh unless they blocked the Tiran Straits. The message indicated considerable Israeli flexibility: it did not include a demand for the return of the UNEF or the withdrawal of Egyptian military presence from the Straits. The government recognized that such a demand was unrealistic. The objective now was therefore only to ensure freedom of shipping in the Bay of Eilat, and no more than that. At the same time, the Israeli government was well aware that a constant Egyptian military presence in the Tiran Straits meant, as Eban phrased it, 'that the sword of Damocles will be suspended day and night [and] the threat [to block the Straits] will never disappear'.[20]

Israel is disappointed by the US stance

From the beginning of the crisis, the main arena of Israeli diplomatic effort was, naturally enough, the United States. The Israeli government believed that only firm US backing could counter what was interpreted as full Soviet backing for Egypt and Syria. Only unequivocal, and preferably public, clarification from the White House and the State Department as to the US commitment to Israel's security and freedom of shipping, could deter Nasser from aggression and from blocking the Straits.[21] Only a resolute US stand could avert the danger, however remote, of Soviet military intervention on the side of the Arabs in the event that war broke out.

However, so far as Israel was concerned, the US stand at this stage was initially disappointing and the State Department even tended to delay supplies of military equipment agreed on prior to the crisis. This attitude was in striking contrast to the readiness displayed by France and Great Britain to expedite supplies of vital equipment.[22] Johnson's first message to Eshkol was blatantly non-committal, and merely stipulated constraints on Israel. The practical implication of the 'consultation' which the US President demanded before any Israeli action, and above all, any military move, was essentially a US right to veto any operative Israeli decision and primarily military action. But there was also another, positive, aspect to the demand for 'consultation'. It implied US readiness for involvement and coordination of moves. Later this approach was famously expressed in the phrase which Johnson reiterated to Eban and Eshkol: 'Israel will not be alone, unless it decides to go alone.'

US policy, up until the stage when the Egyptian President announced the closing of the Straits, and to a large degree afterwards as well, was a cause of concern for Israel. The reports from the embassy in Washington made it clear that the United States was seeking an outlet from the crisis and a way of averting a military clash in the region, even at certain cost to Israel. The Americans did not deny their commitment to freedom of shipping, but clarified to Israeli representatives that it would honour it only if Israel refrained from acting without prior consent. Ambassador Avraham Harman estimated that the aim of the United States was to avoid military involvement and, since it saw no prospect of inducing Nasser or the Soviets to display flexibility, it would pressure Israel to concede.

The Americans did not respond to Israel's demand that they issue a peremptory statement. They preferred quiet diplomacy, and in fact placed their trust at this stage in the UN Secretary-General's mission to Cairo. Nobody could have guessed that Nasser would once again play his cards and announce the blocking of the Straits while U Thant was on his way to Egypt. The assumption was that the Secretary-General's mission was a vital 'time-out' during which a solution might be found or indicated. Among themselves, and at the UN, the Americans had already discussed such possibilities as renewal of the activity of the Israel–Egypt Armistice Commission and the stationing of a UN force on the Israeli side of the border. These ideas were unofficially raised in their contacts with Israel.[23]

Despite the official US stand, as conveyed to Ambassador Harman, there is evidence that, on a less official plane, the US conveyed different messages to Israel. At the Ministerial Committee on Security, Eban quoted a communication from the Under-Secretary of State Eugene Rostow: 'We advise you ... after the entry of an Egyptian force into Sharm al-Sheikh not to act against the Egyptian army until and unless the Egyptians block the Straits.' Eshkol commented that the negotiations with the US were top secret.[24] The Americans may have believed at this stage that Nasser would not give the order to close the Straits, but the message essentially acknowledged Israel's right to act if and when the Straits were closed.

Israeli emissaries in the United States endeavoured to sway US policy, and not only by conventional diplomatic means. Prominent Jews with clout in the administration, in the Democratic Party and in Johnson's circle were asked to operate as an effective lobby on behalf of Israel. Jerusalem encouraged its representatives to step up efforts in this direction in order to create in the United States a climate of public sympathy for Israel which would persuade the administration, and in particular the President, to back Israel. There is reason to assume that these efforts had some impact.[25]

Israel's stand on the UN force

Israel was not particularly troubled by the evacuation of the UNEF in itself. There were some who even thought that it would be to Israel's advantage. But evacuation of the UNEF together with the influx of military forces into Sinai, the propaganda drama and the inflaming of emotions on the Arab side, had a profound psychological impact. It was felt that the blocking of the Straits was liable to occur at any minute and would be a *casus belli*. U Thant was about to leave for Cairo in order to seek a solution to the crisis. It was manifest that in the international arena nobody believed that the status quo ante could be restored, and the prevailing opinion was that the crisis could only be resolved by appeasing Nasser.

The idea of stationing a UN force on both sides of the border, which was raised in diplomatic circles, paid mere lip-service, since there was no practical prospect of its acceptance by Nasser. The solution seemed to be to station a force on the Israeli side alone, and Israel objected to this because it would not solve the Straits problem but would merely restrict Israel's freedom of action and expose it to humiliation and charges that it was sheltering in the UN's shadow for fear of Egypt. The political assessment in Jerusalem was that U Thant would not succeed, perhaps would not even try to remove the Egyptians from Sharm al-Sheikh. At most, he would succeed in obtaining Egyptian consent to some form of UN presence in the Straits alongside the Egyptian presence, but this would require parallel Israeli consent to the stationing of a UN force inside Israel. Eban was of the opinion that this was precisely what U Thant would propose to Nasser, and Nasser would agree. Israel, Eban thought, would find it difficult to withstand such a compromise despite its grave implications. Nasser, he believed, 'has not decided to disrupt shipping. He has decided to be in a situation where he can brandish this sword [at any time].'[26]

Consequently, a day before Nasser's proclamation of the barring of the Straits to Israeli shipping, the prevalent view in the Israeli government was that he was in no hurry to do so. Political logic, as perceived in Jerusalem, would impel Nasser to optimize the Egyptian achievement by forcing Israel to agree to a UN presence on its soil in return for a corresponding presence in the Tiran Straits (but not along the Egyptian side of the border) and revival of the Armistice Commission from which Israel had withdrawn unilaterally.[27] Egyptian military presence at Sharm al-Sheikh, it was assumed, would serve from now on as a 'whip' for Egypt to deter Israel from attacking Syria or any other Arab country, and under these conditions the 'popular struggle' would continue and even intensify – not only from Syria but from the Egyptian-controlled Gaza Strip as well.

The main points of Eshkol's remarks at the Ministerial Committee on Security on 21 May, which were set out on a typewritten sheet,

summarized the evaluation of the situation and the government's objectives at that stage:

> Egypt's strategic aims could be: (a) to destroy Dimona and Israel's
> capability to develop nuclear weapons. (b) the blocking of shipping in
> the Bay of Eilat. (c) an all-out onslaught aimed at defeating Israel. This
> last aim, according to both military and political data, does not appear
> likely even to the Egyptians.... Our political objectives: (a) to achieve
> the withdrawal of concentrations on the borders. (b) to ensure that a
> UN force or presence remains in the Straits. (c) to obtain clarification
> as to the US commitment towards Israel. (d) to ensure maximum inter-
> national pressure on Damascus and Cairo so that Fatah activity will
> not be repeated. (e) to ensure that America clarifies to the Soviet
> Union that it will not permit harm to Israel. (f) to act simultaneously
> in London and Paris to achieve these ends. (g) to activate Jews and
> friends throughout the world to help achieve these aims.[28]

The Dimona issue

While Israel conducted a wide-ranging diplomatic campaign on the blocking of the Straits, discussions on the delicate issue of the Dimona nuclear
reactor were held in the utmost secrecy. The underlying theme in all gov-
ernmental deliberations, and at the General Staff as well, was fear that
Nasser's main intention was to destroy Israel's nuclear capability, thereby
eradicating what was, for Egypt, an intolerable strategic threat, as Nasser
often phrased it. The Egyptian reconnaissance sorties over Dimona[29] provided ostensible proof of this intention. It was evident to the government,
as Israel Galili said,[30] 'that the Dimona subject is a special problem as
regards international relations'. Rabin too believed that the most logical
move so far as Egypt was concerned would be to attack Dimona, an act
which would gain international understanding.[31]

Operationally speaking, the most critical eventuality would be a surprise air raid conducted simultaneously against the reactor and Israeli airfields.[32] This was the 'nightmare scenario' and the prospect of its
occurrence spurred the senior command several days later to urge the
government to take pre-emptive action. Israel had not warned that it
would react with war against an attack on the reactor[33] but in practice
there had been no need. It was clear enough that a military onslaught on
any target whatsoever within Israel's sovereign territory would constitute a
declaration of war. Ministers Pinhas Sapir, Zalman Aranne and Moshe
Kol were opposed to this automatic formula.

The government decided nonetheless that 'if Egyptian aircraft penetrate
Israeli air space and bomb any target whatsoever, the IAF will react with
full force'. What weighed the balance was the need to guarantee Israel's

supremacy in the air. Eshkol explained: 'We have fewer airfields than they do. We have always said that the first five minutes determine the outcome, who is first to bomb airfields.' In any case, Eshkol reassured the 'doves', 'if there is any fundamental issue [i.e. if Dimona is bombed] we will meet again'. But he demanded a decision and it was taken.[34]

In the absence of diplomatic activity in this respect, all that was left was to anticipate the danger to the reactor by reinforcing the anti-aircraft defence measures and the security around the site against possible attack by an airborne Egyptian commando force. However, as noted above, the military preferred not to take risks and favoured a pre-emptive move to achieve decisive aerial superiority as the best guarantee of the safety of the reactor.

Indeed, the question of the reactor was particularly sensitive. Israel was well aware that the prospect of Israeli nuclear capability was regarded by Nasser as a clear 'red line'. An attack on the reactor might be considered 'legitimate' in international eyes. Even the United States would have found it difficult, in light of its emphatic stand against the proliferation of nuclear weapons and against Dimona, to view the destruction of the reactor as an unjustified act of aggression. Moreover, an attack on the reactor might even justify a parallel attack on Israel's airfields in order to neutralize an Israeli counter-attack from the air.

It seems feasible to assume that the reactor was a central objective of Egyptian operative planning. The reconnaissance sorties over the reactor bear this theory out. Why then did Nasser eventually decide to block the Straits and become involved in the issue of free shipping instead of directly attacking a 'legitimate' strategic target? It seems that he erred in his calculations. He preferred to provoke Israel to attack first, confident of his ability to contain the blow and launch a counter-strike in which Dimona would be the prime target.

The government: concern and caution

The mood in Israel in the first week of the crisis was one of alertness and apprehension, but until the closing of the Straits the fear of imminent war was not acute. Abroad, on the other hand, Israeli legations reported growing expressions of solidarity. Eban considered them 'slightly panicky' and his reaction indicates that he was concerned that Israel would be perceived as weak and intimidated, 'the sheep trembling with fear of the wolf'. This image could undermine the credibility of Israel's deterrent power, and therefore it was essential, he said, 'to cause them to believe more strongly that disruption of shipping means war'. Among the other 'dovish' ministers there were already signs of anxiety at the prospect of war.[35] An additional reason for concern was the fact that Britain and France had retreated from the 1950 declaration of the three Western powers guaranteeing the existing borders in the Middle East, and now announced that it was the UN's responsibility to maintain peace in the region.[36]

Despite the political 'time-out', while the outcome of U Thant's mission was awaited, some ministers did not hide their anxiety and demanded maximum restraint in order to avert war. The 'dovish' trend was generally led by the leader of the National Religious Party, Minister of the Interior Moshe Haim Shapira. He proposed approaching the United States and Britain and 'charging them with responsibility for our fate here ... sparing nothing, neither money nor dignity', so that they would expedite the dispatch of tanks, aircraft and ammunition to Israel, and 'demanding of them this basic aid on which our very survival depends'. He feared that the IDF's existing ammunition reserves would not suffice and that 'if we don't destroy their air force ... who knows what will happen to us in the end'.

Other ministers supported Shapira and dermanded the reinforcement of the defensive deployment and restraint insofar as possible with regard to terrorist activity. Zalman Aranne declared: 'I am not willing to accept that, because of sabotage, there will be a war. I am not ready for this, either intellectually or emotionally.' Mordechai Bentov rejected the very idea of a pre-emptive strike: 'I want to assume that all those around this table do not want war. The time is past when it was thought that if there is danger it is best to anticipate it.' Even if the Egyptians bombed Dimona no decision should be taken in advance as to how to respond, Bentov declared. Pinhas Sapir demanded maximum circumspection and proposed that Israel should not rely on Western aid: 'I always think,' he explained, 'that although Israel is not the sole problem in the Middle East, there are certainly some enlightened nations who would be happier if the problem called Israel did not exist.'

In the absence of Yigal Allon, Minister of Labour, who was on a visit to the Soviet Union, Moshe Carmel was the only minister of senior (reserve) military rank. He advocated a forceful approach and demanded discussion without delay of the various possibilities and the formulation of lines of action so that Israel would not be caught unprepared in the event of an unexpected military development, and take hasty decisions.

Eshkol summed up the discussion: the main issue now revolved around Sharm al-Sheikh, but 'for the time being we should not talk too much about this ... it would be better not to allow the Arabs the pleasure of seeing the Jews standing and wailing'. Eshkol found the proper balance between 'doves' and 'hawks'. He stressed: 'My principle is that we do not want war. We are all agreed on this.... We have mobilized in order to prevent it.' But 'if the Egyptians fly over Israeli territory and bomb it, whatever they bomb [even Dimona alone] ... we must take action with the planes that we have, and cause them as much damage as possible'.[37]

At this 21 May session of the government, time was allotted to a survey of the civil emergency measures, which were described as satisfactory. The Minister of Commerce and Industry, Zeev Sherf, surveyed the basic food reserves, quantities which would suffice for five to ten months. The Deputy Defence Minister Zvi Dinstein described the potential output of power-stations, the oil reserves (sufficient for increased consumption for four months) and the state of transport (the Achilles heel was transportation due to the mobilization of a large number of civilian vehicles for the war effort) and also discussed communications and hospitalization needs.[38] In light of the fact that the crisis had been so unexpected, the problems were surprisingly few.

On 22 May in the afternoon, the Prime Minister addressed the Knesset. His speech was cautious and almost conciliatory. Eshkol listed 113 acts of sabotage for which Syria was responsible and thirty-four protests conveyed by Israel to the Security Council. Referring to the Arab states, he declared:

> 'We are not aiming at attack ... we have no interest in striking against their security, their territory or their legal rights. Nor will we intervene in any way in their internal affairs, in their regimes, their regional or international relations. We demand of them on the basis of reciprocity that they honour the same principles where we are concerned.'

Eshkol announced that as a result of Egyptian concentrations of forces on the border and the evacuation of UNEF he had ordered, with the assent of the government, restricted mobilization of reserve forces, and this had already been implemented in full.[39]

Chapter 14

The revision of Intelligence evaluations and the shift to offensive planning

On the morning of 19 May, the Chief of Intelligence, Brigadier-General Aharon Yariv, who a day previously had claimed that the Egyptian deployment was defensive, changed his mind and said that it should be regarded 'as offensive as well'. The continuing deployment of Egyptian forces, the evacuation of the UN Emergency Force, the advance of Egyptian bombers into Sinai, the photo reconnaissance sortie over Dimona and the stationing of Egyptian troops at Sharm al-Sheikh had created a cumulative effect which forced Israel to modify its Intelligence evaluations. Yariv also reported that the Egyptian minister of war was visiting the Gaza Strip with the intention, among others, of curbing any local initiative for terrorist action which might hinder the operational plans of the Egyptian army. Rabin ordered that preparations be made for mobilization of additional brigades, and that the emergency logistic disposition be activated.[1]

That morning, for the first time, the General Staff forum[2] heard that the Intelligence evaluation which had served as the basis for all long-term planning was no longer valid. The Chief of Intelligence defined the most recent Egyptian steps as 'a most drastic change in the line they pursued till now'. It was true, said Yariv, that in the absence of effective inter-Arab cooperation, it could not be assumed that the Egyptians had abandoned their basic view that the time was not yet ripe for a confrontation with Israel. At the same time, the recent Egyptian moves were evidence 'at least of readiness to go very far towards such a confrontation, and perhaps even readiness to initiate it themselves'.

It was Yariv's opinion that it was not only concern for Syria that had changed Egypt's viewpoint and he offered two possible explanations: (1) Egypt had received information or evaluations that Israel was about to implement its nuclear programme and that all the American reassurances on this matter were hollow; (2) the Egyptians believed that a wider conspiracy was afoot, aimed at striking at their efforts in Yemen by combined action, initially against Syria, and perhaps even direct action against Egypt while its main force was involved there. Yariv had gained the impression that 'there is apparently Soviet backing for Egypt and Syria in this situation, although it is not clear how far it is willing to go'.[3] At this stage Israeli Intelligence did not know that Soviet disinformation had sparked off the crisis, but there were apparently some indications of this. As we shall see below, Yariv's evaluation of the role of the Soviet Union weighed heavily on the political decision-makers.

Yariv described the constant expansion of the Egyptian force in Sinai[4] and listed Egypt's possible strategic objectives: (1) Conducting a 'preventive war' with the aim of destroying the Dimona reactor and the Israeli threat of nuclear weapons. They might also seek to achieve additional aims such as a strike against IAF bases and perhaps also occupation of limited areas. (2) Ending Israel's freedom of action and undermining its 'deterrent image'. (3) Halting Israeli shipping through the Straits of Tiran. (4) Launching an all-out attack with the aim of annihilating Israel. This objective, according to military and political information, 'apparently does not seem feasible even to the Egyptians'.[5]

Thus, after three days of crisis, the Intelligence Branch admitted that the firm conviction it had held for some years was no longer valid, namely that Nasser would not involve himself in a war when the timing was not under his control, so long as the crack forces of his army were bogged down in Yemen, the Arab world was deeply divided, and the balance of forces could not guarantee Arab victory. The contention of the military that the struggle against Syria could be permitted to escalate without serious fear of Egyptian intervention had been based on that same inflexible evaluation, which had now suddenly been refuted. It now seemed that Egypt was prepared for a military confrontation, perhaps even prepared to initiate it. Yariv's readiness to admit to all this is noteworthy.[6]

Rabin: 'If it were only possible to turn back ...'

After Yariv had delivered his evaluation, Rabin commented: 'The time has come for us to stop deluding ourselves that someone will come to our aid. I suggest that anyone who is relying on someone else should consider that he is wrong.' Rabin noted that the ideal objective for Israel would be 'first of all, if it were only possible, to turn back'; in other words, to restore the military status quo ante. But since this was mere wishful thinking, it was necessary to deploy a suitable force in the south against Egypt and in the north against Syria. In the centre of the country, facing Jordan, an alert without mobilization of reserve forces would suffice, because it was unlikely that Jordan would attack. Egypt, Rabin declared, would be the target for IDF action, but only if it attacked. At this stage, the Chief of Staff was still contemplating reaction in the event of an Arab onslaught, and not an offensive initiative.

The Chief of Staff demanded that officers and soldiers be made aware 'that we are readying ourselves for war', and that the complacent mood be dispelled. 'We did not choose this war, but ... the situation now is the most serious I can recall since the War of Independence.' He feared that the Egyptians might employ gas, and admitted that the IDF was not effectively prepared for this contingency. He also noted that bombardment of densely populated areas could be anticipated in wartime and stressed the need for the civil defence system to be on the alert. The IDF's small navy, he said, was not capable of providing effective coastal defence against the Egyptian navy and hence he placed his trust in the air force in this respect.[7]

Wide-scale mobilization

Later in the day, Rabin met with Eshkol, together with the chiefs of Operations and Intelligence. They discussed the possibility of issuing a statement that Israel would go to war if the Straits were closed, the aim being to deter the Egyptians from taking this step. Thus it is evident that within the senior command there were those who doubted the wisdom of 'quiet diplomacy'.[8]

Since it was now believed that Egypt's intentions were offensive, Rabin demanded a go-ahead for a major mobilization, which Eshkol gave. Also approved were the photo reconnaissance sorties requested by Intelligence and by the IAF. The IAF was even granted a priori permission to attack Egyptian airfields if the Egyptians bombed the reactor. Thus the change in Intelligence evaluations drastically affected the attitudes of both the Chief of Staff and the Minister of Defence, and the direct outcome was a dramatic increase in the call-up of reserve forces. Some 18,000 reserve troops had already been mobilized, and now instant approval was given for an additional 45,000.[9] Mobilization on this scale could not be concealed. For the first time since the crisis had broken out, the atmosphere reflected awareness that Israel was on the brink of war.

The decision to mobilize on a wide scale was, so far as Israel was concerned, 'a quantum leap'. On the following day, 20 May, the General Staff began to formulate an operational plan for an offensive against Egypt, no longer content with the deployment of Southern Command in accordance with the defensive plan, code-named 'Sadan' (Anvil). This marked a new stage, namely no longer discreet and cautious moves, but the bustle of preparations for a military clash. The mobilization was bitterly censured by former Prime Minister Ben-Gurion, who argued that Israel was escalating the crisis by its own actions and increasing the danger that war would ensue.[10] There is no evidence that Nasser's moves were motivated by Israel's mobilization of reserves. They were apparently influenced mainly by calculations of prestige in the Arab world, by the frenzied popular response in the Arab countries, which restored Nasser's standing, by the expectations aroused by his actions and by what seemed to be a triumph in his gamble in the face of Israel's ostensible display of weakness. In that case, Ben-Gurion's criticism was unjustified.

The mood of heightened tension eased somewhat in the afternoon, when reports were received of the UN Secretary-General's intention to visit Cairo. A lull could now be anticipated, after which the direction of events would become clearer. On the morning of 20 May, after receiving an Intelligence report from Yariv, Rabin set out on a tour of Southern Command with the Prime Minister. During the tour he told Eshkol that there were two possible paths of action for the IDF: one was a major attack in order to destroy the main Egyptian force in Sinai. The second was a limited onslaught for the occupation of the Gaza Strip as a 'bargaining card' in case Nasser closed the Straits. In any event, Rabin explained, the ground operation would be preceded by an air operation aimed at paralysing the Egyptian air force.[11] Eshkol was not enthusiastic about the idea of occupying the Gaza Strip,[12] but did not impose his opinion. Of particular interest is the fact that such a vital issue as the IDF's plans for war was discussed between the Chief of Staff and the Prime Minister informally during a tour rather than at a meeting of the Ministerial Committee on Security, where it was never raised.

Offensive planning

The fact that offensive operational planning was initiated only on 20 May demonstrates that Israel's fears of a sudden deterioration in the situation and a surprise Egyptian initiative notwithstanding, the prospect of war had not been taken seriously until then.

It is self-evident that within the General Staff and its various branches, operational plans to cover a wide range of situations were filed away, ready to be brought out, examined and updated when the 'moment of truth' arrived. The question to be asked before analysing the plans themselves is whether the IDF's operational planning was based on the directives of the political echelon or whether it was the exclusive product of the inner logic of the military.

The answer was supplied by Yitzhak Hofi, Chief of the Operations Department in the General Staff in 1965 to 1967, in a lecture to students of the IDF Staff College:

'As a rule, logic requires that in a democratic country, like the State of Israel ... the strategic objectives of the state be determined by the political authority since it is generally accepted that the military authority is the executive authority and not the authority that determines or should determine the country's political goals. ... In our case the order was generally reversed. The army made up its own operational plans and made its own political assumptions as to those plans. In each of the operational files and operational plans, the first page contained basic hypotheses which the army, in practice, accepted as political hypotheses. In general, once a year the General Staff presented its plans to the political echelon and received its approval and sometimes its comments. But the sole, exceptional case where a political conception preceded an operational plan was the [1956] Sinai Campaign.'[13]

Theoretically, it could be deduced from Hofi's remarks that the army made its own decisions and planned its own moves and objectives without reference to the standpoint of the political echelon. However, this would be too sweeping a conclusion and should be qualified. First, the IDF's operational plan was not 'forced' on the political echelon. It is true that the relevant minister did not convey instructions to the military on operational planning. The army formulated its own political assumptions from which its plans derived, but eventually the plans were submitted for the approval of the Minister.

Second, examination of the concrete political hypotheses of the army reveals that they did not deviate from accepted theories. It may be, therefore, that the reason why the Minister remained uninvolved was due not only to Eshkol's unfamiliarity with military matters but also because the army operated from an accepted starting point.

Third, and most important, the actual planning process did not necessarily determine what would be done in practice when the time came, and the army never questioned the right of the political echelon to decide when it would take action and against which objectives.

Notwithstanding, this was undoubtedly a case of distortion of the proper order and defective civil control and supervision of the army. This resulted not only from the 'civil' nature of Eshkol's government and his lack of military knowledge, but also from the fact that the government essentially perceived the army as the guardian of security and not as an instrument for achieving political or territorial aims. This was the determinant factor: the government, during this period, did not aspire to territorial gains of any kind beyond the borders of the state. Hence, it did not think it necessary to instruct the IDF to pursue any aim other than the fundamental, self-evident aim of defending Israel's territorial integrity, the security of the population and vital national interests. The IDF was required to achieve these aims on the basis of professional considerations and the government considered that its obligation was to supply the military with the necessary instruments, without examining the operational plans.

Therein lay the catch: since the narrow dimensions of the state dictated a doctrine of 'transferring hostilities to enemy territory' the conduct of warfare according to a strategically defensive and operationally offensive approach was, in the final analysis, of territorial significance. The operational principles of offensive warfare called for occupation of territory across the border, which, in retrospect, had far-reaching political implications. The government did not take sufficient note of the significance of the operative planning and left it to the army. During the crisis, the government never held discussions on the objectives of the war, either in plenum session, at the Ministerial Commttee on Security, or in any ministerial or civilian authorized forum. The army debated and wrestled with the question, modifying and altering the operational plan, which received its final form at the very last moment, by then under the penetrating gaze of the new Minister of Defence Moshe Dayan, who was both knowledgeable and involved, and hence exerted some influence on the final version of the operational plan. In the end, as the dust of war settled, the military confronted the political echelon with territorial facts which the latter had never contemplated and for which it was completely unprepared.

'Kardom' (the Axe)

On the morning of 20 May a new stage began in the General Staff – offensive planning. The 'Kilshon' (Pitchfork) plan was now revised and renamed 'Kardom' (the Axe).[14] It was a wide-ranging plan aimed at enveloping the forward Egyptian force by wide pincer movements, the shorter arm – Division 31 under Avraham Yoffe – to be dispatched through the northern routes of the Sinai Peninsula to the rear of the Egyptian force, and the longer arm – the 84th Division under Yisrael Tal – to close it off from the south, and in between, the 38th Division – commanded by Ariel Sharon – would check and immobilize the enemy's main stronghold in the central route of Sinai.

It is noteworthy that the capture of Sharm al-Sheikh which controls the Straits of Tiran was not included in the Pitchfork plan and that the occupation or cutting off of the Gaza Strip was a mere addendum to the plan. Although the defined objective was to take over all of Sinai and stabilize the line at the Suez Canal within six days, inherent in the plan was the assumption that the fighting was likely to cease in the early stages due to international intervention, and hence maximum gains should be extracted in the initial stage of the attack. The gain would not necessarily be measured by the size of the captured area, although this too would be an important factor, illustrating the extent of the Egyptian defeat and serving as a political bargaining card. When the IDF's objectives were weighed in the balance – from occupation of territory to destruction of enemy forces – the greater weight was clearly attributed to the latter. Israel, in the final analysis, had no territorial demands on Egypt and the unwritten assumption was that any area in Sinai captured by the IDF would be restored to Egypt (as was the case in the wake of the 1956 Sinai Campaign). On the other hand, the main objective, according to the plan, was annihilation of the Egyptian army. The IAF, which was assigned the mission of achieving superiority in the air, undertook the mission of destroying the Egyptian air force and aiding ground forces by crushing the Egyptian army in Sinai.

The Kardom plan was intended to trap the Egyptian army in northern Sinai, blocking its paths of escape and forcing it into battle, particularly by armoured forces. If the prime intention had been to achieve maximum territorial gains in the briefest possible time, before external factors intervened, military logic would have dictated that the Egyptians be enabled and perhaps even lured into rapid retreat by employing threatening flanking moves and leaving escape routes open. However, as noted above, since territorial gain was of secondary significance, not likely to endure for political reasons, destruction of the enemy's force was accorded priority and was to be considered the most important strategic gain of the war. The lesson of the 1956 Sinai campaign was that even the loss of territorial assets acquired during the war would not cancel out the long-term impact of the military victory which won Israel years of quiet on the Egyptian front. The conclusion was that the more resounding the military victory and the greater the débâcle of the enemy force, the longer the enemy would desist from military confrontation with the IDF and the greater would remain Israel's effective deterrent power.

The Kardom plan entailed complex logistic problems related to the concentration, movement, activation and provision of supplies to the southern 'long arm' which was to include the main armoured brigades of the IDF.[15] The plan had been based on an envisioned situation which for the time being actually existed, whereby the Egyptian rear in Sinai was void of significant forces. Within two or three days, as the Fourth Division, the main Egyptian armoured reserve, moved into Sinai, the existing format of Kardom became impractical. In the new circumstances, the IDF's 'long arm', in the course of difficult and exhausting movement up from the south for deep flanking of the forward Egyptian forces, was liable to find itself face to face with a strong and fresh Egyptian force. Moreover, later on, as fears grew that war would break out on other fronts as well, and in particular the Jordanian front, the possibility of moving forces from arena to arena along the shortest possible lines had to be taken into account. Thus, to deploy the crack force in the distant south became a less attractive option. For these reasons, the role of the southern arm of Kardom dwindled as planning proceeded and the IDF now focused its efforts on the northern and central axes of Sinai. In the final plan, Nakhshonim, all that was left of the southern arm of Kardom was a secondary move and a deceptive action, important in themselves but by no means decisive.

At noon on 20 May the Head of the Operations Department presented the plan for assault to the Chief of Operations,[16] and the plan was subsequently submitted to the Chief of Staff. After a lengthy discussion of the various aspects of the plan, Rabin approved it, but added, in the margins,

an order which generated alternative and controversial operational planning in the IDF. Rabin said: 'We need also to plan the possibility of annihilating the Egyptian air force and taking the [Gaza] Strip.'[17]

Atzmon

The alternative offensive plan for the Egyptian front was given the code-
name Atzmon and was the reverse of the Kardom plan. In effect, it advocated the continuation of the defensive ground plan with a minor offensive
addition: the occupation of the Gaza Strip.

Rabin's order on 20 May to prepare a limited alternative plan stemmed
from the difficulty in adapting instantly to the swift transition from
defence to comprehensive war. In contrast to his fellow senior officers, the
Chief of Staff was exposed to the reluctance of the political echelon to contemplate war and to the gamut of foreign and internal political considerations discussed by the government. He could not therefore confine himself
to purely military calculations. Atzmon was a minimal plan for a 'small'
war. Rabin knew that the government did not want war of any kind but
he also knew that there would be no escape from a military response to an
offensive Egyptian move or the blocking of the Straits if Israel wanted to
preserve its deterrent power. Atzmon was a hard-pressed possible solution
in such a situation for those who wanted to avert all-out hostilities but
who were required to provide some answer to the Egyptian challenge. The
idea was simple: simultaneously with destruction of the Egyptian air force
(the IAF 'Moked' plan), the IDF would conquer the Gaza Strip and
thereby inflict a blow on Nasser's prestige and provide the Israeli government with a 'bargaining card' against the blocking of the Straits and the
concentration of forces in Sinai.

The great advantage of Atzmon lay in its simplicity, the ability to implement it with relative ease and brevity and the immediate political gain it
ensured, which could serve as a lever for achieving the desired political
objective: restoration of the status quo ante, namely dispersal of the forces
and guarantee of freedom of shipping. And all this without involvement in
large-scale hostilities and with high probability that the other fronts would
remain calm.

The drawback of Atzmon was liable to be the 'squandering' of the
air strike on a minimal ground gain which would not produce the desired
result. Nasser was liable to be unimpressed by the Israeli 'bargaining
card', the Tiran Straits would remain blocked, Israel would be 'stuck' with
the Gaza Strip, with its vast and hostile refugee population, the political
situation would not permit Israel to launch another offensive operation
with the aim of opening up the Straits, Nasser might exploit the passing
of time for purchase of massive military supplies from the Soviet Union
and rehabilitation of the Egyptian air force, and launch a counter-attack

when it suited him in coordination with the other Arab states. Meanwhile the concentrations of forces in Sinai would remain unchanged and might even be reinforced, and Israel would be forced to maintain a high level of alert and mobilization at an intolerably heavy economic and moral cost.

This was apparently the reasoning behind the fierce resistance among the senior military command to the Atzmon plan. The only general who supported the Chief of Staff was Yisrael Tal, whose division was earmarked for action. Tal argued that the occupation of the Gaza Strip was an operative target which could be achieved within twenty-four hours, so that if the fighting was stopped by then due to external intervention Israel would retain 'a tangible gain ... and Nasser who is presented as the warrior of Islam and the shield of the Palestinians will now appear as someone who has not succeeded in defending even those who were under his direct protection in the Gaza Strip'.[18]

With the exception of Tal, the General Staff was overwhelmingly opposed to Atzmon. The relevant criticism was accompanied by a feeling of affront. It was generally believed that underlying the plan was a total lack of confidence in the capability of the IDF. The Commander of Southern Command claimed that he and all the division commanders had been 'shocked.... We had the feeling that the IDF was being shamed ... that they don't believe in the power of the IDF.'[19] A weighty supporter of the critics was Major-General (res.) Moshe Dayan, who on 20 May asked for and received the permission of the Minister of Defence to tour the IDF front. During his tours of Southern Command, Dayan voiced his reservations about the plan to its Commander and the division commanders.[20]

Because of the strong objections to Atzmon, the plan was later expanded while the Chief of Staff was indisposed and without his knowledge, so as to encompass not only the occupation of the Gaza Strip but also an advance along the Sinai northern coast to el-Arish and beyond. In hindsight, this was only a stage in the evolution of the new, wider plan for the Egyptian front, an alternative to Kardom, which shifted the main effort from the southern axis to northern Sinai. The expanded plan was known as 'the extended Atzmon' or Kardom 2 and in its final version as 'Nakhshonim'.

The change in the Intelligence evaluation of the General Staff and the transition to an offensive plan at the end of the first week of the crisis were, naturally, interconnected. Where the Chief of Staff's relations with the political echelon were concerned, it was no less than an 'earthquake'. After years of rigid Intelligence evaluations to the effect that Nasser was not intent on war, Yitzhak Rabin was now obliged to admit to Eshkol and the Ministerial Committee on Security that the conception had collapsed: Nasser was bent on confrontation, and Israel should prepare for war.

The tension left its mark on Rabin. The first sign was his instruction to draw up the Atzmon plan, which reflected his desire to avoid an all-out war even if Nasser blocked the Straits. This new way of thinking accorded with the stance of the majority of the government, but was totally at odds with the mood of the General Staff. Rabin's distress deepened when Nasser announced the blocking of the Straits, and the dilemma took on substance.

Chapter 15

Casus belli

On the evening of 22 May, President Gamal Abdul Nasser, accompanied by Vice-President Abdel Hakim Amer, visited the Egyptian air force base at Bir Gafgafa in Sinai and addressed the pilots and officers. Nasser surveyed the events which had led to his decision to move Egypt's army into Sinai and to evacuate the UNEF. He noted, among other things, that 'Israeli commanders' had proclaimed their intention of conquering Damascus and overthrowing the Syrian regime, and that Eshkol, too, had threatened Syria in the belief that Egypt would not intervene because it was bogged down in Sinai. The bombshell was contained in a single phrase in his long speech, namely: 'Under no circumstances will we permit the Israeli flag to pass through the Bay of Aqaba.'[1]

As significant as the content was the style of the speech, both contemptuous and provocative, throwing down the gauntlet to Israel. 'The Jews are threatening war – we say to them *ahlan wa-sahlan* (welcome)!' Mocking Israel and questioning its military power, Nasser revealed that Israel had agreed to participate in 1956 in the British–French conspiracy against Egypt only on condition that a French squadron was posted to defend Israeli air space, and claimed that he had ordered his army to retreat in order to confront the French and British forces, and hence the claim that the IDF had beaten the Egyptian army in Sinai was baseless. Nasser added challengingly: 'Perhaps war will be an opportunity for the Jews, for Israel, for Rabin, to test their strength against our force and to discover that everything they have written about the 1956 battle and the conquest of Sinai is a collection of rubbish.'[2]

The speech was broadcast after midnight on Radio Cairo, and on the following morning, 23 May, was headlined in the press. All the Egyptian papers published alongside the item a photograph of Nasser and Amer laughing heartily together with the pilots. Radio Cairo and the Egyptian press emphasized that the blockade would apply not only to vessels bearing the Israeli flag but also to those conveying 'strategic materials', such as oil. The psychological impact of the news item was very strong: it whipped up the popular mood in the Arab world to frenzied dimensions, and intensified Israeli fears and awareness that there was almost no escape from war.

The discussion with Eshkol in the Pit

At 03:45 on 23 May, shortly after retiring for the night, Rabin received word from the Chief of Intelligence that, according to Reuters, Nasser had proclaimed the closing of the Straits of Tiran to vessels bearing the Israeli flag. The Chief of Staff's bureau chief informed Eshkol's military secretary, who immediately left for the supreme command post and telephoned Levi Eshkol from there.[3] Shortly afterwards, the Chiefs of Operations and Intelligence, the Commander of the IAF and the head of the Operations Department met with the Chief of Staff in the 'pit', in the course of which they received information that the blockade would also apply to tankers carrying oil to Israel.

The implications, so far as the General Staff was concerned, were clear and self-evident: war. The view that such an Egyptian move would mean war was an axiomatic assumption in the army and had been the proclaimed *casus belli* of Israeli governments for the past decade. The evident conclusion was that Nasser's proclamation amounted to a declaration of war on Israel. This was also the feeling among the general public.[4]

At the same time there were several reasons why Israel could not, for the time being, react automatically with military force to the Egyptian President's declaration: (1) the declaration had not yet been put to the practical test; (2) the US President had urgently requested a 'time-out'; (3) members of the Israeli government were reluctant to go to war; (4) the Chief of Staff, the supreme commander of Israel's armed forces, whose response was anxiously awaited, was by no means in a bellicose spirit.

Yitzhak Rabin started the day in a state of exhaustion as a result of a long and nerve-racking week, drained by lack of sleep and tension, suffering the side-effects of heavy smoking and burdened by guilt feelings. The information on the blockade reached him in the early morning hours when he was emotionally and physically burnt-out and close to collapse. In the course of that critical day he was far from being at his best, and was incapable of instilling confidence in others and displaying the required decisive leadership and composure. All eyes were upon him, and his apparent hesitation and apprehension had an intimidating effect on some of the ministers, enhancing their dread of war. In the end, Rabin collapsed under the pressure and the intolerable burden of responsibility and fell sick. He recovered and began to function again only thirty-six hours later.

In discussions he held from the morning onward in the supreme command post, in which Eshkol, the Deputy Minister of Defence Zvi Dinstein and the head of the Mossad Meir Amit joined him, Rabin emphasized the risks of fighting on at least two fronts. In particular he constantly reiterated his fears of the Soviet Union.[5] In the course of the discussions Eshkol received a message from the US President, conveyed from the Under-Secretary of State Eugene Rostow to Ambassador Avraham Harman and Minister Ephraim Evron, in which Johnson urged the Israeli government not to act for the coming forty-eight hours. The US adminis-tration wanted to gain time in order to weigh up the situation and decide what line to adopt to contain the crisis. The discussion in the 'pit' there-fore revolved around the significance of Johnson's message in light of the new situation and of a previous secret message from Washington which implied that the US administration was reaffirming Israel's right to react with force in the event that Nasser closed the Straits.[6]

Analysing the situation, Rabin concluded that there was no escape from war, but he dwelt on its cost and dangers: (1) if hostilities broke out, they would undoubtedly be waged on two fronts and might even expand to a third front;[7] (2) in the anticipated war, 'We will have to act alone, and it will be a life and death war, a war of to be or not to be'; (3) the main problem, he claimed, was not the Arabs but the Soviets; (4) the settlements in the north would undoubtedly suffer heavy Syrian bombardment which would inflict 'tremendous damage'.[8]

Eshkol, to the dissatisfaction of most of the senior officers, decided not to precipitate matters. 'We have another week until the next oil tanker is due in Eilat,[9] and until then we should exploit the time for political activ-ity.' Thus, Eshkol did not consider Nasser's declaration to be a pretext for war so long as no ship bound for Israel was blocked en route. Summing up the discussion, he said: 'I understand that the army is of the opinion that we should wait no longer.' He was evidently implying that the army's viewpoint would be presented to the government, but that he personally was against immediate warfare, both in light of Johnson's message and because, until the Straits were actually blocked, there was respite for diplo-matic action.[10]

Discussion at the Ministerial Committee on Security

After leaving the 'pit', the Prime Minister convened the Ministerial Com-mittee on Security at 09:00 for a decisive discussion in the Prime Minister's Office in Tel Aviv. It was clear that the question on the agenda was whether to go to war. The tension was high and several of the ministers were in a very nervous state.[11]

The Prime Minister opened the proceedings: 'On our front there is news. . . . It requires consultations and not only consultations but my impression is that it calls for action as well.' With this brief introduction, Eshkol, as Minister of Defence, seemed to be placing himself on the side of the army, though perhaps not decisively so. Immediately afterwards he yielded the floor to the Chief of Staff Rabin, who reported that the Egyptian force at Sharm had been instructed to block the Straits from 12:00 that day, but not to damage in any way vessels escorted by US warships.

He posed the question of 'whether or not to accept this' to the ministers, without himself stating his position, but noted that failure to respond would undermine Israel's deterrent capability. It would be impossible, he explained, to limit the fighting to Sharm al-Sheikh, 'because that means starting the war in the most difficult and worst place for us'. The only possibility was to strike at the Egyptian air force and to advance forces into Sinai. It could be assumed, he added, that the Syrians would intervene with air and artillery attacks, and Israel should take into account that for the first few hours the IDF would not be free to silence Syrian fire. 'The choice is not easy,' Rabin told the ministers. 'I am not suggesting that it will be a stroll in the park.' After observing the anxious expressions of the ministers, Rabin felt the need to qualify his remarks: 'I may have been too pessimistic.'

Foreign Minister Eban spoke after Rabin. He proposed that he be sent on a mission to Washington immediately in order to obtain unequivocal clarification from President Johnson as to whether his government would honour its commitment to Israel and US warships would escort shipping through the Straits. The historical weight of the moment dictated this move, Eban emphasized, even if the prospect of a positive response was very slim. 'I think that for generations to come we will not be able to explain to ourselves and to others [how we missed the opportunity to avert war] without putting this to the test.' Eban interpreted the Chief of Staff's viewpoint as support for a military operation, but argued that his own trip did not rule out this possibility but merely postponed it in order to clarify whether or not there was an alternative.

Once again the 'doves' set the tone at this discussion. Moshe Haim Shapira supported Eban's proposal. If the US escorted Israeli vessels, he said, 'it will be a very grave warning for Nasser', and the longer it was possible to postpone war the better. Yisrael Barzilai feared that a Soviet commitment had motivated Egypt's conduct. He was afraid that Israeli cities would be bombed, and was not confident 'both from the military viewpoint and as regards internal defence'. Zalman Aranne commented that 'this secret of bombing airfields is not an Israeli patent' and feared that the Israeli assault aircraft 'will be so battered by this' that they would be unable to provide protection in Israel's air space. Pinhas Sapir and Yisrael Galili, casting all the weight of responsibility on Rabin, asked him whether a postponement of forty-eight or sixty hours would critically affect the surprise element. Rabin hesitated and his reply was wavering: 'It is a difficult question,' he said. 'It isn't a surprise move. They are ready for this move. They may be more nervous today in anticipation of our response ... to say that 48 hours is fateful.... I can't undertake to answer that.' After Rabin's reply, Galili steered the rest of the discussions: 'Since I hear from the Chief of Staff that a 48 hour postponement, and it will certainly be more, does not mean a decisive failure', Eban's trip should be approved.

After the meeting, the following resolutions were adopted: (1) that the Ministerial Committee on Security regarded the closing of the Straits of Tiran as an act of aggression against Israel; (2) to postpone the decision on this act for forty-eight hours, in the course of which the Foreign Minister would clarify the US stand; (3) to empower the Prime Minister and Minister of Defence to decide on the Foreign Minister's meeting with the US President.[12]

Discussions with the opposition

At the beginning of its session, the Ministerial Committee decided, on the advice of the Prime Minister, that several members would meet the same day with representatives of the opposition. Also invited were the Secretary of Mapai Golda Meir, and the Knesset's Foreign Affairs and Security Committee Chairman David Hacohen, and, from the opposition – Knesset members Menahem Begin, Aryeh Ben-Eliezer, Yosef Serlin and Elimelekh Rimalt of Gahal (Herut–Liberals Bloc) and Moshe Dayan and Shimon Peres of Rafi (Ben-Gurion's 'Israel Workers' Party).

Eshkol asked the Chief of Staff to brief the participants. Rabin described the dilemma: loss of the IDF's deterrent capability or bitter warfare, perhaps on all fronts. Again he pointed out the danger of exposing the settlements in the north to Syrian artillery. His recommendation did not sound decisive: 'It seems to me ... there is almost no alternative but to try and strike a blow at Egypt.'

Eshkol was not pleased with the US stand but explained the problem facing the government, namely whether to accede to Johnson's request to postpone reaction for forty-eight hours lest a refusal cause him to wash his hands of Israel. Eshkol was probably hinting at the possibility that Israel would have need of US aid in order to check Soviet intervention or in the event that the military situation deteriorated. None of the participants at the meeting objected to acceding to Johnson's request. Ben-Eliezer and Hacohen were taken by surprise and were particularly concerned at Rabin's statement, from which they gathered that the IDF was not adequately prepared for a war on several fronts and that the civilian population was liable to remain exposed to attack for a number of hours.

Golda Meir, Begin and Ben-Eliezer, however, opposed the idea that US warships should escort Israeli shipping through the Straits of Tiran. Moshe Dayan, on the other hand, argued for a permanent US presence in the Straits, which would guarantee free shipping. He said: 'More power to them. I'm willing to put my Israeli pride on hold.'[13]

Lior to Eshkol: 'He's not the same Yitzhak'

At noon Rabin again met with Eshkol who approved the mobilization of another 30,000 reserve troops.[14] An additional meeting with the Prime Minister later in the afternoon exposed the differences of opinion between Rabin and Weizman. The Chief of Operations favoured an immediate military operation to culminate in a shattering blow to the Egyptian air force, while the Chief of Staff claimed that war entailed bloodshed which he was anxious to avoid, and hence, so long as there was a prospect of regulating passage through the Straits by diplomatic means, military action should be delayed. Rabin preferred, therefore, to refrain from fighting until diplomatic efforts had been exhausted, and in any event focused only on the minimal plan, Atzmon.[15]

Rabin reported that the Egyptians were constantly reinforcing their units in Sinai, so that it was essential for the IDF to deliver the first blow by employing air power. At the same time, he added, 'The war will not be easy and a great deal of blood will be spilled, and we will have many losses – are we ready for this?'

The Chief of Staff's standpoint apparently instilled a minimalist mood in the other participants as well. Commander of the Southern Command Yeshayahu Gavish said that it was essential to decide which plan was to be pursued: Atzmon or Kardom. Gavish recommended that the IDF start by occupying the Gaza Strip before achieving dominance in the air, and once the latter had been achieved 'to take another serious chunk [of Sinai] without going too far south'. This operation would be code-named 'limited Kardom', He supported General Yisrael Tal's proposal to proceed along the northern axis to el-Arish. This was apparently the first hint of what was to develop into an interim plan, to be called 'extended Atzmon' or Kardom 2, its crux to be the occupation of the Gaza Strip and northern Sinai, a plan which was to gather momentum in the days to come.

Following Gavish, Rabin said:

> 'It's not pleasant to contemplate, but it's a fact that it is not easy to start a war – not only as such but also because of the enemy's deployment. The main condition for success is to achieve superiority in the air and this cannot be achieved rapidly. And it may become necessary to divert air power to Syria.[16] ... Hence our aim is not conquest of Sinai but a blow to the Egyptian air force and armour, while capturing the Strip.'

Rabin was making it clear that the reference was to Atzmon and no more than that.

The notes recorded by the head of the IDF History Department Avraham Elon on the deliberations in the afternoon hours of 23 May, from which the above statements are cited, reflect Rabin's minimalist mood but not his despondency. Yisrael Lior, Eshkol's military secretary, was so troubled by Rabin's weary and stumbling performance that he felt it necessary to drive to Jerusalem and report to the Prime Minister. 'It's hard to define what's going on with the Chief of Staff,' he said, 'but his behaviour has changed. . . . It's not the same Yitzhak.'[17]

Weizman, who was frustrated by Rabin's viewpoint, wondered whether in light of the government decision to exhaust the diplomatic possibilities, it was still urgent to mobilize almost all of the reserve forces. Rabin gave the order to mobilize. In the early evening he met tête-à-tête with Weizman and they apparently discussed what task to assign to Brigadier General Haim Barlev, who was summoned back from his studies in Paris when the closing of the Straits became known. After a talk with Yisrael Galili, Rabin went home. Efrat, his bureau chief, left for the airport to greet Barlev. 'The Chief of Staff is not feeling well and has gone home', Efrat told him.[18] (See Appendix: 'What happened to Yitzhak Rabin'.)

In the evening the Prime Minister addressed the Knesset to sum up the political discussion. In referring to the events of the past day, he spoke in a minor key. He described the blocking of the Straits as 'an act of aggression against Israel', and revealed that the government was in close contact with the countries which had supported the principle of free shipping in the Gulf of Aqaba in 1957, and that 'international support for those rights is serious and quite extensive'. Eshkol appealed to the Superpowers to 'act without delay to maintain the right to free shipping to our southern port'.[19]

Under the new circumstances, and in the absence of effective pressure from the military for an immediate military operation in response to the Egyptian blockade, the Prime Minister had no difficulty in taking time for political and diplomatic action. Without further thought, he dispatched Eban on his diplomatic mission to clarify the degree to which the United States was ready to take action to guarantee freedom of shipping and the practical significance of its commitment to Israel's security. Eban expanded his mission to include Paris and London. The US President had asked for forty-eight hours and Eban's mission doubled the period of time in which the government could not take decisions, and the army could not, of course, take action. During the interval, fears of an initiated Egyptian strike grew in the IDF, and the senior command began to urge Eshkol and the government to permit a pre-emptive Israeli move which would foil the dangerous prospect of an Arab attack.

The stagnation as a result of Eban's mission evoked profound frustration among the senior command. The international diplomatic effort was focused entirely on the problem of free shipping. This problem was, politically speaking, a *casus belli* and, diplomatically speaking, a lever for recruiting international support. But from the military point of view this was of marginal importance. The existential threat to the State of Israel did not stem from the blocking of the Straits but from the massing of forces along its borders and the prospect of a pan-Arab onslaught. Even without an Arab attack, this deployment of forces called for a parallel deployment of the IDF, which meant wide-scale mobilization of reserves and disruption of everyday life, a situation which would prove intolerable in the long run.

The diplomatic effort, therefore, from the point of view of the General Staff, was focused on a barren issue. Even if it succeeded it would not solve the main problem that the IDF faced. But so long as the diplomatic campaign was in full force, and the breaking of the blockade by international force seemed possible, Israel ostensibly had no pretext for war, and the 'dovish' sector of the government foiled decisions on military action. Hence the senior command, as we shall see below, decided to intervene in the diplomatic moves in order, at least, to shift the focus of diplomacy from the secondary issue of the Straits to the main problem: the concentration of forces. They did not succeed in this, but gradually instilled in the political echelon awareness that the tangible threat to national security lay in the latter and not in the former. It was this awareness which eventually impelled the government to decide to go to war.

Chapter 16

The army pressures the government

Gamal Abdul Nasser's declaration about the blocking of the Tiran Straits was greeted in Israel with astonishment. The possibility of a blockade had been contemplated, but nobody had imagined that it would occur while the UN Secretary-General was on his way to Cairo. On the contrary, U Thant's trip had eased the tension and aroused expectations that the diplomatic stage in the crisis was about to ensue. The impact of the shock was manifested in the mood of panic at the civilian level and of indecisiveness at the senior military level. While the most dramatic expression was the physical collapse of the Chief of Staff, the precipitous decision to dispatch the Foreign Minister on a mission to Western capitals was also an instinctive reaction to shock and indicated disarray rather than judicious consideration. Within a day or two the atmosphere in Israel would change. Rabin would rally, the army would adopt a decisive stand and Eshkol would be persuaded that Israel must deliver the first blow against Egypt. However, by then Eban's mission was a diplomatic fact and a liability for the government and its ability to decide on a pre-emptive strike.

The sharp change was wrought by the Intelligence evaluation that Nasser's decision to block the Straits and the subsequent enthusiastic response in the Arab world possibly implied that Nasser no longer feared the prospect of war and might even set it in motion at any moment. But another reason was the return of Minister of Labour Yigal Allon and of Brigadier General Haim Barlev, who had been out of the country since the beginning of the crisis, and whose presence was vitally important to both the government and the General Staff.

From 24 May the military began to exert increasing pressure on the civilian echelon to launch a pre-emptive strike.[1] The evaluation that Nasser was ready for a military clash with Israel and would not rescind his decision to block the Straits meant that war was now inevitable. Since nobody in the General Staff pinned real hopes on international action, Eban's mission was viewed by it as harmful, liable to bind Israel's hands and give the Egyptian army respite to consolidate its positions in Sinai or perhaps even to initiate offensive action. Moreover, military Intelligence was concerned at the growing activity between the Arab states and at the frenetic mood of the Arab world, now rallying around Nasser's leadership and call for war against Israel.

In view of the continual escalation, it was feared that as time passed and the Arab deployment along Israel's borders consolidated, Israel's military situation would become more difficult. The nightmare scenario of the General Staff was the establishment of a coordinated pan-Arab offensive force, to include an Iraqi expeditionary force on the West Bank, and a concerted aerial attack on Israel's few airfields, on the Dimona reactor, and on civilian concentrations and infrastructures. Another possibility was a large-scale renewal of terrorist activity on all the borders, including the Gaza Strip, under cover of the Arab military deployment, forcing Israel to attack and thereby providing the pretext for a pan-Arab onslaught. Even if no Arab action was taken, the presence of an offensive and threatening military concentration, however static, along Israel's borders, would force Israel to maintain mobilized reserves in the long term, thereby paralysing the economy. In order to interrupt this dangerous development in good time, the army considered it essential to take the initiative as soon as possible, and above all to ensure dominance in the air.

Weizman's day

In the absence of Yitzhak Rabin, 24 May was the day of Ezer Weizman, his second-in-command. It may also have been the day which sealed his fate and determined that he would never serve as Chief of Staff. Weizman testified that after visiting the ailing Rabin late on 23 May he had spent a sleepless night.[2] Then he decided that morning 'to take command' and to put the army into action. He had gallantly spurned Rabin's suggestion that he take over command of the IDF, but his instincts told him that he must take immediate initiative, move the forces and send them into action. Weizman probably feared that the atmosphere of inaction and uncertainty would filter down from the General Staff to the field units. He did not share the hesitations and guilt feelings which tormented Yitzhak Rabin, and had been far less exposed than Rabin to political considerations and deliberations of the government and the Ministerial Committee on Security. Moreover, by nature he was decisive, self-confident, impetuous and trigger-happy.

Weizman acted rapidly in order to draw up an operative plan that same day, submit it to the Prime Minister and order a quick movement of units in the south that night to new deployment areas so that they would be ready for battle the next day. However, the outcome was the reverse of Weizman's intention. The government was unable to take a decision during the forced political 'time-out' provided by Eban's mission. The orders issued by the General Staff on Weizman's instructions for urgent futile cross-movements between the divisions stationed in the Negev created a strong impression of disorder and panic. The commanding officer of Southern Command and the division commanders criticized Weizman, and the demand was voiced for the appointment of Haim Barlev as Rabin's deputy.

Weizman resented Rabin's drastic curtailing of the operational plan from Kardom to Atzmon. The latter essentially overturned the objective of the IDF's operational planning, namely to destroy the Egyptian army, and confined itself to the effort to win a dubious territorial 'bargaining card' in the form of the Gaza Strip. Not a single member of the General Staff, with the exception of Yisrael Tal, supported Atzmon. Hence Weizman decided on his own responsibility not to discuss it with the Chief of Staff (whom he visited again that morning), but to formulate an interim plan, whose basic points had been suggested by Gavish and Tal to Rabin the previous day before his collapse – something in between Kardom and Atzmon. This was the 'extended Atzmon' plan or 'Kardom 2'. Its main gist was an aerial attack (Moked) on the Egyptian air force simultaneously with capture of the Gaza Strip and a breakthrough on the northern axis towards el-Arish as the main thrust. Implementation was scheduled for 25 May. The objective was to achieve an immediate 'bargaining card' for political negotiations, to guarantee freedom of shipping and withdrawal of Egyptian forces, on the assumption that the Superpowers would soon impose a ceasefire. The Eighty-fourth (regular) Division, under Yisrael Tal, was assigned to the northern axis. The Thirty-first Division, under Avraham Yaffe, which was to operate on the northern axis, was now ordered to engage in a secondary effort on the southern axis. Only the mission of the Thirty-eighth Division, under Ariel Sharon, remained unchanged – to check and immobilize the massive Egyptian deployment in the Abu Ageila-Quseima sector.

On the morning of 24 May Weizman discussed the new operational plan with a limited General Staff forum. He ordered the IAF Commander to put the force on alert, ready to carry out Moked. By 08:30 the Operations Department had issued a standby order for Kardom 2, including the necessary movement of forces to be carried out on the night of 24/25 May. Generals Gavish and Tal wondered 'If the orders are implementable and if they are not too densely timed'. But there was no time for debate. Weizman wanted the IDF attack to begin the next morning, and he intended to conclude the matter without delay with Eshkol and to submit the operational plan for his approval that day.[3]

By noon Weizman had met twice with Eshkol and reported to him on the condition of the Chief of Staff and on the orders issued in connection with the IDF plan, and it was agreed that the plans would be submitted in the late afternoon for approval by the Prime Minister.[4] Prior to that, the Chief Medical Officer Dr Eliyahu Gilon had reported in private to the

Prime Minister on Rabin's condition and apparently assured him that the Chief of Staff was expected to recover within twenty-four hours.[5]

The plans were presented to the Prime Minister between 17:30 and 20:00 in the supreme command post, and the meeting was attended by most of the generals, including Haim Barlev.[6] It was Eshkol's first meeting with the senior command since the crisis had begun, and in contrast to their future encounters there were no indications of a rift between the General Staff and the Minister of Defence. However, there were initial signs of tension. The generals complained about the attitude of the political echelon and emphasized that the success of an IDF attack was conditional on the go-ahead for war at the earliest possible opportunity. The feeling in the 'pit' was that Israel was on the brink of war. Eshkol knew that it would not be possible to obtain a government decision to launch hostilities while the Foreign Minister was in Washington, but chose not to say this to the senior commanders. Weizman and other generals demanded that Eshkol convene the government that night and that a decision be reached,[7] but the Prime Minister gave no indication that the operation would be approved for the following day. On the other hand, he did not explicitly rule out the possibility.[8] Eshkol left the meeting heartened by the self-confidence of the generals, which contrasted with the hesitations of the Chief of Staff.[9]

On the night of 24/25 May, the forces in the Negev were moved in accordance with Weizman's order (in particular the 200th and 520th Armoured Brigades), but movement was halted towards morning, when it transpired that no go-ahead had been received from the political echelon, and the forces were ordered to move back.[10] The erratic movement convinced the units that the senior command had lost their heads. Weizman's prestige sank to a new low.

The events of the night were described by the Commander of the Thirty-eighth Division, Ariel Sharon, as 'a crazy race of intersecting forces'. He felt 'that everything is collapsing there [in the General Staff]. What particularly affected me was to see those convoys crossing one another and there was mayhem. . . . I had no idea if the General Staff knew what was going on, and we didn't know what was going on up there.' Sharon tried to contact the Chief of Staff but Rabin's secretary, Ruhama Tzafrir, answered that he was ill. Sharon's request to visit Rabin at home was refused. On 25 May in the morning Sharon wrote a note to Avraham Yaffe, Commander of the Thirty-first Division: 'It seems to me that the army is very sick.' Yaffe replied: 'The war yesterday was conducted by our mutual friend [Weizman] and that's exactly what it looks like.' The Command CO, Yeshayahu Gavish, reported that the pointless movements had infuriated him. 'It wasn't simple to move all the units in a single night. It was just someone's lunacy.' The next day Gavish told Rabin: 'I'm sorry, but you need to hurry and appoint Haim Barlev as Deputy Chief of Staff.'[11]

Why did Weizman act so hastily without consulting the Chief of Staff, although they had met that same morning? There were apparently three reasons:

1   Weizman, like most of his colleagues in the General Staff, and unlike Rabin, believed that it was essential to act without delay and to strike at Egypt in reaction to the blockade, in order to maintain the IDF's deterrent capability. As he saw it, from the moment the Egyptians had crossed the 'red line' there was no escape from a clash, and it would be preferable to act while the Egyptian force was unorganized, and to preclude the danger that Egypt would attack first.
2   Weizman felt that in Rabin's present emotional state, when he was even contemplating resigning, it was pointless to discuss the operative plan with him. Weizman must have been shocked by the fact that, at this critical stage, the IDF was suddenly left without a leader, and decided that it was vital to send the army into action at once to overcome the leadership void.
3   On that same day, Weizman became aware of the threatening shadow cast by Haim Barlev, his rival for the post of next Chief of Staff, who had just returned from studies in France and spent the day in the 'pit' studying the plans.[12] Thus, Weizman had an additional motive for taking over command in order to consolidate his status.

There may have been an additional, covert reason for Weizman's desire to send the IDF into action as fast as possible. Unlike his 'ground force' colleagues, he believed wholeheartedly in the IAF. Under his command, the Moked plan for destruction of the Arab air forces had been developed and streamlined, and he must have been eager to put it to the test.[13] Its success, as the war in fact demonstrated, would lay the foundation for ground action and determine the direction the fighting would take.

To say that Weizman's independent moves did not gratify Yitzhak Rabin would be an understatement. In his memoirs Rabin described his emotions with circumspection, merely commenting that 'Ezer acted impetuously'.[14]

The urgent cables: the military intervenes

When the senior command realized that there was no chance of approval for a military move before the diplomatic endeavours had been exhausted, they decided that it was necessary to intervene in order to divert the focus of attention from the issue of free shipping to the main military threat – the concentration of enemy forces and the fact that time was running out.

The first sign of active IDF intervention can be identified in the initiatives of Shlomo Argov, the Foreign Ministry's liaison officer to the

General Staff. Argov criticized the tactics of his ministry, thereby echoing the stance of the General Staff.[15] He even met, on his own initiative, with US Ambassador Barbour, stressed the importance of the time factor and hinted that an IDF operation was imminent, which came as a shock to the ambassador.[16] However, Argov's initiative was merely the overture to direct intervention in the diplomatic process on the part of Yitzhak Rabin.

On 25 May, Rabin returned to his post. His standing had apparently been undermined in the eyes of the political echelon although this was never stated explicitly. In any event, it was important, both for the army and for the general public, to restore effective functioning, even if only to outward appearances. In practice, Rabin was deposed (or perhaps it would be more accurate to say released) from his semi-ministerial status, and from now on was able to represent the army's point of view without 'pangs of conscience'. Nonetheless, the prevailing conviction among the General Staff was that he was not presenting persuasively the decisive demand of the military echelon to take the initiative and launch a pre-emptive strike immediately.[17]

The situation to which Rabin returned was complicated: on the one hand, Weizman had reached agreement, or thought he had reached it, with Eshkol on an operational plan to be put into action without delay once approved by the government. On the other hand, first reports had been received of Eban's meeting on 24 May in Paris with President de Gaulle, which intensified the feeling that the decision to send Eban had been a mistake as a result of which Israel's hands were tied. Third, there was now a greater possibility, in light of the movement of Egypt's Fourth Division into Sinai and additional Intelligence reports,[18] that Nasser was aiming for a coordinated pan-Arab offensive move. Under these circumstances, the military echelon felt it vital to intervene in the diplomatic negotiations and to steer them in the direction they preferred.

After Rabin and Eshkol had met briefly tête-à-tête,[19] they were joined by Weizman, Yariv and Barlev. The Intelligence Chief dwelt on the deterioration in the situation and the possibility of an Arab attack. 'The time factor is vital,' Yariv noted. 'There is reason to assume that Nasser thinks he needn't wait any longer.' He added: 'The problem is no longer the Straits.'[20] His comments underlined the two main arguments which the senior command had presented to the politicians:

1 In view of the real danger of an Arab attack, the IDF must deliver the first blow and launch a pre-emptive strike before the enemy completed preparing its forces. Any delay would not only increase the critical risk of a pan-Arab attack but would improve the logistic and operational organization of enemy forces, thereby placing the IDF at a disadvantage and endangering the success of its efforts even if it acted first.

2   Israeli and international diplomatic efforts, which were at any rate
     being conducted ineffectively and focusing attention on the wrong
     issue (the Straits), could not offer a solution to the central problem:
     the concentration of forces threatening Israel.

The first cable: 'Intentions to launch an all-out Arab onslaught ...'

The Prime Minister accepted the recommendation of the senior officers to
intervene in the diplomatic moves and divert it to the proper channels.
Moreover, details of the conversation reveal that Eshkol was persuaded
that the IDF would be forced to act and the diplomatic conditions should
be prepared accordingly.[21] Eshkol decided to cable instructions immediately to Eban.

Eshkol's cable to Eban began: 'There has been a far-reaching change in
the situation of the Egyptian forces and the inter-Arab military situation',
and went on to describe the amassing of forces and the military
coordination and buildup in the Arab countries, which indicated that 'the
objective now evolving is not the Straits but a total and decisive effort
against Israel ... we are receiving word of intentions to launch an all-out
Arab onslaught on Israel.'

The cable cited the mission of the Egyptian Minister of War to
Moscow[22] as evidence of Soviet–Egyptian coordination, and claimed that
'the deterioration in the Western stance so far has served as a catalyst for
this development'. Therefore,

> it should be made clear to President Johnson that the question is no
> longer the opening of the Straits alone, but first of all the danger to
> Israel's very existence ... every passing hour strengthens their [the
> Arab] forces and increases their appetite, insolence and daring in both
> the diplomatic and the military arena, to the point of involvement in a
> total, I repeat, total military struggle. Can the US President tell us, at
> this eleventh hour, what practical, I repeat, practical steps he is ready
> to take on his part in order to prevent the explosion which is coming
> closer by the hour?[23]

This dramatic cable was dispatched on the morning of 25 May. It is very
likely that the content was influenced not only by the military developments it described but also by the troubling impression gained from the
Eban-de Gaulle meeting, and the pressure which the French President
exerted on Israel not to open fire.[24] It was feared that Eban's diplomatic
mission, which some had thought from the outset to be a mistake,[25] would
impose further constraints on Israel. The 'dovish' Foreign Minister may
have been suspected by the military of deliberately inviting pressure on

Israel to refrain from military action and to conduct the campaign through diplomacy. The diplomatic path, even if it won a vague assurance as to freedom of shipping, would not check the dangers to Israel's existence stemming from the weakening of its deterrent capability, the threatening concentration of forces on its borders, and the inter-Arab militant trends led by Egypt. The military, therefore, thought that Eban should not be content with reassuring slogans and diplomatic procrastination, but must insist on explicit answers and practical moves on the part of the United States, while clarifying that Israel perceived itself as facing an immediate existential threat. The significance of this clarification was, of course, that if the United States was unwilling to guarantee that it would take 'practical steps' at once, Israel would be obliged to act alone, and would then expect the United States to display understanding and to provide full international diplomatic backing.

The second cable: 'Essential immediate implementation of US guarantee ...'

As if his previous cable had not sufficed, the same evening the Prime Minister, under pressure from the Chief of Staff, sent off a second cable to the Foreign Minister, even more urgent and strongly worded than the first.

> In the wake of developments in the past day, we fear an Egyptian-Syrian surprise attack at any moment. Hence the following message must be conveyed urgently to the US Government: there is danger of a total attack on Israel by Egypt and Syria. In this situation it is essential to obtain immediate implementation of the US guarantee, by declaration and immediate, repeat immediate, action, namely, a statement by the US Government to the effect that any attack on Israel will be regarded as an attack on the United States. This statement should be accompanied by instructions to US forces in the region to coordinate action with the IDF against any possible attack. On any response you receive, confine yourself to answering that you will report their response to your Government. In light of the urgency of the situation this information must be conveyed immediately to the highest US echelons, if possible to the President or, in his absence, to Rusk.[26]

These two cables, dispatched urgently on the same day several hours apart, are evidence of the atmosphere of tension, almost panic, in the senior command on 25 May. The fear of immediate attack on the one hand, and the need to await the outcome of the meeting with Johnson on the other, created an intolerable situation. The cables reflected a desperate attempt to extricate Israel from the trap, based on the evaluation in the General Staff that a surprise Egyptian attack was not only possible but likely.

The touchstone for Egypt's offensive schemes was the entry of the Fourth Division into Sinai. Egypt's decision to close the Straits had to take an Israeli military response into account, and it was logical to assume that the Egyptians would not wait for Israel to move but would choose to launch a surprise air attack. The obvious objective was the Dimona reactor, but an even greater fear was severe damage to Israel's few airfields, whose implications in wartime would be inestimably graver.

Particularly interesting was the metamorphosis of the Chief of Staff. Before his collapse, Rabin seemed to be wrestling with the question of which side of the military–political 'seam line' he supported. His semi-ministerial status had accustomed him to the political way of thinking. The pressure from both directions had precipitated his breakdown, but once he recovered he could only take up a position on the military side. His bureau chief testifies to Rabin's close ties with Minister Yigal Allon. Allon's assured and activist views and the reassuring presence of Haim Barlev instilled greater confidence in Rabin and rescued him from his state of isolation.[27]

Rabin displayed greater decisiveness this time in the face of speculations that an Egyptian attack was imminent. He challenged Eshkol:

> 'We are on the verge of an explosion. The question is – what are we waiting for and for how long? The problem is not the Straits. The problem is willingness or unwillingness to decide. The Straits have become a secondary issue. If the Americans are ready to issue a declaration that any attack on us is an attack on the United States, that might be a reason to wait. Otherwise – no!'[28]

The key point in the second cable was the forlorn hope that the US administration would announce that an attack on Israel would be considered an attack on the United States and accompany the announcement by orders to the Sixth Fleet to coordinate its activities with the IDF. Eshkol and Rabin knew only too well that this was unlikely to happen. Hence the cable had a twofold objective: first, to curb the Foreign Minister so that he would not accept a diplomatic formula which would impose restraints on Israel. Second, to release Israel from its commitment to the United States if and when the Israeli demand was rejected.

Genuine anxiety or a diplomatic manoeuvre?

The perplexing question is: What evoked the atmosphere of critical emergency on 25 May?

One possible answer may be sought in the testimony of Egyptian Chief of Staff General Mahmoud Fawzi to the effect that an Egyptian air attack was scheduled for 27 May, and that the relevant orders had already been signed by Abdel Hakim Amer when Nasser ordered its cancellation on 26 May.[29] If this evidence is reliable, there must have been some military activity in Egypt on 24 and 25 May which served Israeli Intelligence as 'indicators' of a possibly imminent Egyptian onslaught. The agitated mood of the senior command on 25 May was certainly no coincidence, and was probably based on firm evidence.[30]

It was not without good reason that Rabin warned: 'we are on the verge of an explosion!'; not without good reason that Eshkol decided to dispatch urgent cables to Eban about the events of 24 and 25 May noting 'intentions to launch an all-out Arab onslaught on Israel', 'the explosion which is coming closer by the hour?' and 'the danger of a total attack on Israel by Egypt and Syria'. These moves cannot be perceived as mere diplomatic manoeuvres without factual backing. It is more feasible to assume that the Eshkol–Eban cables were not only intended to ease US pressure on Israel but also expressed genuine distress and authentic fears.

The American threat

If Nasser did in fact plan to attack on 27 May, as Fawzi claimed, what caused him to change his mind and cancel the attack at the last moment?

The answer should be sought in Washington, where Eban received the cables, was stunned, and hastened to alert the Americans.[31] They took the warning seriously and acted swiftly, instantly assigning military experts and Intelligence bodies to examine and evaluate the information. Concurrently, on instructions from the President, they took immediate drastic steps in the diplomatic sphere: Under-Secretary of State Eugene Rostow urgently summoned Egyptian Ambassador to Washington Mustafa Kamel late at night on 25 May and conveyed, on behalf of the President, a grave warning to his government. According to information transmitted by the Israelis, said Rostow, the Egyptians were about to attack Israel. The Egyptian government should be aware that such an attack would impel the United States to activate its commitment to Israel's security, and this would amount to 'suicide' on the part of Egypt.[32]

This grave warning, with its almost explicit threat of US military action against Egypt, must have had an impact on Nasser's calculations, particularly in view of the deep suspicion and mistrust which prevailed between Nasser and Johnson and Johnson's 'wild' reputation as a president capable of anything.[33]

The most likely scenario is as follows: after the decision to evacuate the UN Emergency Force on 18 May and the announcement of the blocking of the Straits of Tiran on 22 May, the Egyptian President decided to go one step further (perhaps with the intention of forestalling Israel's anticipated reprisal attack), and to launch a surprise strike against Israel on 27 May. The timing was probably no random decision: the Egyptians could not have taken action before then while Eban was on his mission and the UN Secretary General had not yet returned from his trip to Cairo. They did not want to wait any longer after that for fear that Israel would steal a march on them and attack.

The core of the Egyptian attack was apparently intended to be an aerial operation against the Dimona reactor and Israeli airfields. As backing, Nasser moved the Fourth Division into Sinai on 24 May in order to secure the rear in Sinai, in addition to the mass forward deployment of forces along the Israeli border. The aim of this deployment was to absorb the anticipated IDF counter-blow. In Israel there were increasing indicators on 25 May of an imminent enemy attack, but the government was unable to act because of the mission of the Foreign Minister, who had already arrived in Washington but had not yet met with the President. In these circumstances, an Israeli pre-emptive strike would have been perceived as a treacherous act, a kind of 'Pearl Harbor'. The only way out of the trap was to alert the United States that Israel was under imminent threat of attack and to demand that the US immediately honour its commitment to Israel's security. The US administration could not have acted before examining the information provided by Eban, and even if it had been convinced of the authenticity of the data, US military intervention would have entailed complicated constitutional procedures in view of the Vietnam situation. The administration could not, of course, declare that an attack on Israel would be considered tantamount to an attack on the United States, as Israel requested. It did, however, do something relatively close and no less effective. Together with the urgent scrutiny of the information by army and Intelligence bodies, it dispatched a grave warning to the Egyptian government, which implied that the US would intervene in support of Israel in the event of an Egyptian attack, and that this would amount to 'suicide' for Egypt. It is doubtful whether this threat would have been put into full effect, but it did the job: Nasser retreated from his intention to attack, cancelled the attack scheduled for 27 May and decided to change tactics. He would wait in defensive deployment while continuing to amass forces on Israel's borders and would increase pressure, in the hope that one of two things would happen: either international intervention would enforce a solution which would extract a price from Israel and grant Nasser a prestigious diplomatic triumph, or Israel would attack and then the Egyptian army would contain the blow and launch a coordinated all-Arab onslaught under political conditions advantageous to the Arabs.

There is no way of knowing if the above-described scenario is an accurate reflection of events. It may well be that Nasser took his secrets with him to the grave. However, it is highly feasible. If indeed such was the chain of events, then the Israeli military's intervention in the diplomatic process had dramatic results, far beyond the original intentions of Israel's Chief of Staff. It would have denied Egypt military initiative and provided the IDF with the chance to deliver the first decisive blow several days later.

Meanwhile, on 26 May, the urgent dispatch of cables appeared to be an embarrassing fiasco resulting from unjustified Israeli hysteria. In Washington, military and Intelligence experts, headed by the Chairman of the Joint Chiefs of Staff, General Earl Wheeler, pored over the data in parallel teams, and arrived at the joint conclusion that the Israeli evaluation of an imminent Arab attack was unfounded. Eban had the impression that they suspected Israel of having handed over erroneous information with the aim of involving the United States. The US experts declared that even if the Arabs were the first to attack, the IDF could still prevail over any possible coalition of Arab armies.[34]

Abba Eban, both in reports to the government and in his memoirs, did not conceal his incredulity at and criticism of the hysterical cables he received, whose refutation by the Americans he considered personally humiliating.[35] He was not fully aware of the fact that the greatest gain of his trip – the grave US warning to Egypt (which he defined in his memoirs as 'a superfluous diplomatic gesture'!) – was achieved thanks to that same 'hysteria'. US deterrence 'compensated' entirely for the undermining of Israel's deterrent capability in the course of the crisis and apparently prevented an initiated Egyptian attack.[36]

Is it surprising, therefore, that the Egyptians accused the United States of a plot against them? As far as they were concerned, when the US administration laid a heavy restraining hand on them it freed Israel of restraints and enabled it to exploit the vast advantage of dealing the initial blow. This fact, which is true in itself, was the basis for the charges against the United States of a 'conspiracy' with Israel against the Arabs, claims in which the Egyptians believed wholeheartedly.[37]

The brewing crisis atmosphere and Israel's intensive diplomatic efforts accelerated diplomatic activity between the two Superpowers.[38] As a result, urgent personal messages from Soviet Premier Alexai Kosygin were handed to Nasser and Eshkol simultaneously during the night of 26/27 May. Eshkol received an additional message from Lyndon Johnson, who made him privy to his own secret correspondence with Kosygin, and urged him to refrain from initiating action. The Soviet message, when added to the direct US warning, apparently had a restraining effect on Egypt.[39] The Israeli government was deeply influenced, as we shall see below, by the US message, and decided to wait and hope for an international solution of the crisis.

The reasonable conclusion is that Eban's diplomatic mission and the intervention of the IDF in the diplomatic efforts had weighty consequences. They led to urgent Superpower intervention at the highest levels aimed at curbing both sides to the Middle East crisis. At the same time, as will be seen below, developments in Washington and in the region several days later led to the relaxing of US pressure on Israel. Israel gained thereby; Egypt felt betrayed.

At the time, and from the viewpoint of the IDF General Staff, Eban's mission was a mistake from the outset, brought no advantage, and caused nothing but harm by restricting Israel's freedom of action. The Foreign Minister, so it seemed, had failed abysmally. Not only had he weakened Israel's deterrent capability by appearing to plead for international protection, failed to win Israel space for manoeuvre, or to prepare the ground for IDF action, but he had also clung to the dubious promise of an international solution. He had given Nasser precious time for organization and consolidation, improvement of deployment and tightening of the siege around Israel, thereby limiting the IDF's options and increasing the danger of an all-Arab attack.

As if this was not enough, Eban had failed even in the important mission of shifting the focus of attention from open shipping routes, which the army considered secondary, to the concentration of forces, which it perceived as the main problem. The message Eban brought back with him, namely that the United States seriously intended to guarantee freedom of shipping through the Straits, was regarded by the army as insignificant and missing the target. His diplomatic efforts had been conducted, according to the army, on marginal issues, supplying a confused government with the excuse to evade the vital decision, and interfering with the IDF's desire to act against the main, existential danger.

Chapter 17

The politicians' quandary

Yitzhak Rabin writes that on 25 May, Eshkol rejected decisively the pressure being brought to bear by the IDF.[1] The extant documents contradict Rabin's version of events, and reveal that Eshkol did not reject the pressure on that day. On the contrary, he was persuaded by the senior command and by Yigal Allon's arguments that Israel was under immediate and critical danger of attack and hence it was vital for the IDF to strike the first blow. Eshkol wrestled with the issue and contemplated convening an urgent session of the government to take the necessary decision. However, there was no way of escaping the trap created by Eban's mission, and there was now no alternative but to wait until he returned or, at least, until after his meeting with the US President. The senior commanders gritted their teeth and waited, believing that every passing hour increased the danger and would make it harder for the IDF to conduct itself in the inevitable confrontation. When Eban eventually returned, and the government decided to go on waiting, a full-blown crisis erupted between the political and military echelons.

The activist front – Yigal Allon and the military leaders

Thus, on 25 May, Israel was on the verge of deciding to go to war, and if Eban's mission had not complicated the situation, Eshkol might have mustered a majority for such a resolution. The sharp change of direction stemmed from the Intelligence evaluation, stance of the military, and shift in the balance of opinions in the Ministerial Committee on Security as a result of Allon's return. Since he was considered to be the government's greatest authority on military and security matters, his resolute and uncompromising views tipped the balance.

Immediately after arriving in Israel, Allon plunged into the thick of events, met with the Chief of Staff and members of the General Staff, and advocated an assertive activist policy. At the same time, the General Staff had been reinforced by the presence of Haim Barlev, who shared the views

of Allon, his former commander in the Palmach. Rabin was no longer isolated and could share responsibility with those who agreed with him. The
activist front consisted of Rabin, Barlev, Weizman and Yariv in the military as well as, in the Ministerial Committee, Yigal Allon, backed to some
degree by Yisrael Galili and Eshkol. Allon regarded himself as a greater
authority than his colleagues and set the tone at ministerial deliberations
and at the political committee of the Mapai-Achdut Ha-Avoda Alignment
Party. He strongly disapproved of the decision to dispatch Eban to the
Western capitals, and proposed that Israel take immediate offensive action.

The leader of the 'doves', National Religious Party leader Moshe Haim
Shapira, was greatly troubled by the change in the internal balance of the
government and plunged into feverish activity in order to check what he
regarded as a dangerous, foolhardy line of thinking. The sole authoritative
counterbalance to Ahdut ha-Avoda in matters of national security was the
Ben-Gurionist Rafi Party. Shapira's fear that the 'hawks' would win the
day impelled him to confront Eshkol with what was almost an ultimatum
in order to ensure that the government was expanded. Shapira wanted
Ben-Gurion himself to take the helm, since he trusted him to counteract
the Ahdut ha-Avoda hawks, but was willing to settle for the appointment
of Ben-Gurion's trusted disciple Moshe Dayan as Minister of Defence.

That Shapira wanted to see Gahal (the right-wing Herut-Liberals)
represented in the government was ostensibly surprising in view of his
dovish views. In practice, however, since the beginning of the crisis, Gahal
had displayed considerable restraint, and its Chairman, Menahem Begin,
also favoured entrusting the premiership to Ben-Gurion though the latter
made no secret of his opinion that Israel should avoid becoming involved
in hostilities. Thus, in the general turmoil in the political arena, part of the
Left was more hawkish in its views than the Right, and the representative
of the most important dovish central party sought right-wing reinforcement in order to counterbalance the shift towards the army's viewpoint.

Shapira's efforts to curb the domination of the Palmach veterans
extended beyond the political sphere into the military arena. He objected
to the appointment of Haim Barlev as Deputy Chief of Staff and
demanded that Weizman be appointed to the post. Weizman was no less
of a hawk than Barlev, but he was not a 'Palmachnik' and hence was not
suspected of being a blind follower of Allon. In view of Rabin's difficulties,
Allon proposed on 25 May the immediate appointment of Barlev as
Deputy Chief of Staff. Allon had apparently already discussed the matter
with Eshkol, since the latter responded that 'it has almost been arranged',
but had not yet been finally settled with Rabin. Weizman appealed to
Shapira for backing, but without success.[2]

The day after Allon's return from abroad, he accompanied Eshkol,
Rabin and Barlev on a tour of the headquarters of the Eighty-fourth Division in the south, close to Ofakim. The Prime Minister had just concluded

a tense meeting with Shapira,[3] the demand for the appointment of Dayan as Minister of Defence was gaining momentum, and Eshkol was still resolutely opposed to yielding the position. His appearance in the field, accompanied by Allon, the hero of the War of Independence and former Commander of the Palmach, was intended to instil in the Israeli public confidence that Israel's security was in reliable hands.[4]

Although Allon told the senior officers that there was no choice but to wait until after Eban's meeting with President Johnson,[5] this was not exactly the viewpoint he presented to civilian forums where he called for immediate action. At an evening meeting of the Alignment Party political committee[6] on 25 May, Allon explained that Egypt had already supplied the pretext: two German ships passing through the Tiran Straits that day en route for the Jordanian port of Aqaba had been examined by an Egyptian patrol. 'So the blockade is in operation', Allon said. Nasser's motive was clear, he said. 'I think that Nasser is perturbed by the state of the Dimona reactor' – and he was evidently preparing an attack. Allon concluded that it was essential to launch a pre-emptive strike the next morning, or at the latest immediately after the Eban-Johnson meeting, in order to destroy the Egyptian air force on the ground and to commence a ground attack simultaneously. He was not as concerned for the fate of the settlements in the north as were the 'dovish' ministers. Settlements close to the Syrian border 'will get a hard knock and go into the shelters', and then the IDF could attack the Syrians as well. As for the Superpowers, Allon claimed that 'once we start acting, and not a moment sooner, we should inform [them] that we have received reliable information that the Egyptians were about to launch a total onslaught within an hour or two. We had no choice and we took action.'

The urging of the senior command convinced Eshkol, and he considered convening the government and even representatives of the opposition in order to take a crucial decision. 'The army claims that for every hour that we delay we are playing with Israeli lives', he told his colleagues. But the main dilemma he faced was related to Eban's mission. If Johnson demanded time in order to convene the Security Council, Israel would be in danger. 'We are in an unfortunate situation,' he said. 'It has even been suggested that I summon the government tonight, that we act tomorrow and tell Eban to return home.' Eshkol's misgivings and hesitations reflected the degree of pressure being exerted by the military: 'If the army agrees to the day after tomorrow perhaps that will be easier for Eban as well [because his visit will end by then]. But there is certainly danger that by then the Egyptians will have launched their attack on us.'

Despite representation of the army's viewpoint by Allon and, to a lesser degree Eshkol, the feeling of entrapment lingered. Shaul Avigur said that 'Eban should not have been sent. But if he's there, we must not act before he sees Johnson.' Allon retorted: 'Let's assume that it's definite that the Egyptians are going to attack. Wouldn't you act then? That's what we must do! Let Eban stay there and explain that meanwhile the situation has changed.'[7]

Eshkol is undecided

Eshkol's hectic consultations that day reflected his state of uncertainty. Anxious to convene the government, he told his close advisers that the General Staff 'are pleading with us not to waste a single hour'.[8] Foreign Ministry Director-General Aryeh Levavi cautioned against the 'Pearl Harbor syndrome' if Israel acted while Eban was caught up in his mission to the United States. The Director-General of the Prime Minister's Office, Yaakov Herzog, opined that Eban could not inform Johnson without minimal notice that Israel was about to act. This implied that the IDF would not be able to go into action immediately after the Eban–Johnson meeting. Eshkol wondered if the government had not erred when Nasser announced the closure of Tiran in acceding to the US request to wait for forty-eight hours.[9]

The possibility was discussed of dispatching an Israeli vessel to the Straits both in order to test the Egyptian declaration and to ensure that blame for aggression would clearly fall on Egypt. The head of the Mossad, Meir Amit, quoted a CIA representative who had asked Israel to postpone its decision and to act only if the Egyptians actually barred an Israeli vessel from passing through the Straits.[10] Levavi said that a ship should be sent to the Straits: 'If it's stopped – well and good, that's a *casus belli*. If not – too bad, but we will have lifted the blockade.' However, Rabin rejected the idea for fear that Nasser would view it as provocation and launch an attack 'not necessarily at Tiran, but all over the country'.[11] Yariv also dismissed the idea of sending a test vessel to the Straits in order to prepare the ground for the IDF operation. The generals argued, with considerable logic, that this would serve as a clear indication to Nasser of Israel's intention to attack.

The threat of aerial attacks

The literature on the 1967 war has not dwelt sufficiently on the dread of Arab aerial attacks evinced in Israel by both ministers and generals during the waiting period. After the event, the pre-war panic was seen as excessive and unrealistic, and few admitted to its existence. Yet study of the Minutes of government sessions, the Foreign Affairs and Security Committee, and the General Staff indicates unquestionably that there was considerable trepidation.

In the absence of strategic surprise, tactical surprise remained a vital element of the IDF's operational planning and it was on this that the IAF's Moked plan was based. The ground forces' representatives in the General Staff recognized the crucial importance of Moked and the zero hour for the ground attack was scheduled at the request of the IAF. Since, however, there was some scepticism as to the degree of success which could be anticipated, special forces were put on stand-by for a complementary ground operation (Operation 'Bluebird') which was to target airfields in Sinai. The Chief of Intelligence even voiced his suspicion that the Moked plan might have been leaked to the Egyptians by Soviet Intelligence. Due to its small number of airfields and dense concentration of population and infrastructures in a narrow strip of territory close to the border, Israel would be highly vulnerable if it did not gain complete supremacy in the air.

The second Egyptian aerial incursion

On 26 May Eshkol held a government meeting, during which a dramatic development altered the atmosphere and instantly restored the mood of anxiety and urgency. The Chief of Staff received a report of an infiltration of Israel's air space by four Mig 21s flying at a great height. One pair of aircraft performed a photographic sortie over Dimona and a second pair turned south. Rabin conveyed the content of the report to the ministers in brief and left the meeting. The ministers began to discuss the next item on the agenda – the proposal to expand the government. At this stage, only the National Religious Party favoured coopting Rafi and Gahal on to the government and appointing Ben-Gurion or Dayan as Minister of Defence. Shapira said that this would equip the government with 'broad shoulders', irrespective of whether it decided to go to war or not. The other ministers were ready to bring in the opposition to take part in the consultations and share the responsibility but without changing the composition of the government. Finance Minister Sapir labelled the National Religious Party proposal 'ousting' and said it would 'undermine the government instead of reinforcing it' while Agriculture Minister Gvati called it 'a crime'. Eshkol complained that while Egyptian aircraft were photographing Dimona, 'here we are, sitting and discussing Ben-Gurion'.[12]

The Chief of Staff and the Chief of Operations returned to the meeting to give a more detailed report on the infiltration, and Rabin requested an immediate discussion with the Prime Minister. Eshkol left the meeting in order to confer with him.[13] Rabin reported to Eshkol that a 'strange and worrying broadcast referring to coordination between bombers and fighter planes' had been monitored and could be connected to a planned Egyptian attack on Dimona. He noted, at the same time, that Egyptian ground forces were not at that moment deployed for offensive action. Weizman was blunter: 'All the signs indicate that they intend to attack Dimona'. Eshkol asked: 'Can it be understood that you want to attack today?' (i.e. without waiting for the Eban-Johnson meeting). In view of the political constraints, Rabin proposed waiting until after the Washington meeting. Weizman too realized 'that at the moment we can't take action', but proposed that the latest date for action be 'tomorrow morning'.

Back at the government meeting, Minister of Education Zalman Aranne spoke with great emotion, and his remarks deserve to be quoted because of his frank admission of the fears of the 'doves'. Aranne was afraid of the Soviet Union, which he described as a 'cosmic force'. While the United States was submerged in Vietnam, the Soviet Union was enjoying freedom of action. Aranne's misgivings were profound and agonizing: 'It may well be,' he confessed,

'that with a broken heart, I, a member of this government, will be obliged to agree that we have to shift over to the offensive. . . . I shall mourn this, because all the time inside I can feel what war in 1967 will mean for us, with what we have, with what we don't have, with what the other side has, and the other side in not just one side, it is a wall of steel and fire. Russia is behind them. . . . I can envisage before me our cities, our settlements, perhaps civilians, civilian victims perhaps several times more than the number of victims in the front line. All those who keep urging us, can they arrange it all in three days?!'

Aranne argued that the viewpoint of the army did not represent the feelings of the troops. 'I can't believe that the army of civilians standing at this moment on the border is raring to go into battle', he declared. Alluding to the demand for changes in the government, he said that the cry 'Bring us a saviour' did not reflect the wishes of the army, because 'this is an army of the people, not professionals'. Aranne objected vehemently to handing over the conduct of affairs to Ben-Gurion or Dayan. That would mean a change-over of government and would weaken its status both externally and internally. And, he added bitterly, the situation was not 'ripe for a dictator'. He suggested that the government confine itself to appointing military advisers to Eshkol, namely Allon, Yadin and Dayan.

Now came the turn of the 'hawkish' ministers, Ahdut ha-Avoda's Yigal Allon and Moshe Carmel. Under the impact of the incursion by Egyptian aircraft, Allon emphasized the urgency of a decision. He protested the fact that at such a critical time, the subject on the agenda was the expansion of the government. 'I envy you,' he told his colleagues, 'for being so courageous as to think that this [the decision to go to war] can be discussed in twenty-four or forty-eight hours' time . . . while the other side is now in a state of ecstasy.' He explained that the side which was the first to shatter the air force of the other side would win the war. 'And I don't know if [the Egyptians] won't decide to do it tonight, in an hour's time, tomorrow, whoever is first by even half an hour, which means that their aircraft won't be on the ground when the attack comes, will win the day.' Allon said he was afraid that, while the government was in session, it would become clear 'that the Egyptian air force has taken off, and when it takes off – it will be too late'. He urged the ministers: 'Leave ideology aside. We're not divided into a peace party and a war party, into heroes and cowards. On this matter, I'm a coward.' Allon 'begged' the Prime Minister to empower three or four ministers after the meeting to take decisions in light of developments.

Moshe Carmel supported Allon. He warned against a surprise Egyptian air attack on Dimona and various airfields, after which achievement of an Israeli victory would entail 'intolerable bloodshed'. He demanded that the government 'formulate now' the order to the Minister of Defence and the Chief of Staff to take action, because, 'Whoever says that we should postpone the discussion to Saturday evening or Sunday doesn't know what world he's living in'. When it came to military matters, he claimed, the worst scenario and not the best should be contemplated.

Shapira tried in a conciliatory tone to persuade his colleagues to accept Ben-Gurion: 'This isn't an expression of non-confidence', he said, but rather a demand for a unification of forces. He begged them to set aside reckonings of prestige and of 'Ben Gurion – yes or no'. His remarks, however conciliatory, nevertheless angered Eshkol, who claimed that Shapira had treated all his explanations 'like chaff before the wind'. He read out a note he had received from Dayan, asking to be recruited for active service 'so that my presence in military units will be entirely kosher'. As for Ben-Gurion, Eshkol was unequivocal: 'I will not be part of a Government with him in it ... until the very last moment there was talk of a deceptive Government, of cheats, of liars, and tomorrow or in a week's time we are supposed to conduct a war together?! ... Nobody can demand of me that I turn myself into a doormat.'

One resolution passed at the end of the meeting was to empower Eshkol to coopt representatives of Gahal and Rafi on to the Ministerial Committee on Security. And on the most crucial issue on the agenda, the government's resolutions reflected the dovish stand. It was decided: (1) to authorize the Minister of Defence and the Chief of Staff to decide to take action if Israel was attacked; (2) that if the Minister of Defence wanted to launch a strike he would convene the Ministerial Committee on Security; (3) the government would be convened again on Eban's return.[14]

That evening the Chief of Staff met with Yigal Allon and senior Foreign Ministry officials Moshe Bitan and Yosef Tekoah, to evaluate a message from the Egyptian Embassy in Washington, intercepted by Israeli Intelligence, reporting that an official in the State Department had informed them that the United States would not fight in order to open the Straits.[15] Later, the Chief of Staff held a 'fateful' conversation with Eshkol and Allon at which they weighed up the possibility of convening the government that same night in order to take the decision to attack the next morning, 27 May.[16] However, the postponement of the meeting between Eban and Johnson, whose outcome would only be known in the early morning hours, again foiled this possibility.[17] Everyone was now awaiting the report on the White House meeting.

Chapter 18

The height of the diplomatic campaign – and the outcome

It was a day of tense anticipation when the Foreign Minister met with President Lyndon Johnson on 26 May. Reports received from the embassy in Washington on contacts of Eban and senior Israeli representatives with White House and State Department officials made it clear that the Americans were unconvinced by the Israeli estimate that an Egyptian attack was imminent, and were even suspicious of Israel's motives.[1] Eban conferred with Defence Secretary Robert McNamara and Secretary of State Dean Rusk. The latter dismissed the Israeli evaluation and, on behalf of the President, voiced uncompromising objections to preventive action on Israel's part and rejected the Israeli demand for a US declaration that any attack on Israeli would be tantamount to an attack on the United States. Eban pointed out to Rusk that he needed to return home urgently in order to attend the decisive government session. The government's decisions, he emphasized, would be based on whatever Johnson told him, and the only thing that could prevent war would be 'the President's assurance that he has taken a resolute and unconditional decision to open the Straits, including a declaration and a detailed letter to the Prime Minister'.[2]

The White House was irritated by the attempt to pressure the President. Walt Rostow told Evron that the President was contemplating postponing the meeting with Eban for several hours and that he was not happy with 'the theatrical atmosphere' surrounding the meeting. He also cited the need to study the UN Secretary-General's report on his visit to Cairo and his conclusions.[3] The Americans exerted themselves in order to persuade the Israeli representatives that they were firmly resolved to open the Straits and to promote efforts, together with Britain and other countries, to organize an international maritime task force for this purpose. However, not all the reports received in Israel confirmed the US statements. In London Ambassador Aharon Remez met with Minister of State for Foreign Affairs George Thomson, and deduced that not only was there no consensus among the maritime nations with regard to the need for action, but no vessels were ready if it was decided to act immediately.[4] The Israeli military attaché in Washington, General Yosef Geva, cabled the Chief of

Staff his impression that 'there is almost no chance of independent American action on the Straits, and it is not even clear to the military people here that they will hasten to our aid if the Egyptians attack. General Wheeler ... clarified that we are capable of defeating the Egyptians alone even after suffering the first blow.'[5] The Pentagon, so it appeared, was not eager to risk an additional military involvement at the time and was anxious to convey this message to Israel.

Johnson: 'Israel will not be alone unless it decides to go alone'

At 19:00 hours (Washington time), President Johnson received Eban in the White House for a talk which lasted close to two hours. Also present were McNamara, the Rostow brothers (Walt, the President's Special Assistant, and Eugene, Under-Secretary of State), Assistant Secretary of State Joseph Sisko and Press Secretary George Christian. Eban was accompanied by Ambassador Avraham Harman and Minister Ephraim Evron.[6]

In Israel the problem of the Straits was now considered secondary, and the urgent cables Eban received had related to the immediate military threat. Notwithstanding, Eban focused almost entirely on the problem of the Straits in his talk with Johnson. This was probably not because he had decided to ignore instructions from Jerusalem, but because, after what the Secretaries of State and Defence and the Chairman of the Joint Chiefs of Staff had said concerning the threat to Israel, he felt that there was no point in discussing the matter further with the President.

Eban explained to Johnson that on the question of freedom of shipping Israel had to choose between capitulation and fighting and, while determined not to yield, wanted first to examine the possibility of an international solution to the blockade and whether the United States was resolved to promote such a solution. He asked, 'Will we fight alone or are you with us?' and what practical form the US commitment to Israel would take.

Johnson promised to bring the full influence and efforts of the United States to bear in order to open the Straits but emphasized that he required the backing of Congress and of the public. He did not hold a high opinion of the effectiveness of the UN, but it was essential initially to exhaust all possible moves there and meanwhile to put together an effective force in order to lift the blockade. As for the US commitment to Israel, he said:

> 'We reviewed everything that this country has said in relation to Israel. Truman through Eisenhower and Kennedy and what I have said. All this is important but I tell you that this is not worth five cents unless I have the people with me.'

Johnson reassured Eban that the time for action was not far off, but, he said, 'Would it be wise at this moment, as we say in the language of poker, to call Nasser and raise his hand?'

The President was unwilling to provide Israel with the ultimate commitment it requested and described as unrealistic the proposal that he declare that an attack on Israel would be tantamount to an attack on the United States. On the other hand, Johnson was resolute in his commitment to open the Straits to Israeli shipping: 'I'm not a feeble mouse or a coward and we're going to try. What we need is a group, five or four or less, or if we can't do that then on our own.'

At the same time, the President pointed out to Eban that constitutional constraints obliged him to recruit the support of Congress for any warlike move. 'I'm not a king', he said.

Only towards the end of the meeting did Eban raise the main subject on the agenda in accordance with the cable from Jerusalem. He asked: What if the Israeli assessment was true, and stressed that Israel had to take the matter seriously since Nasser had made it clear that the UAR objective was the destruction of Israel. McNamara replied that all the Intelligence agencies had assessed the situation and could see no indication of 'imminent offensive action' on the part of the Arabs.

At the end of the meeting, Johnson handed Eban a written note, containing the essence of the US stand: the United States was bound by certain constitutional procedures, efforts at the UN had not yet been exhausted, and the United States intended to take vigorous action to guarantee that the Straits would remain open. The concluding paragraph was the most important.

> I must emphasize the necessity for Israel not to make itself responsible for the initiation of hostilities. Israel will not be alone unless it decides to go alone. We cannot imagine that it will make this decision.[7]

The outcome of Eban's mission

What were the results of Eban's mission? He had seemingly achieved nothing and merely accumulated 'prohibitions and tribulations' as opposition leader Menachem Begin put it. De Gaulle's stand was negative, Harold Wilson was sympathetic but not influential, while Johnson had merely reiterated the US standpoint and rejected the possibility of independent Israeli action.

Practically speaking, however, the mission had one very important result: it essentially forced the Israeli government to take a 'time-out' and thus precluded a pre-emptive Israeli strike around 25 to 26 May. At this time, as noted above, Eshkol seemed likely to succumb to the pressure of the military and to approve a pre-emptive strike (it is another question whether he would have won a majority in the government for such a step, or whether he would have been content with a narrow majority, which is by no means certain). The main reason for the postponement of the decision was Eban's mission. Not only was Eban's meeting with Johnson a senior-level direct, personal and vital dialogue at a critical moment, but it also sharpened the commitment of the US and of the President in particular. As a result, the government decided after Eban's return to take a risk and give diplomatic efforts a chance to resolve the crisis.

Eban's mission was also significant so far as Egypt and other Arab countries were concerned. It created the impression that the Israeli government was hesitant and was courting international protection in order to evade Arab fury. This further strengthened Nasser's standing and Arab cohesion. The strong warning dispatched by the United States to Nasser apparently served as a powerful deterrent and important consideration in Nasser's decision not to open fire first, but it certainly did not enhance Israel's image in his eyes. He could assume that Israel feared confrontation. As a possible result, Nasser preferred for Israel to initiate hostilities and isolate itself, while Egypt would contain the first onslaught and launch a crushing counter-attack which would defeat Israel.

To sum up, therefore, Eban's mission had a profound impact on the timetable of the crisis, and its most important consequence, as it now appears, was the postponement of both Israeli and Egyptian military moves. This conclusion suggests that the implications of the mission were far-reaching: if Israel had initiated hostilities on 25 to 26 May, the war would probably have been confined to the Egyptian front, and then only to the northern Sinai sector and the Gaza Strip (this was the IDF's operative plan at the time). Jordan would most probably have remained outside the fray, and on the Syrian border there would have been at most a few skirmishes and an attempt to occupy the demilitarized zone. The IDF might even have confined itself (according to the Atzmon plan) to a strike against the Egyptian air force and occupation of the Gaza Strip alone as a dubious 'bargaining card'. On the other hand, if the Egyptians had been first to launch an aerial and ground onslaught, the war would undoubtedly have taken a different turn.

The urgent messages sent to Eban, instigated by the IDF, read like SOSs and added a touch of drama to the mission, spurring the Americans to vigorous action, pregnant with consequences, both towards Egypt and in the Superpower arena.

Washington's aim was to achieve an understanding with Moscow as swiftly as possible in order to check the crisis before it veered out of control. The United States hoped initially that the UN Secretary-General would find the magic remedy, even though Nasser had already announced the blockade. But before U Thant's return and before he could report on his talks with the Egyptian President, Eban arrived at the White House armed with alarming information on an imminent Egyptian attack. Although US experts did not verify the data, the administration felt the need not only to direct a grave warning at Egypt, but also to establish a dialogue with Moscow at the highest level. Johnson and Kosygin reached agreement to the effect that each side would restrain its own 'client'. The equation, however, was not symmetrical. The United States curbed Israel and severely cautioned Egypt. The Soviet Union proved effective in restraining Egypt but much less so as far as Israel was concerned.

The Soviet message

Very late on the night of 26/27 May and in parallel to Dimitri Pojidaev, his counterpart in Cairo, the Soviet Ambassador to Israel Sergei Chubakhin brought an urgent personal note from Soviet Premier Alexei Kosygin to Prime Minister Eshkol. According to information in the possession of his government, Kosygin wrote, the situation in Israel was 'sharpening as though there was no alternative to acts of war'. Kosygin's style was firm rather than blunt, and the impact of the message was, in the end, paradoxically, placatory rather than deterrent. The inevitable comparison was with Premier Nikolai Bulganin's brutal and alarming missive of 5 November 1956,[8] and the difference was great.

'It would be a tremendous error,' Kosygin warned, 'if circles eager for battle and unrestrained by serious political thought had the upper hand in such a situation, and arms were to begin talking', He called for all possible measures in order to prevent a military conflict and cautioned that 'it is easy to ignite a fire but putting out its flame may not be nearly as simple as those pushing Israel to the brink of war imagine'. The demand to Israel not to be the party responsible for launching hostilities was phrased in a moderate and minor key: 'We hope that following a serious consideration of the evolving situation and of the responsibility lying on the shoulders of that side which will initiate the aggression, the Government of Israel will do everything in its power to avoid a military conflict in the Middle East.'[9]

The Soviet stance on the crisis evoked various questions and surmises in Israel. It was manifest that Moscow's policy was hostile, but its motives were not clear, and its tepid reaction roused suspicions that a Soviet plot was afoot. The Israeli Embassy in Moscow was isolated and its reports were sombre. It was unable to supply reliable information on the mood of the Kremlin. On 27 May, Ambassador Katriel Katz sent a cable, which was not grounded on concrete information, reporting that the situation was

> the outcome of a joint conspiracy and plan of the Soviets and Syria, Egypt, Iraq and Algeria to drive the West away from the oil resources

and from the vicinity of Turkey and Iran. Israel is intended to be the victim of this crusade, on the assumption that the Arab–Israel war will restore the revolutionary states to leadership of the entire Arab world, and UN intervention will be paralyzed by a Soviet veto and the Western powers will hesitate to intervene both for fear of Soviet intervention and because they themselves are occupied elsewhere.

The Ambassador proposed a campaign to expose this conspiracy.[10] However, most of the evaluations of the Soviet Union's role from other Israeli legations, particularly Paris, London and Washington, pointed to a cautious Soviet approach, granting the Arabs diplomatic backing while striving to consolidate the Egyptian achievement and stem the downward slide into armed conflict.[11]

Nasser: our fundamental objective – the destruction of Israel

On 26 May, Gamal Abdel Nasser voiced the most direct, explicit threat against Israel since the crisis had begun. Appearing in Cairo before the representatives of the Arab Trade Union Confederation, the Egyptian President sounded determined to take the risk of a full frontal clash with Israel, in full confidence of victory:

> 'The Arab world today is different from the Arab world of ten days ago, and the same is true of Israel. The Arabs are firmly resolved to realize their rights and they will restore the rights of the Arabs of Palestine. We are confident of victory over Israel ... the blocking of the Straits means entering into an all-out battle with Israel. This requires preparations. When we felt ourselves to be ready, we did this.... If we are attacked, it will be war and our fundamental objective will be the destruction of Israel.'[12]

On the same day, Nasser's associate, Muhammad Hasanin Heikal, editor of the daily *al-Ahram*, published an article which made a strong impression in Israel. Heikal showed a profound understanding of the psychological element in Israel's security conception and his conclusion was that Israel had to go to war. If we can trust General Mahmoud Fawzi's testimony that Egypt was about to inflict a surprise blow on Israel on 27 May, and Nasser cancelled it at the last moment due to the US warning, then Nasser's speech may be interpreted as handing on the US caution. The United States had warned Egypt that an attack on Egypt's part would be tantamount to 'suicide'. Nasser readdressed the same threat to Israel. If the US threat was intended to enable Israel to deal the first blow, that would constitute suicide on Israel's part, Nasser cautioned.

From the viewpoint of Israel where the atmosphere was one of acute tension and anxiety, Nasser's threat was interpreted literally as a 'declaration of intent'. The feeling was that the country's leadership was confused, astray and helpless, concentrating on lobbying efforts and displaying weakness and cowardice, and thereby spurring Nasser to escalate his threats and to challenge the very existence of the state. Nasser was escalating the crisis a step at a time, and there was reason to fear that he did not intend to halt and that the next step would be a surprise attack on Dimona and IAF airfields. The jingoistic atmosphere in the Arab world, the continuing influx of forces and the increasing inter-Arab coordination had rendered the existential threat tangible and critical.

Israeli diplomacy was endeavouring to neutralize the UN as a mediatory factor in view of Israel's basic mistrust of that organization and in order to avoid freeing up the United States from its direct commitment to Israel's security. The efforts were focused mainly on Washington.

After the Eban–Johnson meeting, Ambassador Harman and Minister Evron conferred with Eugene Rostow, and Evron reported to Jerusalem on the talks, and on the anticipated scenario: publication of an international declaration on the right to freedom of shipping, organization of an international maritime force concurrently with recourse to the various procedures at the Security Council. All this was to occur in the course of two or three weeks during which the two sides would be required to agree to a 'moratorium': the Egyptians would not activate the blockade and Israel would not try to challenge it. Rostow even added a bonus: an Israeli naval vessel would be invited to join the international expeditionary force. He also promised that immediate steps would be taken to ensure liaison in the sphere of military Intelligence.[13] The idea of the 'moratorium' had already been proposed by U Thant at his meeting with Nasser, who agreed instantly.[14] In Israel the whole 'moratorium' idea was greeted with derision: Israel was asked not to send vessels through the Straits so that Nasser could display 'benevolence' and not prevent passage.

The night of 27/28 May: the government is split

The government was convened again on Saturday night, 27 May, as an extended ministerial committee on security. The meeting took place in the Minister of Defence's office in Tel Aviv and lasted all night. Foreign Minister Eban, whose report was awaited, arrived straight from the airport shortly after the meeting began.[15] At this tense marathon meeting the government was split between the 'hawks', who supported the army's views, and the 'doves', who were adamantly opposed.

Yariv's survey at the meeting was intended to lead the government to an inevitable conclusion. He reported that the influx of forces into Sinai and the Straits was continuing and the Egyptians were investing effort in obtaining a large supply of weapons, and were trying meanwhile to play for time with Soviet support. On the other hand, he pointed out, there had been no explicit Soviet guarantee of military intervention on Egypt's side. Yariv explained that the Egyptian deployment in Sinai had been built up hastily and was not yet balanced, but as time passed it would be improved and reinforced, and more Arab expeditionary forces would join it. He added: 'We know for certain that their decision is first of all to send the air force into action. It is also clear what the significance will be if they succeed in employing their air force before we put ours into action.'

Yitzhak Rabin was more explicit. He spoke of 'a noose which in my opinion is tightening around us', and the increasing difficulty of removing it as time passed. Rabin had already hinted that there were indications of US courtship of Nasser.[16] The Chief of Staff noted that he was not suggesting an easy alternative. But to wait idly meant in fact to help the enemy to deploy their forces and thus to intensify the danger to the State and increase the number of casualties and the scope of devastation which the inevitable war would cause. 'If we go into action tomorrow – we will spare ourselves casualties', Rabin said. Zalman Aranne disagreed and thought that Johnson's courtship of Nasser was intended rather 'to dissuade him from warlike action'.

At this stage, Abba Eban arrived. His report was intended to create the opposite effect to that produced by the reports of the military. Eban told the ministers that de Gaulle had been 'shocked and alarmed', and had cautioned: 'It will be a tragedy, a tragedy, if you are the first. Never be the first. You must fight only if others attack you. You cannot imagine the disaster for you and your lives if you don't observe that rule.'

Eban's remarks reflected his disapproval of the urgent cables he had received. The Americans, he said, had dismissed all the evaluations they contained and had even suspected Israel of slanting the reports in order to prepare the ground for an Israeli attack and perhaps even to entangle the United States. Eban described Johnson's viewpoint as persuasive, and the various stages of the proposed solution, without specifying the time framework: (1) efforts to win the backing of Congress ('This stage is almost complete'); (2) full exploitation of the procedures at the Security Council; (3) and simultaneously, a declaration by the maritime nations to be followed by the assemblage of a flotilla of vessels to break through the blockade.

The 'dovish' ministers were greatly encouraged by Eban's report, which seemed to bear out their own views. Minister of Religious Affairs Zerah Wahrhaftig said that it was evident that an initiated military action would isolate Israel. 'It would be an adventure, simply an adventure.' On the other hand, international action in the Straits would damage Nasser's prestige and Israel would suffer no losses. Housing Minister Mordechai Bentov and Health Minister Yisrael Barzilai concurred.

Yigal Allon was the strongest champion of the army's cause. If it were a matter of the Straits alone, he would not rule out international action, but the issue was the realization of an existential threat to Israel, namely a massive onslaught on all fronts. He dwelt on the critical significance of granting offensive initiative to the enemy and of the destruction of the IAF and asked a rhetorical question: 'Does anyone around this table imagine that we, under any circumstances, will permit the enemy to be first, merely in order to prove to the world that they began?!' Allon noted that the United States had not yet had the final word on the Dimona reactor and the refugee issue. 'And I'm not sure if the Egyptian alert is not also connected to their assumption – which need not necessarily be true – that we have arrived at a critical stage at the reactor.' He did not rule out a coordinated bombing attack on the reactor and – simultaneously – in order to forestall reaction – the bombing of IAF bases, 'and Nasser will even emerge as a hero who saved the Middle East, as it were, from nuclear weapons'. Allon was anxious to persuade the irresolute ministers that he had examined the situation with the eyes of a military expert and had no doubt that the IDF was capable of inflicting a heavy blow on the Egyptian air force and armour, whose rehabilitation would require years. 'And if this job is done by purely Hebrew labour, without pretensions of occupying Sinai and annexing of Sinai, but just the necessary minimum in order to shatter the enemy's power, to hold on to the minimum territory as a bargaining card for a settlement to prevent war – then all the Powers will sing a different tune.'

Allon's confident remarks impressed but did not convince the 'doves'. Minister of Finance Pinhas Sapir defined himself 'as someone who has been torn in the past four days between yes and no', but his remarks implied a relatively conclusive 'no'. 'It was very hard for us to win ourselves a state, to lose it – would be very easy', Sapir said. He protested against the excessive self-confidence of Allon's statement at a time when the fate of the country was being weighed in the balance. 'It is all constructed on the fact that we have X planes and we can sweep the skies clean. What happens if, Heaven forbid, someone else sweeps the skies?' Sapir admitted that, unlike Allon, he understood nothing of military matters, but as an expert in the security economy he understood 'that if we destroy 100–150 planes, within two or three weeks they will have Mig 21s instead of Mig 17s and 19s'. Sapir envisaged a remorseless scenario of bombing of civilian settlements. He described his meeting with Shimon Peres prior to the government meeting.[17] Peres had spoken with great emotion and warned that, militarily speaking, Israel was facing disaster, 'and this is not mere party tactics', Sapir commented.

Minister of Agriculture Haim Gvati, one of the 'hawks' in the government, said that the advocates of waiting were not thinking of forty-eight or seventy-two hours, because even after a month the conditions would remain unchanged. There was no country in the world which wanted war to break out here, said Gvati, and all of them were ready for Israel to pay the price. Johnson's proposals, he thought, were meaningless. 'Nothing will happen. Time will pass, there will be discussions, and they will grow accustomed to it all.' He was afraid that a decision not to act would be a grave turning point for the country's destiny and would turn it into a protectorate. Nasser's prestige was rising, and he might even take over Jordan 'while we sit and argue whether it is permissible for us to be first'. Gvati referred to the danger of demoralization:

> 'Today the nation is mobilized. . . . I don't know when we can repeat this and how the people will respond. I want to warn against missing this hour, squandering the vast effort. . . . Let us not delude ourselves. . . . We must decide tonight if we are taking action or bringing the forces back home. I am in favour of taking the risk. To me it seems much smaller than the danger of dispersing our forces today.'

The most emphatically dovish line was led, as usual, by Moshe Shapira of the National Religious Party. He reminded his colleagues that Israel had never gone to war alone, and that during the War of Independence it had been backed by the Soviet Union and Czechoslovakia. Israeli initiative meant that the United States would adopt a negative stance and the Soviet Union would support the Arabs. He did not believe that Israel would be able to withstand this. Israel would lose planes, ammunition would run out, and, on the other hand, the IDF would not conquer Cairo or destroy the Egyptian army and air force, and Russia was even liable to send 'volunteers' to Egypt. The Americans must be trusted to open the Straits and not to play into the hands of Nasser, who was waiting for the IDF to attack so as to isolate Israel. Shapira demanded patience and reliance on diplomatic tactics.

The Chief of Staff intervened at this stage of the discussion and reported a personal note he had received from the Italian Chief of Staff, according to which in the next four or five days no Arab attack should be expected, but 'anything could happen' after that. Rabin may have been trying to say that although he was in favour of an immediate Israeli strike the hourglass would not run out in the coming forty-eight or seventy-two hours. But he cautioned against the danger of leaving the initiative to Nasser. Regarding the 'doves', he commented that they were implying that the State of Israel could not survive through its own efforts. On an offended note, he added: 'If the State of Israel thinks that its existence is conditional on an American commitment and not on its own might – I have nothing to add.' The army's sense of affront was voiced even more clearly by Operations Chief Ezer Weizman, who reminded the ministers that the IAF had downed eleven enemy aircraft without losing a single aircraft of its own. He had no doubt, he said, 'that this is the bitterest war that this nation has ever fought, in the air as well. If I had to choose a confrontation with Egypt, I would want to catch them under more propitious conditions, but war does not always occur the way you plan it.' He expressed his complete confidence in the ability of the IAF to break the Egyptian air force. 'It is doing an injustice [to the IDF] – which may stem from lack of knowledge – not to trust in our strength', Weizman declared.

Eshkol sided with the army. He pointed out that Johnson was now focusing on the Straits and asking for time. If it was only a case of the shipping issue so be it, Eshkol said; Israel could have waited a week or two. But the problem was Israel's deterrent capability. Minister without Portfolio Yisrael Galili also sided with the advocates of immediate military action, mainly on the grounds that Israel's regional and international standing and deterrent capability would be weakened if it failed to act, and due to the imminent prospect of an all-out Arab attack aimed at annihilating Israel. Transport Minister Moshe Carmel argued that to refrain from action would inevitably lead to the worsening of the security situation 'and total collapse of Israel's element of deterrence'. The closing of the Straits would be followed by disruption of Israeli shipping in the Mediterranean, and Israel would be forced to fight under much worse conditions. 'I have heard what is going on here now in Arab villages [in Israel]', Carmel added. And echoing the Chief of Staff, he added: 'Whoever says that we cannot stand alone is saying that we will not survive here.'

The Minister of Justice, Yaakov Shimshon Shapira, favoured waiting forty-eight hours for action so that it would not occur too soon after Eban's return. 'How can we withstand all the Arab states?' he sighed. Eshkol closed the meeting at 04:00 with the proposal that the government reconvene a few hours later. Aware that the ministers were exhausted, he said: 'I would not like to take a vote now, but to let colleagues sleep on it.... Eban too will do some thinking. As to what [Yaakov Shimshon] Shapira said [that we should not act immediately after Eban's return] – there is something in it.' Every day was vital, but 'I would not want to antagonize the US President too much'.

The balance is tipped: Johnson's note

On 28 May at 05:30, an hour and a half after the government meeting ended, US Ambassador Walworth Barbour brought Eshkol a personal note from Johnson, dated 27 May. In it Johnson made Eshkol privy, discreetly and on a personal basis, to the content of a message he had received from Soviet Premier Alexai Kosygin. The Soviets had received information that Israel was preparing a military operation. The Arabs did not want a military clash. Therefore, if Israel took action, the Soviets would extend aid to the countries under attack. The Soviet Union asked the United States to take all the necessary steps to prevent such a clash, and gave its assurance that it too would take steps in that direction. Johnson added: 'As your friend, I repeat even more strongly what I said yesterday to Mr. Eban. Israel just must not take any pre-emptive military action and thereby make itself responsible for the initiation of hostilities.'

To underline these remarks, Barbour added a message dictated by Secretary of State Dean Rusk to the effect that the United States and Britain were continuing feverishly to prepare the military aspects of an 'international naval escort plan', and hence 'with these assurances of international determination to make every effort to keep the Straits open to the flags of all nations – unilateral action on the part of Israel would be irresponsible and catastrophic'.

It seems that Rusk's veiled threat had more impact than Johnson's confidential message. It served, perhaps, as a counterweight to the grave warning that the Administration had addressed to the Egyptians. The statement that unilateral action on Israel's part would be 'irresponsible and catastrophic' could not be ignored.

The communications from the United States tipped the balance, and changed the stance of the government and the balance of views within it. Indirectly, it also determined the future composition of the government. Within four days Eshkol was to give up the defence portfolio, but during this brief period other developments affected the attitude of the United States.

The government meeting was resumed on 28 May at 15:00.[18] The IDF representatives present were Rabin, Barlev, Weizman and Yariv. Opening the proceedings, Eshkol asked the Foreign Minister to report on the notes from the US President and from the Embassy in Washington. Under the strong impact of Johnson's and Rusk's words, Eban argued that a decision to postpone military action was self-evident, and Eshkol advanced the obvious conclusion: in view of what Johnson had told Eban, Kosygin's message to Johnson and the latter's personal message to him, 'I don't think we can fail to take note'. It was evident to all that something was being done to ensure free passage through the Straits of Tiran, Eshkol emphasized, despite fears that it would 'melt away'. On the other hand, a time limit should be set 'for us and for them' of two or three weeks, so that there would be no foot-dragging procedures, such as submission of the freedom of shipping issue to the International Court of Justice in The Hague,[19] and at the same time the army should remain mobilized in order to forestall danger. The waiting period should be exploited for a major fund-raising campaign to finance military needs, and the fact 'that we are good little children' should be exploited to expedite military purchases, particularly of aircraft and ammunition.

In contrast to the meeting of the previous night, there was now almost complete unanimity of opinion. The 'doves' breathed a sigh of relief, and even Yigal Allon did not challenge them. He supported Eshkol's stand, albeit unenthusiastically, well aware that the reinforced commitment of the United States obliged Israel 'to give the US, as far as possible, the chance to honour its commitment', but Allon had grave doubts 'as to how this exercise will end'. He feared that at the very last minute the Americans would stipulate conditions unacceptable to Israel, such as international inspection of Dimona. Allon's 'interim conclusion' was gloomy: it was an impressive Arab diplomatic gain and a heavy blow for the prestige and deterrent capability of the IDF.

The Chief of Staff tried in vain to alter the balance. 'I am not saying that the alternative is easy,' Rabin asserted, 'but I do say that in my opinion to delay the blow against Egypt will take us back to the pre-1956 situation, because I don't believe that the world will open the Straits for us. I am convinced that in two or three weeks we will face the same problem under worse political circumstances and worse military conditions.'

Eshkol responded peremptorily and put Rabin in his place: 'I don't want to do what I did with regard to others [i.e. the ministers], bring pressure to bear on you and ask you a simple question, yes [respond to Johnson's appeal] or no? Even if you say yes, I'm not interested in that!' He was making it abundantly clear, therefore, that Rabin's viewpoint was irrelevant. Eshkol wanted the civilian echelon to decide the matter. His remarks clearly indicate his resentment at the intervention of the military in the decision-taking process and their pressure for action.

The only minister who fully supported the army's stance was Moshe Carmel. He cautioned that the government was making a grave and dangerous mistake, and would eventually face the need to confront the Egyptians under much graver conditions. Carmel understood the sense of relief at the postponement of the confrontation, 'but relief is not a solution and doesn't and won't provide a solution for Israel's survival and security unless we shatter the Egyptian forces. From this point of view I think that now is the best time and the opportunity will not return in the near future.' Carmel explained that he had met with officers who gave him details of the Israeli deployment and spoke of the excellent and unique prospects for success. He was aware, he said, that he had no chance of changing the opinions of most of his colleagues, but asked that his views be recorded in the Minutes.

Eban attacked Allon and Rabin scathingly. The rule was, he said, that one did not conduct a war over prestige (i.e. the IDF's deterrence capability) but over vital interests. 'There are no widows and orphans of prestige,' said Eban, 'and I am afraid that if we carry out this blow, since we are not living alone in this world, by acting today we will be isolating ourselves from all our existing and possible allies, with everything this entails as regards supplies of arms and equipment.' He agreed with the Chief of Staff that the government was taking a risk by deciding not to act, but the decision to act was also risky, and what was required was 'to measure the relative weight of the risks'. At this stage, Eban said, he believed that the danger of action was greater, but the situation could change within a week or ten days, and 'if it turns out that all this is deception or illusion – then we will sober up'.

After the meeting, at 17:15, it was resolved that 'in view of the prospects for the activity of the US Government, together with other Governments or on its own, to open the Straits, Israel will refrain from taking initiated military action until a new decision is taken, within three weeks of the present meeting'.

Chapter 19

Waiting

On 26 and 27 May both the General Staff and the government nervously awaited the results of the Foreign Minister's meeting in Washington. The basic operational plan remained unchanged at this stage – Moked in the air and Kardom 2 on the ground – but at the suggestion of the Operations Department the possibility was contemplated that Arab forces might move into the West Bank, thereby turning the Jordanian front into a theatre of war. Additional plans were also drawn up for the Egyptian front. The planned transfer of an Egyptian armoured assault force, under General Saad a-Din a-Shazli, from the northern sector of the front to the south,[1] and the border patrols conducted by Egypt in order to locate breaching points, suggested an Egyptian intention to cut off the southern Negev. The Egyptian propaganda machine prepared the ground for this move by claiming that the conquest of Eilat by the IDF in 1949 had been illegal, because it had occurred after the signing of the Egyptian–Israeli armistice agreement.[2] An Egyptian attempt to cut off the southern Negev triangle appeared to be the logical strategic move: it could create the desired territorial continuity between Egypt and the eastern Arab expanse, deny Israel its outlet to the Red Sea, and render the Straits issue irrelevant. Such a territorial bridge would reflect Egypt's intention to win direct access to Jordan, Syria and Iraq, to encircle Israel and to impose Egyptian hegemony over the entire Fertile Crescent.[3]

Tactically speaking, on the other hand, the IDF was anxious to lure Egyptian forces away from the northern axis – where the main effort was to be focused according to Kardom 2 – southward, in order to facilitate the breakthrough into Sinai. This was the task of a special unit named 'the fraudulent division', whose aim was to mislead the enemy into thinking that the IDF was planning to launch its main effort on the southern axis into Sinai. However, the luring of the Egyptian forces to the south created a threat to Eilat, which greatly concerned the General Staff and was exacerbated by the signing of the Jordanian–Egyptian defence pact on 30 May (see below) which put the Jordanian armed forces under Egyptian command.[4]

Yigal Allon was the only minister who, undoubtedly with Eshkol's permission, was in constant contact with the General Staff, and in particular with Rabin, Barlev and Yariv. At a meeting with the latter two in the Pit on 27 May, Allon examined the operative plans and noted the need to make it appear as if the enemy had opened hostilities. He surmised that on the following day, after Eban's return, the government would adopt a positive resolution, and added: 'If the Syrians intervene – we should go up on the [Golan] Heights and dig in.'[5] Under Allon's influence, Eshkol took Barlev into his confidence and was greatly impressed by his unique qualities and by his confidence and cool demeanour in sharp contrast to the confusion and anxiety all around him.

On 27 May Eshkol invited Barlev to a private lunch, and heard his evaluation of the situation. Barlev apparently supported an early Israeli attack, but did not try to pressure the Prime Minister. An additional issue which must have arisen in the course of the meeting was Eshkol's intention, voiced the previous day at the political committee of the Alignment Party, to appoint Barlev Deputy Chief of Staff. After the lunchtime meeting, Eshkol held a private talk on the same subject with Ezer Weizman.[6]

Eshkol broadcasts to the nation

The government decision of 28 May to allow a three-week period for international efforts to solve the crisis was, as noted above, completely at odds with the army's position on the matter. The Chief of Staff, who was aware of the mood of the General Staff, asked the Prime Minister to meet with the generals immediately and explain the government decision to them. The senior commanders were summoned urgently to a meeting in the Pit without being told why.[7] However, while en route to the meeting, Eshkol was obliged to perform another important task: to broadcast to the nation and explain the government's decision.[8]

Tremendous significance has been attributed to Eshkol's ill-fated address, which was broadcast live from the Kol Israel radio studios in Tel Aviv during the main 20:30 evening news.[9] It is indisputable that the broadcast had a detrimental impact on morale. Eshkol had never been a skilled orator, and his weary tone and hesitant and faltering delivery of an obviously unfamiliar text depressed his listeners. The Israeli public as a whole, in the front line and at home, were pinned to their radio sets, waiting tensely for the Prime Minister's message, and what they heard was severely discouraging.

Eshkol did not grasp the gravity of the mishap at first. It was only the savage criticism in the press of the following day which brought it home to him. However, the problem apparently lay in content no less than in delivery. The Prime Minister had no uplifting message to offer. The danger was great, Eshkol said. The blocking of the Straits was an act of aggression. The government had heard the Minister of Foreign Affairs' report – particularly on his talks in the US capital – and had formulated instructions for further diplomatic efforts in the international arena. Eshkol's speech was replete with such phrases as 'the IDF is completely ready' and 'the firm resolve of the people',[10] but this alone could not suffice to conceal the fact that the Israeli government had placed its trust in foreign elements and not in the IDF's might.

It was this fact, more than Eshkol's hesitant speech, that determined the response. The entire Zionist Israeli ethos was on trial: independence, self-reliance, national pride and, above all, the invincible IDF which had been elevated to the status of myth. All this appeared to have been abandoned in an instant in light of the threat, and the new Jew seemed to be reverting to being the old, Diaspora Jew, namely helpless, and begging for protection by foreigners.

This now was the image of Eshkol's government, and it was in sharp contrast to the self-image of Israelis, particularly of the IDF commanders and soldiers in the field. Intolerable tension was created between the pale, elderly, confused and seemingly panic-stricken civilian leadership, engaged in a desperate effort to avert war, and the IDF, the supreme expression of the new Israeli essence that was young, daring, belligerent. The confrontation between the military and political echelons was now inevitable.

The Israeli press did not spare Eshkol and was harshly critical of his stammered address. One newspaper wrote that the speech 'evoked horror in Israel ... it surprised a nation, whose nerves and muscles were strained to breaking point. It was in a pathetic tone, accompanied by inarticulate and disgraceful mumbling, like some bad provincial theatre.' Another described the speech as 'The most shameful symptom of the Government's lack of talent ... the listener received the impression that his Government is headed by a broken man, stammering out with difficulty a text written by someone else ... at this fateful emergency hour, when all nerves are stretched, this is a terrible thing.'[11]

Confrontation in the Pit

Eshkol came to the Pit, accompanied by Yigal Allon, immediately after the broadcast to the nation from the nearby Kol Israel studio. The generals awaited him, already aware that the government had decided not to approve the pre-emptive strike. The group dynamic must have intensified their sense of affront and fury, but beyond this they were convinced that the government, in its confusion, had acted irresponsibly, thereby placing the very survival of the State at risk. Eshkol had no idea what was awaiting him. Rabin, on the other hand, sensed the atmosphere and, against custom, did not open the meeting with his own remarks.[12]

There was international readiness to solve the Straits problem, Eshkol explained, unaware that he was not touching on the main concern of an audience which did not consider freedom of shipping to be the main issue. Eshkol described his meeting with the Soviet Ambassador and the note he had received from the Soviet Premier, de Gaulle's negative response, the top-secret message from Johnson about the Soviet decision to extend aid to the Arabs if Israel attacked, and Johnson's caution that preventive action on Israel's part would be catastrophic.

He dwelt on the preparations of the 'maritime powers' for organization of a maritime expeditionary force to pass through the Straits of Tiran, and mentioned the US promise (which was based on half a sentence which Eban had heard from Johnson but not really confirmed) that if the international effort failed the US would act alone. Under these conditions, he emphasized, it would not be politically, diplomatically and morally logical to launch warfare. He expressed his understanding of the disappointment of the generals, but demanded of them 'military and political maturity'.

The senior officers who took the floor all attacked the government decision. No one, neither Rabin nor Allon, came to Eshkol's rescue. Generals Gavish, Ze'evi, Yaffe, Tal, Matti Peled, Narkis and Elazar did not question the government's authority, but emphasized that the problem was not the Straits but the existential threat to Israel. They spoke of the loss of deterrent capability, of the critical significance of inflicting the first blow, of the inability to maintain a mobilized reserve army in the long term, and insisted that the IDF would prevail only if permitted to take action in good time. Their remarks reflected the affront and frustration of the army, prevented from carrying out its supreme task due to the vain hope that others would do the job for them and save the country.

The bluntest of all was Ariel Sharon: 'Today we have sawed away the IDF's deterrent power with our own hands', he said. The IDF was capable of destroying the Egyptian army, but in the future this would extract a much more costly price, and to concede now would open up the prospect of Israel's demise. The people were ready to fight a just war, and the government decision had disheartened them. This decision, he cautioned, could also lead to a renewal of fidaiyun terror attacks. Sharon denounced the diplomatic efforts to open up the Straits by means of an international force. The damage to Israel from the Sinai Campaign, he argued, had stemmed from collaboration with France and Britain. Pleadings for help (he used the Hebrew word 'shtadlanut' which has negative connotations originating in the Diaspora Jewish communities' pleas to the authorities) were mere demonstrations of weakness, and the government's decision not to send the IDF into action was a manifestation of impotence, presenting Israel as an empty vessel, as a powerless country which had never before suffered such degradation.

Eshkol was infuriated by this criticism and his response was sharp, reflecting the chasm between the views of the military and the civilian echelons.

Eshkol attacked the impatience of the senior command. 'We need a long breath. Nobody ever said we are a preventive army.' On the contrary, he stressed, the concept of preventive war was unacceptable to the government. The fact was that the Sinai Campaign – a preventive war – had left Israel with empty hands, apart from the passage through the Straits, as the result of international pressure. Eshkol even hinted that, so far as he was concerned, the Straits issue was not critical.[13] Particularly significant was Eshkol's reply to the claim of the generals that Israel had forfeited deterrent capability. He retorted that the generals had received everything they demanded in order to build up deterrent power, with the central objective of preventing war. He was implying that the IDF – and not the government – had failed to actualize its deterrent power, and in any event the test of deterrence now was to allow the government room for manoeuvre, and not automatically to initiate hostilities.

> 'You need more weapons? OK. You wanted 100 aircraft? You got them. You wanted tanks. You got them so that we can win if it becomes necessary. You didn't get all that so that we could get up one day and say: "Now we can destroy the Egyptian army – and we'll do it".... I never imagined that if there was a large Egyptian army close to our border, we would get up at night [immediately] and destroy it.... Deterrence doesn't mean that one has to act.... I believe that deterrent force should be capable of waiting and enabling exploration of all other possibilities.... This may irritate the generals, who have been trained all their lives for attack, for war, but we [the government] talked of deterrence [to prevent war].... Are we to live on our swords all our lives?'

The Prime Minister's military secretary, who was present, described the atmosphere as fraught with tension, almost intolerably so. The tone of the generals' statements reflected not only criticism but also mistrust and even contempt for the government. The situation was on the verge of explosion. At this stage, Yigal Allon intervened and proposed that the meeting be suspended. Rabin, tactlessly, immediately requested a meeting with the Prime Minister 'to take decisions'. Eshkol refused angrily.[14]

The General Staff discusses the military significance of waiting

When Eshkol and Allon left the meeting, the General Staff members were left to discuss the military significance of waiting. The first problem was the morale of the army. 'What do we say to the troops?' asked Rabin.

'The decision [of the civilian echelon] is [the conclusive] decision, but what will keep the country going or bring about its downfall is the IDF. Our problem – how to maintain the IDF [in a high state of readiness and morale].... The present situation is a crisis [of morale] much greater than the withdrawal from Sinai [in 1957].... If there is any prospect for this army it is in maintaining its morale.'

The fear, therefore, was that morale in the army might slacken while the danger of a surprise Arab attack remained. General Yisrael Tal suggested that any release of reserve troops should be postponed. 'We need to say [to the soldiers] that the danger has not passed. For political reasons we were not allowed to act at this stage, but the situation has not changed.' The Chief of Staff adopted General Tal's view and ordered that the brigade commanders be convened the next day and briefed accordingly.[15]

As a result of the government's decision to wait, the Prime Minister had approved the immediate demobilization of 30,000 reserve soldiers, but their release was delayed and mobilization continued. In view of the crisis of confidence between the General Staff and the government, the Prime Minister's office regarded this as a serious contravention by the military of the orders of the political echelon.[16] However, Rabin's discussion with the generals after the meeting with Eshkol, which focused on the negative impact on morale of a waiting period, revealed that the delay in releasing reserve units was not a rebellious move but one due to fears that such a step would weaken the armed forces. The senior command invested considerable effort in the maintenance of morale and readiness.[17] The demobilization was implemented subsequently in stages, and by the time war broke out some 50,000 reservists had been demobilized, the great majority of them older veterans.[18] In retrospect, it transpired that their demobilization helped to promote the element of surprise when hostilities were eventually launched.

The day after the government decision and the stormy meeting with the Prime Minister, the General Staff held a lengthy discussion on the military implications of waiting. As usual, the Chief of Intelligence began with a briefing on the enemy's deployment. He explained that, if the IDF waited for two to three weeks, the Egyptian deployment in Sinai would be consolidated, reinforced and strengthened. The Egyptian hold on Sharm al-Sheikh would improve and large consignments of weapons would flood in from the Soviet Union and be absorbed rapidly. Yariv particularly feared additional aircraft purchases, the improvement of the absorption capacity of the Egyptian air force and the supply of sophisticated electronic equipment to the Egyptian army. The longer the crisis, said Yariv, the more intense the wave of extreme nationalist emotion sweeping the Arab states and the greater the danger to Hussein's regime in Jordan.

According to top-secret information, Hussein had informed Nasser that day that he was ready to establish a 'national government' and had proposed a meeting between them. Nasser had agreed to a meeting on several conditions, including the non-entry of Saudi troops into Jordan. Yariv surmised that the Egyptians were liable 'to initiate large-scale action, even if not within two or three weeks', and to precede it with terrorist activity. Egyptian action, he estimated, would begin with an attack on Dimona and on Israel's airfields. Yariv described the Egyptian forces in northern Sinai as in a state of 'total chaos' due to frequent changes of objective, but this situation would end, he argued, if the Egyptians had time to organize.

The Egyptians assumed, Yariv said, that the IDF would attack along the northern and southern axis, and hence had reinforced their units on both of these axes. The Egyptian deployment did not permit an immediate shift to attack mode, apart from limited missions such as the occupation of Eilat, but the introduction of additional units into Sinai and evacuation of additional forces from Yemen would change this situation. Yariv added that a training course for operators of tactical Soviet-made Frog surface-to-surface missiles was due to end and expressed the fear that the Egyptians would dispatch missiles for exhibition purposes and psychological effect. He also feared that the Egyptians might employ poison gas. He concluded: 'As regards the military and political picture of the enemy, it is clear that postponement of action will make things very difficult for us.' In response to the question of how soon the Egyptians could switch over to attack, Yariv said: forty-eight hours.

The Chief of Staff wanted to sharpen his remarks so that they would be understood by the political echelon, and to clarify the grave implications of waiting for another two to three weeks, since the delay was liable to reinforce the Egyptian deployment in Sinai and lessen the IDF's ability to confront it. He had already admitted to the government, he said, that 'we cannot open the Straits of Tiran ... but we can perhaps deliver a blow'.

The discussion reflected the profound frustration of the military in view of what appeared to them to be lack of comprehension on the part of the political echelon which was missing the opportunity to deliver a resounding blow to the Egyptians. The generals expressed various views on what might be expected to happen in the interval, but all of them predicted that severe restraints would be imposed on Israel, obliging it to make do with a partial gain such as occupation of the Gaza Strip.

Hod feared that an aerial attack would be more difficult to carry out in two or three weeks' time, but his greatest fear was provocation and an initiated attack on the part of the Egyptian air force. Elazar said that he had told the Prime Minister 'that the day will come when, if we attack, it will be a question of a pyrrhic victory'. He thought that the army 'unlike the Government, should think ahead'. The conduct of the United States was also a cause for concern. The Commander of the IAF feared that the Sixth Fleet might be withdrawn while Rabin feared that the United States might impose an embargo on Israel. In view of the possibility that the regime in Jordan might collapse, Ze'evi and Horev proposed conquering the West Bank and preparing for defence against an Egyptian attack.

Yariv commented: 'It's good that the politicians aren't here, because the problem is what impression they gain – and they don't always understand.' Rabin backed him: 'The economic ministers didn't understand the implication of keeping an army mobilized [in the long term] and they voted against action.' And Yariv added:

> 'What we need to present [to the government] is that the army thinks that we need to attack now. The two weeks will cast a heavy question mark on [our status and on] our prospects for the future [to survive in this region] not only with regard to the Arabs, but also the Turks, the Persians, the Africans and the West.'

Ezer Weizman was the bluntest of all. He argued that the General Staff should force the government to act. 'We need to attack and we need to discuss in a smaller forum how to guarantee that we will attack within a week ... at that forum we need to find a solution as to how to bring the Government to a decision.' Weizman's prediction was accurate. Exactly a week later the IDF went to war.

The waiting period: the Intelligence appraisal

In the wake of the government's decision, it was decided that the Intelligence Branch would draw up a document analysing the grave implications of the decision to wait another 'two or three weeks'. This unsparing document attributed weighty responsibility to the political echelon. Its preparation, by order of the Chief of Staff and the Chief of Intelligence,[19] was intended to exert pressure on the government to alter its decision, but since it was an internal document – in which the professional military echelon made recommendations to the decision-making politicians – this was a legitimate move. If these were in fact the views of the senior command, and there is no evidence to the contrary, it was their professional duty to point out to the government the possible grave consequences of its decision.[20]

The gist of the document is that, when it came to a direct clash with Arab armies, Israel had nothing to gain from 'freezing' the situation. On the contrary, drastic changes could be anticipated in the coming few weeks in the military deployment of the enemy and the general political situation, and this would be to Israel's detriment. The main points were as follows:

1   In the coming few weeks, the Egyptian deployment in Sinai and Sharm al-Sheikh would soon be organized, reinforced, equipped and consolidated through entrenchment, mining and fortification. Additional

forces would be transferred from Yemen, additional divisions would be built up and new equipment would be absorbed. A highly effective organization of the Egyptian air force and rapid supply of new aircraft and electronic systems would increase its offensive and absorptive capacity, and every passing day would weaken the prospects of the IDF to achieve supremacy in the air. Strengthening the Egyptian maritime deployment in the Suez Canal and at Sharm al-Sheikh could also be expected.

2   The more protracted the crisis, the greater the damage to Israel's prestige, its deterrent capacity would wane, and the regional standing of the West, particularly the United States, would be undermined. A wave of nationalist fervour was sweeping the Arab masses, and Hussein's regime in particular was in danger. In light of the evolving inter-Arab situation, the United States might find itself totally isolated in the arena alongside Israel, and this would sap its readiness to act independently and forcefully in order to lift the blockade or to hasten to Israel's aid in the event of a military clash.

3   In the course of two or three weeks, it was unlikely that Egypt would initiate terrorist activity from the Gaza Strip, but in the longer term this policy could change. On the other hand, the stepping-up of sporadic terror on the part of Palestinian organizations could be anticipated, due to the popular mood and the decreased readiness of the Jordanian and Lebanese authorities to curb it. Syria was liable to continue its basic path of 'popular struggle' and to seek to involve Egypt by means of terrorist activity directed against Israel.

4   The possibility of movement by Iraqi ground and aerial forces into Jordan and Syria, and Jordanian military intervention on Egypt's side, was becoming increasingly likely.

5   'Egypt's finest hour' and a wave of uninterrupted gains could persuade its leaders to 'exploit the success' and launch additional action, such as promoting serious fidayeen activity or inflicting a blow on the Dimona reactor and Israel's airfields.

The document detailed the Egyptian ground deployment vis-à-vis the IDF's possible modes of operation and the additional forces and military equipment which were expected to flood into Sinai. Special emphasis was placed on the operational readiness of the Egyptian air force, its modernized equipment, intensive training, successful photo reconnaissance flights and anticipated reinforcement. 'In practice, there are more than 20 indicators of the readiness of the Egyptian air force for attack', the document noted, and it was also stressed that a tactical early warning would not be easily achieved in the event of an initiative on the part of the Egyptian air force.

A detailed clause in the document was devoted to the highly sensitive situation in Jordan, and cast considerable doubt on the ability of the regime there to survive. The document also listed the possible paths of action for the Syrian and Iraqi armies, and noted the possibility of employment of non-conventional weapons by Egypt: chemical weapons (gas) and even 'primitive radio-active weapons', all this to be accompanied by developed psychological warfare methods.[21]

Thus the IDF senior command greeted the government decision to wait with deep frustration, anger and affront. The universal feeling among the generals was that the government was placing the very existence of the state at risk and the ability of the IDF to win the inevitable war. The Intelligence evaluation was intended to detail the dangers and to bring home to the government the gravity of the responsibility it was undertaking when it rejected the General Staff's proposal to launch a pre-emptive strike. These feelings and evaluations indubitably seeped from the senior military command to the political establishment, because Israel's military and political elites had never been detached from one another. Eshkol was not yet aware of the fact, but he was about to lose the basis of his political power and his grasp on the defence portfolio.

Chapter 20

Establishment of a national unity government

The military aspect

Having decided to wait three weeks to test the international efforts under US leadership to open the Straits, the government might have been expected to be exempt for the time being from the army's unremitting pressure to attack at once. Once a decision was taken, the army was obliged to obey it, albeit unwillingly. However, the pressure did not ease, and the government, and in particular the Prime Minister, were not accorded a single moment of grace. They were flung together with the entire political establishment into a vortex of growing public demands for a government of national emergency. The government's decision, the veil of secrecy over its considerations and Eshkol's faltering speech to the nation, robbed it of its remaining credit. The demand focused on the replacement of the Minister of Defence, and the remainder was of secondary importance. The idea of establishing an emergency government began to take shape on 22 May, and gathered momentum as the crisis deepened, and Eshkol and his ministers appeared increasingly baffled and helpless. The political leadership tried for ten days to manoeuvre between various possibilities: bringing in the opposition, establishing an advisory security team for the Prime Minister, exchanging portfolios among ministers, reinforcing the government, and finally even entrusting the defence portfolio to Yigal Allon. It was all to no avail. The pressure was coming from below, from the street, from the ranks of the army, and it focused on one charismatic personality: the man with the eye-patch, the hero of the Sinai Campaign – Major General Moshe Dayan. Four days after the decision was taken to wait, and after every effort and manoeuvre to avoid it had failed, Eshkol bowed to the inevitable.[1]

On 1 June at 16:15 he summoned Moshe Dayan and offered him the defence portfolio. The national unity government was established on the same day. Moshe Dayan of the Rafi Party became Minister of Defence. Menahem Begin, the Gahal (Herut) leader, and Yosef Sapir of the Liberal Party, were appointed ministers and members of the Ministerial Committee on Security. The appointment of Dayan was greeted with great enthusiasm by the public and the army. Four days later Israel went to war.

We are not concerned here with the political crisis which generated the national unity government,[2] but rather with the influence and involvement of the army, if such there was, in the political crisis which led to Dayan's appointment.

Moshe Haim Shapira attempts to restrain the army

The strangest phenomenon in the process of establishment of a national unity government and the appointment of Dayan was the fact that its strongest advocate, National Religious Party leader Moshe Haim Shapira, the Minister of the Interior, was the most consistent and vehement opponent of the IDF's activist tendencies. The drafting of 'hawks' into the government appeared to be blatantly inconsistent with Shapira's efforts, as one of the chief 'doves' in the government (others were his fellow party member Zerah Wahrhaftig, Mapai ministers Zalman Aranne, Abba Eban and Pinhas Sapir and Mapam and Independent-Liberal ministers) to curb the army and prevent war. Shapira himself provided the answer to the riddle, in response to a direct question from Eshkol.[3] Only an activist public figure, he trusted, could tell the public the unpopular truth, namely that it was impossible to go to war under prevailing conditions and it was essential to find a political solution and guarantee international and Superpower backing. The figure Shapira was thinking of was David Ben-Gurion, who had already voiced his emphatic views to that effect. If it was not possible to bring him in, then his loyal protégé and member of his party Moshe Dayan could replace him.[4] Shapira apparently thought that Dayan would accept Ben-Gurion's authority, and may have been impressed by Dayan's trenchant criticism of the IAF operation of 7 April and his acceptance of the government's decision to wait.[5]

Shapira even asked former Chief of Staff Haim Laskov, who came to see him on 28 May, to recommend the establishment of an emergency government with Ben-Gurion and Dayan, if Dayan did not tend to be hasty in his decision-making and what Dayan's stand was on diplomatic moves. Laskov assured him that, first and foremost, Dayan supported diplomatic efforts.[6] However, Dayan was not necessarily Shapira's ideal choice. He wanted to bring the Rafi Party into the government as a counterbalance to the strong support of Ahdut ha-Avoda (especially Allon and Carmel) for the activist trends of the IDF senior command. He was ready to accept any arrangement which would expand the government and achieve that goal.

Shapira did not want Eshkol as Minister of Defence for the simple reason that he did not trust him on military matters. Eshkol was neither a 'dove' nor a 'hawk' but, to Shapira's mind, he had leaned towards the army too often and had entangled Israel in a risky situation. What was needed, therefore, was an authoritative security figure who could restrain the army, and the only candidates were Ben-Gurion or Dayan. Shapira did not consider Allon to be a suitable candidate, not necessarily because he lacked the public aura of the other two, but because Allon totally identified with the stance of the General Staff. 'Allon is too extreme', Shapira claimed in explaining his strong objections to Allon's appointment as Minister of Defence.[7]

Hence, on 31 May and 1 June, when the proposal to appoint Allon was on the agenda, Shapira cast a veto. He informed Eshkol that if the portfolio was not entrusted to Dayan, the National Religious Party would leave the government. This was no idle ultimatum. Eshkol's coalition rested on the support of seventy-two of the 120 Knesset members, and the departure of the eleven NRP members would have almost certainly led to the coalition's collapse and the government's fall, particularly since within Mapai itself there was increased support for a response to the public demand for Dayan's appointment. All Eshkol's attempts to persuade Shapira, emphatically ('strongly advise ... it's impossible to accept dictates on your part all along the line') and imploringly ('respected Moshe Shapira, help me. I am the one who has been injured ... help me, we can go forward together') were unsuccessful. Shapira was impervious to Eshkol's reproaches and pleas.[8]

As for Menahem Begin, who had always been regarded as an extremist 'hawk', his participation in the government would not necessarily alter the balance, according to Shapira. First, Begin was not earmarked for a position in the leading political and security team, apart from membership of the expanded Ministerial Committee on Security. Second, the Begin of May 1967, leader of Gahal, was poles apart from the Herut leader of the 1950s. Throughout the crisis Begin maintained a low profile, issued no militant declarations, and even tried to secure the appointment of his great rival David Ben-Gurion, opponent of war, as Prime Minister or Minister of Defence.[9] In any event, the most critical front was the Egyptian front, where even the Herut movement had no significant territorial aspirations.[10] Nonetheless, Shapira should have anticipated that if not Dayan then certainly Begin would sympathize with the military's viewpoint after joining the government.[11]

Was it the IDF's senior command, as some argue, which plotted to strip Eshkol of his position as Minister of Defence and bring in Dayan?[12] No proof could be found of such a plot, and the composition of the General Staff (most of whose members were Palmach veterans) suggests that, if asked, their probable choice would have been Yigal Allon – not Dayan.[13]

The only direct evidence of recommendation of Dayan by a general on active service was that of OC Central Command Uzi Narkis, on a personal basis. Narkis had been closely associated with Dayan when he served as Head of the Operations Department, and Chief of Staff Dayan tended to sidestep his deputy Haim Laskov and the Chief of Operations Yosef Avidar to work directly with Narkis.[14] On the morning of 1 June, Dayan visited him at Central Command. Shortly afterwards Narkis was asked in a telephone conversation with the Mapai Central Office (perhaps by his father-in-law, Knesset member David Hacohen) whether to prefer Allon or Dayan. He recommended Dayan, arguing that 'the problem today is to check the wave of extreme nationalism, the Arab self-confidence, and only one man can do that. Nobody knows Yigal Allon. So – it's Dayan. Vote Dayan!!!'[15]

To conclude that the military meddled improperly in politics for Dayan's sake[16] would be an overstatement. In general one can say that the army chiefs were concerned not with personalities but with issues. They wanted to overturn the government's decision to wait, and they succeeded in doing so.

Ben-Gurion fears a military coup

The crisis of confidence between the military and the political echelon influenced Ben-Gurion's standpoint and he cited it as the reason for his change of opinion and eventual agreement to the appointment of Dayan as Minister of Defence in Eshkol's government. Ben-Gurion, whose relations with his successor had been clouded since 1964, was uncompromising in his total invalidation of Eshkol, and the emergency situation intensified his savage criticism rather than moderating it. 'It would be disastrous and impossible for the Government of Israel to be headed by a liar', the 'old man' declared. 'We must rid ourselves of this man who is a political and military danger. . . . It will be an unparalleled sin against the nation if we do not continue to urge for the removal of this prime minister. . . . If we do not remove this disgrace which is hanging over the country.'[17] This categorical approach negated any possibility of inviting Ben-Gurion to join a unity government, whether as Prime Minister or Minister of Defence, and left the road open for Dayan. The 'old man' remained adamant till the very last moment in his demand for the removal of Eshkol as a condition for Rafi's joining the government, but when he realized that the majority of his faction were in favour of Dayan's appointment, he changed his mind and explained that it was necessary to instil in the army confidence in the civilian leadership.[18]

It seems, nonetheless, that Ben-Gurion was sincerely and deeply disturbed at what appeared to him to be the danger of a military coup. The day after the generals met with Eshkol in the Pit, Ben-Gurion told the former head of the Mossad, Isser Harel: 'There is some talk of [a military coup] . . . that would be the final disaster. That's all we need. It's a kind of mood in the army, and it worries me. I am very anxious.'[19] Later that day Ben-Gurion convened a press conference in the Knesset and read out a statement without answering questions. He said: 'To our gratification we have an army we can trust ... but two things of fateful significance should be remembered:

1   The army in a democratic state does not act on its own initiative or that of its military commanders, but with the knowledge of the civilian government and according to its instructions....
2   War is not conducted solely through military activity. A defensive war – and Israel will not become involved in any campaign which is not defensive – is not conducted merely by military force, particularly in the case of a small nation like Israel. It also requires diplomatic activity.'[20]

In practice, Ben-Gurion was supporting the decision of the Eshkol government to opt for diplomacy, despite his sweeping and indiscriminate criticism of Eshkol. But more than this, the venerable leader was defending Israeli democracy against the danger of a military take-over or unauthorized action by the army. Two days later, in the Rafi faction, Ben-Gurion again voiced his profound concern at the developments he anticipated within the IDF. On the basis of information he had received on the generals' meeting with Eshkol on 28 May, he predicted grave events in reaction to the omissions of the political leadership. Ben-Gurion said that if his forecast proved correct, the result would be 'a stain on the State of Israel from which it will never cleanse itself'. It was his opinion that there was only one way of saving the situation and that was the appointment of Dayan as Prime Minister.[21]

On the evening of 1 June, the Rafi Knesset members met in Ben-Gurion's home and discussed the question of joining the coalition and Dayan's appointment as Minister of Defence representing Rafi in the expanded government, as Eshkol proposed.[22] Ben-Gurion announced that he had considered the question and now supported Dayan's appointment. He continued to demand that Eshkol be deposed from the premiership, but it was clear that this was a hopeless demand, and that the die had been cast. Ben-Gurion explained that his change of attitude stemmed from anxiety in view of the prevailing mood in the IDF. 'Who knows what will happen and what will occur within the army. We need an army with trust [in the leadership] and that is what it will be when Moshe is minister of defence.'[23]

Allon's hour

The final and decisive stage of the hectic debates within the political establishment concerning the establishment of an emergency government raged in the forty-eight-hour period between Tuesday (30 May) and the afternoon of Thursday (1 June). It began with a meeting of the Mapai-Achdut ha-Avoda Alignment faction in the Knesset, where Eshkol realized that a 'coup' was being conducted against him by his most loyal colleagues, as the majority of the faction supported Dayan's appointment. Eshkol still emphatically refused to relinquish the portfolio.[24] The next day, 31 May, the leaders of the Alignment discussed the issue at length and sought a solution. Eshkol stuck to his guns and insisted on the appointment of four security advisers (Allon, together with former Chiefs-of-Staff Dayan, Yigael Yadin and Laskov). He tried to persuade his colleagues that 'if we let Dayan in we are opening the gates ... to Rafi, who will claim that they saved the country with the force we prepared'. The Mapai Secretary-General, Golda Meir, was even blunter. 'We are not going to be the first party which hands over rule to fascism without a fight', she said. But now Eshkol understood that even his senior ministers thought that he should yield the defence portfolio. Most of them supported the appointment of Yigal Allon to the post. Eshkol himself gave them the pretext when he said: 'It would be more convenient and desirable for me to work with Allon than with Dayan.' He was referring explicitly to the idea of making Allon privy to security matters rather than to handing over the portfolio to him. However, Zalman Aranne seized on the statement and proposed that Allon be appointed 'full minister of defence'. Aranne explained that 'we need a minister of defence who is a professional'. He argued the need for 'recovery from the psychological state of the nation' (i.e. the lack of confidence in Eshkol as Minister of Defence), but referred also to Rabin's difficulties:

> 'For the Chief of Staff as well, this crisis seems to be too much. He also gave the strong impression that he has doubts as to whether we can endure it. When the situation is that our Chief of Staff, who should be made of steel, is not steel, and when our Minister of Defence is the Prime Minister and not a professional, I started thinking.'

Additional advocates of Allon's appointment were Shaul Avigur, Zeev Sherf, Yisrael Galili and Moshe Carmel. Only Knesset Speaker Kadish Luz supported Dayan and only in lukewarm fashion. Among the Alignment ministers and the Mapai leadershp there was a consensus that it was essential to bring in Dayan one way or another in view of the pressures of the political establishment and of public opinion. Yaakov Shimshon Shapira proposed appointing Dayan as Foreign Minister and Eban as Deputy Prime Minister. Eshkol, for his part, had an original suggestion: he proposed Allon as Deputy Prime Minister and Dayan as 'minister of the army', emphasizing that 'this has nothing to do with the Minister of Defence and the Ministry of Defence'. From here on a strange discussion ensued on the possibility Eshkol had cited, until Avigur stated decisively:

'There is no clarity in the Prime Minister's proposal.' The hierarchy, he said, was unclear, and, considering Dayan's personality, 'it will start being Hell. Who will give the orders?' It would be preferable for Dayan to be appointed Minister of Defence than 'minister of the army', Avigur declared.

In the end, Allon addressed Eshkol directly: 'If you offer me the Ministry of Defence – I will accept with responsibility and loyalty'. This was a hint that he would be more loyal than Dayan. Allon rejected the proposal that Eban be relieved of the Foreign Affairs portfolio. His view was that Dayan should be offered the deputy premiership and participate with the Prime Minister in all war efforts. He believed that Dayan would agree.[25]

After the meeting, Eshkol and Avigur met with Moshe Dayan and proposed that he join the government as Deputy Prime Minister. Dayan rejected the offer, saying that he was 'a man of action'. He was angered to learn from Eshkol that Allon was earmarked for Minister of Defence. He expressed the opinion that Yigal Allon was more suitable than he for an advisory position. Dayan also spurned the proposal that he become Foreign Minister and said that he preferred to be 'commander of the southern arena'. In any case, he added, even 'if you make me minister of defence I want you to know that I will leave Tel Aviv and go down to the Negev and pass the war there'. Dayan recommended that his appointment to a position on active service should not be publicized, lest it be interpreted in Egypt as a challenge.[26]

Shaul Avigur proposed that Allon be appointed Minister of Defence immediately and that Dayan's proposal be accepted, and he be drafted 'for special tasks in the General Staff', the underlying intention being to appoint him eventually as commander of the southern front. Eshkol grumbled to his associates: if the Dayan matter was settled, what was the point of depriving him of the Defence portfolio? But this sounded like a faint protest. Eshkol was beginning to resign himself to the fact that he must give up the Defence portfolio. All that remained was to arrange the matter with the Chief of Staff.

Rabin offers Dayan the post of Chief of Staff

Although he had served under Allon in the Palmach, Yitzhak Rabin was not on close terms with his former commander. Nonetheless, Allon usually backed Rabin at government meetings, supporting the army's viewpoint. When Allon returned to Israel on 24 May he immediately plunged into the thick of events, updated himself on the Intelligence picture and the operational plans and held frequent meetings with Rabin, Barlev and Yariv. This being so, it is easy to suppose that Rabin preferred Allon as Minister of Defence over Dayan, with whom he had never had 'chemistry'.

When Eshkol summoned Rabin in the middle of a meeting with the Alignment ministers in order to sum up the details of Dayan's appointment as commander of the southern front, Rabin did not reject the idea out-right, although it was liable to come as a shock to the CO of Southern Command, Yeshayahu Gavish.[27] It is unlikely that Rabin was trying thereby to blaze the trail for Allon. It is more feasible to assume that Rabin, who was certainly aware of the political furore and the pressures brought to bear on Eshkol, did not dare to refuse the Prime Minister. There is no evidence to suggest that Rabin did not have full confidence in Gavish. Be that as it may, Rabin did not take a forceful stand in defence of the CO Southern Command. This was apparently one of the manifesta-tions of Rabin's weakness during the crisis.[28]

Rabin asked Eshkol to summon Dayan for a joint talk before he gave his answer. In the course of the conversation, to Eshkol's aggravation, Rabin asked Dayan again and again 'sincerely' if he wanted to become Chief of Staff in his stead. Dayan rejected this and stressed that he was interested only in the southern front, would act under the command of the Chief of Staff, and was willing for Gavish to be his deputy. After the meeting, Rabin said that if the government took the decision and he received the order, he would carry it out despite the unpleasantness involved with regard to Gavish. He expressed the hope that Gavish would agree to work alongside Dayan.[29]

The proposal to Dayan that he take over as Chief of Staff was the most striking manifestation of Rabin's condition. Whereas his offer to Weizman on 23/24 May that he take over as Chief of Staff was made at a time when he was exhausted and depressed, the proposal to Dayan was the outcome of sober calculation, merciless towards himself, but perhaps based on his sense of responsibility. Rabin knew that he was not at his best and that the burden resting on his shoulders was intolerable.[30] He was apparently ready 'to sacrifice' himself for the good of the cause, both because of his sense of guilt and because he was aware that in his condition he was not entirely qualified to command the army in wartime.

The end of the race: Dayan wins

Once the Chief of Staff had agreed, the picture appeared complete: Eshkol, Prime Minister; Allon, Minister of Defence; and Dayan, Commander of the southern front. Eshkol convened the government late that night in order to announce the decision, though with a heavy heart. But his trou-bles were not yet over. There was fierce opposition in the government to Eshkol's proposal, particularly on the part of the National Religious Party ministers, which developed into a sharp exchange of words between the ministers and in particular between Eshkol and Moshe Haim Shapira. The latter presented an ultimatum, his main argument being that so long as Eshkol was opposed on principle to separating the portfolios of Prime Minister and Minister of Defence, his standpoint made sense. But once

Eshkol had agreed to waive the Defence portfolio, Shapira argued, why had it not been offered to Dayan, thereby facilitating the establishment of a government of national unity?[31]

The next morning, 1 June, the Mapai Secretariat convened for a stormy marathon session where a bitter debate raged between the supporters of Allon and Dayan's champions, in which the latter won the day.[32] At noon, Eshkol and a team of coalition representatives met with the Gahal leaders, who – having meanwhile coordinated their moves with the Rafi leaders – declared that they would only join the government if Dayan served as Minister of Defence.[33] Now the Independent Liberals as well added their voices to the demand for Dayan's appointment.[34] Street demonstrations and petitions also made an impact.[35] An additional difficulty arose from the direction of the army. Rabin summoned Gavish in the morning and informed him of the intention to appoint Dayan over him. Gavish responded on the spot that he was not ready to serve as deputy to Dayan and would immediately resign from his post. The rumour of the new 'arrangement', which meant the deposing of the CO Southern Command, spread like wildfire through the army and evoked angry responses. Rabin told Eshkol that he was finding it difficult to make the changes.[36] Eshkol, realizing that he had no room left for manoeuvre, felt it necessary to consult the Mapam leader Yaakov Hazan, who assured him that his faction would back him even if he decided to entrust the portfolio to Moshe Dayan.[37] Eshkol decided to summon Dayan and ask him to join the government as Minister of Defence.

Weizman's outburst

While Dayan was on his way to Eshkol's office, the Chief of Operations, Ezer Weizman, burst into the office in a state of great emotion. The description provided by Eshkol's military secretary Yisrael Lior, who was an eyewitness, may seem melodramatic, but there is no reason to doubt its reliability. The very fact that Weizman burst in without scheduling a meeting or coordinating it with the Chief of Staff was an extraordinary move.

Weizman already knew that Barlev had been promoted over his head to the post of deputy Chief of Staff and would be the next Chief of Staff. He felt deeply injured. Only a week previously, when Rabin collapsed and he had taken over for him, Weizman had appeared to be within arms' length of the position. He was now, as he himself said, 'in the mood of a beaten cur'.[38] His outburst was undoubtedly an expression of his personal distress, but more than that it reflected the cumulative pressure within the General Staff directed at the political echelon, at a time when the military threat was increasing. The impulsive Weizman could no longer bottle up his emotions, and in any event had nothing to lose.

Lior relates that Weizman broke into the office of the Prime Minister, who was lunching at the time with the Minister of Justice Yaakov Shimshon Shapira. Weizman burst into tears. 'The country is being destroyed. Everything is destroyed', Weizman roared into the astonished faces of Eshkol and Shapira. He shouted: 'Eshkol, give the order and the IDF will go to war! Why do you need Moshe Dayan? Who needs Yigal Allon? We've got a strong army and it's only waiting for your order. Give us the order and we will win. We will win and you will be the Prime Minister of the victory government.' At that moment, Shapira also burst into tears, and Weizman, still agitated, left the room and tried to tear his brigadier general's insignia off his shoulder. The emotion in the office was high. This dramatic episode marked the very peak of the crisis.[39]

The establishment of the national unity government

Once Eshkol had decided to offer the Defence portfolio to Moshe Dayan, events proceeded at a dizzy pace. Within a few hours the government of national unity had been established and met the same evening for its first session.

At first, Eshkol conferred with Dayan and invited him to join the government as Minister of Defence. Dayan agreed, but asked Eshkol if he was being invited on an individual basis or as a member of Rafi. Eshkol replied that he was being invited as a representative of Rafi,[40] but if Rafi refused to join the government he would invite Dayan personally.[41] The Rafi faction met in Ben-Gurion's home, and in the course of the meeting the 'old man', as noted above, changed his mind and agreed to Dayan's participation in the government. Dayan paid lip-service to the venerable leader, and declared that he would act under Ben-Gurion's close guidance.[42] The Gahal leadership met concurrently to decide who to send to the government of unity.[43] Eshkol summoned the members of the political committee and the Alignment ministers, who already knew that they were facing a fait accompli.[44] As the meeting began, Allon announced that he was withdrawing his candidacy and Eshkol thanked him warmly.[45]

The government convened at 21:30 and began the meeting by discussing the planned expansion of the government.[46] Dayan and Begin joined them after half an hour. Eshkol opened the first session of the expanded government in ceremonious fashion. 'We will call it the Government of national cohesion', he said.[47]

First discussion of the military situation

Finally, after four days of political upheaval during which the government and Ministerial Committee on Security had no respite to discuss the military situation, Eshkol proposed that the government convene next morning in the supreme command post.[48] The Chief of Staff and the Chief of Intelligence attended this first meeting of the new government. Rabin described the deployment of the Egyptian army in Sinai and noted that, for the time being, it was defensive. The Syrian army had moved two additional brigades forward to the Golan Heights and steered its armoured 'shock force' in the direction of the Jordan Valley. The Jordanian army, Rabin said, was still in its usual deployment, but an Iraqi divisional force had begun to concentrate in the border area and was liable to enter Jordan within five to ten days. 'The question now arises: What is the significance of the entry of foreign forces into Jordan?, he asked, implying that a pre-emptive move should be considered.[49]

The Chief of Staff went on to give details about the deployment of Israel's mobilized forces. He emphasized the time element, in particular where the IAF was concerned, and explained that the key to ground action was the achievement of supremacy in the air. The IAF enjoyed a qualitative advantage at the present time, he said, despite its quantitative inferiority. However, the Egyptian air force was engaged intensively in preparations for absorption of new planes and in offensive organization and planning. 'I think that in the past one or two weeks the Egyptian air force has trained for offensive action more than in the entire past year', he noted. Rabin wanted to emphasize the central point in the army's demand for a pre-emptive strike: real concern lest the Egyptians make the first move and attack from the air, leaving the IDF with poor opening conditions. Eshkol reinforced Rabin's statement about the importance of the time element by adding that the morale of the troops would be damaged if they were mobilized for a lengthy period and remained idle. The enemy, he explained, was exploiting the time in order to consolidate and reinforce its deployment in a manner which would greatly hamper an IDF attack.

Moshe Dayan, speaking for the first time as a member of the government, analysed the situation, ostensibly without taking a stand. He explained that the Egyptians had blocked the Straits by offensive action and were deployed for defence with large forces in order to anticipate any Israeli attack. Now the Israeli government must decide how to deal with the situation: 'Whether or not we need to swallow the Straits affair without going into battle.' This was a political question and the army should not voice an opinion on the matter, Dayan emphasized. He was thereby putting the army in its place and preventing it from pressuring the government. What the army should do was to bring before the political echelon its evaluation of the balance of forces, military data and considerations of space and time. On these matters, Dayan said, a separate discussion should be held at the earliest possible opportunity.

However, Dayan was also indicating clearly what his stand would be. He explained that if the government did not intend to decide on attack, half of the reserve force should be released and the remainder should dig in and be prepared in defensive positions. On the other hand, 'if there is any thought that we want to attack', every day that passed made a great difference and rendered the assignment increasingly difficult, because the more the enemy improved its deployment, the more difficult it would be for the IDF to break them. 'And I think that we are arriving at a fantastically absurd situation because we are not setting ourselves an objective', he asserted.

The Foreign Minister, surveying the political situation, also refrained from adopting a stand. He spoke of 'two clocks' with no coordination between them: the diplomatic clock ticking in Washington, which in the next two weeks could lead to international action for opening up the Straits, and the local military clock moving forward at a faster pace. Dayan, in a question, emphasized the pointlessness of diplomatic effort focused on the Straits. What did the Israeli government expect the United States to do about the 1,000 tanks and 80,000 Egyptian soldiers entrenched in Sinai? he asked. Eban replied that the Americans were convinced that Israel was capable of defending itself and winning.

The Prime Minister described the dilemma of the government, which had decided only four days before to allow three weeks for exhausting the international options and had informed the powers of this decision. 'How can we extricate ourselves [from the trap] so that they will not complain to us that we promised to wait?!'

Due to the lateness of the hour, Eshkol decided to close the meeting and convene the expanded Ministerial Committee on Security the following morning in the supreme command post.[50]

Chapter 21

The strategic turning point
The Egypt–Jordan defence pact

On 30 May a dramatic development occurred which expedited the political and military timetable and very soon overturned the government decision of 28 May to await the outcome of the diplomatic efforts. King Hussein succumbed to intense internal pressure and 'went to Canossa' to his sworn adversary, the Egyptian President.

He flew his own royal plane from Amman to Cairo, accepted all the conditions stipulated by Nasser, and the two leaders signed a bilateral defence pact identical in content to the Egyptian–Syrian pact. The agreement placed the Jordanian army under Egyptian command and Hussein was forced to agree to the entry of Egyptian and Iraqi forces into Jordan and to reconciliation with his bitterest enemy in the inter-Arab arena, PLO Chairman Ahmed Shukeiri.[1] This exceptional development further validated the standpoint of the military and civilian opponents of the government's approach. It heightened the level of anxiety of the Israeli public and the feeling that the noose was tightening. Within two days, as mentioned above, Eshkol was obliged to hand over the Defence portfolio to Moshe Dayan.

The risk that Jordan would intervene in the event of war had always been taken into consideration. However, the deep rift between Jordan and Egypt and Jordan's Western orientation gave Israel reason to hope that Hussein would remain aloof from the hostilities. At most, he would be content with a few 'gun salutes' as a gesture of solidarity. The Jordanian–Egyptian agreement made it clear that the Jordanian arena would be active in the event of a flare-up. The placing of the Jordanian army under Egyptian command and the anticipated movement of Iraqi troops into Jordan created an ominous potential strategic threat to Israel, whose 'green line' border was extremely vulnerable and left it no choice but to launch a pre-emptive counter-attack.[2]

Thus it appears that it was on 30 May, and not before, that Israel faced up to its lack of an alternative. The influx of Egyptian forces into Sinai had generated the crisis and impelled Israel to mobilize its reserve forces, bringing the national economy to a virtual standstill which could not be sustained for long; the blocking of the Straits was less an act of military and economic significance than a challenge to Israel's deterrent capability, a proclaimed *casus belli*; fear of an initiated Egyptian air attack on the reactor and airfields prompted the military to exert pressure on the government to give the go-ahead to a pre-emptive attack. None of these developments, however, sufficed to force the government to yield to pressure. The Nasser–Hussein pact turned the tables on the government. The nightmare scenario of massed Iraqi, Egyptian and Jordanian forces on the West Bank, facing Israel's 'soft belly' – its dense population concentrations and infrastructure – was intolerable. It was the combination of all of these factors which finally spurred Israel to take action, but the Jordanian–Egyptian defence pact of 30 May was the final straw. It could even be claimed, with a slight degree of exaggeration, that it was Hussein's initiative which ignited the Six Day War.[3]

Hussein's surprise move, which altered the strategic equation, was almost certainly the consequence of Israel's decision to wait. Nasser's meteoric rise, Israel's bewildered and apprehensive appearance, the huge enthusiasm generated by the Nasserist challenge throughout the Arab world in general and among Hussein's Palestinian subjects in particular, the intoxicating anticipation of 'the liberation of Palestine' – all these compelled the King to seek some form of 'life insurance' for himself.[4] If Hussein had hoped secretly that Israel would make the first move and crush Nasser before the Hashemite regime tottered,[5] the Israeli government's decision of 28 May dispelled his illusions. He swallowed his pride in order to save his regime, and perhaps his life as well.

The Hussein–Nasser pact which, in practice, placed the Jordanian army under Egyptian command, the immediate dispatch of Egyptian commando battalions to Jordan and the imminent entry of Iraqi expeditionary forces into that country heightened the sense of emergency in Israel and instantly put an end to the phony lull in the wake of the government's decision. Not only Israel, but the United States as well, was influenced by the new circumstances. There were sudden indications from Washington that the administration was no longer so resolutely opposed to an Israeli military operation.[6] The US efforts to set up an international maritime 'task force' were proceeding at a snail's pace, and it was now evident that they would not keep step with the dizzying pace of events in the region. The Americans apparently realized that to bind Israel's hands would shift the heavy responsibility on to the United States. This might force the US – bogged down as it was in the Vietnamese morass – to become involved militarily in an additional region, with all that this implied in the international arena and for its relations with the Arab world.

For the time being, however, so long as no threatening forces were amassed on the Jordanian border, the Egyptian front remained the main priority for the General Staff, and this was still the situation when war broke out. Nonetheless, the Jordanian front now replaced the Syrian front as the second priority.[7]

The fact that despite the Egyptian–Jordanian pact, the IDF did not shift the centre of attention from the south to the east is highly significant in view of the theory that the General Staff was eager from the outset to complete the unfinished business of 1948 and to extend Israel's eastern border.[8] Both Chief of Staff Yitzhak Rabin, and Moshe Dayan, who was to be appointed Minister of Defence on 1 June, made it abundantly clear that the main campaign was to be waged against the Egyptian enemy, and all the rest was secondary.[9] On 5 June when the war began, the Israel government, with the approval of all its members (including Allon and Begin!), made a sincere effort to exclude Jordan from the hostilities.[10] It was, above all, Hussein's disregard for Israel's appeals (whether because he was misled at the beginning of the war into thinking that Egypt had the upper hand, because events veered out of his control, or because he believed – apparently with some justification – that he had no choice but to join in the fighting) which determined the long-term consequences of the Six Day War. Israeli action, in response to Jordanian fire, commenced with limited offensive moves in the Jerusalem and northern Samaria sectors in order to achieve local tactical objectives.[11] What ensued was the – unpremeditated – conquest of the entire West Bank. In the last few days before the war, the General Staff did begin to draw up an operative offensive plan for the Jordanian front, but it had not been completed when war broke out, and forces needed for the conquest of the West Bank had not in fact been shifted to this sector. The IDF continued to face southward.

Pargol (The Scourge) – planning the conquest of the West Bank

The first Intelligence reports on Hussein's overtures to Nasser roused the General Staff, whose efforts had been almost entirely focused up until now on the Egyptian front, to pay serious attention to the eastern front as well. After an inexplicable delay, the General Staff was 'reminded' that it was necessary to prepare a concrete operational plan for the grave contingency that this front would be not only active but perhaps even the main arena. The underlying assumption was that by the end of the three-week waiting period decided on by the government, the IDF would face a combined Jordanian–Egyptian–Iraqi army amassed along Israel's eastern border.

On the afternoon of 30 May, before the details of the Jordanian–Egyptian pact were even known, a preliminary meeting was held at the Operations Branch to discuss the situation on the Jordanian front. Lt. Col. Haim Nadel, who chaired the proceedings, opened:

'Due to the situation, Hussein may fall. Syrian and Iraqi forces are liable to enter Jordan. This being so, we must plan for the conquest of the West Bank. The precondition is supremacy in the air.... In the course of occupying the West Bank – it will be necessary to rein in on the other fronts.'[12]

This discussion is particularly interesting because for the first time since the crisis had begun a General Staff forum, though at relatively junior level, was discussing a plan to occupy the West Bank. The basic operative plan for conquering the West Bank was code-named *Pargol* (The Scourge). This discussion and those which ensued dealt therefore with revising the plan and deciding which force would carry it out. The planning was based on an aerial attack on the Arab air force bases in order to ensure supremacy in the air and on deployment for defence and interception on the Egyptian and Syrian fronts, during the conquest of the West Bank.

The underlying assumption of *Pargol* was, therefore, that the Jordanian front would become the central arena if and when foreign troops moved in. At this stage, the discussion was defined to planning 'on paper' without actually transferring forces from Southern Command to Central Command and without affecting the existing operative planning on the Egyptian and Syrian fronts.

The head of the Jordanian 'desk' in the Intelligence Branch, Zeev Bar-Lavi, estimated that 'in light of the situation, Hussein fears for his regime – which is why he has visited Nasser and accepted his conditions.... The conditions that Nasser stipulates will eventually topple Hussein's regime.' He surveyed in great detail the deployment of the Jordanian armed forces and its possible modes of action.[13] The head of the Operations Branch described the proposed order of battle which called for the shifting of large-scale forces including the regular Thirty-fifth Parachute Brigade and the regular Seventh Armoured Brigade from the other commands to Central Command. The composition of the forces stemmed from the view of the Jordanian arena as 'the main effort'. The participants went on to discuss the preferred breakthrough routes from the south, north and west for conquest of the West Bank.[14]

It is noteworthy that in addition to the *Pargol* contingency plan for occupation of the West Bank, there was also a 'mini-*Pargol*' plan aimed at breaching the entrenched Jordanian deployment in Jerusalem by employing infantry and armoured units and linking up to the Israeli enclave on Mount Scopus. Narkis revealed later that Ben-Gurion's instruction during the upheaval in Jordan in the spring of 1963 had been to reinforce Israel's standing in Jerusalem in case Hussein was overthrown, by linking up with Mount Scopus (and not the conquest of the West Bank). Narkis described in detail how various other plans had evolved from this basic objective, thereby expanding the 'mini-plan'. As for the Old City of Jerusalem, it was to be 'dealt with separately'. Narkis gained the impression that Ben-Gurion's intention was to avoid becoming entangled in the Old City.[15]

While preliminary plans were being formulated for the Jordanian front on 30 May, the IDF remained deployed for a lengthy wait. The Operations Branch issued orders for defensive deployment under the *Sadan* (Anvil) plan and for the release of part of the mobilized reserve force. One of the clauses in the order charged the Eighty-fourth Division, the regular division under the command of Southern Command, with the task of planning offensive deployment in the Jordanian sector, while coordinating between Southern and Central Commands. It should be emphasized that this order related to planning alone.[16]

The following day, 31 May, discussions of the Jordanian arena continued among the General Staff, with emphasis on Jerusalem. The gamut of opinions ranged from conquest of the entire West Bank to limited actions such as 'skirmishes' around Jerusalem, as part of the defensive efforts.[17] The Chief of Operations Ezer Weizman led the maximalist line. He expressed the hope that 'Out of the strong will come forth sweetness'. It was his view that 'war will come at any event, because otherwise the State of Israel will not survive'. The enemy was gaining strength with every passing day, but 'on the other hand, the fruits of victory and international sympathy will be greater and more profound'.[18] Rabin explained that if the Jordanian–Iraqi threat materialized on the eastern front, the IDF's operative targets would be occupation of the West Bank and the Gaza Strip and an attack on the Egyptian air force. However, at this stage he was opposed to directing the main thrust in the Jordanian arena. For purposes of action on the Jordanian front, he said, the Central and Northern Commands would have to make do with the forces allotted to them within the framework of the *Sadan* defensive plan, with the addition of an armoured brigade and airborne forces. Rabin summed up the situation: the main enemy was Egypt. The Eighty-fourth Division (the IDF's strongest armoured force) would not be redirected to the Jordanian front.[19]

On 1 June, the Operations Branch issued an order for the planning of Operation *Pargol* which defined the objectives as follows:

> The IDF will attack the West Bank within 36 hours of receipt of the order to act with the aim of precluding a Jordanian attack on Jerusalem or on the centre of the country, while at the same time carrying out *Kardom* offensive plan in Southern Command and *Sadan* defensive plan in the Syrian sector.[20]

This planning order did not evolve into an operational order until war broke out, and the IDF's moves during the Six Day War on the West Bank were essentially without overall orderly planning.

The change in political circumstances as a result of the Jordanian–

Egyptian pact, the United States' qualified approach to its commitment to opening up the Straits, and the faltering of the plan for an international maritime force, reinforced the army's demand for a military initiative. In the late afternoon of 1 June, and also in view of the anticipated changes in the government's composition, Rabin was 'optimistic' that the government would soon decide on the IDF initiative. At a meeting with the Chiefs of Operations and Intelligence, the Quartermaster Branch and CO IAF, the re-examination of all plans was discussed, as was a possible 'pretext' for attack, including the possibility of staging the shelling of an Israeli settlement.[21]

The Foreign Minister changes his mind

At 18:30 the Prime Minister informed the Chief of Staff of Moshe Dayan's appointment as Minister of Defence, and invited him to attend the government meeting planned for the same evening. Before the meeting, Rabin and Yariv conferred with Eban and the Director-General of the Foreign Ministry Arie Levavi to evaluate the situation. After Rabin and Yariv had surveyed the evolving deployment of the Arab armies in the wake of Hussein–Nasser alliance, Eban announced that he had changed his mind. He was now persuaded that the diplomatic efforts had been exhausted and from now on it was necessary to accord priority to operational military calculations.[22] This turn-around by Eban, who until then had headed diplomatic efforts to solve the crisis, was a milestone which augured the upheaval in the balance of power in the government.

Eban was the main target, immediately after Eshkol, for criticism of the government's policy of waiting. When the generals referred mockingly to 'humiliation' and shameful pleading for outside help they were referring to Eban's shuttle diplomacy. De Gaulle's bluntly negative approach had come as a shock to Israel and had been perceived, unjustly, as a failure on Eban's part. Even de Gaulle's embargo on arms consignments to Israel was attributed, apparently erroneously, to the fact that Eban had expressed gratitude to the French President for supplying arms to Israel, thereby drawing his attention to the issue.[23] It was as if Eban had undertaken the mission to seek an audience with the Western heads of state on his own initiative. There were those who thought that it would have been preferable to send someone of unofficial status, such as former Foreign Minister Golda Meir,[24] but Eban refuted the proposal emphatically and hastened to establish facts. His trip was frowned on not only by the army, but also by those in government and opposition circles.[25] In hindsight, it can be determined that the mission was a correct diplomatic move which prepared the political conditions for an IDF attack and imposed greater constraints on Egypt than on Israel. However, at the time it was believed to be working against Israel's supreme interest, as seen by the army – namely to deliver the first blow. Eban's standing was undermined to such a degree that at a certain stage the proposal was raised to dismiss him and appoint Moshe Dayan in his place.[26] The mission angered the advocates of immediate action to the point where they hurled accusations not only at the decision to send him but also at the contents of his reports.[27] There is no evidence to support the charge that Eban deliberately misled the government. Even if his report dwelt on de Gaulle's declarations of amity, it did not gloss over the President's strong objections to Israeli action.[28] Eban could not have envisaged that de Gaulle would take such a drastic step as imposing an embargo on Israel. As for Johnson's commitment to Israel, while he had indeed told Eban that if no international maritime task force could be assembled the United States would act alone, he had said so halfheartedly,[29] and was not voicing the explicit stand of the administration. On this point, there is apparently some justification for the claim that Eban's report was over-optimistic. Indeed, when Eshkol, in a communication to Johnson, tried to pin down that commitment, he encountered disappointing reservations which cast serious doubts on US resolve and did not gain Eban additional credit.[30] Eban presented the messages he had received from de Gaulle and Johnson in a fashion which reinforced his own anti-war stance and that of the other 'doves' in the government. It was only natural for the 'hawks' to be highly critical of him.

It seems feasible that the change in circumstances due to the Hussein–Nasser pact and the evident change in Washington's stance would, in any case, have led the government to alter its standpoint and order the IDF to act, particularly since, after expansion, it was now more 'hawkish' in character. But it is indeed noteworthy that Foreign Minister Eban was the first to sense, with accurate timing, that the time had come to put diplomacy on the back burner and hand over the helm to the security leadership.

Chapter 22

The decisive meeting in the Pit

The Ministerial Committee versus the General Staff

On Friday, 2 June 1967 at 09:25 the expanded Ministerial Committee on Security met with the General Staff forum in the Pit war room. The government decision five days earlier to agree to a respite for international action under US leadership was still in force. The second meeting of the week between the military and civilian echelons (following the General Staff meeting with Eshkol on 28 May) also developed into an incisive clash between the two sides. What the generals had to say instantly dispelled the celebratory mood of the ministers, who only the evening before had raised their glasses to the establishment of a government of national unity.

They were now faced with the demand for an immediate decision to send Israel to war. Before the meeting, the Prime Minister appeared relaxed and told the ministers 'that for the time being things are going to ease up'.[1] However, by the end of the intriguing encounter the general feeling was that the die had been cast.[2] Two days later the government voted by a large majority to go to war the following day.

Yariv: 'The United States will not constitute the main obstacle to our action'

The Chief of Staff opened the meeting and said that the aim was 'to display the picture to the Government the way it appears to the IDF'.[3] The Chief of Intelligence read out the main points of the Intelligence Research Department's evaluation dated 31 May. He went on to analyse the American stand on the basis of reports from the Israeli Embassy in Washington and media sources. Yariv concluded that the United States had no intention of taking serious action to lift the maritime blockade by force and in fact, he said, the Americans were increasingly convinced that Israel must act alone. The US had no desire to become entangled in regional hostilities and many members of the administration would consider Israeli action as a convenient solution to the problem. In Washington, unlike Paris, Israel could wield influence on the administration.[4] He believed, on the basis of 'hints' received, that if Israel acted judiciously and speedily, the 'United States will not be the main obstacle to our action'.

Rabin described the situation in all its gravity, and distinguished between the problem of the Straits, whose significance lay in the effect on Israel's deterrent capability and what he saw as the main problem, namely 'the military and political situation evolving around us, in which time is not on our side'. He spoke in terms of a dynamic process of a massing of military forces on the Egyptian and Jordanian fronts and increased inter-Arab cooperation. He anticipated the possibilities of Egyptian attacks, terrorist action, renewal of the water diversion efforts, and even prevention of the passage of the fortnightly convoy to Mount Scopus. 'The members of this forum [the IDF General Staff], and I first of all ... don't want war for its own sake', Rabin stressed, but, he added, the noose was tightening around Israel, the enemy had proclaimed their objective of annihilating Israel and time was on their side. Israel's leaders did not have the right to wait until the enemy had gained decisive superiority, thereby placing Israel's survival at grave risk. It was crucial to act immediately and to inflict 'a resounding blow' on Nasser, which would transform the entire Middle Eastern situation. The implications of taking the initiative, particularly where the IAF was concerned, would be critical for the outcome. Today, Rabin declared, the IDF could still do the job, even if forced to act on a limited scale, and to suffer some damage on the Syrian and Jordanian fronts.

In answer to a question from Eshkol, Rabin emphasized once more that every additional day of inaction 'impedes the implementation [of the IDF plan] and makes it more costly'. The CO Southern Command illustrated this viewpoint by depicting three scenarios: the situation on the day the blockade was announced ('if we had taken the offensive then, it would have been a walkover'); the situation 'on the day it was decided [28 May] not to carry out the attack', and the current situation. Still, Gavish explained, 'an attack launched tomorrow will differ significantly from an attack in four days' time when the situation will be much more serious'. Yariv backed Gavish, noting that 'Cairo is urgently cramming forces into Sinai. In some cases, the troops go without food and water for 48 hours because the urgency and disorder are so great. That's not bad for us, and again it's all a question of time.'

Rabin summed up this section of the meeting: 'Mr Prime Minister, we have presented the matter to you. The question is, what does the Prime Minister want to happen here at this forum?' Eshkol did not reply and an open discussion ensued in which the senior command again voiced their views unrelentingly and imperatively. In a desperate attempt to gain time, Minister of the Interior Moshe Haim Shapira further exasperated the generals by asking a question which seemed to rebut all their explanations: If in any case the Egyptians had already concentrated almost all of their army in Sinai, 'what difference can it make [if we launch an attack] now, in a week or ten days? ... On the other hand, we are liable to lose the political campaign ... if we act immediately.'

Sharon: 'Who is more qualified than we are to tell you that the army is ready for war?'

Brigadier General Avraham Yaffe, the first speaker in the discussion, emphasized the need to take the initiative:

> 'I have been sitting in the Negev for 14 days with the units and the reserve forces.... Our feeling there ... is that we have failed to seize the initiative all along the front.... We must snatch the initiative from the Egyptians. If we can gain it by diplomatic means – well and good ... but so far all our initiative is in the shape of the Foreign Minister's trip to the United States.'

Yaffe did not rule out the idea of confining action to an IAF attack without bringing any other forces into play. The main thing, he said, was 'to do something, to exploit our initiative and to change this situation where we can see the clouds gathering and approaching and we are sitting idle'.

Yaffe's minimalist approach was anathema to Ariel Sharon. He started out by declaring that 'the IDF forces are readier and abler than ever before to destroy and to repel an Egyptian attack'. The objective, Sharon clarified, 'is no less than total annihilation of the Egyptian forces'. The gravest issue, as he perceived it, was the loss of Israel's deterrent capability, which was weakening day by day due to 'the hesitations and foot-dragging [of the government]'. He tried to persuade the ministers, who were afraid of heavy casualties, that due to the situation's gravity, 'there is moral justification for the decision-taking echelon to approve an operation which will entail more losses'. Sharon objected in particular to Israeli dependence on the Superpowers:

> 'Any link-up on our part with other powers is a mistake of the first order. Our aim is to make sure that in the coming ten or twenty years or generation or two, the Egyptians will not want to fight us. Any link-up on our part with other powers or action against marginal objectives [e.g. attacks on Egyptian airfields and conquest of the Gaza Strip alone] instead of focusing on the central objective of destroying the Egyptian army will prove that we are weak. That was the main damage caused by the Sinai Campaign. We could have gone it alone. The fact that we linked up with others showed us up as helpless.'

Sharon emphasized that only a resolute stand in defence of Israel's rights, one of which was freedom of shipping, could guarantee the state's long-term survival. He alluded mockingly to Eban's mission: 'Our scurrying about – and I won't use the word "shtadlanut" – [begging for help from rulers] among the Superpowers and pleading for rescue are not part of our stand in protection of our rights.' Sharon rounded off his remarks by assuring the ministers that the IDF was ready for action, equipped with a sturdy fighting spirit and decisive military superiority. 'Who is more qualified than we are to come and tell you that the army is ready for war?' he asked. He warned that any attempt to postpone the date of the attack in hope of receiving more tanks and aircraft would be a grave error. 'Today nothing can have any effect except for a rapid and courageous, timely decision on the part of the government. The rest can be left to our forces. I can assure you that it will be carried out in the best possible fashion.'

Minister of Defence Moshe Dayan now took the floor. He said little but it was evident that he was siding with the General Staff although, ostensibly, he confined himself to a 'technical explanation'. He explained to Moshe Haim Shapira the connection between the consolidation of enemy forces, and the high number of casualties which would result from an attack on their fortified positions. Dayan claimed that the IDF would have limited time at its disposal until the fighting was halted by anticipated international intervention. The deeper the Egyptian entrenchment, the more time would be needed to defeat them. Dayan added that even if everything went well, there would still be the need for a second stage to conquer Sharm al-Sheikh and open up the Straits, since this could not be achieved at an early stage. If the first stage was drawn out due to Egyptian entrenchment, there might not be enough time for the second stage, and the Straits would remain blocked when the ceasefire was imposed.

Peled: 'We are entitled to know why we are suffering this disgrace'

The Chief of the Quartermaster Branch, Brigadier-General Matti Peled, was the bluntest of all in his attack on the government. For two weeks, morning, noon and night, he said, the army had been contending that time was working against Israel. But the General Staff had not received a single word of explanation for the wait. 'I can understand that we are waiting for something to happen. If so, let us in on the secret and then we will know why we are waiting!' Peled denied the importance of international action for lifting the blockade: 'We have heard something regarding Tiran, which lost its significance long ago. It was not important to start with and is even less important now.' The entry of an Egyptian force into Sinai was nothing new for the IDF, having been anticipated and planned for in various exercises and war games. The only surprise, he stressed, was Nasser's audacity, since it was well known that his army was not ready for war. Peled had an explanation to offer for Nasser's moves:

'In my opinion he was relying on the hesitation of the Israeli government. He acted in the confidence that we would not dare to hit at him.... Nasser moved an army which was not ready to the border and he derived full advantage from the move. One fact is acting in his favour and that is the fact that the Israel government is not ready to act against him.'

Peled interpreted the questions the ministers had raised during the meeting and on previous occasions as manifestations of a lack of confidence in the IDF. 'What has the IDF done wrong to deserve these doubts as to its capability? What more does an army need in order to win the confidence of the government but to win every battle?'

As the officer responsible for logistics, Peled permitted himself to brandish the economic argument and point out the impact of the deteriorating economic situation on the morale of the troops:

'The economy is in an intolerable condition. Food supplies scarcely manage to reach the places where they are needed. How long will it be before our soldiers in the frontline are affected by the situation in the home front? ... How long can they sit there when everything we left behind is collapsing? ... The State of Israel does not have infinite stamina. The IDF will be able to beat the enemy in three weeks' time as well, but I don't know what will happen in the interior.... It is not clear to me if the government has an accurate picture of what is going on internally. I now meet with directors of government ministries on an almost routine basis, and their representatives know what is going on. If you only knew ... you would ask why we are not acting faster. The enemy is digging in and growing stronger and the economy is growing weaker and all this for an aim which nobody can explain to us.'

Peled concluded on a sharp note: 'We deserve to know why we are suffering this disgrace. Perhaps, on this occasion, we will receive an explanation. Why are we waiting?'

The Prime Minister hastened to sum up the discussion and to defend the government. It was clearly evident that Sharon and Peled had infuriated him. Having already resolved to send the IDF into action, he did not want to be misunderstood. Hence, he began by declaring: 'What I am about to say is not intended to explain what we are going to do tomorrow or the next day.'

First, he replied to Sharon, who had denoted the diplomatic efforts 'scurrying about'. 'Everything we have vis-à-vis the material strength of our army came as a result of this scurrying about,' he said in reproof. 'Let's not forget that and let's not regard ourselves as Goliaths as a result. Barefisted, unequipped and unarmed – we have no strength.' He was reluctant to place unqualified faith in the army's evaluations. 'With all the evaluations and data of Intelligence there are several things of which it can be said that they could end in this way or that', in particular what the Soviet Union was liable to do.

In a country of two million citizens, he told the generals, a man needed to ask himself:

'Let us assume that we break the enemy's might today. Tomorrow we need to start building up our power anew, because we too will have lost forces ... and then, if every ten years we need to fight we will have to consider whether we have an ally who can aid us.... Sometimes the difference of a day and an hour can be decisive in the sense that not everyone in the world will fall on us us like a pack of wolves.'

Eshkol noted in particular the importance 'of whispering in Johnson's ear so that he won't claim that we cheated him, because we may still need him. Let's hope we won't need him in the middle of the fighting'. At the same time Eshkol hinted that there was a limit to waiting and the hour of action was close at hand.

The Prime Minister was apparently deeply hurt by Peled's remarks and answered him in a defiant spirit:

'I permit myself to think that you know no more than we do about what is going on in government ministries, what this country has and what our reserves are ... in the civilian sphere. I don't think we are less equipped now than ten years ago [during the Sinai War] and perhaps even more. Therefore, one can say that two days more or one day less will not decide the campaign.'[5]

Eshkol, as the greatest authority on economic affairs insisted that the Achilles heel was not the economic situation and that it was important to preserve Israel's relations with its friends throughout the world so that the IDF's strength could be built up after the war. A military victory would not end the dispute 'because the Arabs will still be here', he argued.

Rabin expressed the hope that the government would convene that same day and make a decision, but Eshkol declared that a government meeting would be held, as usual, on Sunday. Thus the meeting ended on a similar note to the meeting in the Pit five days previously. Eshkol may have replied in this fashion in order to give vent to his resentment at the IDF's pressure but in fact he had resolved to wait no longer.

At noon Eshkol conferred with a limited forum consisting of Dayan,

Eban, Allon, the Director-General of the PM's office Yaakov Herzog, and Rabin. It was decided unanimously that the time had come to go to war. Dayan and Allon favoured an immediate attack,[6] as did Rabin. Eshkol was already leaning in this direction, and Eban voiced no objections. The impact of the meeting with the General Staff had decided the issue. However, it was agreed that the attack would not begin 'before Monday [5 June]'.[7]

The army's influence: legitimate, borderline legitimate or illegitimate?

This is the place to sum up and evaluate the role which the army commanders played in persuading, or perhaps forcing, the government to decide to go to war. Was the pressure they exerted beyond the bounds of the legitimate constitutional framework, or did the IDF act within the permissible framework in accordance with the rules of conduct in a 'mature' democratic political culture?[8]

In order to answer this question it should be noted that, as we have shown, the military perceived the situation as acute and feared that they were liable to face the difficult choice between constitutional loyalty, which dictated full submission to the elected civilian authority, and a higher loyalty to the very existence of the state and their duty to protect it and the lives of its citizens. Such a situation is liable to evoke activist symptoms even among a professional officer class.[9]

The General Staff was entirely convinced that the government was endangering the country. From 22 May, the date on which Nasser proclaimed the closing of the Straits of Tiran, the senior command was united in the belief that there would be no escape from a military confrontation. The government's indecision, so it seemed, was encouraging Nasser to act even more audaciously and granting his army time for organizing, consolidating, reinforcing and re-equipping its own army as well as rallying allied Arab armies around Israel's borders. The most feasible assumption, based on 'indicators', was that Nasser would direct an initial blow at the atomic reactor and IAF airfields. It was feared also that concentrations of population and infrastructure would be bombed and that the Arab armies, enjoying air superiority, were subsequently liable to launch a coordinated offensive simultaneously on all fronts, thereby forcing the IDF to split its defensive efforts. This nightmare scenario included the possibility of wide-scale terrorist attacks and an uprising of Israel's Arabs. A situation might develop, the generals asserted, whereby the IDF would not be able to win the inevitable fight.

Moreover, a crisis of confidence now became apparent between the military and political echelons. On the one hand, the government's confidence in the army was shaken, due to the rebuttal of the Intelligence evaluation, the collapse of the deterrent capacity, the unexpected downward slide to the verge of war, and Rabin's hesitations and breakdown.[10] On the other hand, and above all, the army did not trust the government to act judiciously, and considered it to be confused, panic-stricken, spineless and incapable of making decisions. It was not only the army which had lost confidence in the civilian leadership but also the anxious general public at home and the mobilized troops on the front line.[11]

The paternal, anti-charismatic and irresolute image of Levi Eshkol did not answer the psychological need for confident and persuasive leadership. The frenzied atmosphere in the Arab world, the blunt threats that Israel would be destroyed and its citizens slaughtered, had touched a very sensitive nerve in Jewish consciousness. Eshkol's standing was at its lowest ebb due to the economic recession which had created a gloomy atmosphere well before the crisis,[12] the savage criticism levelled against him by the opposition and the media (and in particular the charge that he was responsible for a 'security mishap'), the deterioration of the security situation due to increased terrorist activity, and finally his faltering address to the nation which appeared to reflect helplessness, a plea for outside rescue, and an affront to the Israeli ethos.

The army believed that it held the solution to the situation, that the nation was pinning its hopes on its fighters, and only the government was delaying action and casting doubt on the IDF's ability to save the country from disaster. Victory depended to a critical extent on the IAF's ability to achieve aerial supremacy and this in its turn was conditional on achieving the vital element of tactical surprise. Hence the government's 'delaying tactics' and in particular the incomprehensible decision of 28 May were perceived by the army as potentially disastrous.

In the severe crisis which ensued, the army could have been strongly tempted, in light of its perception of the circumstances, to seize the initiative, and 'intervene' to deliver the nation from danger. *The crucial fact is that this did not occur.* The army was confronted with a supreme test of its loyalty to the laws and constraints of the democratic framework, and that framework was preserved and did not crumble.

Still, what did the army do and to what extent – if at all – was there ever a danger of illegitimate 'intervention' on its part?

First, it should be pointed out that the tension between the military and civilian echelons did not extend through the entire three-week period of the crisis – 15 May to 4 June. It began only after Nasser's announcement of the closure of the Straits and the dispatch of Foreign Minister Eban on his diplomatic mission to seek support from the Western heads of state. The government's marathon discussions on 27 and 28 May which resulted in a decision to wait three weeks, in total disregard for the army's view, created a situation which the IDF found unacceptable. The tension between military and government reached its peak during the four days that were marked by two highly charged meetings in the Pit: between Sunday evening, 28 May, when the generals met with the Prime Minister, and Friday morning, 2 June, when they met the expanded Ministerial Committee on Security. Between these two dates, the military echelon took the following steps:

1 Immediately after the meeting with Eshkol in the Pit, Rabin ordered that steps be taken to forestall inertia (a slackening of alertness) in the army and to maintain high morale, both through propaganda and through a strict military routine and intensive training regime.[13]
2 The Intelligence Branch issued a very sombre evaluation on the military and diplomatic implications of a three-week wait.
3 Several of the generals were recruited for a 'propaganda campaign' in order to persuade the political establishment to change the government decision. To this end, several meetings took place between senior officers and political figures.[14]

Of these three activities, only the third appears to be somewhat problematic, because it seemingly points to IDF intervention in politics, particularly when the demand had been raised to relieve Eshkol of the Defence portfolio. But even if several officers tried to influence the appointment of a new Minister of Defence, their impact was infinitesimal and in no way undermined the supremacy of the political echelon. The move to appoint Dayan to the post was inspired by pressure of public opinion and the political establishment and not necessarily by the urgings of the senior command.

And yet one may still ask whether there was ever a danger – even if it came to nothing – of improper intervention by the IDF?

We have already noted Ben-Gurion's dread of unauthorized action on the part of the army as the result of its lack of confidence towards the civilian leadership, an act which would constitute 'a stain on the State of Israel from which it will never cleanse itself'. It is noteworthy that there is no evidence that at any stage whatsoever the General Staff intended to take action against the government and overrule its decisions. However, the fact that several generals, in the course of charged encounters with the political echelon, felt the need to emphasize that the army was subordinate to the government,[15] and the fact that the Prime Minister felt it necessary to put the military in their place indicates that a certain fear, however faint, was hovering in the atmosphere.

The generals who led the Israeli army in battle in the June 1967 war are unanimous in their view that there was never any danger of a 'putsch'.[16] This conviction is clearly verified by what the army did and by what it refrained from doing. Nonetheless, Ezer Weizman was quoted as having said that Israel was never closer to a military coup than on the eve of the

Six Day War.[17] According to one source, the American Intelligence services estimated that such a danger existed.[18]

That the possibility was contemplated and actually broached out loud at the senior military level during the tense and frustrating encounters with the political echelon is attested to by only one member of the IDF General Staff at that time – Ariel Sharon. His exceptional testimony deserves to be quoted in full:

'After the first meeting with Eshkol [in the Pit on 28 May] ... I must say that I myself, and I also discussed it with the Chief of Staff, for the first time had the feeling, and this must be admitted, we sometimes asked whether in the State of Israel a situation was possible whereby the army would seize power. Could there be a situation where the army takes decisions without the government ... and I always said that it wasn't possible, that in Israel such a thing couldn't happen. And here, after the meeting on 28.5 ... I told the Chief of Staff and the other people there that in fact this is the first time where a situation had arisen where this was possible, and it would be accepted positively. That means that for the first time a situation had arisen in Israel where seizing of power [by the army was possible] not for purposes of desire for power but for decision-making. The basic decision [i.e. to go to war] could be taken without the government, for the first time. And I don't remember whether he [Rabin] agreed or not, but I think that he saw it like that as well. I don't think that anyone talked of practical matters, whether it was possible to carry it out, but from the viewpoint of the situation which existed ... the first meeting on 28 May ... we didn't finish discussing the subject. After the meeting on 2 June [with the expanded Ministerial Committee on Security] ... we [the generals] stayed behind to talk afterwards, and I said that if we had been at a certain stage, what we started talking about afterwards, we would have stood up and said [to the Ministers], listen, your decisions are endangering the State of Israel, and since the situation is now very grave, you are requested to step into the next room and wait there, and the Chief of Staff will go over to Kol Israel [national radio] and broadcast an announcement [on a decision taken by the army to go to war] ... they [the Ministers] would have accepted it with a sense of relief. That was my feeling.'[19]

Sharon's testimony may be seen as the expression of an individual line of thought or mood which he shared with the Chief of Staff and colleagues in the General Staff. It should be noted that this was not a unique thought because Sharon raised it in the Pit twice within five days. But it was an aberrant expression, no more than 'thinking out loud'. A similar thought may have gone through the minds of other generals, but Sharon was the only one who voiced it. Perusal of the documentation reveals no evidence that there was ever any practical outcome.

The question of the limits of obedience of a soldier to the democratically elected civilian echelon is not a simple one.[20] The existence of some kind of limit is accepted. No soldier is called upon to 'blindly obey', and under extreme circumstances he will be fulfilling a higher obligation if he gives priority to moral or professional considerations and to his ultimate responsibility towards the state and the security of its inhabitants.

The outcome of the Six Day War has clouded comprehension of the extreme situation at the time, because the fact that Israel enjoyed decisive military superiority became evident only post factum, so that the claim of the General Staff that it would be disastrous to wait was disproved. In fact, most of the generals admitted later that the waiting period – in addition to its vast diplomatic advantages – strengthened the IDF, enabled it to complete its operative planning, to lay out the logistic deployment, to organize and train forces, and to transform the reserve forces as well into a kind of regular army. In retrospect, nobody claimed that the army had been correct in its evaluations. The way in which Eshkol and his government conducted the crisis came to be regarded, in the end, as political sagacity at its best.

This was not the way things appeared before the war. The General Staff, as noted, was convinced that the government was endangering the country. They raged, they exerted pressure, they exhorted, but they did not take illegitimate or provocative action in order to confront the political echelon with a fait accompli. There is no way of knowing for sure what would have happened if the government had persisted in its policy of waiting despite the deterioration in the military situation (the entry of Iraqi forces into the West Bank, further reinforcement and consolidation of the Egyptian force in Sinai and so on), in a manner which would have aggravated the army's dilemma even further. But there is no reason to assume that even in that case the army would have acted of its own accord and not on the basis of the decisions of the government. It is an incontrovertible fact that the IDF began to release reserve forces and to prepare for a long wait. The shortening of that period from three weeks to one was due to IDF pressure, promoted by the change in the composition of the government, and the 'yellow light' from Washington. But the most important factor was the Hussein–Nasser alliance and its strategic implications, which tipped the balance.

On 28 May 1967 the Israeli government (with the exception of Moshe Carmel) voted unanimously to wait. Exactly a week later, on 4 June, almost the entire government (with the exception of two Mapam ministers) decided unanimously to go to war immediately. The army had brought pressure to bear and got what it wanted, even though several days late and only after the existential threat loomed larger. The General Staff did not need to recourse to unconstitutional measures. This possibility, even if contemplated for a moment by one general or another, was never actually on the agenda.

Restricting the powers of the Minister of Defence

Once Dayan was appointed it was necessary to decide on the division of authority between the Prime Minister and the Minister of Defence and in particular the restrictions on the latter's freedom to issue orders to the army. The procedures were formulated by Yigael Yadin, former Chief of Staff, who was trusted by both Eshkol and Dayan.[21]

1　The Minister of Defence will not act without the approval of the Prime Minister as regards the following:

- launching general hostile action or war against any country whatsoever;
- taking any military action in the course of war which oversteps the bounds of action as determined by the government.
- launching military action against any country which has not, until that moment, participated in hostilities.
- bombing important cities in enemy territory if the act has not been preceded by bombing of Israeli cities by that same enemy.
- launching retaliatory action in response to incidents.

2　The Prime Minister can, with the knowledge of the Minister of Defence, summon the Chief of Staff, the Chief of Intelligence, the Director-General of the Ministry of Defence or the Assistant Minister of Defence in order to receive information.

This hastily drawn-up procedure can scarcely be regarded as a comprehensive series of instructions for defining the subordination of the Minister of Defence to the Prime Minister. In any event, all the actions listed in Clause 1 were subject to the approval of the government plenum or the Ministerial Committee on Security. This was not an orderly division of authority but rather a document aimed at dispelling fears, which were not explicitly expressed, that the Minister of Defence might make his own decisions and take action after consulting the army, without informing the government and its head.[22] Dayan himself ignored the agreed procedure when he gave direct orders to the CO Northern Command on 9 June to attack the Syrians on the Golan Heights, thereby contravening the government's decision of the previous night not to launch such an attack (in fact, at the government meeting of 8 June Dayan was the most vehement opponent of an attack on Syria).[23]

'Presentation of plans' to the Chief of Staff and Minister of Defence

That evening the Southern Command's plans were presented to the Chief of Staff and a discussion was held with the participation of the Deputy Chief of Staff, Chief of Intelligence, CO Southern Command and southern divisional commanders Tal (Eighty-fifth Division), Sharon (Thirty-eighth Division) and Yaffe (Thirty-first Division). An hour later they were joined by the Minister of Defence, who also perused the plans and took an active part in the subsequent deliberations and helped determine the outcome. This discussion was the decisive stage in consolidation of the ultimate operational plan 'Nakhshonim', which was implemented in general lines on the southern front.

It is seemingly surprising that at this late stage, almost three weeks after the crisis had begun, and after endless deliberations and planning, the IDF did not yet have a definite operational plan for a ground offensive on the Egyptian front. The reasons lay in the rapid changes in the situation which required flexibility and adaptation of plans as well as allocation of forces and tasks. Within Southern Command there was an ongoing struggle between the divisional commanders. Ariel Sharon was pressing and demanding expansion of his division's assignments and the aims of the war in general, while Yisrael Tal, whose division was earmarked for the main thrust, favoured more modest objectives. In the end, Avraham Yaffe, who was more passive, was left with a depleted division. His spearhead brigade (200th Armoured Brigade under Yiska Shadmi) fought in the breakthrough stage in Sharon's sector with a brilliant incursion movement in Wadi Hareidin, and should logically have been under Sharon's command.[24]

This was not the first time that operational plans had been presented to the civilian echelon but, unlike Eshkol, Dayan, as former Chief of Staff and the man who had waged warfare in Sinai only a decade previously, had something to say about the planned moves and objectives. The General Staff was therefore now facing a new situation, in which it needed to persuade a Minister of Defence with professional experience and background and to adapt the operational plans to his instructions. Until then under Eshkol the Chiefs of Staff had been 'exempt' from all professional intervention, and the government had never troubled to define the objectives of the war. Its defensive tenet and the ministers' lack of military know-how (apart from Allon and Carmel) had left the General Staff devoid of strategic instruction and without definition of the objectives of the war. In its present plight, the government wanted only for the army to remove the threat. Beyond that, it devoted little serious thought to the tactics of warfare and its possible outcome.

Moshe Dayan issued three basic instructions for the General Staff stemming from the political evaluation. It is noteworthy that they were not deliberated and decided by a government forum but originated in Dayan's own personal perception and were undoubtedly coloured by his experience as Chief of Staff and inspired to some extent by Ben-Gurion. The issues were:

1   The Gaza Strip – the debate between the generals on the need to conquer the Gaza Strip was based entirely on military considerations. Tal feared that 'if we do not deal with the Strip it will cause mayhem in our settlements'. Gavish too was concerned for the fate of the settlements along the border with the Gaza Strip, and Barlev insisted that the Sixtieth Brigade should be brought in for rapid action to capture the Strip, where two Palestinian brigades were deployed, within two hours. Rabin, on the other hand, was ready to forgo the conquest of the Strip in order to focus the armoured effort on the conquest of el-Arish and the destruction of the bulk of the Egyptian force. Ariel Sharon thought that 'the Strip will fall in any case' and there was no need to invest unnecessary effort for that purpose. Only the Assistant Chief of Operations, Rehavam Ze'evi, exceeded the purely operational calculations and commented that 'it would be a pity to forfeit the headline: Gaza is ours!'[25]

    Moshe Dayan was opposed to the conquest of the Strip but not for military reasons. 'The Gaza Strip issue is problematic because of the refugees', he said. He was afraid that the capture of the Strip would force Israel to undertake the burden of supporting the refugees, and he preferred to leave this to the UN Relief and Work Agency (UNRWA). Only in one case, Dayan explained, would Israel be obliged to occupy the Strip – if the Egyptians stationed foreign forces there. This would be a total violation of the armistice agreements and an excellent rationale for Israeli action, but in this case as well no action should be taken against the Strip in the first stage of the fighting, only later.[26]

2   The Suez Canal – the Suez Canal was not defined as an objective in the operative plans submitted by the Command, but reaching it was not ruled out. Dayan now clarified this point: 'The Canal is not an objective. We must keep our distance from it after cleaning out the routes leading there. This is because of its value to the entire world, with which we must not enter into conflict.' When the Head of the Operations Branch commented that 'to sit beside the Canal could be a bargaining card for Sharm al-Sheikh', Dayan reiterated his opinion, and went on to explain: 'A threat against the Canal can only cause us harm. Those who are capable of removing us from Sinai will not be the Egyptians [but the great powers] and it is in their interest that we should not threaten the Canal. On the contrary, it would be a pretext for action against us.' Dayan, therefore, was contemplating the post-war diplomatic campaign and estimating that Israeli presence on the

banks of the Suez Canal or near it would help to intensify pressure on Israel to withdraw from Sinai.[27]

3   Defining the minimal territorial gain necessary – Dayan wanted to annihilate as many Egyptian forces as possible but he was intensely aware of the limitations of diplomatic time. He accepted the assumption that within seventy-two hours international intervention would enforce a ceasefire, and declared that during this period a minimal territorial gain should be achieved – the conquest of northern Sinai as far as el-Arish – even if the blow against the Egyptian armour was not complete.[28]

The discussions in the General Staff that night and on the following day consolidated the final operative plan, which was code-named 'Nakhshonim'. It was based on Kardom 2, in other words a main thrust along the northern axis to be executed by the Eighty-fourth Division and the cream of the armoured forces, but with an additional effort along the central axis, including a complex breakthrough by the Thirty-eighth Division and the penetration of an armoured brigade of the Thirty-first Division to destroy the forward Egyptian deployment. Of the southern arm, which had been earmarked in Kardom 1 to the main thrust, there now remained only one armoured brigade, the Eighth Brigade, facing Shazli's force.

The encounter with the generals in the Pit pushed Eshkol and his ministers to the brink of the fateful decision. The IDF was now consolidating the final plans under the eye of the new Defence Minister. The scene was set for war. There was only one last point to clarify and weigh heavily before the die was cast: the US position on an Israeli pre-emptive strike.

Chapter 23

The decisive stage
War

As noted, the turning point, which induced the Israeli government to shorten the waiting period, was the signing of the Hussein–Nasser pact on 30 May. This surprising development had an immediate impact on Washington. Israel's Intelligence services suddenly received indications ('hints', as Yariv denoted them at the Ministerial Committee on Security) that US objections to an Israeli pre-emptive strike were less steadfast than before. These indications were at variance with the official messages transmitted through diplomatic contacts.

From the outset the Departments of Defence and State had not been of one mind as regards employment of an international 'armada' to open the Straits of Tiran. President Johnson supported the plan initially, despite the reservations of the Defence Department, although it is unlikely that he intended to carry it through. He favoured it mainly as a means of exerting pressure on Nasser. Due to the altered circumstances in the Middle East, the President now accepted the recommendation of the Defence Department 'to unleash Israel'. And yet the State Department continued to caution Israel not to open fire first, and to argue – less and less convincingly – that they were still investing effort in organizing an international maritime force.[1] There may have been some form of coordination between the various sectors of the administration, a kind of 'division of labour': on the official diplomatic plane, the United States continued to warn Israel against taking action and, simultaneously, unofficially and discreetly, conveyed different messages.

The American perspective

The decisions taken by the Israeli government during the crisis were closely connected to the standpoints of the United States. This was also true of the fateful and historic decision taken by the government of national unity on 4 June 1967 – namely to go to war. The majority of Eshkol's government, who were not spoiling for a fight and feared the outcome, were particularly anxious at the prospect that their country might go to war alone and without Great Power backing. From the moment the Straits were barred to Israel, the government sought support in Washington and received it on condition that Israel did not fire the first shot. The restrictions on Israel, at a time when the existential danger was increasing, imposed a heavy responsibility on the United States. Eventually the view that it would be advisable to allow Israel free action prevailed in Washington.

US documents on the period under discussion were recently opened to the public. This abundant documentation casts light on US diplomacy, Intelligence evaluations, reports from embassies in the Middle East, discussions and decisions of senior officials and the White House. They also reveal aspects of Israeli diplomacy from the American angle. This rich archival material helps to illuminate the background to the change in the US approach, a change which made it easier for the Israeli government to make its fateful decision.

Johnson: 'The transcendent objective: the avoidance of hostilities'

The objectives of the United States in the first two weeks of the crisis (15–29 May) were to prevent war, and in the third week (30 May to 4 June) – to be absolved of responsibility for the war which was now unavoidable. When the crisis erupted, the United States passed pacifying messages from Jerusalem to Cairo, to the effect that Israel had no intention of attacking Syria, there were no concentrations of Israeli forces on the Syrian border, and, if no infiltration and sabotage were perpetrated there was no cause for concern.[2] Israel still perceived the crisis in the context of terrorist activity, and, in a note to President Johnson on 18 May, Eshkol expressed concern that the concentration of Egyptian forces in Sinai might encourage Syria to resume terrorist acts under the false impression of immunity.[3] The hasty decision of UN Secretary-General U Thant to evacuate the UNEF from Sinai took Washington by surprise, and Israel hastened to caution against blocking shipping in the Bay of Aqaba, a warning which the United States immediately transmitted to the Soviet representative at the United Nations.[4] Israel's Ambassador in Washington, Avraham Harman, asked Under-Secretary of State Eugene Rostow for confirmation that the United States' 1957 commitment to freedom of shipping was still valid, and Rostow reassured him on that point, but said that it should be perceived within the framework of the President's demand for 'immediate consultation' in the event that Egypt interfered with free passage.[5] Johnson dispatched a message of reassurance to Eshkol. He did not mention freedom of shipping explicitly, but rather his commitment and that of his predecessors to Israel and his support for retaining an 'important and desirable' UN presence in Sinai.[6] Concurrently, Johnson dispatched a conciliatory note to Nasser, urging him 'to set as your first duty ... this transcendent objective: the avoidance of hostilities', and proposing to send Vice-President Hubert Humphrey to Cairo.[7] On the eve of U Thant's trip to Cairo, US Ambassador to the UN Arthur Goldberg conveyed to him his country's support for freedom of shipping and views on the need to retain an effective UN presence at Sharm al-Sheikh and in the Gaza Strip.[8]

When Nasser announced the closure of the Straits to Israeli shipping and to 'strategic materials' earmarked for Israel, US diplomacy went into high gear in order to dissuade Israel from starting a war, and to prevent Egypt from blocking the Straits.

The designated ambassador, Richard Nolte, conferred in Cairo on 23 May with Egyptian Foreign Minister Mahmoud Riad, while US Ambassador to Moscow Thomas Thompson held an urgent meeting with Foreign Minister Andrei Gromyko, who assured him that the Soviet Union opposed the war and, as anticipated, blamed Israel for the crisis.[9] The President himself appeared that day on radio and TV and declared that the Bay of Aqaba was an 'international waterway', where freedom of shipping was a vital interest for the international community, and blocking would be an illegal and destructive act against peace.[10] The attempts of the United States to summon an urgent session of the Security Council encountered Soviet resistance.[11] The Soviet Union also rejected the French initiative, which Britain favoured though the United States was unenthusiastic, to hold discussions among the four Powers on a resolution of the crisis.[12]

The British formula fails

US documents reveal that the idea of opening up the Straits by employing an international armada was conceived by the British. On 24 May, before the United States had had time to contemplate possible paths of action, British Minister of State in the Foreign Office George Thomson landed in Washington straight from a government meeting in London (Foreign Secretary George Brown left for Moscow simultaneously) with a plan for action. It seemed that Abba Eban, who visited London that same day, had not wasted his time there. The main points of the British plan were: formulation of a declaration in support of freedom of shipping and recruitment of widespread international support among the maritime nations for an 'escort operation' in the Straits of Tiran, backed by a show of strength in the Eastern Mediterranean. President Johnson was sceptical as to the possibility of rallying a multinational force, while Secretary of State Dean Rusk argued that military action would require the approval of Congress, which would involve some delay.[13] However, in the absence of any other option, the Americans pinned their hopes on the faint hope of consolidating international support and participation in the venture, in the vain hope that they could thereby pressure Nasser into retreating. Rusk presented the alternatives to Johnson: to permit Israel to act (Rusk himself was vehemently opposed) or to take action in accordance with the British plan, without final commitment. The need to persuade Israel not to attack, however, induced the President to present a committed stand to the Israeli Foreign Minister.[14] For a week the British plan was under consideration in Washington as the sole operative possibility. Officially, it was not shelved until fighting broke out. In practice, it was defunct from the end of May.

The British–US plan was effective up to a certain stage, only in order to be brandished at Israel in order to persuade it that the administration was determined to open up the Straits. Nasser was much less impressed. The opposition of Egypt and the Arab world, and of the non-aligned nations and the Eastern Bloc, precluded widespread support for the proposed 'declaration of the maritime nations'. The text of the declaration was agreed on and conveyed to US legations in the maritime countries only on 31 May, when the administration was already seeking other solutions.[15] On 2 June the Americans and British agreed to defer for the time being military planning of a joint operation, for fear of leakages. In Congress, which had learned the lessons of Vietnam, support was expressed for US participation in military effort but only within the framework of the UN or a multinational coalition, and under no circumstances as unilateral action. The Department of Defence pointed out the many difficulties and dangers entailed in a military venture, in the absence of sufficient forces in the Red Sea arena.[16] The plan now seemed less attractive, and the administration was left with no alternative apart from granting Israel licence to act.

Evaluation: Israel will win

One of the important factors which eventually led the United States to consent in practice to permit Israel to solve its problems alone was related to the evaluation by Intelligence sources in the Department of Defence and the CIA that Israel would prevail. Dean Rusk claimed that the worst eventuality from the point of view of the United States would be if the Arabs defeated Israel and were close to driving it into the sea. Secretary of Defence McNamara claimed that the reverse was the most likely scenario: the United States would be in a tight spot if the Soviet Union hastened to rescue a defeated Egypt from Israel. The Intelligence Services did not change their attitude throughout the crisis, and continued to assert that the IDF could beat any Arab military coalition even if the Arabs inflicted the first blow. Israel's appeals for aid were 'a gambit' intended: (1) to persuade the United States to provide military supplies; (2) to extract more US public commitments to Israel; (3) to receive American approval for Israeli military initiatives; (4) to put more pressure on Nasser.[17] The military deployment in Sinai was perceived by the Americans as defensive in nature. Without entirely ruling out other calculations on Nasser's part (such as bringing forward the inevitable clash with Israel before the latter had acquired nuclear weapons), the possibility that Nasser was seeking a 'military show-down' with Israel was defined as highly unlikely, and Soviet opposition was also anticipated. The most likely course was that Nasser would drag out the situation, so that the long-term mobilization of reserve forces would have an increasingly adverse effect on Israel's economy.[18] At the same time, the Americans were convinced that Israel was in a state of great nervous tension and an 'apocalyptic' atmosphere (as Abba Eban called it in his talk with Dean Rusk),[19] and could not be restrained for long.

It is interesting to note that the US administration and the Intelligence appraisals did not attribute malicious intent to the Soviet Union or claim that it had instigated the crisis and had prior knowledge of Nasser's decision to close the Straits. They also ruled out any Soviet intention to foment a flare-up in the Middle East. The Soviets, it was assumed, regarded the crisis as 'a godsend' and were trying to derive the maximum political benefit at the expense of the United States in the region, but they did not want war. Rusk believed, notwithstanding, that if Israel attacked Egypt and won the day, the Soviets would do 'something', though he was not clear as to what.[20]

Israeli diplomacy – the view from Washington

Israel's diplomatic strategies have already been surveyed, but it is worth noting several points which emerge from the US documents:

1   Foreign Minister Eban endeavoured to boost the American commitment to Israel's security by asserting that the decisions of the Israeli government were guided by the requests and guarantees of the United States.[21] His message to the Americans was: it's your responsibility.
2   Eban permitted himself to take issue with the style Eshkol adopted in his urgent cables. He told Dean Rusk that the messages would have been phrased differently if he himself had been in Israel.[22]
3   Eban was apparently unconvincing in his rejection of the proposal to station a UN force on both sides of the Israel–Egypt border and perhaps only inside Israel. Rusk may have gained the impression that Israel would not reject the idea outright.[23]
4   The position Eban represented in Washington on 26 May was that the freedom of shipping issue was the central problem, and was 'far more serious than terrorist attacks or troop deployments, for its consequences would be to cut Israel off from one-half of the world and leave it crippled'. This stance, as noted above, was at variance with the views of the General Staff. Four days later, Eban told Ambassador Barbour the opposite: the concentration of forces on the border was more dangerous than the blocking of the Straits.[24]
5   The Israeli Minister in Washington, Ephraim Evron, adopted bold,

possibly unauthorized diplomatic initiative on 2 June. He met, at his own request, with Walt Rostow, the President's Assistant for National Security and emphasized that he was not speaking in the name of the Israeli government. Evron wondered aloud whether, in light of its relations with the Arab world and the Soviet Union, it would not be more advantageous for the United States if an Israeli vessel, rather than an international flotilla, tested the blockade. Egyptian fire directed against the vessel would trigger an Israeli military reaction and a general flare-up. Evron asked whether, in such a case, the United States would honour its 1957 commitment and acknowledge Israel's right to self-defence, and whether it would curb Soviet intervention. Rostow reported this to the President.[25] Was Evron acting off his own bat? It is hard to believe that a senior experienced diplomat would have conceived of such an idea without sanction, but on the other hand, I have found no evidence that he was ever authorized to convey such a message to the Americans. The IDF objected to the dispatch of a vessel to the Straits for fear of exposure of intent, and the government had not decided on such a move. It is barely conceivable that Evron received personal instructions from Eban to put out feelers in that direction. A day previously Eban had met with Rabin and informed him that the possibilities of diplomatic action had been exhausted and it was now yielding place to military considerations. Perhaps Eban wanted to ensure that the now inescapable war would not commence with Israeli action. As we shall see below, at the pivotal government session on 4 June, Eban sided with the ministers who advocated sending a vessel to the Straits so that Israel would not fire the first shot.

6   On the military level, the US documents reveal that apart from the above-mentioned 'aid package', discussions of which began before the crisis, Israel asked the US for the 'loan' of 150,000 to 200,000 gas masks, in addition to the 20,000 already supplied during the crisis. The Americans agreed but the masks were never sent.[26] Israel also requested the immediate supply of a Hawk battery and a hundred missiles, 140 M-60 tanks and twenty-four Skyhawk aircraft. The administration turned down the request for missiles and planes and agreed to consider the request for tanks,[27] but this too was not implemented by the time hostilities broke out.

Messages from Arab capitals: the standing of the US is in danger

A crucial reason for the administration's eventual decision to abandon the British–US scheme for opening up the Straits were the messages received from Arab capitals, which stressed that the United States would pay a heavy political and economic price for support of Israel, and that there was no likelihood that Nasser would rescind the blockade. Among the crucial points were the following:

1   The Saudi Minister of Petroleum Ahmed Zaki Yamani estimated on 24 May that the crisis would culminate in war. He recommended that the United States keep its hands off and act only within the UN framework without trying, as he put it, to act the 'policeman'. He warned that if the United States supported Israel on the issue of freedom of shipping, it would be 'finished' in the Middle East. Two days later King Hussein conveyed a similar message, and later declared that Nasser would not back down from the blockade and proposed that Washington declare its neutrality and opposition to any party which started a war.[28]

2   The designated ambassador to Cairo Richard Nolte conveyed his recommendation that the United States dissociate itself from appearances of support for Israel, remain neutral and step in only as peacemaker if hostilities erupted. 'Otherwise, we foresee heavy cost to the US for relationships in the Arab world. . . . Equally, see little chance viable future for Israel save as armed beachhead, guaranteed by US.'[29]

3   The US Ambassador to Damascus Hugh Smythe expressed his profound dismay at Washington's disregard for the appraisals and recommendations dispatched by its representatives in the Arab countries for a 'hands-off policy' in the dispute. He claimed that the US must abandon its guarantee to freedom of shipping in the Straits in view of the destructive consequences, and sharply criticized his country's support for Israel which he described as an 'unviable client state'.[30]

4   The Department of Defence and the CIA estimated that the passage through the Straits of an oil-tanker headed for Eilat flying the US flag or escorted by American warships would show up the United States as the enemy of the Arabs and evoke outraged responses and grave political and economic damage. 'The Arabs have smelled blood', according to the CIA, and euphoria and victorious emotion were sweeping even Nasser's bitterest enemies against their will into his camp. The Arabs were anticipating that the United States and Britain would hasten to Israel's aid and were preparing for that eventuality. The anticipated reactions included blocking of the Suez Canal, stoppage of oil supplies to the West, a ban on anchoring of vessels in Arab ports, a commercial boycott, the closing of the Wheelus US air base in Libya, nationalization of oil companies and assets, and attacks on US and British installations and institutions throughout the Middle East.[31]

5   Secretary of State Dean Rusk felt the need to write a personal reply to the US ambassadors in Damascus and other Arab countries and try to persuade them, citing numerous examples, that US policy in the Middle East was balanced. The long-term stance of the United States,

he explained, was based on two principles: preserving the independence and territorial integrity of all countries in the region, and defending the basic interest of the international community to maintain freedom of shipping. The United States could not go back on this basic stand, which had been proclaimed by all its presidents in the past two decades, particularly since its support for free shipping through Tiran had been proclaimed in return for Israel's consent to withdraw from Sharm al-Sheikh in 1957.[32]

6   The conclusion drawn by the US administration after receipt of the message from the pro-Western Arab states was that an Israeli military operation was to be preferred to US action. Walt Rostow wrote to the President on 4 June: 'The moderate Arabs – and, in fact, virtually all Arabs who fear the rise of Nasser as a result of this crisis – would prefer to have him cut down by the Israelis rather than by external forces.'[33]

The American emissaries to Cairo

Two senior US emissaries were dispatched to Cairo during the crisis. The first was the diplomat Charles Yost, a Middle Eastern expert and former ambassador to Damascus. He was sent by the Secretary of State to reinforce the legation in the Egyptian capital, then headed by a new and inexperienced ambassador who had not yet submitted his letter of accreditation. The second – and more senior – emissary was Robert Anderson, former Secretary of the Treasury, who had already tried his hand at mediation between Israel and Egypt in 1956.[34] Anderson, who travelled to the Middle East on business, was asked by President Johnson to visit Cairo and meet Nasser. The following are the main points of the reports submitted by the two emissaries:

1   Charles Yost, who met with Foreign Minister Mahmoud Riad among others, reported his impression that Nasser would not back down from the blockade, was showing no indications of readiness to compromise, would not be deterred by threats and might even welcome a military confrontation with Israel. US support for freedom of shipping in the Bay of Aqaba would severely undermine if not destroy its standing in the Middle East, and the forced opening up of the Straits would only strengthen Nasser. If the US continued to pursue this tactic, Yost warned, it would suffer the same fate as Britain and France in 1956. Yost even estimated that Nasser would extend his demands beyond restoration of the status quo ante the Sinai Campaign. He defined his recommendations as 'limiting damage': stationing a UN force in Israel, supplying Israel with oil from other ports, and renewed guarantees of Israel's existence and integfrity.[35]

2   Robert Anderson met with Nasser for two hours on the night of 31 May. Nasser explained in detail his motives and moves since the beginning of the crisis and clarified that he would not be the one to initiate war. He did, however, voice his fear that Syria was liable to take military action and involve him in a confrontation, and added that he had no control over the Palestinian organizations which were eager to fight. Nasser admitted that any conflict that would break out on the Syrian or Jordanian border would inevitably lead to Egyptian intervention. He appeared relaxed and confident as to the outcome of any military clash between the Arabs and Israel. As for the Tiran Straits – his sole aim was to revert to the 1956 status quo, which had been altered as a result of aggression. The Straits, he said, were in Egyptian territorial waters, and his army would prevent Israeli shipping, oil transportation and weapons supply to Israel through the Straits. To the question of whether he would agree to direct the issue to the international court at The Hague (the US commitment to Israel in 1957 had included the proviso that it should not conflict with decisions of the international court), Nasser replied that he was not interested in foot-dragging. He hinted that in effect his hands were tied: the Arabs as a whole would not accept any consent on his part to compromise. Anderson asked Nasser if he would agree to accept Israel as an established fact. Nasser replied that this depended on Israel permitting a million Palestinian refugees to return to their homeland. The refugees, he said, would not be content with compensation and would insist on returning because the Arabs were deeply attached to their land. The practical result of the meeting was a decision to dispatch the Deputy Egyptian President Zakaria Mohi al-Din to Washington. On 2 June Nasser sent a note to President Johnson, expounding his country's stand on the dispute with Israel. He noted that he would welcome a visit by Vice-President Humphrey (as proposed by Johnson in his note of 22 May). The US Embassy in Cairo reported that Mohi al-Din would leave for Washington on 7 June, and intended to discuss with his hosts a range of issues relating to the Palestinian problem, resolution of which would make it possible to resolve the Tiran shipping issue as well.[36]

Washington's recipe for compromise

In parallel to the decline of the British–US plan, the administration sought a compromise formula of some kind, which would not oblige Nasser to back down completely on the Straits issue, and which Israel could live with. The formula, in whose devising Israel played no part, was intended to award Nasser a symbolic victory and to avert substantial damage to Israel. The idea was to enable free passage of vessels of all countries through the Bay of Aqaba, including oil-tankers, with the exception of Israeli vessels. The issue of Israeli shipping would be discussed separately, possibly at The Hague court, when the crisis ended.[37] The assumption was that the actual damage to Israel from the blockade would stem mainly from the barring of oil-tankers from Iran, which supplied the bulk of Israel's oil requirements. Johnson told Eban that the United States was 'not going to say it's all right if the rest go through, but Israel's ships cannot',[38] but this was deliberately vague diplomatic talk. The Americans had received no indication that Nasser would be ready to accept such a compromise, and were probably planning to discuss the matter with Mohi al-Din. They surmised that if Nasser was reconciled to this idea (and the prospects were very slim), they would be able to exert pressure on Israel to accept it, even as a provisional arrangement. They were too late.[39]

The conclusion: let Israel act

Washington never took a formal decision to allow Israel to act. Officially, the British–American plan was never taken off the agenda. The 'declaration of the maritime nations' continued to be discussed through diplomatic channels until the outbreak of the fighting and signatures were collected, with scant success. Only two countries – Australia and Holland – displayed readiness to participate in the multinational armada. The date for the commencement of joint military planning was set for 6 June, and nobody was eager to take part. The administration knew that time was running out. The Americans estimated that Israel would not wait beyond 11 June, two weeks after it had promised to wait. The recommendation that Israel be allowed to act was formulated and argued in the best possible fashion by a member of the National Security Council, Harold Saunders, on 31 May.

The United States, Saunders wrote, had reversed the policy of twenty years in the Midde East and was now committed 'to a course that will more likely than not lead us into a head-on clash with a temporarily united Arab world'. The US should have allowed Israel to launch a strike on 21 May when Egypt was not yet ready and then intervened as peacemaker. 'It seems that the UAR has won all the chips to date, but Israel may really be the big winner', having won what the US steadfastly refused to give for twenty years: a special relationship and a security guarantee. 'Whoever is the bigger winner, we are the sure loser,' Saunders claimed. 'If we follow our present course, we stand to lose economically ... and to suffer substantial Soviet gains. If we back away from Israel, we're a paper tiger.' It was now clear that Nasser had no intention of backing down. The Arab world was united in its resolve to take drastic steps against the United States. Other maritime powers were not willing to join the 'regatta'. And Congress would not approve independent action. 'The other choice is still to let the Israelis do this job themselves.' Eshkol had stated that he was willing to go it alone if the United States did not produce results. He 'is correct that we don't have any right to hold him back longer while his enemy gets stronger unless we're willing to take on the Arabs ourselves. Pretty soon we'll have Soviet warships in the Red Sea. We ought to consider admitting that we have failed and allow fighting to ensue.'[40]

The Saunders report was written from a personal viewpoint but it reflected the mood of the administration at the end of May. Rusk wrote on 3 June to US ambassadors in Arab countries: 'You should not assume that the United States can order Israel not to fight for what it considers to be its most vital interests.'[41]

The mission of the head of the Mossad

Because of the conflicting messages received from the United States, the Chief of Intelligence proposed to Eshkol that he send the Mossad head, Meir Amit, to Washington to ascertain directly the administration's stand.[42] His mission was interpreted as an expression of non-confidence in Foreign Minister Eban, who had returned from Washington only four days previously, and in his ministry.[43] This, however, was apparently a misinterpretation. Between 26 May, when Eban met with Johnson, and 31 May, when Amit left Israel, the circumstances had changed entirely with the signing of the Egyptian–Jordanian pact. The indications of a change in the US stance called for discreet and clandestine enquiries at the highest level. This was the goal of Amit's trip.[44]

Amit left for the United States on 31 May,[45] and on the day he arrived in Washington, his first meeting was with the CIA's Intelligence experts for a comparison of Intelligence data and estimates, which turned out to be very similar. At a meeting with Richard Helms, head of the CIA, Amit discovered to his surprise that no command had been set up to plan the blockade-lifting operation. At his request, a brief meeting was scheduled for the following day with Defense Secretary Robert McNamara. According to Amit, he exceeded his authority by telling McNamara that Israel could not wait three weeks, but three to four days at most. Israel did not want a single US soldier to fight on its behalf, he stressed, but it wanted three things from the United States:

1   Isolation of the arena from any Soviet attempt to intervene.
2   Diplomatic backing at the UN in the course of the military operation, in order to enable the IDF to achieve its objectives.
3   To restock the IDF's arms depots after the war.

McNamara asked only two questions: how long would the fighting last and what was the anticipated scope of casualties. Amit estimated that the fighting would last a week and casualties would be lower than in Israel's War of Independence (in which it lost about 1 per cent of its population). 'I read you loud and clear', said McNamara, who expressed no reservations whatsoever. During the meeting, he contacted Johnson and reported to him. A note was passed in to him on Dayan's appointment as Minister of Defence. He stood up and embraced Amit. 'You should go home. Your place is there', he told him.

If Amit's description is accurate, the United States was indicating through this channel that, so far as it was concerned, Israel had the green light for a pre-emptive strike. It should be pointed out, however, that the summary of the conversation as it appears in the US documents is not identical to Amit's version, and does not necessarily suggest a hint to Israel.[46]

And in fact, the messages from the United States were not yet unequivocal. It was manifest that the US had withdrawn its veto on an Israeli attack, but the administration feared that this move would appear to be part of a US–Israel conspiracy. Consequently, the State Department continued to urge Israel not to fire the first shot. The Americans now thought it preferable for Israel to send a vessel to the Straits of Tiran so that Egyptian fire would serve as the direct pretext for warfare.

Unlike Defence Secretary McNamara, Secretary of State Rusk was considered by Israeli diplomats in Washington to be aloof and chilly in his attitude towards Israel.[47] In fact, Rusk was entirely fair in his dealing with the crisis and tried to find a solution which would prevent a conflagration. As noted above, it was the State Department which broached the plan to open the Straits by bringing in an international maritime force, while the Defense Department had misgivings about it. At first, Rusk did not share the view of the Defense Department that it was preferable to leave it to Israel to act. The peremptory note he appended to Johnson's message to Eshkol, in which he asserted that Israel action would be 'catastrophic', helped persuade Israel on 28 May to decide on a waiting period. On 30 May, however, Washington's evaluation was amended. The organization of an international armada (scarcely a serious idea from the outset) and the moves at the UN and in Congress were proceeding at snail's pace, and lagged behind the feverish pace of events in the Middle East. Now the Secretary of State had no alternative but to acquit the United States insofar as possible of the responsibility for the inevitable conflagration.

At a meeting on 2 June with Ambassador Harman and Minister Evron, Rusk and Eugene Rostow tried to gain time and deter Israel from action. The plan for an armada was proceeding apace, the Americans said, and the test in the Straits was scheduled for seven to nine days' time. The Soviets had promised that the Egyptians would not attack, Rusk noted, and although this couild not be relied on, 'if it was necessary to enter into a military confrontation with the Russians, he would think twice'.

The Ambassador commented that Israel surmised that the Soviet Union would not intervene, and Rusk responded that 'a lot depends on the question of who starts the war'. [48]

The message to Israel was that it should not be the first to open fire. The American 'whip' was the implied threat that if Israel started a war and the Soviets intervened, the United States would be absolved of the commitment to Israel, which had ignored its advice.

On the following day, 3 June, Eugene Rostow contacted Evron and asked urgently whether the Israeli 'test' vessel (the *Dolphin*) had in fact left the Eritrean port of Massawa headed for Egypt (it had not).[49] It is possible that the Americans were trying to hint as to how they thought Israel should act. The recommendation to Israel to dispatch a vessel flying its flag to the Straits, so that the Egyptians would fire the first shot, was also conveyed directly, though unofficially.[50]

The Johnson note: 'A yellow light'

On 3 June Johnson sent Eshkol an additional message, the last before the war. It seemingly contained nothing new. Johnson reiterated the main points he had voiced to Eban eight days earlier and the written message he had given him. He reaffirmed the intention of his administration to continue its vigorous efforts at the UN and elsewhere to guarantee freedom of shipping through the Straits of Tiran, and explained his constitutional constraints. At the same time, however, there were two important points in the message. The President emphasized that Israel should not be responsible for launching hostilities (and repeated the mantra that 'Israel will not be alone unless it decides to go it alone'). In the second paragraph he conveyed a heavy hint that the true message from the United States was being carried by the head of the Mossad: 'We have completely and fully exchanged views with General Amit.'[51]

Towards evening on Saturday, 3 June, before receipt of Johnson's note, Eshkol convened a meeting at his home, attended by Dayan, Allon and Rabin.[52] Analysis of the cables and messages from the United States left the participants confused. Eshkol complained that Washington was focusing only on the problem of the Straits and ignoring the main problem – the massing of forces. Foreign Ministry Director-General Arie Levavi said he was afraid that if Israel acted, the United States would regard itself as released from the obligation to extend help, while the Soviets might 'go far'.[53] Meir Amit's return was tensely awaited. Close to midnight, Amit and Harman arrived directly from the airport.

Amit said that he had found no differences between the information and evaluations of Israeli Intelligence and those of US Intelligence. As for the maritime task force, he revealed 'that there is no body dealing with the matter in serious fashion', and added that he thought the armada would never materialize, and in any event 'the Americans are anxious for us to unburden them of the armada'. As for independent Israeli action, the head of the Mossad had gained the impression 'that the Americans would welcome any action as long as we succeed in smashing Nasser'. But he had understood from his interlocutors in Washington that Israel must first implement the *casus belli* in the Red Sea (namely, send a vessel through the Straits, which would come under Egyptian attack). Amit recommended waiting an additional week (to complete at least a two-week waiting period) and only then to exploit the pretext for war. In view of the hints that the Americans were ready to help, the head of the Mossad had asked his hosts for 'weapons, money and political backing'. He concluded: 'If we launch warfare and succeed – everyone will be with us. If we do not succeed – things will be hard.'

Ambassador Harman described the political situation in the US capital. There was considerable support for Israel, he said, and Johnson would have 'a political problem' if he did not succeed in finding a solution to the crisis. His conclusion was that the President should be granted a respite of 'seven to nine' days before Israel took any decision to act, and recommended in particular 'making sure that we do not fire the first shot'.

Having delivered their reports, Harman and Amit were submitted to a cross-fire of questions, in particular from Dayan and Allon who attacked both the idea of sending a ship through the Straits for fear that it would constitute disclosure of intent, and the recommendation to continue waiting. Harman and Amit tried to defend themselves and said that the additional wait was important from the diplomatic viewpoint in order to win the backing of the US President. Dayan was furious: 'The true altern-ative,' he said, 'is for [the Egyptians] to attack, but then we lose Eretz Israel. Anyone who waits for the Egyptians to take action must be aware that thereby we will lose Eretz Israel. We don't give a damn about the Americans. In this situation it would be stupidity to wait!'

The Chief of Staff Yitzhak Rabin explained that every passing day made the IDF's task harder in view of the buildup of Egyptian forces, their con-solidation and improved disposition. In particular, he pointed to the divi-sional Iraqi task force and the Egyptian commando battalions and fighter planes which were arriving in Jordan. Dayan reinforced Rabin's remarks and stressed the danger to Eilat and the price of waiting, which he said would result in a mortality rate of thousands more.[54]

Finally, Eshkol seemed to be convinced. He asked how long it would take the IDF to launch an offensive, and even queried if it was possible to act immediately – 'this morning'. In the end it was agreed that the decision to go to war would be submitted to the government at its weekly meeting due to convene in a few hours' time, on Sunday morning, 4 June, so that the attack could commence the following day.[55]

Johnson's note reached Eshkol only on 4 June, at the height of the government meeting,[56] and made very little difference. In contrast to the previous note, it contained nothing which was likely to defer the decision the government was about to take.

The government debates and decides: War!

The Ministerial Committee on Security convened at 08:30 on Sunday, 4 June.[57] The Foreign Minister delivered a political survey in which he noted that since the signing of the Egyptian–Jordanian pact, the United States had realized that Israel might act independently,[58] while emphasizing that Israel should not be the first to open fire. The assumption in Washington was that the Soviet Union would not intervene, although the Secretary of State was careful not to say so explicitly, in order to leave his country uncommitted and to pressure Israel not to be the first to fire. President de Gaulle, who had imposed an embargo on arms consignments to Israel, had again warned Israel against war (at a chance meeting with Ambassador Walter Eytan).

The Chief of Intelligence stated that he had 'a very clear picture of Egyptian military strategy': Egypt considered a clash to be inevitable, and hence was cramming more and more forces into Sinai and investing considerable effort on additional fronts. He referred 'to de facto [Egyptian] domination of the Jordanian army', to the imminent entry into Jordan of a large Iraqi task force, to the orders issued by General Riad to initiate wide-scale hostile actions when fighting broke out, and to the danger posed by the Egyptian commando battalions which had already arrived in Jordan. 'I don't want to create panic', Yariv emphasized, but his conclusion was clear: from minute to minute the prospect of Egyptian offensive initiative was growing, and it was self-evident that the IDF must deliver the first strike.

Menahem Begin commented at this point that Israel could send a vessel to Egypt, and if the Egyptians shelled it, Israel would then have the right to defend itself. Eban underscored this, saying that in such an event, Israel would enjoy US support. These statements angered the Minister of Defence.

Dayan: 'We are at the limit of our ability to win a war'

Dayan was more categorical: 'Nasser has to pay the promissory notes he signs', he argued, and his offensive intentions were obvious. Nasser's most likely targets were airfields ('to do to us what we want to do to them') and Jerusalem and Eilat. If the war began with an enemy air attack, the IDF would have forfeited its main weapon. If the enemy took the initiative, or commando battalions attacked in Jerusalem ('they could go through Bet Safafa into the heart of Jerusalem and perpetrate a massacre'), or Eilat was captured ('it's a question of one push [for the Jordanian army] in order to join up with the Egyptian forces'), Israel would lose the initiative, its operative planning would go awry and it would be driven to defence in the rear, 'which is almost all of Israel's territory'. As time passed, the enemy forces were building up and consolidating and the cost of fighting would mount by thousands. Dayan furiously rejected the demand to wait, to dispatch a vessel to Egypt and to refrain from firing the first shot: 'The stupidest thing possible would be to ask us now not to fire the first shot. It would mean that in the present situation we should allow the other side to fire the first shot.' The Egyptians, Dayan stressed, were tracing every vessel which set out from Massawa and would exploit the early warning in order to launch hostilities, the scope, location and timing of which they would choose, while Israel would be abandoning the element of surprise. 'I am sitting here listening and I can't believe what I'm hearing – allow the Egyptians to start the fighting at will, to destroy our air force!'

Dayan added that there was a limit to the IDF's ability to overcome the Arab armies, both due to the limited geographic dimensions of the state and because of the cost in blood. 'We are at the limit of our ability to win a war', he cautioned. He therefore proposed taking the initiative and acting as soon as possible in order to cut the military noose now tightening around Israel, even if thereby Israel found itself in a complicated diplomatic predicament. 'Afterwards we will launch our diplomatic campaign from a poor position, but it will be possible to survive where the military situation is concerned', he said.

Eshkol: 'What will happen afterwards?'

Eshkol, who had not yet received Johnson's note, said that it was his impression that 'something all the same is softening in the President's tough stand'. He said he would have wanted to wait another week if he hadn't seen 'the life-and-death danger' to Israel from the tightening noose.

Eban interrupted Eshkol and reported the content of Johnson's note which he had just received. Continuing his remarks, Eshkol did not disguise his fears as to 'what will happen afterwards?' if Israel was charged with aggression and deprived of military supplies. He thought there was a certain logic in de Gaulle's question: 'Assuming that you win, what will happen in ten to fifteen years' time?'

Eshkol was in distress[59] but saw no way out. If the Americans had been ready to provide Israel with an overt guarantee openly by means of the Sixth Fleet, he said, he would have been content with that.[60] But in the absence of such a guarantee he proposed allowing the IDF to decide on the timing and method of the offensive.

Allon: 'Better for them to condemn us and for us to live than for them to lament us'

Allon, who from the outset had favoured a pre-emptive strike, said that the Johnson note and the reports of Amit and Harman were evidence that the United States preferred to leave the job to Israel. The diplomatic possibilities had been exhausted, Allon declared, and it was essential to act because of the mortal danger. 'Better for them to condemn us and for us to live than for them to lament us' he said, and added that the Egyptians had crossed three red lines: the blocking of the Straits, the concentration of an offensive force and violation of the status quo in Jordan. He considered the Jordanian border to be the greatest danger and estimated that an instant Israeli victory at the beginning of the offensive against Egypt could deter Hussein from opening up a third front.

There was no serious debate at the Ministerial Committee on Security. Even Zalman Aranne, the ultimate 'dove', now supported early launching of hostilities. Zerah Wahrhaftig appealed for the dispatch of a vessel to the Straits, so that Israel would not be the first to open fire. Dayan and Allon, however, dismissed his proposal. 'It would be like cabling the Egyptian command that the Israelis are planning to attack on such and such a date. It would be total suicide', said Dayan.

Considerable circumspection was displayed by the new minister, Menahem Begin. He proposed sending Meir Amit on an additional secret mission to Paris, London and Washington in order to explain Israel's predicament and to seek the understanding of the leaders. His proposal was apparently greeted with derision, and he agreed to withdraw it if such a move was liable to have a negative impact on IDF operations. He too was convinced that the government should give the army the signal to launch an all-out offensive against the Egyptian army. Such an attack, he said, should not be immediate but should take place in the coming week.[61]

After the Ministerial Committee on Security concluded its meeting, the government plenum then convened as an expanded Committee, to discuss the situation.[62] Yariv began with an Intelligence survey and concluded: 'Not only is the picture changing from minute to minute and critically to our detriment ... but from hour to hour the possibility of offensive Egyptian, Jordanian and Syrian initiative is growing.' He was followed by Eban, who surveyed the political picture. He described the change in the US stance, but noted that the US advocates of Israeli action were requesting that events be manipulated so that the Egyptians would fire the first shot. The view in Washington, he said, was that the Soviet Union would not intervene in the fighting and lacked the tools to do so, but this was only a surmise and there was no certainty of this. Eshkol again spoke about the 'tightening noose' which must be cut as early as possible.

The dovish ministers Bentov and Moshe Haim Shapira acknowledged the gravity of the situation but asked for a deferment of action for another week in order to enable the United States to act, and proposed that Israel should not be the first to open fire. Their main concern was that an embargo might be imposed on arms supplies to Israel.[63] However, the majority of the ministers now backed the Israeli offensive initiative. The most profound impression was made by Dayan's purposeful remarks.

Dayan explained the critical significance of the first blow in light of Israel's lack of reserves and the limitations on its power. He described the protracted process of buildup and organization of the forces confronting Israel in terms of thousands of additional Israeli casualties in the inevitable war. He also dwelt on the danger to Jerusalem, Eilat and the coastal plain from Arab offensive initiative, which could disrupt any IDF operative planning. What was on the cards was the first blow, he stressed. A surprise blow, he explained, could put a hundred enemy planes out of action and he added mockingly: 'Those one hundred planes are worth more than all the additional arms which the Minister of the Interior [M.H. Shapira] or Knesset Member Ben-Gurion [who opposed going to war] can obtain in the coming six months.'

Dayan's strongest argument was the limited ability of the IDF to prevail if the war was conducted on enemy initiative and in arenas determined by the enemy. 'Our only chance of winning a war is to be the initiators and to conduct it according to our own direction', said Dayan. 'There is a limit to our ability to win', and in any war conducted on the enemy's initiative, Israel was liable to suffer defeat.

'The government has decided to take military action'

After Dayan had spoken, there was no further debate within the government. All the ministers, excluding the two Mapam representatives, rallied around Dayan's draft proposal, the main points of which were:

> The government has decided to take military action which will liberate Israel from the military noose tightening around it ... the government hereby empowers the Prime Minister and Minister of Defence to approve for the General Staff the date of the operation.[64]

The crisis which led up to the Six Day War lasted for three weeks, and IDF forces were mobilized almost in full for about two of those weeks. Away from the feverish activity in the political and diplomatic arenas, the IDF concentrated on preparations for war. The waiting period was exploited for training, stock-up of equipment, and logistic and operational planning – all of which improved the IDF's fighting capability.[65] In contrast to the apprehensive mood on the home front, the mobilized troops were in high spirits and confident. The press and radio, of vital importance during the crisis, generally considered themselves to have been enlisted to the cause in order to uplift national morale, maintain contact between the front line and the home front and alleviate anxiety.[66] The former chief of Intelligence Brigadier-General (res.) Haim Herzog was summoned to Kol Israel, the national radio service, to broadcast reassuring reports and evaluations to the nation.[67] Popular songs were composed to boost the public mood and the sense of shared destiny was reflected in manifestations of fraternity, volunteering and mutual aid. The strongest boost for morale was undoubtedly the establishment of the national unity government and the appointment of Moshe Dayan, hero of the Sinai Campaign, as Minister of Defence.

In short: by the time the government decided to go to war, the nation was well prepared. The army was tensed like a coiled spring. The home front was united, and convinced that the war was justified and that there was 'no alternative'.[68]

Towards evening on 4 June, the Operations Branch issued the order for Operation Nakhshonim. In essence, this order was of mere historical value, and constituted a general summary of the framework of the planned IDF operation. The IDF offensive was intended for the Egyptian front alone. Central and Northern Commands were assigned exclusively defensive missions. The execution of local 'skirmishes' on the Jordanian front, in the event that the Jordanian army opened fire, was to be conditional on approval of the Operations Branch.[69] The zero hour had been chosen in accordance with the plan for the IAF's Operation Moked, namely a surprise attack for destruction of the Egyptian air force in its home. The stopwatches of the air, ground and naval forces were set at 07:45.[70]

Few were in on the secret; the forces were resting before going into action and last-minute preparations, communications or troop movements were avoided as liable to arouse the suspicion of the other side. Consequently, the last night was quiet.

On 5 June at 07:45 as the IAF's Moked Operation against Egyptian air bases commenced, the siren alert sounded throughout the country. The Assistant Chief of Operations, Brigadier-General Rehavam Ze'evi, conveyed to the Southern Command the order: 'Nakhshonim, we wish you success, action!'[71]

The war had begun.

Afterword

The war which began on the morning of 5 June 1967 was regarded by the generation of Israelis who experienced it in the front line and on the home front, as well as by the government and the IDF General Staff, as a war of 'no alternative'. It was born out of authentic feelings of deep anxiety and existential threat, and its sole purpose was to eliminate that threat and lift the blockade without territorial aspirations or definition of political objectives for the post-war future. In fact, the Eshkol government never discussed the objectives of the war, even when that war appeared inescapable. All the government wanted was to ward off hostilities, and when it was compelled to take the decision to fight, it phrased it in simple terms: 'The government has decided to take military action which will liberate Israel from the military noose tightening around it.'[1]

The aim, so it was implied, was to restore the status quo ante and no more than that. The military moves very soon confronted the government with facts which required it to take decisions for which it was unprepared. The first day of fighting raised the issue of the conquest – Menahem Begin asked that it be referred to as 'liberation' – of the Old City of Jerusalem. The government deliberations on the issue reflected, above all, incertitude, and National Religious Party leader Mosh Haim Shapira advocated internationalization of the Old City.[2] Dayan displayed scant enthusiasm for the conquest of the Old City, and his secretary Haim Yisraeli reported to Ben-Gurion: 'Moshe doesn't want to conquer it because he doesn't want to have to give back the Western Wall.'[3]

Eshkol summed up the order of priorities: the first priority was the Sinai front and the occupation of Sharm al-Sheikh, while

> 'in the Jordanian sector we are going forward in the prior knowledge that we will be obliged to leave [East] Jerusalem and the West Bank. On the Syrian [front] we need to take the Banias [springs].... It is not worth entering the el-Hamma [enclave in the demilitarized zone] because it is a "hole" [i.e. too remote], it's worth [however] finishing

off [i.e. capturing and controlling] the [other parts of the] demilitarized zones [along the Israel–Syria border].'[4]

The army carried out its tasks on the Egyptian and Jordanian fronts in accordance with operative plans and the nature of the terrain and of the enemy forces confronting it, irespective of political objectives. The offensive on the Syrian front was postponed to the fifth day of the war, and was launched on 9 June on the personal initiative of Defence Minister Dayan, contrary to the uncompromising stand he had held at the previous evening's meeting of the Ministerial Committee on Security, which had thwarted the decision to approve such an attack.[5] Although the IDF action was conducted without the framework of orderly political decisions, at the conclusion of the brief war Israel held all the cards it required to make far-reaching political decisions and to shape a new political reality in an attempt to resolve the Arab–Israeli dispute.

On 12 June 1967, a few hours after the fighting ended, Dayan held 'consultations on the conquered territories'. Senior army officers hastened to submit various proposals. The Head of the Intelligence Branch's Research Department, Col. Shlomo Gazit, opined that Israel had no interest in conquest and in expanding its territory at the expense of the Arabs and that there was room only for border revisions based on negotiations. He proposed solving the problem of the Palestinian refugees by establishing a demilitarized Palestinian state on the West Bank and in the Gaza Strip. Col. Yuval Neeman, who had been recruited as special adviser to the Intelligence Branch, proposed, on the other hand, delineating 'natural' borders for the State of Israel, identical to the ceasefire lines, including the whole of the Sinai Peninsula, the Gaza strip, the West Bank and the Golan Heights. He suggested the establishment of an autonomous Palestinian state with federative links to Israel and without common borders with any Arab state.[6] The Assistant Chief of Operations, Brigadier-General Rehavam Ze'evi, proposed establishing an independent Palestinian state in Samaria, with Nablus as its capital, and even provided a name, 'Medinat Yishmael' (The State of Ishmael). Ze'evi declared that the new state should be established as soon as possible and warned that 'protracted Israeli military rule will enhance the hatred and deepen the rift between the [Palestinian] inhabitants of the West Bank and Israel, because of the objective steps it will be essential to adopt in order to ensure order and security'.[7]

Dayan had already judged at this stage that any Israeli political scheme would be dependent on the support of the United States. He, who as Chief of Staff in 1957 had harshly criticized Ben-Gurion's 'capitulation' to American pressure to withdraw from all territory captured in the Sinai Campaign, now assumed that Washington would not permit Israel to establish political facts as it saw fit. The only real debate at the Ministerial Committee on Security was conducted on the future of the West Bank between ministers who favoured the 'Palestinian option', namely the establishment of an independent or autonomous Palestinian state, and those who advocated a settlement with Jordan. Eshkol wanted Israel to decide rapidly on its position. It was his view that Israel should annex only East Jerusalem and the Gaza Strip, although he had doubts as to the latter. Due to the controversy, the government passed a unanimous secret resolution on 19 June 1967 relating only to Egypt and Syria. It stated that Israel proposed peace treaties on the basis of the international border and demilitarizing arrangements in Sinai and on the Golan Heights, a guarantee of freedom of shipping through the Suez Canal and the Bay of Aqaba, and non-interference with the flow of the Jordan source waters. The government decision was transmitted by the United States to Egypt and Syria. Despite the generous Israeli proposal offering the return of all the Egyptian and Syrian territories, the uncompromising response was a demand for unconditional Israeli withdrawal.[8] The political initiative of the Israeli government and the response it received dispelled fears of American pressure for early withdrawal. Israel now toughened its stand on the future of the occupied territories and the decision of 19 June was no longer compatible with the new position. The mood in Israel was euphoric, and Dayan's declaration that the Arabs should make the first phone call[9] turned into a policy. Levi Eshkol, the ailing Prime Minister, was losing his grip, and Dayan became the dominant figure in determining Israel's security policies and how the occupied territories were to be administered. The pivotal resolution adopted by the national unity government immediately after the war was the unification of Jerusalem. The decision to apply the 'jurisdiction and administration of the state to East Jerusalem' was formulated by 11 June. On 27 June, the government approved the decision and drew the municipal boundaries of the united city. The Knesset passed the law on the unification of Jerusalem the same day.[10]

In contrast to the prevailing view, I believe that the establishment of the national unity government on 1 June 1967 did not have a decisive impact on the decision to go to war or on the way in which that war proceeded. The Eshkol government would most probably have arrived at its decision even without the Rafi and Gahal representatives. There was no escape from war, not necessarily because of pressure from the IDF, but due to a combination of reasons: Nasser's resolve to maintain the blockade in Tiran and the dissolving of the plan for an international armada; the clustering of hostile Arab forces along Israel's borders; the exacerbation of the threat after the signing of the Egyptian–Jordanian pact and the anticipated entry into Jordan of a large Iraqi task force; the inability to maintain long-term mobilization of reserve forces; and finally, the indications from Washington that Israel was free to act as it saw fit. The war would probably have been conducted in the same fashion even if Dayan had not taken over the Defence portfolio from Eshkol. On the other hand, the expansion of the government had an extensive impact on Israel's post-war policy. It is unquestionable that a government without the dominant war hero Moshe Dayan, and without the influence of the Gahal ministers, would have conducted itself differently, thereby holding out better prospects for the Jordanian option.[11] It is a moot question whether this path of action would have tempered the influence of the generals, who had been transformed in public eyes by the intoxication of victory into all-powerful heroes incapable of error. The disillusion came only six years later, when Israel was stunned by the outbreak of another war in the middle of the holiest day in the Jewish calendar: Yom Kippur.

In summing up the facts presented in this book, my conclusion is: in the four years preceding the Six Day War, the military activism of the General Staff had a detrimental impact on the attainment of the security policy goals. While the army was subordinate to the political echelon, it was not subjected to effective control and often exceeded the bounds of the government's intentions. The senior command did not intend deliberately to bring about war in order to expand Israel's borders. In light of the forced withdrawal in 1957 from all the territorial gains of the Sinai Campaign, the accepted assumption was that there was little chance of preserving such gains in 1967. What was required, according to the Chief of Staff, was forceful action in order to maintain Israel's deterrent capability and force the authorities in Amman, Beirut and in particular Damascus to put a stop to terrorist action against Israel. Hence, the military demanded a strategic military response to a tactical military problem. In light of the flawed nature of civilian control and the absence of an effective diplomatic means of tackling the problem of terrorism, the expansion of military action was inevitable. Consequently, the army (at Samu and in determining the scope of aerial operations) slid unintentionally from the tactical to the strategic sphere. The military triumph of the Six Day War should not be allowed to obscure the fact that the army failed to achieve the strategic objective of the government's security policy – protection of the status quo, putting an end to the terrorist activity and the prevention of war.

What remains is value judgement: given the circumstances, conditions and Intelligence evaluations which faced the military command, did it act fittingly? Did it act properly or improperly?

Chief of Staff Yitzhak Rabin, a sensitive and conscientious man, took upon himself the full burden of responsibility and admitted honestly: 'I entangled the State of Israel because of a series of mistakes I made' (see Appendix). There can be almost no doubt that Rabin was referring to the military operations – in particular the IAF operation of 7 April 1967 – which led to escalation and embroilment in war. Rabin was the government's trustee on security matters, charged with the task of dealing with challenges in a manner which would forestall war. This was in fact his intention, but he failed. The narrow line between increasing deterrence and worsening escalation was crossed unwittingly. Let it be said in Rabin's defence that he was relying on a hidebound Intelligence evaluation to the effect that Nasser did not want war and hence Israel had considerable leeway for action against Syria without real danger of becoming involved in war. In the period under discussion (and later too) the IDF Intelligence Branch enjoyed a monopoly regarding national evaluations and the collating of databases and conclusions. The fundamental error did not stem, therefore, from the level of strategic intentions, but from misguided Intelligence evaluations. The problem lay not in the abundant raw field of Intelligence material which the secret services supplied to the IDF, whose quality was vindicated during the war, but in the ability to foresee the intentions and moves of the other.

The result, as noted above, was total failure of Israel's security policy, whose supreme aim had been the deterrence and prevention of war. Rabin considered himself responsible for this failure. But while there may be some justification for blaming the military leadership for causing the May 1967 crisis, no fundamental defect can be perceived in the standpoint of the military during the crisis and in the pressure it brought to bear on the government to launch a pre-emptive strike. The subjective sense of existential danger was authentic, and not unjustified. Nasser had crossed the 'red lines' and posed an insupportable challenge to Israel's deterrent capability, which was its main barrier against Arab hostile initiative to alter the status quo and carry out the proclaimed intention of annihilating Israel. The closing of Arab ranks around Nasser, the ecstatic bellicose atmosphere in the Arab world and the gradual buildup of forces around Israel's long borders dramatized this danger and created tremendous psychological pressure on Israel. The many expressions of sympathy and support from world public opinion were no substitute for the absence of military guarantees on the part of the Powers for Israel's security. The diplomatic efforts merely proved that it was impossible to place trust in external aid. Under these conditions, the decision to wait seemed disastrous, both because it granted the enemy respite for further troop buildups, consolidation and organization, and – and this was the main point – because it left the enemy the initiative for striking the first blow. The critical significance of the first blow under Israel's geographic conditions at the time was self-evident. The balance of forces between Israel and the Arab states in arithmetic terms was considered potentially critical and liable to have a crucial effect on the course and outcome of the war if the Arabs were first to attack. The desire of the senior command to act first was therefore entirely justified. The war, in the final analysis, bore this out.

One may conclude by stating that the military leadership, to a large extent, 'entangled' the State of Israel (to quote Rabin) in escalation which generated the crisis which culminated in an unpremeditated war, a war which from the outset was unwanted and non-essential. But from the moment the crisis erupted and the threat emerged, the military's advocacy of offensive initiative was correct. During the war itself, the IDF, as is well known, carried out its mission in the best possible fashion.

Appendix
What happened to Yitzhak Rabin?

Yitzhak Rabin was a very strong Chief of Staff. He was authoritative, professional, dominant, charismatic,[1] and unquestionably had the greatest personal impact on the military forces which won the 1967 war so decisively. For eight years (more than any of his predecessors or successors), as Chief of Operations, Deputy Chief of Staff and Chief of Staff, Rabin was in charge of all the crucial tasks of preparing the army for war. If there is one individual, more than any other, who deserves the credit for the efficient functioning and resounding victory of the IDF in the Six Day War, it is, without a doubt, Yitzhak Rabin. But while this is true of the preparations for war, the same cannot be said of the way in which the crisis and campaign of May to June 1967 were managed by Rabin. He was not at his best then.

Yitzhak Rabin was more a 'builder of force' than a 'user of force'.[2] He was extremely methodical, calculated, analytical, measured, sensitive and cautious, but he was not a commander who galvanizes his men and stirs them for the fight. His lengthy military career notwithstanding, Rabin's biography did not include the command of combat divisions in wartime, apart from a very brief period during Israel's War of Independence when he commanded the Harel mini-brigade which battled heroically to save Jerusalem from falling. During the Sinai Campaign Rabin was CO Northern Command and outside the battle area.

As Chief of Staff, Rabin enjoyed unprecedented status. Minister of Defence Eshkol left the military arena to him. Eshkol's military secretary, Yisrael Lior, testified that Eshkol placed his trust in Rabin 'uncritically', abided by his advice almost without discussion and accepted his opinion 'with closed eyes'. The impression was gradually created that the Chief of Staff was essentially functioning as a quasi-Minister of Defence. Rabin permitted himself to issue declarations and grant numerous interviews to the press and on more than one occasion gave free rein to his opinion to an extent which embarrassed the political echelon and earned him a discreet private reprimand from the Prime Minister. Among the general public, however, his prestige was high. He was, as Lior put it, 'astoundingly popular', and sought after by the media. His handsome appearance, deep voice, and the professional authority and responsibility which he radiated, won him great popularity. In these respects, Rabin was a very 'political' Chief of Staff and, in the contest for public adulation, he left the Prime Minister and the political leadership far behind.

Rabin's quasi-ministerial status, his regular participation in meetings of the government and the Ministerial Committee on Security, and the fact that he was the supreme military authority in the eyes of the army and the civilian echelon, contributed to the blurring of borderlines, which was the source of his predicament during the crisis.[3] In the course of his deliberations with ministers, Rabin was privy to a wide range of government calculations, and internalized not only the complexity and implications of the security policy and foreign relations, but also apparently some of the anxieties of several senior ministers. Until a certain stage in the crisis, Rabin responded to the prospect of imminent war with a degree of 'fear and trembling'. He particularly dreaded the possibility of heavy casualties, and his sense of responsibility overpowered him. From this point of view, he ceased to be the assertive representative of the army's stand, and began to share the misgivings of the government. Several of the generals felt that the message he was conveying to the politicians was not sufficiently emphatic and clear, and there were also reverberations to that effect in the political echelon.[4]

Above all, it seems, Rabin was burdened by a consciousness of failure due to the fact that Israel was on the verge of a war which the government did not want and the army had not prevented – in fact, had helped to precipitate. Despite his quasi-ministerial status, his subordination to the political echelon was solid and unshaken. It was precisely his unique status which intensified his sense of responsibility towards the government. Rabin was well acquainted not only with the Prime Minister and Minister of Defence but with all the ministers as well. He knew that the government relied on him and looked to him to offer solutions to the security problems which would not embroil the country in war. He had gained their full confidence when he succeeded by simple means in solving the water diversion problem, which had threatened to plunge the region into a military confrontation. He also proposed a solution to the problem of terrorist activity which seemingly did not involve large-scale hostilities, namely a fierce and swift blow against Syria. The government was not easily persuaded, both for fear of exacerbating the situation and because of Soviet patronage for the Syrian regime. Rabin, equipped with Intelligence evaluations, tried for months to convince the ministers that there was nothing to fear. Egypt, Rabin told the ministers, was bogged down in Yemen and the Soviet Union would not intervene in a local problem. The Syrians would learn their lesson and stop supporting guerrilla activities or else the regime in Damascus would collapse. The continuation and worsening of terrorist action created expectations in Israel that Syria should be punished, which in their turn brought pressure to bear on the government. The incident of 7 April 1967 and the seemingly cautious and moderate reaction of Egypt and the Soviet Union appeared to validate the claim that Syria could be attacked with impunity. In the absence of any other solution to the terror problem, the government was on the verge of deciding to accept Rabin's viewpoint, on the basis of his firm and well-argued evaluation that such a move would not lead to war.

When the crisis broke out in mid-May 1967, the general feeling for two or three days was that Nasser's moves were a mere 'exercise' and the Egyptians were still loyal to their basic strategy which ruled out war before the time was ripe. This was initially the Intelligence Branch view. Rabin was troubled and adopted the necessary cautious measures, but the evaluations continued to rule out war. It was only when the evaluation was amended on 19 May, to the effect that Egypt was now ready to fight Israel, that Rabin was shaken. The entire theory which he had constructed and presented to the government was suddenly debunked and collapsed. Rabin's policy of controlled escalation against Syria, which had peaked on 7 April and was intended to isolate the Syrian arena and call a halt to terrorist action, had come to nothing. Not only had it failed to check hostile terrorist action, but it was about to embroil Israel in a war which the government did not want and, on the contrary, feared. Yitzhak Rabin felt that by erring in his evaluation, he had misled the government.[5]

The Chief of Staff was now obliged to appear before the government and inform it that the country must prepare for war, and it would be for the best if the IDF dealt the first blow. The government itself was in a state of confusion and distress. The ministers were unprepared 'emotionally and intellectually' (to quote Minister of Education Zalman Aranne) for war. In their resentment, they demanded that the Chief of Staff at least avoid disrupting diplomatic efforts to solve the crisis. Although the diplomatic timetable was out of step with the military timetable, Rabin could not object to it. Moreover, his attempt to restrict the war, if it proved inescapable, to a 'small war' in order to gain 'bargaining cards' was more congruous with the government's tendencies than with the military logic and mood of the General Staff. Rabin, therefore, was trapped in a mesh of contradictions. He was desperate for a prop, for encouragement, to unburden himself of some of the terrible weight of responsibility.[6] In his distress, he even contemplated resigning and thereby ridding himself of the burden.

On 21 May Rabin requested a meeting with Ben-Gurion.[7] Rabin admired 'the old man', and even owed him his promotion to a position which had guaranteed him the highest IDF post. However, under the circumstances, Rabin's initiative was both out of order and inexplicable. Ben-Gurion had long since become the most unrelenting critic of his successor, Eshkol. Seeking Ben-Gurion's advice was an expression of Rabin's personal distress, but perhaps no less an act of defiance of Eshkol, for placing him in a situation where he was directly exposed to government criticism. He was now nostalgic for the previous Ben-Gurion model whereby the Chief of Staff was insulated from the government and received 'clear instructions' conveyed through the Minister of Defence.

Ben-Gurion was blunt in his deprecation of the government and of Eshkol in particular, and severely criticized the decision to mobilize reserve forces and also the large-scale IAF operation on 7 April, the cause of the escalation. 'You [Rabin and Eshkol] have reduced the country to a very grave condition, you bear responsibility,' Ben-Gurion charged and added: 'We mustn't go to war. We are isolated.'[8] 'Yitzhak was depressed', he wrote in his diary.[9]

Next day, Rabin, again on his own initiative, met with Dayan. To Dayan's query as to his impression of Ben-Gurion, he replied that Ben-Gurion had not displayed an understanding of military matters, but 'it was a pleasure to talk to a man who speaks plainly, in terms of "yes" and "no", what to do and what to avoid doing (compared to Eshkol, who is the complete opposite)'. Rabin, who chainsmoked throughout the meeting, appeared to Dayan not only exhausted but also confused, indecisive, tense and depressed, and far from eager for the fray. If this was the impression he made when he met with his subordinates, it was not a good thing, Dayan concluded.[10]

An interesting point which arose at the Dayan–Rabin meeting related to the causes of the crisis. Rabin argued, which seemed strange to Dayan, 'that if we had inflicted a **heavier blow** on Syria [emphasis in original] we could have avoided the present situation'. Dayan easily refuted the logic of this argument.[11] This suggests that Rabin was still trying, with the last vestiges of his energy, to champion the theory he had been advocating to the political echelon for some time, although events had now clearly disproved it. It is not surprising that he did not sound convincing.

On 23 May, after the tense meeting of the Ministerial Committee on Security, Rabin sought out Moshe Haim Shapira, the most consistent anti-activist, in the hope of finding a sympathetic ear. Instead, he received a chilly reception and angry accusations, which discouraged him even further. Shapira's stern remarks were particularly painful for Rabin, as he later admitted, because they targeted his deepest misgivings and hesitations and his feeling of guilt. He remembered the traumatic exchange in detail, and described it in his memoirs: 'How dare you?' Shapira asked. How did Rabin and Eshkol dare to do what the Dayan–Ben-Gurion team had not dared to do, and place the survival of the state at risk by involving the country in war, possibly on all the fronts, at a time when Israel was totally isolated. Ben-Gurion, Shapira said, had waited five years after the closing of the Straits in 1951, and launched a military operation only after - guaranteeing great power backing and protection of Israel's air space. The blocking of the Straits was not an existential threat, he claimed, and to go to war in the prevailing circumstances would be madness. 'Dig in!' Shapira enjoined him. Israel should dig in and fortify its positions and repel attack, but under no circumstances should it fire the first shot.[12]

This conversation shook Rabin, already exhausted and tormented by severe misgivings, and his functioning was visibly affected. Eshkol's military secretary, Yisrael Lior, who was present at the General Staff deliberations in the afternoon of that day, was so concerned that he decided to go up to Jerusalem especially in order to report personally to Eshkol.[13]

In the investigation conducted by the History Department, the head of the Chief of Staff's office Rafi Efrat testified laconically: 'In the evening the Chief of Staff felt ill and went home.'[14] Leah Rabin mentioned the incident in her memoirs very briefly. On 23 May in the evening, she wrote, Yitzhak broke down as the result of a combination of reasons: the distressing conversations with Ben-Gurion and Shapira, the doubts gnawing at him, his sense of heavy responsibility and his extreme exhaustion over the previous week. According to Mrs Rabin, her husband arrived home that evening 'dazed with exhaustion' and told her that he was leaving for Southern Command. She immediately decided 'that the time had come to switch off the engine and above all, let him rest', and summoned Dr Eliyahu Gilon, the Chief Medical Officer. Gilon gave Rabin a sedating shot and he slept until the following afternoon.[15] Gilon diagnosed 'acute anxiety' and conferred next morning with Weizman and Efrat. It was decided to report to Eshkol and to disseminate the story that the Chief of Staff was suffering from nicotine poisoning.[16]

According to Weizman, Rabin telephoned him at 20:00 on 23 May and asked him to come to his home immediately. When he arrived (apparently before Gilon's visit), he found Rabin 'broken and very depressed'. They were left alone and Rabin said to him: 'I got the State of Israel into a mess because of a series of mistakes I made [which brought us to the brink of the] most difficult war Israel has ever known. In this war – everything depends on the air force. It will decide the outcome of the war. I believe that whoever has made a mistake, should go. I made a mistake. Will you take over from me as Chief of Staff?' Weizman, so he claims, spurned Rabin's offer and encouraged him to rally. Next morning he visited Rabin again and repeated his refusal.[17]

It is hard to question Weizman's testimony even if it was written many years later. This was not the kind of incident one forgets. It is feasible that Rabin actually said, 'I got the State of Israel into a mess', admitted to mistakes and declared that 'whoever has made a mistake should go'. It is true that he had no authority to offer Weizman his post, but in the given situation of 23 and 24 May, Weizman was the Number Two in the IDF senior command, and his rival, Haim Barlev, had only just returned from Paris. The fact is that Rabin's resignation would immediately have placed

Weizman in a favourable position to become the supreme commander of the IDF.

Rabin's version of the incident does not contradict Weizman's, although he does not mention asking Weizman to replace him. 'I was very tired, and in a black mood,' Rabin wrote. 'Not often in my life have I permitted myself this weakness, allowing someone to share my innermost feelings, trying to ease the heavy burden by exposing my thoughts to someone else. I am an introvert. This time I felt the urgent need.' Rabin writes that he did not tell Weizman about his talks with Ben-Gurion and Shapira, but said that he felt that he was sharing with the political echelon responsibility for the fact that Israel was now in the worst predicament it had faced since the War of Independence. 'Am I perhaps to blame?' he asked Weizman. 'Would it perhaps be better if I resigned?' Weizman, according to Rabin, tried to persuade him to stop talking of resignation, and said he was confident that Rabin could lead the IDF to great victory.[18]

Rabin's version suggests that he was contemplating resigning but had not yet decided and was seeking Weizman' reassurance,[19] which he received. Seven years later, when the story was published, Rabin thought, and rightly so, that Weizman had broken faith with him, although he never claimed that the story was untrue.[20]

At the time, Rabin's brief breakdown remained a deep secret among the military and political elite. It was not leaked to the local or international press and did not diminish Rabin's prestige. Only in April 1974, when Rabin was candidate for the premiership after Golda Meir's resignation, did Weizman expose the story, as proof of Rabin's unsuitability for the post. The revelation aroused sensation and the pros and cons were debated in the press, but it did not prevent Rabin's election for his first term of office as Prime Minister (1974–1977).

After thirty-six hours' absence and rest, Rabin recovered and returned to duty. He was 'different from in the past', according to Weizman.[21] The Chief of Staff had undoubtedly been in urgent need of rest in order to recuperate, but this was not apparently the main reason for his recovery. The most important reason is connected to the fact that during his absence, two central personalities had returned home, who provided Rabin with support and vital reinforcement, in both the military and the political spheres. Barlev rapidly became the dominant figure in the General Staff, gradually superseding Weizman, and to a large degree covering for Rabin's weakness.[22] Allon immediately became the leading figure among the government hawks, backing the army's viewpoint. Rabin was rescued from his state of isolation. He could now cease vacillating between government and General Staff and decided where he stood. From now on he was unequivocally the spokesman for the IDF.

Rabin's time-out left its mark and affected the standing of the Chief of Staff.[23] This fact was not always stated explicitly, but may be discerned in various statements made after his return to duty. There were also several indications:

- The documents in the IDF archives on the May/June 1967 crisis indicate that Rabin was displaying a lower profile in General Staff deliberations, in his control over subordinates, and the gradual shift of the focus of power in Barlev's direction.
- A blunt and untypical remark by Eshkol at a decisive government debate on 28 May to the effect that he was uninterested in Rabin's opinion whether or not to accept Johnson's plea to Israel not to initiate hostilities.
- Rabin's request that Eshkol appear before the General Staff forum the same day and explain the government decision.
- Remarks of various politicians about the Chief of Staff.[24]
- Rabin's response to Eshkol's appeal to appoint Dayan as CO Southern Command in place of Gavish.
- Rabin's proposal that Dayan replace him.
- Rabin's order to Gavish to submit to the new Minister of Defence the more comprehensive plan, in contradiction of his previous stand.

Dayan's appointment to the Ministry of Defence spelled the end of Rabin's quasi-ministerial standing,[25] and during the war he played a secondary role in decision-making and conducting the campaign. After the war the laurels of victory sufficed for all those who had been involved, and naturally enough Dayan and Rabin received the greatest share of glory. But towards the end of Rabin's term of office, between June and December 1967, Dayan was indisputably the more dominant of the two.[26] Although the post-war period is outside the context of this book, it seems that Rabin's standing in the General Staff and the IDF in general was not affected by his difficulties during the crisis. In the eyes of the general public, who at the time and long after knew nothing about the secrets of the Pit, Rabin remained, and rightly so, the hero of the war and the champion of the glorious victory.[27]

Biographical notes

Yitzhak Rabin (born 1921) – completed his term of office as Chief of Staff on 31 December 1967 and was replaced by his deputy, Haim Barlev. Served as Ambassador to Washington (1968–1973), Prime Minister (1974–1977), Minister of Defence (1984–1989), and Prime Minister and Minister of Defence (1992–1995). Reached an agreement with the PLO (1993) which established an autonomous Palestinian authority in the West Bank and Gaza Strip, and signed the Israel–Jordan peace treaty (1994). Recipient of the Nobel Peace Prize (1994). Assassinated on 4 November 1995 by a Jewish assassin opposed to his concessions to the Palestinians of territory conquered during the Six Day War. Was succeeded by Shimon Peres.

Levi Eshkol (born 1895) – continued to serve as Prime Minister until his death in February 1969. Was succeeded by Golda Meir.

Moshe Dayan (born 1915) – continued to serve as Minister of Defence until Golda Meir's government resigned in 1974 as the result of the public storm around the recommendations of the Commission of Inquiry (headed by Supreme Court Justice Shimon Agranat) on the mishaps of the Yom Kippur War. When the Likud came to power in 1977, he was invited by Prime Minister Menahem Begin to serve as Foreign Minister in his government. Played an important role in achieving the peace treaty with Egypt (1979) under which Israel withdrew from the Sinai Peninsula conquered during the Six Day War. Resigned in October 1979 and died two years later.

Yigal Allon (born 1918) – appointed Deputy Prime Minister (1967) and served in this position and as Minister of Education in Golda Meir's government (1969–1974) and Foreign Minister in Rabin's first government (1974–1977). Died in 1980.

Abba Eban (born 1915) – served as Foreign Minister until 1974. Was Chairman of the Knesset Foreign Affairs and Security Committee

(1974–1977), then retired from political life and devoted himself to writing, lecturing and presenting TV documentary programmes and series. Died in 2002.

Moshe Haim Shapira (born 1902) – continued to serve as National Religious Party Chairman and Minister of the Interior until his death in 1970.

Menahem Begin (born 1913) – Minister without Portfolio in governments of Eshkol and Meir. Resigned in 1970 due to his opposition to the cease-fire agreement with Egypt. Led the Likud Party to victory in the 1977 and 1981 elections and served as Prime Minister. Signed the peace treaty with Egypt (1979) which included full withdrawal from the Sinai Peninsula and evacuation of Jewish settlements there. Recipient of the Nobel Peace Prize (1979). Due to PLO terrorist action from Lebanon ordered the controversial invasion of Lebanon which claimed numerous casualties. As a result he sank into a depression, resigned in 1983, and remained secluded at home until his death in 1992.

Haim Barlev (born 1924) – appointed Chief of Staff on 1 January 1968. The war of attrition between Israel and Egypt was waged during this period (1969–1970). On retirement from the army he was appointed Minister of Trade and Industry in Meir's government (1972–1974) and later Minister of Police (until 1977). In 1992 he was appointed Israeli Ambassador in Moscow and served there until his death in 1994.

Ezer Weizman (born 1924) – continued to serve as Chief of Operations until 1969. On retirement from the army, he joined the Likud Party and served as Minister of Transport in Meir's government until the Likud left the coalition in 1970. When the Likud came to power in 1977, he was appointed Minister of Defence and played a major role in achieving the peace treaty with Egypt in 1979. Resigned in 1980. In 1993 he was chosen as seventh President of Israel and served until 2000. Died in 2005.

Aharon Yariv (born 1920) – continued to serve as Chief of Intelligence until 1972 and on retirement was appointed Adviser on Intelligence and Counter-terror to PM Golda Meir (until 1973). Between 1974 and 1975 he served as Minister of Transport and Minister of Information in the governments of Meir and Rabin. He then retired from politics and established the Center for Strategic Research at Tel Aviv University, which he headed until his death in 1994.

Ariel Sharon (born 1928) – served in the IDF until 1973, retiring as CO Southern Command (1970–1973). Resigned from the IDF after he was passed over for the position of Chief of Staff. He then initiated the establishment of the Likud Party. During the Yom Kippur War (1973) he was a division commander and played a central role in the crossing of the Suez Canal and transfer of the fighting to the Egyptian hinterland, a move which tipped the balance and brought the Egyptians close to defeat. In 1981 he was appointed Minister of Defence and in 1982 initiated the IDF invasion of Lebanon in order to uproot the PLO terrorist bases. In 1983 he was forced to resign in light of the conclusion of the commission headed by Supreme Court Justice Y. Kahan which investigated the massacre of Palestinians in the Sabra and Shatila refugee camps in Beirut by Lebanese Christian militias operating in an Israeli-controlled area. Until 1992, and again between 1996 and 1999, he served in various ministerial positions and was the central figure in the widespread establishment of Jewish settlements in the West Bank and the Gaza Strip, territories conquered during the Six Day War. In 2001 he was elected Prime Minister, and initiated the disengagement plan from the Gaza Strip and northern Samaria and the evacuation of the Jewish settlements there, a plan which was implemented in 2005. Prior to the 2006 elections he seceded from the Likud and established the Kadima Party, but in January 2006 he suffered a brain haemorrhage and lapsed into a coma. He was replaced by his deputy, Ehud Olmert.

Notes

Preface

1 See G. Ben-Dor, 'Israel in 1967: international standing and self image on the eve of war' in Asher Sessar (ed.) *Shisha Yamim – Shloshim Shana (Six Days – Thirty Years)*, Tel Aviv: Am Oved, 1999, pp. 31–44.
2 S. Shamir, 'Decline of Nasserist messianism' in S. Shamir (ed.) *Yeridat ha-Nasserism (The Decline of Nasserism)*, Tel Aviv University, 1978, pp. 1–60. On Nasser–Kennedy, Nasser–Johnson relations, see M.H. Heikal, *The Cairo Documents*, New York: Doubleday, 1973, pp. 187–249.
3 See report of US Ambassador to Cairo, Lucius Battle, April 1967, and in particular a missive from his deputy David Ness, 11 May 1967. Both predicted that Nasser would launch a risky undertaking in order to extricate himself from his predicament. W. Quandt, *Peace Process*, Washington, DC: The Brooking Institute, 1993, pp. 26, 508.
4 Quandt, *Peace Process*, pp. 58–62. See also A. Ben-Zur, *Gormim Sovietiim u-Milkhemet Sheshet ha-Yamim (Soviet Elements and the Six Day War)*, Tel Aviv: Sifriyat Hapoalim, 1976, and G. Golan, *Soviet Policies in the Middle East from World War Two to Gorbachev*, Cambridge: Cambridge University Press, 1990, pp. 58–67; J.D. Glassman, *Arms for the Middle East: The Soviet Union and War in the Middle East*, Baltimore, MD: Johns Hopkins University Press, 1975, pp. 22–64.
5 A. Lall, *The UN and the Middle East Crisis 1967*, New York: Columbia University Press, 1968. Odd Bull, *War and Peace in the Middle East*, London: Leo Cooper, 1973. See also I.J. Rikhye, *The Sinai Blunder*, Oxford and New Delhi: IBH, 1978.

Introduction

1 T. Herzl, *Der Judenstaat*, Leipzig: M. Breitstein's Verlags Buchhandlung, 1896. T. Herzl, *Altneuland*, Leipzig: Seeman, 1900.
2 See S. Huntington, *The Soldier and the State*, New York: Random House, 1957. M. Janowitz, *The Professional Soldier*, New York: Free Press, 1960. S. Feiner, *Ha-Ish al Gav ha-Soos (The Man on the Horse)*, Tel Aviv: Maarakhot, 1982. A. Perlmutter, *Military and Politics in Israel*, London: Frank Cass, 1969. Y. Peri, *Between Battles and Ballots*, Cambridge: Cambridge University Press, 1983. See also Y. Peri, 'The patterns of connection of the IDF to the political establishment in Israel' in *Milkhemet Breira (A War of Choice)*, Tel Aviv: Hakibbutz Hameuhad, 1985, pp. 31–55. Y. Ben-Meir, *Civil–Military Relations in Israel*, New York: Columbia University Press, 1995. M. Lissak (ed.) *Israeli Society and its Defence Establishment*, London: Frank Cass, 1984.

3 See A. Shapira, *Me-Piturei ha-Rama ad le-Piruk ha-Palmach (From the Dis-missal of the Head of the National Command to the Disbanding of the Palmach)*, Tel Aviv: Hakibbutz Hameuhad, 118–159. See also in contrast, Y. Gelber, *Lama Pirku et ha-Palmach? (Why Was the Palmach Disbanded?)*, Jerusalem: Schocken, 1986. M. Bar-Zohar, *Ben-Gurion*, Tel Aviv: Am Oved, 1975, pp. 700–813. See also Peri, *Battles and Ballots*, pp. 54–57.

4 Ariel Sharon in an interview in *Yediot Aharonot*, 30 May 1997. For similar remarks by Ezer Weizman, see *Lekha Shamayim Lekha Aretz (Heaven and Earth are Thine)*, Tel Aviv: Sifriyat Maariv, 1975, pp. 239–240.

5 See M. Golani, *Dayan Leads to War, Iyunim bi-Tkumat Yisrael (Israel Independence Studies)* 4, Sdeh Boker: Ben-Gurion Heritage Centre, 1994, pp. 117–135.

6 Y. Tal, *Bitakhon Leumi (National Security)*, Tel Aviv: Dvir, 1996, p. 51. On security theory, security policy and military doctrine, see ibid., pp. 43–116, and A. Levite, *ha-Doctrina ha-Tzvait shel Yisrael (Israel's Military Doctrine)*, Tel Aviv: Hakibbutz Hameuhad, 1988, pp. 22–90. A. Yaniv, *Politika ve-Astrategia be-Yisrael (Politics and Strategy in Israel)*, Tel Aviv: Sifriyat Hapoalim, 1994, pp. 13–34. D. Horovitz, *Ha-Tfisa ha-Yisraelit shel Bitahon Leumi (The Israeli Conception of National Security)*, Jerusalem: Hebrew University, 1973.

7 Tal, ibid., pp. 52–53.

8 The expression is used by Emmanuel Vald in *Kilelat ha-Kelim ha-Shvurim (The Curse of the Broken Vessels)*, Jerusalem: Schocken, 1987, p. 14. See also pp. 80–81, 84, 193.

9 R. Parker, *The Politics of Miscalculation in the Middle East*, Bloomington: Indiana University Press, 1993, pp. 245–246.

10 Ben-Gurion said to Rabin on 21 May 1967: 'We both know that this is the destruction of the Third Temple.' This is attested to by Azariyahu Arnan, a close associate of government minister Galili, in an interview in *Maariv*, 13 May 1986. Rabin himself does not mention this in his memoirs.

11 Weizman, *Heaven and Earth*, p. 258. See also Sharon's reference to the restricted operational plan 'Atzmon' (IDF Archives 192/74/1038).

12 The more pessimistic assessment was apparently given by Brigadier-General (ret.) Yehoshafat Harkavi, former Chief of Intelligence. D. Kimche and D. Bavli, *Sufat ha-Esh (The Storm of Fire)*, Tel Aviv: Am ha-Sefer, 1968, p. 102. See also *Ben-Gurion's Diary*, 21 May 1967; Bar-Zohar, *Ha-Khodesh ha-Arokh be-Yoter (The Longest Month)*, Tel Aviv: Lewin-Epstein, 1965, pp. 140, 153–155. Z. Wahrhaftig, Minister of Religious Affairs in the Eshkol government and member of the Ministerial Committee on Security, asked Rabin how many victims were predicted. Rabin replied: 10,000. Author's interview with Wahrhaftig, 24 August 1998.

13 When the May 1967 crisis broke out, efforts were made to purchase gas masks from Germany, the United States and Great Britain. Bar-Zohar, *op. cit.* See also A. Barzilai, 'Chief Lord of the Flies', *Haaretz*, 5 November 1998. The CIA estimated that the Egytians would not use gas. Rabin, *Pinkes Sherut (Service Card)*, A, p. 168. And see below.

14 On fears in Israel that Nasser possessed a 'secret weapon', see Bar-Zohar, *Longest Month*, p. 140. Foreign diplomats in Cairo were of the same opinion. See Parker, *Miscalculation*, p. 90.

15 *Yediot Aharonot*, 30 May 1997. For criticism of this approach within the IDF (represented by Ariel Sharon), to the effect that 'all our problems can be solved through the rifle sights', see M. Amit, *Rosh be-Rosh (Head On)*, Or-Yehuda: Hed Artzi, 1999, pp. 41–45.

16 On the defence budget during this period see Y. Greenberg, *Kheshbon ve-Otzma (Calculations and Power)*, Tel Aviv: Ministry of Defence, 1997.

17 Haber, *Today* ... Tel Aviv: Idanim, 1988, p. 197.
18 Z. Lanir, 'The political objectives and military goals of Israel's wars', in *Milkhemet Breira (A War of Choice)*, pp. 126–133. See also Ben-Meir, *Civil–Military*, pp. 143–148.
19 Chief of Staff Zvi Zur reported to Ben-Gurion on 'great anxiety among the military', *Ben-Gurion's Diary*, 18 June 1963. Bar-Zohar, *Ben-Gurion* (p. 1556), relates that Rabin was in tears. Rabin, in *Service Card*, confesses that he was very moved. See also Weizman, *Heaven and Earth*, p. 236.
20 See e.g. *Ben-Gurion's Diary*, 17 November 1963 to 25 November 1963.
21 Ben-Meir, *Civil–Military*, pp. 31–32. On the 'de-Ben-Gurionization' of security under Eshkol, see Peri, *Battles and Ballots*, pp. 78–80.
22 Weizman, *Heaven and Earth*, pp. 240–241. Rabin lauded Eshkol's approach 'marked by readiness for more varied deployment of IDF might'. Y. Rabin, 'Eshkol, my Minister of Defence', *Bamahaneh*, 14 February 1963.
23 This was Rabin's claim, and it is borne out by Dayan's close associates, Meir Amit and Haim Yisraeli. Ben-Meir, *Civil–Military*, pp. 107–108.
24 Peri, *Battles and Ballots*, p. 162. Ben-Meir, *Civil–Military*, p. 107. Bar-Zohar, *Longest Month*, pp. 68–70. Kimche and Bavli, *Storm of Fire*, p. 99.
25 Peri, *Battles and Ballots*, ibid. Haber, *Today*, pp. 146–147. Hanna Zemer at a study meeting at the Ben-Zvi Institute, 18 February 1997.
26 Peri, *Battles and Ballots*, p. 160. Haber, *Today*, pp. 145–146 and see below.
27 Rabin, *Service Card*, A, p. 114.
28 Author's interview with Tal, 14 January 1999. A similar story on the requirements of the IAF is cited by Weizman, *Heaven and Earth*, pp. 241–242. See also p. 254 and Haber, *Today*, p. 68.
29 Peri, *Battles and Ballots*, p. 162. M. Peled, 'How Israel did not prepare for war', *Maarakhot*, 289–290, pp. 25–28. Haber, *Today*, pp. 41–42, 67, 97, 146–147. For criticism of the excessive power of the Chief of Staff see E. Vald, *Kilelat ha-Kelim ha-Shvurim (Curse of the Broken Vessels)*, Jerusalem: Schocken, 1987, pp. 163–169.
30 N. Safran, *ha-Imut ha-Aravi–Yisraeli 1948–1967 (The Arab–Israel confrontation, 1948–1967)*, Jerusalem: Keter, 1960, pp. 258–259.
31 Tal, *Bitakhon Leumi (National Security)*, Tel Aviv: Dvir, 1996, pp. 110–111. Vald, *Curse*, p. 19 and M. Van-Creveld, 'The Citizen and the Military Science', *The Israel Manual of Public Administration*, No. 15, Jerusalem, 1976, p. 82.
32 On the deterioration of relations between Ben-Gurion and Eshkol, see Bar-Zohar, *Ben-Gurion*, C, pp. 1560–1586.
33 Haber, *Today*, pp. 43–44. Peres claims that the 'omission' to which Ben-Gurion was referring was Eshkol's decision to cut down on the missiles project. Author's interview with Peres, 29 October 1998. Peri writes that BG was referring to two 'blunders'; the greater one was the slowdown of the nuclear programme and the more minor blunder was the Ben-Barka affair. Peri, *Battles and Ballots*, pp. 78–79, 240–244.
34 Safran, *op. cit.*
35 Eshkol headed three governments: the continuing government after Ben-Gurion's resignation in June 1963; the government of December 1964 after his resignation due to the dispute with Ben-Gurion and the government he established in January 1966 after the November 1965 elections to the Knesset.
36 On the 'permanent state of tension' between the military and civil levels, see Weizman, *op. cit.*, p. 240.
37 A. Shapira, *ha-Halikha al Kav ha-Ofek (Walking on the Horizon)*, Tel Aviv: Am Oved, pp. 23–71, and, in particular, A. Shapira, *Kherev ha-Yona (The Sword of the Dove)*, Tel Aviv: Am Oved, 1992.

38 Author's interview with Ze'evi, 3 September 1998. Zerach Wahrhaftig, Minister of Religious Affairs and a member of the National Religious Party, was Polish-born, short and bespectacled, a moderate anti-activist. For the generals, he personified the Diaspora Jew.
39 See below. See also Yehuda Ben-Meir's remarks in a discussion (2 March 1978). *Gevulot Bitahon (Security Borders)* Malle Researches, Tel Aviv University, 1978.
40 After the war, Dayan said: 'The person who decided, or was forced, to give me the Defence portfolio, understood that it wasn't in order to support the policy of diplomatic meetings without military decisions or a policy of evasion'. *Yediot Aharonot*, 16 June 1967.
41 *Maariv*, 12 May 1967.

I Personnel changes in the defence establishment

1 Z. Shalom, 'Ben-Gurion's resignation from the government', in *Iyunim bi-Tkumat Yisrael (Studies in Israeli Independence)* 5, pp. 608–614. N. Yanai, *Kera Batzameret (A Rift at the Top)*, Tel Aviv: Lewin-Epstein, 1969, pp. 11–44. See also Bar-Zohar, *Ben-Gurion*, pp. 1554–1559.
2 I. Harel, *Mashber ha-Madanim ha-Germanim (The German Scientists Crisis)*, Tel Aviv: Sifriyat Maariv, 1982. For a conflicting version see M. Amit, *Rosh be-Rosh (Head On)*, Tel Aviv: Hed Artzi, 1999, pp. 101–125. M. Bar-Zohar, *Ben-Gurion*, Tel Aviv: Zmora Bitan, 1975. pp. 1529–1545. See also S. Aronson, *ha-Politika veha-Astrategia shel Neshek Garini (The Politics and Strategy of Nuclear Weapons)*, Vol. 1, Jerusalem: Akademon, 1994, pp. 221–257, 308–323, and Vol. 2, pp. 43–48. See also M. Bar-Zohar, *Tzayd ha-Madanim ha-Germanim (Hunting the German Scientists)*, Jerusalem: Schoken, 1965, pp. 199–221.
3 On the 'tripartite union', see M. Kerr, *The Arab Cold War 1958–1967*, New York: Oxford University Press, 1967, pp. 58–126.
4 Bar-Zohar, *Ben-Gurion*, pp. 1550–1554. Ben-Gurion's missives were sent without consultation with the professional diplomats in the Foreign Ministry. See G. Raphael, *be-Sod Leumim (In the Confidence of Nations)*, Jerusalem: Idanim, 1981, pp. 116–117.
5 A. Cohen, *Israel and the Bomb*, New York: Columbia University Press, 1998, pp. 99–136. On Kennedy's policy on the Middle East and Israel: M. Gazit, *President Kennedy's Policy toward the Arab States and Israel*, Tel Aviv University, 1983.
6 Bar-Zohar, *Ben-Gurion*, pp. 1524–1526.
7 Ibid., pp. 1526–1529.
8 On the IDF deployment in light of the volatile situation, particularly on the Jordanian front, see Minutes of the General Staff meeting of 6 May 1963.
9 Cohen, *Israel and the Bomb*, pp. 119–123.
10 Yanai, *A Rift*, pp. 293–296.
11 Cohen, *Israel and the Bomb*, pp. 223–239.
12 *Divrei ha-Knesset (Knesset Minutes)*, Vol. 37, pp. 2158–2162.
13 Quotes are from Minutes of the General Staff meetings 1, 8, 15 July 1963.
14 In an interview shortly before the Six Day War, Ben-Gurion was asked by Geula Cohen what he would reply to his grandson if asked what the borders of the homeland were. He replied: 'I would say, the borders of your homeland, my child, are the borders of the State of Israel as they are today. That's it.' See interview in *Maariv*, 12 May 1967. See also Weizman, *Lekha Shamayim Lekha Aretz (Heaven and Earth are Yours)*, Tel Aviv: Sifriyat Maariv, 1975, pp. 200,

208–209, 243–244. U. Narkis, *Khayal shel Yerushalaim (A Jerusalem Soldier)*, Tel Aviv: Ministry of Defence, 1991, p. 327.

15 Levi Eshkol had a particular affinity for water questions. He founded the national water company Mekorot and as Minister of Agriculture and Minister of Finance devoted considerable attention to promoting Israel's water projects.

16 Weizman at the General Staff meeting 8 July 1963.

17 Peres believed that 'modern strategy ... is the transition from the theory of decision-making with the aid of the armed forces to the theory of decision-making without war; how to build up power without using it, so that it will be effective "in advance".' S. Peres, *ha-Shlav ha-Ba (The Next Stage)*, Tel Aviv: Am Hasefer, 1965, p. 116.

18 Peri, *Bullets*, pp. 249–250. P. Seal, *Assad – ha-Maavak al ha-Mizrakh ha-Tichon (Assad – the Struggle for the Middle East)*, Tel Aviv: Maarakhot, 1988, pp. 141–142.

19 Rabin at the General Staff meeting on his first day as Chief of Staff, 1 January 1964.

20 See e.g. U. Narkis, *Akhat Yerushalayim (Jerusalem is One)*, Tel Aviv: Am Oved, 1975, p. 44.

21 See e.g. Robert Slater, *Yitzhak Rabin – Biografia (Yitzhak Rabin, a Biography)*, Jerusalem: Idan, 1977, pp. 54–56.

22 On Rabin's appointment as Deputy Chief of Staff, see Rabin, *Service Card*, pp. 109–113. See also *Ben-Gurion's Diary*, 11 October 1963.

23 *Ben-Gurion's Diary*, 7 November 1963. Without saying so explicitly, Ben-Gurion was probably implying that it was not desirable for two former Palmachniks to head the army.

24 *Ben-Gurion's Diary*, 25 November 1963. BG considered 41-year-old Elrom to be 'too old', and wrote of Weizman: 'I was surprised to hear that he is already forty.' *Ben-Gurion's Diary*, 3 June 1964. On BG's campaign to bring younger men into the senior command and its implementation by Dayan, see Tevet, *Dayan*, pp. 402–407.

25 Rabin, *Service Notebook*, pp. 117–118. Weizman, *Heaven and Earth*, pp. 233–239.

26 Rabin at the General Staff meeting 1 January 1964.

2 Basic security issues

1 J.D. Glassman, *Arms for the Middle East – The Soviet Union and War in the Middle East*, Baltimore, MD: Johns Hopkins University Press, 1975, pp. 22–64.

2 R. Yakar, *Yakhasei Yisrael–Artzot ha-Brit: Hebet ha-Rekhesh, 1955–1967 (Israel–US Relations: the Purchase Angle, 1955–1967)*, Documentation and Historical Research Unit, Ministry of Defence Publishing House, 1995.

3 S. Aronson, *Neshek Gar'ini ba-Mizrakh ha-Tikhon (Nuclear Arms in the Middle East)*, B, Jerusalem: Akademon, 1995, pp. 13–166.

4 M. Pa'il, 'BG's policy and strategy at the end of the War of Independence', *Iyunim bi-Tkumat Yisrael (Israel Independence Studies)*, 1995, pp. 37–90.

5 S. Golan, *Gvul Kham, Milkhama Kara (Hot Border, Cold War)*, Tel Aviv: Maarakhot and Ministry of Defence Publishing House, 2000, pp. 320–378.

6 I. Rabinovitz, *ha-Shalom she-Khamak (The Peace that Eluded Us)*, Jerusalem: Keter, 1991.

7 M. Bar-Zohar, *Ben-Gurion*, Tel Aviv: Zmora-Bitan, 1975, p. 1365.

8 For theoretical and strategic substantiation of the 'defensive-offensive' conception, see Y. Ber, *Bitkhon Yisrael Etmol, ha-Yom, Makhar (Israel's Security Yesterday, Today, Tomorrow)*, Tel Aviv: Amikam, 1966.

9 Golan, *op. cit.*, p. 240.

10 Amiran Oren, 'Fighting Order of Battle – Situation Estimate 1953–1960 as a Turning Point in Security Policy and Expansion of the IDF in the Fifties', *Iyunim bi-Tkumat Yisrael (Israel Independence Studies)*, Vol. 12, 2002, pp. 123–145.

11 A. Levite, *ha-Doctrina ha-Tzvayit shel Yisrael: Hagana ve-Hatkafa (Israel's Security Doctrine: Defence and Attack)*, Tel Aviv: Hakibbutz Hameuhad, 1988.

12 M. Bar-On, *Sha'arei Aza (The Gates of Gaza)*, Tel Aviv: Am Oved, 1992, pp. 91–106.

13 A. Yaniv, *Politika ve-Astrategiya be-Yisrael (Politics and Strategy in Israel)*, Tel Aviv: Sifriyat Hapoalim, 1994, pp. 156–158.

14 Ibid.

15 Stuart Cohen, 'Who needs surface–air missiles?' in Z. Lachish and M. Amitai (eds) *Asor lo Shaket (An Unquiet Decade)*, Tel Aviv: Ministry of Defence, 1995.

16 Y. Goldstein, *Eshkol*, Jerusalem: Keter, 2003, pp. 460–463.

17 Peres contemplated establishing what he called a European 'enclave' in the Middle East through the Common Market. For his letter to Eshkol containing the main points of his security outlook, see N. Yanai, *Kera ba-Tzameret (Rift at the Top)*, Tel Aviv: Lewin-Epstein, 1969, pp. 130–133.

18 Peres confirmed in a private conversation with the author (23 May 1999) that he was in conflict with Ben-Gurion on this matter. Rabin notes in his memoirs that Ben-Gurion, unlike Peres, understood the importance of the United States, and his meeting in March 1960 with Eisenhower resulted in US consent to sell Israel advanced radar systems. Peres and Weizman tried in vain to delay the purchase: Rabin, *Pinkes Sherut (Service Notebook)*, Tel Aviv: Ma'ariv, 1979, pp. 105–106.

19 S. Peres, *ha-Shlav ha-Ba (The Next Stage)*, Tel Aviv: Am Hasefer, 1965, pp. 114–117.

20 On his speech in the Knesset on this subject, described as one of the most important delivered in the Knesset at that time, see *Haaretz*, 26 June 1963.

21 For Peres' version of his consent to serve as Deputy Minister of Defence under Eshkol, see M. Golan, *Peres*, Jerusalem and Tel Aviv: Schocken, 1982, pp. 128–129. On Eshkol–Peres relations, see Yanai, *op. cit.*, pp. 128–133, 252–254. On the circumstances in which Peres was forced to resign due to the rift between Eshkol and Ben-Gurion, see ibid., pp. 217–218.

22 Peres at General Staff meeting, 24 June 1963. See also his remarks at the meeting of 15 July and 28 October 1963, and Peres, *op. cit.*, pp. 47–48, 135–139.

23 Eshkol at General Staff meeting, 15 July 1963.

24 Rabin at General Staff meeting 1 January 1964. In his memoirs, Rabin described his standpoint as much more resolute. See Rabin, *op. cit.*, pp. 105–106.

25 Goldstein, *Eshkol*, pp. 477–482.

26 See mainly: S. Aronson, *Nuclear Arms*; Cohen, *Israel and the Bomb*, New York: Columbia University Press, 1998.

27 Aronson, ibid., and S. Aronson, *Israel's Nuclear Programme, The Six Day War and its Ramifications*, London: Kings College, 1998. See also S. Aronson, 'The Sinai Campaign and nuclear arms', *Yahadut Zmaneinu (Contemporary Jewry)* 13 (1999), pp. 37–73.

28 Bar-Zohar, *Ben-Gurion*, pp. 1388–1394; Zaki Shalom, 'Reaction of the Great Powers to revelation of the construction of the Dimona reactor in the sixties', *Iyunim bi-Tkumat Yisrael (Israel Independence Studies)* 4 (1994), pp. 136–174.

29 Shalom, ibid., pp. 167–169; Cohen, *Israel and the Bomb*, pp. 108–111.

30 Z. Shalom, 'The Kennedy Administration and its Attitude towards Israel's Nuclear Activities', *Iyunim bi-Tkumat Yisrael (Israel Independence Studies)* 5 (1995), pp. 126–164; and A. Cohen, 'Kennedy, Ben-Gurion and the battle for Dimona, April–June 1963', *Iyunim bi-Tkumat Yisrael (Israel Independence Studies)* 6 (1996), pp. 110–146.

31 See extensive quotes from Eshkol's consultation with Deputy Prime Minister Abba Eban, Foreign Minister Golda Meir, Minister of Agriculture Moshe Dayan, Deputy Minister of Defence Shimon Peres and Chief of Staff Zvi Zur. Cohen, *Israel and the Bomb* (Hebrew edn), pp. 217–220.

32 Ibid., pp. 223–226.

33 Ibid., pp. 159, 197.

34 See *FRUS*, 1964–1968, Vol. 18 throughout the volume, and particularly Doc. 169, 214, 269, 415.

35 M. Shemesh, 'The Arab struggle for water against Israel 1959–1967', *Iyunim bi-Tkumat Yisrael (Israel Independence Studies)* (1997), pp. 103–168; Samir Mutawi, *Jordan in the 1967 War*, Cambridge: Cambridge University Press, 1987, pp. 22, 58–62.

36 Rabin, *Service Notebook*, pp. 128–130.

37 Ibid., p. 128.

38 *FRUS*, 1964–1968, Vol. 18, Doc. 146–185.

39 A. Cohen, *ha-Hagana al Mekorot ha-Mayim (Defence of Water Sources)*, Tel Aviv: Ministry of Defence, 1992.

40 Aronson, *Nuclear Arms*, A, pp. 232–308. Bar-Zohar, *Ben-Gurion*, pp. 1529–1545. I. Harel, *Mashber ha-Mad'anim ha-Germanim (The German Scientists Crisis)*, Tel Aviv: Ma'ariv, 1982, pp. 17–18.

41 There were those who charged Peres with launching the Shavit 2 missile on the eve of the elections for electoral purposes, thereby spurring the Egyptians to accelerate their efforts to develop ground-to-ground missiles. See Harel, ibid., pp. 19–22; Monia Mardor, *Rafael*, Tel Aviv: Ministry of Defence, 1981, pp. 319–348.

42 Cohen, *Defence . . .*, p. 155, according to the fiftieth anniversary volume of the Dassault concern in France. English translation of the relevant chapter: Pierre Landereux, 'France: Dassault publication reveals secret Israeli missile program', *FBIS Report*, FBIS-EST-97-008. The item was published in full in the Israeli press on 11 December 1996. See also Aluf Ben, 'Missiles on the nudist beach', *Haaretz*, 17 December 1996; see also Aronson, *Nuclear . . . A*, pp. 269–270; Peres, *Next Stage*, pp. 97–100.

43 See e.g. *FRUS*, 1964–1968, Vol. 18, Doc. 7, and Johnson-Eshkol talk, ibid., Doc. 65.

44 See Chapter 1, n. 8.

45 S. Cohen, 'Who needs . . .' in Lachish and Amitai, pp. 249–282.

46 Bar-Zohar, *Ben-Gurion*, C, pp. 1525–1526. On the Johnson's administration's reconnoitering on the Palestinian refugee question and Egyptian and Israeli reactions see *FRUS*, 1964–1968, Vol. 18, Doc. 25, 70, 291, 297, 323.

47 E. Barak, 'The forgotten struggle: Israel, Egypt and free shipping through the Suez Canal', *Iyunim bi-Tkumat Yisrael (Israel Independence Studies)*, 1991, pp. 81–131.

48 Cohen, *Defence . . .*, pp. 176–177, 319–324, 326–327; see also *FRUS*, 1964–1968, Vol. 18, Doc. 22, 24, 50, 52, 96–98.

49 A. Levite and E. Landau, *be-Einei ha-Aravim – Dimuya ha-Garini shel Yisrael (In Arab Eyes – Israel's Nuclear Image)*, Tel Aviv: Tel Aviv University, 1994, pp. 39–42, 71–76, 183–184; Cohen, *Defence . . .*, pp. 315–332.

50 General Staff meeting, 19 May 1965.

51 General Staff meeting, 10 October 1966.

52 The Lebanese newspaper *al-Nahar* wrote (end of May 1967) that the Dimona reactor was a prime target for an Egyptian attack – quoted in *Davar*, 30 May 1967.
53 M. Mardor, *Rafael*, Tel Aviv: Ministry of Defence, 1981, pp. 497–499.
54 S. Peres, *Battling for Peace*, New York: Random House, 1975, pp. 166–167. See also Ben-Gurion's Diary, 2 June 1967. Dan Margalit notes that Peres perceived the rejection of his proposal, aimed at preventing war, as one of the two main failures in his career (the other was the foiling of the London agreement with King Hussein in 1987). Margalit, *I Saw Them*, p. 69.
55 See Y. Greenberg, *Khesbon ve-Otzma (Calculations and Power)*, Tel Aviv: Ministry of Defence, 1997; Yakar, *Israel–US Relations*; Zohar Levkovitz, *be-Mivkhan ha-Milkhama – ha-Ma'arakh ha-Logisti be-Tzahal be-Milkhemet Sheshet ha-Yamim u-Milkhemet ha-Hatasha (The Test of War – the IDF's Logistic Set-up during the Six Day War and the War of Attrition)*, Tel Aviv: Ministry of Defence, 1995.
56 On the full buildup of the Arab armies in 1964 to 1967 see *Rabin Report*, pp. 11–20. See also Levkovitz, ibid., pp. 29–41, 43–86. Trenchant criticism of the pace of purchase of aircraft and the considerable investment in the reorganization of the navy was voiced by Moshe Dayan at the Foreign Affairs and Security Committee of the Knesset – E. Gluska, *ha-pikud ha-tzva'i veha-hanhaga ha-medinit shel Yisrael le-nokhakh baayot ha-bitakhon 1963–1967 (Israel's Military Command and Political Leadership Face Security Problems 1963–1967)*, Ph.D. dissertation, Hebrew University, 2000.

3 Escalation – Stage I: from skirmishes in the demilitarized zones to aerial sorties

1 A. Shalev, *Shituf Pe'ula be-Tzel Imut: Mishtar Shvitat ha-Neshek Yisrael-Syria 1949–1955 (Cooperation in the Shadow of Confrontation: the Armistice Regime Israel–Syria 1949–1955)*, Tel Aviv: Maarakhot, 1989.
2 Lior was Eshkol's military secretary in the year and a half preceding the Six Day War. He continued to serve under Golda Meir until her resignation in 1974. His diaries were edited in book form, and were an important source for the present book. E. Haber, *ha-Yom Tifrotz Milkhama (Today War will Break Out)*, Tel Aviv: Idanim, 1998.
3 In the deliberations of the government and the Ministerial Committee on Security, Allon adopted the most hawkish positions. See A. Cohen, *Defence*, and see below.
4 Mordechai Kidron, who was Head of the Armistice Department of the Foreign Ministry from 1963 to 1966, says that policy in the demilitarized zones was dictated by the IDF. Y. Melman, 'The hornets' nest of the demilitarized zones', *Haaretz*, 16 June 1995.
5 Haber, *Today*, p. 116. On Eshkol's unease, see ibid., pp. 95–97.
6 Odd Bull, *War and Peace in the Middle East*, London: Leo Cooper, 1973, pp. 51–52.
7 R. Tal, 'Moshe Dayan – self-reckoning, *Yediot Aharonot*, 27 April 1997.
8 Cohen, *Defence*, pp. 13–16.
9 For a survey of the events and discussions where the deployment of aircraft was discussed before the period under discussion, see Cohen, *Defence*, 1992, pp. 13–66.
10 M. Greenberg, *ha-Ezorim ha-Mefurazim bi-Gvul Yisrael–Syria B (The Demilitarized Zones on the Israel–Syria Border B)*, General Staff, History Deptartment, 1993, pp. 54–55.

11 Cohen, *Defence*, pp. 75–76.
12 H. Bartov, *Dado*, Tel Aviv: Sifriyat Maariv, 1978, p. 115.
13 Bartov, ibid., pp. 106, 109–110.
14 S. Tevet, *Khasufim ba-Tzariakh (Exposed in the Turret)*, Jerusalem and Tel Aviv: Schocken, 1968, pp. 81–88, 121–126. Rabin, *Service Notebook*, p. 122. Bartov, *Dado*, p. 110.
15 For a detailed description of the operation, see Cohen, *Defence* ..., pp. 77–117. See also Rabin, *Service Notebook*, pp. 122–124.
16 Ibid. and Rabin at the General Staff meeting, 16 November, 1964.
17 *IDF Archive*, files 103/67/40 and 103/67/140.
18 Cohen, *Defence*, pp. 112–114.
19 See comments of Zvi Dinstein, who served as Deputy Minister of Defence under Eshkol. Peri, *Battles and Ballots*, p. 162. See also Haber, *Today* ..., p. 43.
20 See Ben-Gurion's remarks to Dayan, Cohen, *Defence*, p. 31.
21 Cohen, ibid., p. 47.

4 Escalation – Stage 2: diversion

1 Moshe Shemesh, 'ha-maavak ha-Aravi al ha-mayim neged Yisrael 1959–1967' (The Arab struggle over water against Israel, 1959–1967), *Iyunim bi-tkumat Yisrael (Israel Independence Studies)* 7 (1997), pp. 103–168; Itamar Rabinovitch, 'Ha-maavak al mei ha-Yarden ke-markiv ba-sikhsukh ha-Yisraeli-Aravi' (The struggle over the Jordan waters as a component of the Israel–Arab conflict), *Artzot ha-galil (Land of Galilee)* B, Haifa University, 1983, pp. 863–868. S. Golan, 'Ha-maavak al mei ha-Yarden (The struggle over the Jordan waters), ibid., pp. 853–862. S. Blass, *Mei meriva u-maas (Disputed Waters)*, Ramat Gan: Massada, 1973.
2 *FRUS*, 1952–1954, Vol. 9, pp. 103–114.
3 *Haaretz*, 2 January 1965.
4 Rabinovitch, *The Struggle over the Jordan Waters*, ibid.
5 The significance of Israel's water scheme was inflated because of inter-Arab relations. See debate in the UAR government in 1959 between Deputy President Akram el-Horani of Syria and President Nasser. Quoted in S. Yitzhaki, *Be-ainei ha-Aravim (In Arab Eyes)*, Tel Aviv: Ministry of Defence, 1969, pp. 30–31. See also Shemesh, *Arab Struggle*. ...
6 I. Rabinovitch, *Syria under the Baath*, Jerusalem: Israel University Press, 1972. The basic tenets of the Baath Party are cited in A. Gilboa, *Shesh Shanim Shisha Yamim (Six Years, Six Days)*, Tel Aviv: Am Oved, 1968, pp. 274–276.
7 On the 'Union' and its collapse, see M. Kerr, *The Arab Cold War 1958–1967*, Oxford: Oxford University Press, 1967, pp. 58–126. On the Arab summit conferences before the Six Day War, see A. Sela, *Ahdut be-Tokh Perud ba-Ma'arekhet ha-Bein-Aravit (Unity in Division in the inter-Arab System)*, Jerusalem: Magnes, 1983, pp. 6–7, 26–63.
8 Kerr, *The Arab Cold War*, pp. 127–133. On additional reasons for the convening of the Arab summit, ibid., pp. 133–136. On the background and preparations for the first conference in Cairo see Sela, *Unity in Division*, pp. 26–29.
9 On the discussions and resolutions of the Cairo summit conference, see Kerr, ibid., pp. 29–37.
10 Rabin at the General Staff meeting, 28 December 1964.
11 Rabin feared, so he said, that the Americans would say to Israel: 'Friends, why go to war for 15–30 million cubic meters of water? We can desalinate water for you!' Rabin, General Staff meeting, 11 January 1965.

12 On the diversion work in Lebanon under pressure from the Arab states, see Intelligence Branch document 2 July 1965, *IDF Archive* 758/67/73. See also Shemesh, *Arab Struggle*.
13 General Staff meeting, 25 January 1965.
14 Moshe Dayan, 'Diversion of the Jordan sources', *Haaretz*, 29 January 1965.
15 Rabin at General Staff meeting, 1 February 1965.
16 Rabin at General Staff meeting, 22 February 1965. The General Staff did in fact hold a detailed discussion at that meeting on readiness of the various branches of the armed forces. Ibid.
17 Barlev at General Staff meeting, 8 March 1965.
18 Rabin at General Staff meeting, 8 March 1965.
19 Rabin at General Staff, 15 March 1965. See also *FRUS*, 1964–1968, Vol. 18, Doc. 170.
20 Rabin, *Service Notebook*, p. 124. Cohen, *Defence*, p. 123.
21 Routine security report of Chief of Operations, General Staff meeting, 12 April 1965.
22 Rabin at General Staff meeting, 19 April 1965.
23 Rabin at General Staff meeting, 3 May 1965. On 9 April 1965 the Minister of Defence had approved Rabin's plan for attacking the diversion equipment in Lebanon.
24 Minutes of Eshkol–Rabin conversation of 26 February 1965, *Eshkol Archive*.
25 Minutes of the Eshkol–Rabin conversation of 13 May 1965, *Eshkol Archive*. Rabin's remarks indicate that if the Syrians, contrary to expectations, were not provoked into opening fire by the patrol's fire, 'then in any case we must stage something'. Ibid.; and see Shemesh, *Arab Struggle*, pp. 155–159.
26 Rabin at General Staff meeting, 17 May 1965.
27 Minutes of Eshkol–Rabin conversation, 19 May 1965, *Eshkol Archive*.
28 Buffer fire was first employed in 1962 and on various occasions after that, on various sectors, and was ceased due to UN intervention. For details see letter from Bureau Chief of Head of Operations to Bureau Chief of Staff, 27 January 1967 headed 'Buffer fire – a historical survey', IDF Archive, 117/70/63.
29 Head of Operations routine security report, General Staff meeting, 12 April 1965.
30 Yariv at General Staff meeting, 24 May 1965.
31 General Staff meeting, 24 May 1965. The US protest was submitted both through the ambassador in Tel Aviv and also in Washington. See also *FRUS*, 1964–1968, Vol. 18, Doc. 219.
32 E. Gluska, *ha-Pikud ha-Tzvai veha-Hanhaga ha-Medinit shel Yisrael le-Nokhakh Ba'ayot ha-Bitakhon 1963–1967 (The Military Command and Political Leadership of Israel in Light of Security Problems 1963–1967)*, dissertation, p. 81, n. 61. Shemesh, *Arab Struggle*, pp. 144–158.
33 Rabin at General Staff meeting, 12 July 1965.
34 Rabin at General Staff meeting, 2 August 1965. The Israeli press refrained from reporting on cessation of work in Lebanon as a result of a request by the IDF to the editors.
35 Operation Moznayim (Scales), night of 27/28 October 1965.
36 Barlev at General Staff meeting, 2 August 1965.
37 Shemesh, *Arab Struggle*, p. 159. Report and photographs of the incident of 12 August 1965 in IDF Archive, 758/67/65.
38 Ze'evi and Rabin at General Staff meeting 16 August 1965. See also Cohen, *Defence . . .*, pp. 126–127.
39 *Rabin Report*, p. 33.
40 Rabin, General Staff meeting, 8 November 1965.

41 Yariv, General Staff meeting, 7 March 1966.
42 General Staff meetings, 13 June 1966, 28 March 1966. At the beginning of 1967 the Chief of Intelligence even felt the need to ask his fellow members 'not to forget the diversion subject'. Yariv, General Staff meeting, 2 January 1967.
43 *FRUS*, 1964–1968, Vol. 18, Doc. 45, 110–111, 115, 125, 127–128, 192–193, 197–198, 215.

5 The dispute with Syria worsens

1 P. Seale, *Assad of Syria: The Struggle for the Middle East*, London: Tauris, 1988.
2 A. Shalev, *Shituf Peula be-Tzel ha-Imut (Cooperation in the Shadow of Confrontation)*, Tel Aviv: Maarakhot, 1989, pp. 254–256.
3 Seale, *Assad* (Hebrew edn), pp. 210–314.
4 S. Segev, *Milkhama ve-Shalom ba-Mizrakh ha-Tikhon (War and Peace in the Middle East)*, Tel Aviv: Tversky, 1965, pp. 34–40, 49.
5 A. Sela, *Akhdut be-Tokh Perud (Unity in Division)*, Jerusalem: Magnes, 1983, pp. 50–55. On the Bourguiba affair, see also D. Kimche and D. Bavli, *Sufat ha-esh (The Storm of Fire)*, Tel Aviv: Am Hasefer, 1968, pp. 22–25. Segev, *War and Peace*, pp. 40–42. In a speech in the Knesset, Eshkol responded to Bourguiba's proposals with a peace plan of his own, based on territorial integrity of all the states and minor border adjustments. *Haaretz*, 18 May 1965.
6 On the Casablanca summit deliberations, resolutions and results, see Sela, *Unity*, pp. 55–63.
7 Yariv at General Staff meeting, 13 December 1965. Later, the Jordanian premier Wafsi Tal revealed that a detailed plan was drawn up there for the liberation of Palestine. *Haaretz*, 7 August 1966. See also Shemesh, 'The Arab struggle for water against Israel', *Iyunim bi-Tkumat Yisrael (Israel Independence Studies)*, 7 (1997), pp. 103–168.
8 A. Cohen, *ha-Hagana al Mekorot ha-Mayim (Defence of the Water Sources)*, Tel Aviv: Ministry of Defence, 1992, p. 127. *Haaretz*, 20 September 1965.
9 P. Seale, *Assad*, pp. 97–123. Rabinovich, *Syria under the Baath*, Jerusalem: Israel University Press, 1972, pp. 189–208.
10 Yariv at General Staff meeting, 28 February 1966.
11 Hasnin Heikal described the group which had seized power in Damascus as 'fanatic and irresponsible'. M.H. Heikal, *ha-Sphinx veha-Commissar (The Sphinx and the Commissar)*, Tel Aviv: Am Oved, 1981, p. 149.
12 Segev, *War and Peace*, pp. 52–53. S. Yitzhaki, *be-Einei ha-Aravim (In Arab Eyes)*, Tel Aviv: Maarakhot, 1969, pp. 30–38.
13 Yariv at General Staff meeting, 18 April 1966 and 30 May 1966. Rabin at General Staff meeting, 2 May 1966. Heikal in *The Sphinx* presents the problematic relationship between the Soviet Union and the Arabs as stemming to a large extent from the duality of the Soviet approach: on the one hand a world power with strategic calculations in the power struggle with the United States, and on the other hand, the homeland of the revolution, committed to its ideological and universal mission and its connections with communist parties. Against this background, the participation of the Communist Party in the Baath government in Syria was very important for the Soviets. See also Seale, *Assad*, p. 17.
14 Yariv at General Staff meeting, 4 July 1966. See also Chapter 2 above.
15 Rabin at General Staff meetings, 13 June 1966 and 27 June 1966.
16 On Bunche's visit, see O. Bull, *War and Peace in the Middle East*, London: Leo Cooper, 1973, pp. 95–96. Eshkol and Eban expressed to him their strong

objections to the intention to reduce the United Nations Emergency Force and to evacuate it from Sharm al-Sheikh.

17 General Staff meeting, 11 July 1966. Among the supporters of evacuation of the UNEF was MK Moshe Dayan, at the Foreign Affairs and Security Committee, 17 May 1967, Chapter 12 (below) and Dayan's remarks at the American Zionist Conference, *Maariv*, 28 November 1966.

18 Debriefing on the air force operation of 14 July 1966 in the IDF Archive, 192/74/1393.

19 Cohen, *Defence*, pp. 138–148.

20 *IDF Archive*, 192/74/1393.

21 Rabin at General Staff meeting, 25 July 1966. The Syrian Chief of Staff called for 'a popular war for the liberation of Palestine'. *Haaretz*, 19 July 1966.

6 Escalation – Stage 3: 'harassment'

1 The definition 'intolerable' from Israel's viewpoint was, of course, subjective, but this is the clear impression gained from the General Staff deliberations (see below in this chapter). See also E. Landau, 'Four stages in the terror warfare', *Maariv*, 19 May 1967. From the Arab point of view, the acts of sabotage were not serious, and merely served Israel as an excuse for implementing its expansion aspirations. See e.g. P. Seale, *Assad*, Tel Aviv: Maarakhot, 1993, pp. 135–136.

2 M. Shemesh, *The Palestinian Entity 1959–1974 – Arab Politics and the PLO*, London: Frank Cass, 1988, pp. 1–94. Y. Arnon-Ohana and A. Yodfat, *Ashaf – Dyokno shel Irgun (The PLO – Portrait of an Organization)*, Tel Aviv: Maariv, 1985, pp. 29–41.

3 In response to criticism to the effect that terrorist activity would evoke Israeli military reaction which could end in Arab defeat, the Fatah replied in 1963 in almost 'prophetic' fashion: 'The revolution will last a year, two years, up to twenty or thirty years. On the contrary, let the Zionists conquer the West Bank. . . . History has never yet witnessed the failure of popular revolutions.' A. Yaari, *Fatah*, Tel Aviv: Lewin-Epstein, 1970, p. 38. Precisely thirty years later, it was agreed at Oslo to establish an independent Palestinian Authority.

4 Yariv at General Staff meetings, 11 January 1965 and 18 January 1965. The name *Fatah* first appeared in the Israeli press on 15 January 1965 (e.g. in *Haaretz*), where it was described as an organization established by the Syrians under Palestinian cover.

5 Yaari attributes the Fatah's success and Egypt's withdrawal in 1966 from its objections to terrorist activity, to the *excessive caution* of Israel, which confined itself to very restricted operations and did not punish Syria. Yaari, *Fatah*, pp. 65–66. He is expressing the standpoint of the Intelligence Branch and the General Staff.

6 On the Fatah, its structure and aims and the differences between the Fatah and the PLO, see Yitzhaki, *be-Einei ha-Aravim (In Arab Eyes)*, pp. 38–56. On the Fatah from the IDF's viewpoint and details of its activities, see *Rabin Report*, pp. 34–68.

7 The Fatah's first experience of terrorist activity was the laying of detonation charges in the National Water Carrier, some 3.5 kilometres west of the Ilabun tunnel. It did not explode and was discovered on 4 January 1965, several days after it was laid, by a Border Police unit. *Rabin Report*, pp. 34–84.

8 Yariv at General Staff meeting, 8 March 1965.

9 Yohai Bin-Nun at General Staff meeting, 19 July 1965.

10 General Staff meeting, 19 July 1965.

11 Rabin at General Staff meeting, 27 June 1965.
12 For details of hostile terrorist activity in this period from Jordan, see *Rabin Report*, pp. 86–87.
13 Rabin at General Staff meeting, 6 September 1965. In the course of the operation, an IDF force dispersed warning leaflets in Arabic: 'We hope we will not be forced to visit you with stronger punitive measures. You have been cautioned, and the cautioner had done his duty.' Photograph of leaflet in *Al Hamishmar*, 7 September 1965.
14 Yariv at General Staff meetings, 15 November 1965, 13 December 1965.
15 Rabin pointed this out at General Staff meeting on 31 January 1966. See also *Rabin Report*, pp. 85–87.
16 *Rabin Report*, pp. 88–89.
17 General Staff meeting, 2 May 1966, and debriefing on Operations Joseph and Alpha, IDF Archive, 192/74/1440.

7 The General Staff wants a 'frontal clash'

1 See e.g. Matti Peled's remarks: 'Syria is standing in line to get the lesson they evaded in 1948'. General Staff meeting, 4 October 1965; see also testimony of Lior on the 'Syrian syndrome': E. Haber, *ha-Yom Tifrotz Milkhama (Today War Will Break Out)*, Tel Aviv: Idanim, 1988, pp. 95–97.
2 A. Cohen, *ha-Hagana al Mekorot ha-Mayim (Defence of the Water Sources)*, Tel Aviv: Ministry of Defence, 1992, pp. 18–27. Y. Rabin, *Pinkes Sherut (Service Notebook)* A, Tel Aviv: Maariv, 1979, pp. 97–98.
3 General Staff meeting, 25 July 1966.
4 Yariv at General Staff meeting, 8 August 1966.
5 General Staff meeting, 8 August 1966.
6 Rabin at General Staff meetings, 8 August 1966 and 15 August 1966.
7 For a detailed description of the incident, including background, maps and details of the General Staff debriefing, see *IDF Archive* 1192/74/1390 and 192/74/1387. See also A. Cohen, *Defence ...*, pp. 149–156, E. Weizman, *Lekha Shamayim Lekha Aretz (Heaven and Earth are Yours)*, Tel Aviv: Maariv, 1975, pp. 252–253.
8 In the course of the incident, the Chief of Staff, the CO Northern Command, the Chief of Operations Branch and other officers, in civilian clothes or swimsuits, boarded a boat on the Lake, and were caught in the lens of a Syrian camera. Years later, the photograph was discovered among documents collected by the IDF on the Golan Heights and appeared in the press about a month after the Six Day War. See, for example, the front page of *Yediot Aharonot*, 10 July 1967.
9 The full story of the acquisition of the Iraqi Mig through the Mossad was exposed more than thirty-one years later. See U. Dan, '1966, the Iraqi Mig lands in Israel', *Maariv*, 20 September 1998. It is given in even greater detail in a book by the then head of the Mossad, Meir Amit, *Rosh be-Rosh (Head On)*, Tel Aviv: Hed Artzi, 1999, pp. 179–203.
10 See above, Chapter 5.
11 Rabin at General Staff meeting, 22 August 1966.
12 Weizman at General Staff meeting, 22 August 1966.
13 Ibid.
14 *Bamahaneh*, 18 September 1966.
15 Y. Peri, *Between Battles and Ballots*, Cambridge: Cambridge University Press, 1983, p. 160. Peri says that Eshkol contemplated deposing Rabin, but did not want Weizman as Chief of Staff, and the Ahdut ha-Avoda ministers persuaded

him to refrain from this step. It is hard to believe that Eshkol could have deposed Rabin, who was highly popular, because of his remarks. Neither the army nor the public would have accepted it.

16 Rabin at General Staff meeting, 26 September 1966.
17 The text of the statement in handwriting (apparently that of Minister without PortfolioYisrael Galili) in the IDF Archive, 9/96/54; see also Haber, *Today*, pp. 146–147.
18 File of meetings with the Chief of Staff, *Eshkol Archive*.
19 Haber, *Today* . . ., pp. 104–105.
20 Yariv at General Staff meeting, 10 October 1966.
21 Rabin at the General Staff meeting, 10 October 1966.
22 Ibid.
23 The UN deliberations in October to November are well documented in an unpublished manuscript by Abba Eban, *The Six Day War* (ms. 1969), pp. 27–29.
24 The Chief of Intelligence listed some twenty various organizations, the dominant among them being Fatah. He said that the PLO had also begun to establish underground units, despite Egyptian domination of the organization and the instruction to avoid entanglement. General Staff meeting, 31 October 1966.
25 Rabin at General Staff meeting, 31October 1966.
26 S. Yitzhaki, *be-Einei ha-Aravim (In Arab Eyes)*, Tel Aviv: Maarakhot, 1969, pp. 76–81. Full text of pact, ibid., pp. 224–226.

8 Israel–Jordan: the Israeli dilemma, the Jordanian dilemma

1 On the history of relations between Israel and Jordan up to the signing of the peace treaty, see M. Zak, *Hussein Oseh Shalom (Hussein Makes Peace)*, Ramat Gan: Bar-Ilan University, 1966. See also Y. Melman, *Shutafut Oyenet – ha-Ksharim ha-Sodiim bein Yisrael le-Yarden (Hostile Partnership – the Secret Ties between Israel and Jordan)*, Tel Aviv: Metam, 1987.
2 A. Sela, *mi-Magaim le-Masa u-Matan: Yakhasei ha-Sokhnut ha-Yehudit im ha-Melekh Abdullah, 1946–1950 (From Contacts to Negotiations: The Jewish Agency and King Abdullah, 1946–1950)*, Tel Aviv University, Shiloah Institute, 1985. A Shlaim, *Collusion Across the Jordan*, New York: Columbia University Press, 1988. S. Golan, *Gvul Kham, Milkhama Kara (Hot Border, Cold War)*, Tel Aviv: Maarakhot, 2000, pp. 111–139.
3 On border problems with Jordan in general and the 'urban line' in Jerusalem in particular, see U. Narkis, *Akhat Yerushalayim (Jerusalem is One)*, Tel Aviv: Am Oved, 1975, pp. 21–55.
4 For a detailed and interesting description of routine activity on Mount Scopus up to 1967, see M. Gilat, *Har ha-Tzofim (Mount Scopus)*, Ramat Gan: Massada, 1969.
5 Narkis, *Jerusalem*, p. 52.
6 M. Zak, *Hussein*, pp. 39–44. M. Zak, 'The change in BG's attitude to the Kingdom of Jordan', *Iyunim bi-Tkumat Yisrael (Israel Independence Studies)*, 6 (1996), pp. 85–109.
7 Ibid., pp. 58–66. Melman, *Hostile Partnership*, pp. 56–60. In a private conversation with the Israeli historian Avi Shlaim in 1996, Hussein described and detailed all the secret meetings from 1963 on with Israelis. A. Shlaim, 'Hussein without censorship', *Yediot Aharonot*, 6 April 1999.
8 M. Amit, *Rosh be-Rosh (Head On)*, Tel Aviv: Hed Artzi, 1999, pp. 80–82. The participation of the Chief of Intelligence is mentioned in the summary of the weekly meeting of the Chief of Staff and the Minister of Defence on 4 June 1965. File of meetings with the Chief of Staff, *Eshkol Archives*.

9 Hussein did not forgive Israel for its 'treachery' at Samu. Melman, *Hostile Partnership*, pp. 61–62. On Samu and the rift with Hussein, see Zak, *Hussein*, pp. 83–102. For Hussein's version of Samu, see E. Kam (ed.) *Hussein Poteah be-Milkhama (Hussein Starts a War)*, Tel Aviv: Maarakhot, 1974, pp. 37–41.
10 See S. Mutawi, *Jordan in the 1967 War*, Cambridge: Cambridge University Press, 1987, pp. 54–55, 77–78.
11 Narkis, *Jerusalem*, pp. 21–42. For details of the incidents and raids through the period in all sectors, see *Rabin Report*, pp. 47–64, 83–94.
12 Armistice Commission files, IDF Archive, 758/67/65, 758/67/66, 103/67/32, 103/67/40, 9/69/58.
13 General Staff meeting, 4 October 1965.
14 Debriefing on incident, *IDF Archive*, 9/69/54.
15 A detailed description of the operation and debriefing in the *IDF Archive*, 192/74/1401, 192/74/1398, 192/74/1410, 9/69/47.
16 See Shemesh, 'After the Samu raid: nationalist renaissance on the West Bank and a change in Hussein's attitude towards Israel and the West Bank', *Iyunim bi-Tkumat Yisrael (Israel Independence Studies)*, 10 (2000), pp. 123–164.
17 Rabin at General Staff meeting, 14 November 1966.
18 Yariv at General Staff meeting, 14 November 1966.
19 *IDF Archives*, 192/74/1401.
20 Rabin at General Staff meeting, 5 December 1966. On the 'Stratum' affair see *IDF Archive*, 192/74/1415.
21 Rabin at General Staff meeting, 21 November 1966. US President Lyndon Johnson felt it necessary to dispatch an appeasing message to Hussein on 23 November 1966. See text in Zak, *Hussein*, p. 57. Washington's concern for the stability of Hussein's regime led to the dispatch of urgent military aid to Jordan and anger at Israel which was not easily dispelled. Letter from Israeli Minister in Washington E. Evron to the Deputy Director General of the Ministry of Foreign Affairs Moshe Bitan on 'The Pentagon and its attitude to Israel', 2 January 1967, *IDF Archive*, 117/701114.
22 Rabin at General Staff meeting, 5 December 1966.
23 Ibid.
24 *FRUS*, 1964–1968, Vol. 18, Doc. 388.
25 General Staff meetings, 13 February 1967, 20 February 1967.
26 Weizman at General Staff meeting, 12 December 1966.
27 Moshe Dayan used this contemptuous term to denote the PLO at the onset of its activities. Eshkol reminded him of this at a meeting of the Knesset Foreign Affairs and Security Committee on 17 May 1967. Minutes of meeting, *Eshkol Archive*.
28 General Staff meeting, 12 December 1966.

9 The clash with Syria approaches

1 Suidani at a briefing for Egyptian journalists in April 1967. E. Yaari, *Fatah*, Tel Aviv: Lewin Epstein, p. 78. On the alliance between Suidani and the Fatah, ibid., pp. 39–40.
2 P. Seale, *Assad*, p. 137.
3 On the deliberations of the Committee against the background of events along the Syrian border in January 1967, see A. Cohen, *ha-Hagana al Mekorot ha-Mayim (Defence of Water Sources)*, Tel Aviv: Ministry of Defence, 1992, pp. 158–162.
4 General Staff meeting with the Prime Minister and Minister of Defence, 23 January 1967.

5 Between the end of January and beginning of April 1967 there were ten terror incidents. For details of terror activity from 1 January 1964 to 15 May 1967 see *Rabin Report*, pp. 83–94.

6 The talks were held, as noted above, on Syrian initiative, but formally speaking, the two sides responded to a missive sent on 15 January 1967 by the UN Secretary-General, *IDF Archive*, 117/70/114.

7 Moshe Sasson in conversation with the author, 28 July 1997.

8 A summary of the meetings between the Syrian and Israeli delegations appeared in the *Weekly Letter* No. 82 of the Director-General of the Ministry of Foreign Affairs on 5 February 1967, *IDF Archive*, 117/70/114. See also O. Bull, *War and Peace in the Middle East*, London: Leo Cooper, 1973, pp. 101–103.

9 Yariv at General Staff meeting, 13 February 1967.

10 *Rabin Report*, pp. 67–91.

10 Conflagration

1 The prepared text of Eshkol's speech in the speeches file, *Eshkol Archive*. Interview with Mrs Eshkol, *Yediot Aharonot*, 23 October 1998; see also E. Haber, *Ha-Yom Tifrotz Milkhama (Today War will Break Out)*, Tel Aviv: Idanim, 1988, pp. 133. See Ze'evi's testimony, M. Sheshar, *Sikhot im Rehavam 'Gandhi' Zeevi (Talks with Rehavam 'Gandhi' Zeevi)*, Tel Aviv: Yediot Aharonot, 1992, p. 167.

2 *Rabin Report*, pp. 87–94.

3 General Staff meeting, 13 March 1967. In the March 1967 activity report of the Head of Public Relations in the Ministry of Foreign Affairs, P. Eliav listed the lectures and symposia organized by the Ministry throughout the country. The 'routine' question asked was: 'When will the IDF act against the Syrians?' *IDF Archive*, 117/70/114.

4 General Staff meeting, 3 April 1967, *IDF Archive*, 117/70/114.

5 Minutes of Eshkol-Rabin conversation, 1 April 1967, file of meetings with the Chief of Staff, *Eshkol Archive*.

6 Reference is to three plots which were not considered to be particularly problematical, but the Syrians were in the habit of firing on Israeli workers in the demilitarized zones at that time, in reaction to Israeli buffer fire. See also A. Cohen, *ha-Hagana al Mekorot ha-Mayim (Defence of the Water Sources)*, Tel Aviv: Ministry of Defence, 1992, p. 163.

7 Ibid. See Haber, *Today*, p. 142.

8 A. Cohen, *Defence*, pp. 164–165. Haber, *Today*, p. 143. General Staff meeting, 10 April 1967.

9 A. Cohen, ibid.

10 For a full description of the events of 7 April 1967, and particularly the role of the IAF, see A. Cohen, *Defence*, pp. 163–180.

11 A. Cohen, *Defence*, pp. 166, 175.

12 Ibid., p. 173.

13 A. Cohen, *Defence*, pp. 178–179.

14 Testimony of Brigadier-General Hod, *IDF Archive*, 192/74/1156.

15 A. Cohen, *Defence*, pp. 164–165. See also remarks of the Head of the Air Department, Colonel Menahem Bar, at the debriefing, ibid., p. 175.

16 At the press conference summing up the events of 7 April, the Chief of Staff said that he had ordered the CO IAF not to restrict his pilots from advancing to Damascus if the circumstances dictated this. *Maariv*, 9 April 1967, but there is no confirmation for such an order, and Rabin was apparently merely providing Hod with backing in hindsight.

17 What is more, as a gesture to the IAF for its performance on 7 April, Hod's promotion to the rank of Brigadier-General was brought forward to 10 April. General Staff meeting, 10 April 1967. *Haaretz*, 11 April 1967. *Bamahaneh*, 19 April 1967.

18 General Staff meeting, 10 April 1967.

19 Rabin commented on fears expressed by several ministers: 'There are several Jews here [i.e. ministers] who think they understand the Americans. The Americans are not going to say to us: "Go get them!" but when we do get [the Syrians] – they're delighted, even if they don't say so.' Rabin at General Staff meeting, 10 April 1967.

20 Yariv at General Staff meeting, 10 April 1967.

21 Rabin at General Staff meeting, 10 April 1967.

22 Weizman, *Lekha Shamayim Lekha Aretz (Heaven and Earth are Yours)*, Tel Aviv: Maariv, 1975, p. 254.

23 A. Cohen, *Defence*, pp. 178–179.

24 Carmon at General Staff meeting, 24 April 1967. He could not say whether an attack on Kuneitra or on Syrian airfields would be considered a 'total onslaught' requiring Egyptian intervention, but his remarks indicate what type of action was being contemplated.

25 Ibid. The complacency in Israel where an Egyptian reaction was concerned was in line with the Intelligence Branch assessment, and was reflected in newspaper headlines. The main headline in *Haaretz* on 14 April 1967, for example, announced that the Egyptian delegation had informed Damascus that Egypt would not launch a 'second front' because of the war in Yemen.

26 There were fourteen terrorist incidents between 7 April and 9 May from Jordan, Lebanon and Syria, *IDF Archive*, 117/70/64.

27 M. Brecher and B. Geist, *Decisions in Crisis*, Berkeley: University of California Press 1980, p. 36. On the other hand, on 9 May Eshkol declared in the Knesset that he could not say how the government intended to deal with the situation because the matter had not yet been discussed. Minutes of Foreign Affairs and Security Committee, 9 May 1967, *Eshkol Archive*.

28 Letter from Odd Bull to the Head of the Armistice Commissions Department of the Foreign Ministry, Moshe Sasson, 4 May 1967, *IDF Archive*, 117/70/85.

29 Foreign Affairs and Security Committee Minutes, 9 May 1967, *Eshkol Archive*.

30 As early as October 1966 Dayan stated in the Knesset that there was no need to get excited about 'a few dozen bandits' of the Fatah. Quoted in A. Eban, *The Six Day War* (manuscript, 1969), p. 25. When the crisis erupted, Eshkol mocked Dayan: 'There was a time, not so long ago, when Knesset Member Dayan said that it was a matter of a few bandits so why were we making a big deal of it? But it developed and grew.' Foreign Affairs and Security Committee Minutes, 17 May 1967.

31 Ibid.

11 The trigger

1 For a description of the Six Day War as the fruit of prior Israeli planning, see e.g. A. Nutting, *Nasser*, London: Constable, 1972, pp. 383–424; also M. Abdel-Kader Hatem, *Information and the Arab Cause*, London: Longman, pp. 223–230; H. Cattan, *Palestine and International Law*, London: Longman, 1974, pp. 126–135. On the theory of an Israeli–US conspiracy, see N.H. Heikal, *Ha-sphinx veha-Commissar (The Sphinx and the Commissar)*, Tel Aviv: Am Oved, 1981 (in particular pp. 172–189). For a description of the war as the product of a conspiracy between the Israeli military establishment and

the US administration, against the will of the Israeli government, see Yitzhak Laor, 'Creating Corpses', Kol Ha-Ir, 30 September 1994. A conspiracy between the Mossad and the CIA is postulated by A. and L. Cockburn, Dangerous Liaison: The Inside Story of a US–Israeli Covert Relationship, New York: HarperCollins, 1991, pp. 125–154. The Soviet conspiracy is cited in Abd al-Rahman Rahmi, The Egyptian Policy in the Arab World, Washington, DC: University Press of America, 1983, pp. 232–235. A more developed theory of a Soviet conspiracy against the background of power struggles in the Kremlin is presented by A. Ben-Zvi, Gormim Sovietiim u-Milkhemet Sheshet ha-Yamim (Soviet Elements and the Six Day War), Tel Aviv: Sifriyat Hapoalim. A brilliant satirical description of the war as the outcome of a sophisticated Israeli conspiracy appeared during the war in a column by Ephraim Kishon, 'Had Gadya', Maariv, 8 June 1967.

2 A developed 'nuclear theory' is presented by Aronson in Neshek garini ba-mizrakh ha-tikhon (Nuclear Weapons in the Middle East), Jerusalem: Akademon, 1995, in particular Vol. 2, pp. 13–166, and S. Aronson, Israel's Nuclear Programme: The Six Day War and its Ramifications, London: Kings College, 1998.

3 The testimony and discussions were published in an illuminating book. See R. Parker (ed.) The Six Day War – A Retrospective, Gainesville: University Press of Florida, 1996.

4 See, in particular, R. Parker, The Politics of Miscalculation in the Middle East, Bloomington: Indiana University Press, 1993, pp. 3–122.

5 In both of his above-cited books, Parker made a serious attempt to clarify the Soviet role. See also A. Ben-Zvi, Gormim Sovietiim u-Milkhemet Sheshet ha-Yamim (Soviet Factors and the Six Day War), Tel Aviv: Sifriyat Hapoalim, 1976.

6 On the open and clandestine ties between Israel and Iran over the years see S. Segev, The Iranian Triangle, New York: Free Press, 1988. Meir Ezri, 'Who is There Among You of His People', Or Yehuda: Hed Artzi, 2000; U. Bialer, 'Oil from Iran – Zvi Duriel's mission in Teheran 1956–1963', Iyunim bi-Tkumat Yisrael (Israel Independence Studies), Vol. 8, pp. 150–180 and Vol. 9, pp. 128–168. Y. Nimrodi, Masa Khayei (My Life's Journey), Tel Aviv: Maariv, 2003, pp. 308–311.

7 Segev, Iranian Triangle, pp. 27–69. S. Segev, ha-Kesher ha-Irani (The Iranian Connection), Jerusalem: Domino 1989, pp. 70–71.

8 The details below are from the Chief of Staff's report of his visit to Iran. General Staff meeting, 24 April 1967, and cf. Y. Nimrodi, My Life's Journey, pp. 308–311; Segev, Iranian Triangle, pp. 68–69.

9 He was speaking at a discussion on Intelligence evaluations, General Staff meeting, 21 February 1963.

10 This was the view expressed by Minister Eliyahu Sasson at a government meeting on 21 May 1967.

11 On the riots in Syria in the wake of the article and its attribution to the CIA, see W. Laqueur, The Road to the 1967 War, London: Weidenfeld & Nicolson, 1968, p. 77.

12 On the Soviet reaction to the 7 April events, see Y. Govrin, Yakhasei Yisrael–Brit ha-Moatzot 1953–1969 (Israel–Soviet Relations, 1953–1969), Jerusalem: Magnes, 1990, pp. 252–257.

13 Yariv at General Staff meeting, 3 April 1967. See also Heikal, ha-Sphinx veha-Commissar (The Sphinx and the Commissar), pp. 168–169.

14 Yariv at General Staff meeting, 24 April 1967.

15 Rabin at General Staff meeting, 24 April 1967.

16 D. Kimche and D.Bavli, *Sufat ha-Esh (The Storm of Fire)*, Tel Aviv: Am Hasefer, 1968, p. 43. A. Yariv, 'The background to war', *Dapei Elazar (Notes on Elazar)*, 10, Tel Aviv: 1988, pp. 15–23.

17 At the height of the alert after 7 April the IDF reinforced the line with two tank companies and all in all there were some seventy tanks on the line. When the situation calmed down on the eve of Passover the force was reduced. Weizman at General Staff meeting, 24 April 1967. Yariv at General Staff meeting, 17 May 1967.

18 On 25 April the Communist Party Secretary-General Brezhnev demanded the withdrawal of the Sixth Fleet from the Mediterranean. Eban, *Six Day War* (ms. 1969), p. 32.

19 M.A. Gilboa, *Shesh Shanim Shisha Yamim (Six Years Six Days)*, Tel Aviv: Am Oved, 1968, pp. 94–95. See also n. 13 above.

20 See e.g. headline in *Lamerhav*, 9 May 1967.

21 See headlines of Israeli press on 12 May 1967. In the wake of Arab protests, U Thant issued a clarification on 13 May whose intention was not to sanction Israeli use of force. Gilboa, *Six Years*, pp. 97–98.

22 From April to mid-May 1967 there were sixteen terror incidents, including two skirmishes with armed infiltrators. *Rabin Report*, pp. 91–94.

23 *Al Hamishmar*, 14 May 1967. Gilboa, *Six Days*, pp. 99–100.

24 Rabin's remarks at the press conference, Maariv, 9 April 1967. Eshkol's remarks in the Knesset, Maariv, 10 April 1967.

25 Abba Eban wrote in his memoirs: 'If there had been a little more silence, the sum of human wisdom would probably have remained intact.' A. Eban, *An Autobiography*, New York: Random House, 1977, p. 319.

26 *Haaretz*, 14 May 1967.

27 *Davar*, 12 May 1967.

28 *Al Hamishmar*, 14 May 1967.

29 See e.g. headlines in *Lamerhav*, *Haaretz* and *Jerusalem Post*, 12 May 1967.

30 *Maariv* and *Lamerhav*, 14 May 1967.

31 *Lamerhav*, 14 May 1967, and compare *Bamahaneh*, 18 September 1966 and see above, Chapter 7.

32 The text of the UPI report of 12 May 1967 appears in *Middle East Journal*, Vol. 46, No. 2, p. 174. The quotation is from the recording in J. Cooley, *Green March, Black September*, London: Frank Cass, 1973, p. 160. See also *Middle East Record*, Vol. 3, p. 187. On 13 May 1967 the *New York Times* published a front-page report, taken from Yariv's briefing, under the heading 'Israelis ponder blow at Syrians'.

33 Mahmoud Riad, Egyptian Foreign Minister in 1967, cites an ostensibly direct quote from Rabin's remarks on 12 May. 'We will conduct a swift operation against Syria and conquer Damascus. We will topple the regime there and return.' M. Riad, *The Struggle for Peace in the Middle East*, London: Quartet Books, 1981, p. 17. Nasser made this claim in his 22 May speech when he announced the blocking of the Tiran Straits (see below). In 1968 as well Nasser explained his moves by saying: 'Eshkol said: We will go to Damascus. Rabin said: We will go to Damascus, and Egypt had to fulfil its obligation.' S. Segev, *Milkhama ve-Shalom ba-Mizrakh ha-Tikhon (War and Peace in the Middle East)*, Tel Aviv: Tversky, 1968, p. 70.

34 For a thorough investigation of the information the Soviets conveyed to Egypt, including the various theoretical motives on the basis of existing literature and interviews with those involved, see Parker, *Miscalculation*, pp. 3–35.

35 Ibid., pp. 8–9.

36 See above, Chapter 7. In his memoirs Eban expressed veiled criticism of Rabin.

Eban, *Pirkei Khayim (Chapters of a Life)*, B, Tel Aviv: Maariv, 1978, p. 314.
M. Bar-Zohar, *ha-Khodesh ha-Arokh be-Yoter (The Longest Month)*, Tel Aviv:
Lewin Epstein, 1968, p. 19.

37 Ibid., pp. 8–9.

38 On the threats as a trigger for the crisis, see also S. Shamir, 'The origin of the
May 1967 escalation: the claim of the Israeli threat' in A. Sassar (ed.) *Shisha
Yamim – Shloshim Shana (Six Days – Thirty Years)*, Tel Aviv: Am Oved, 1999,
pp. 56–75.

39 Rabin at General Staff meetings, 18 March 1965 and 15 March 1965.

40 Nevertheless, several foreign guests did attend the parade including the Deputy
President of Malagash, the Chiefs of Staff of Chile and Liberia, General Pierre
Koenig and others. *Davar*, 16 May 1967. On international objections to
holding the parade in Jerusalem and the discussion at the Israel–Jordan
Armistic Commission, see Odd Bull, *War and Peace in the Middle East*,
London: Leo Cooper, 1973, pp. 105–106, and J. Rikhye, *The Sinai Blunder*,
London: Frank Cass, 1980, pp. 12–13. On deliberations of the US administra-
tion on whether the US Ambassador Walworth Barbour should attend the
parade since Britain and France had decided not to send their ambassadors, see
FRUS, 1964–1968, Vol. 19, Doc. 5.

41 *Yediot Aharonot*, 9 May 1967, and see in particular letter of Ben-Gurion to
Davar, 17 May 1967. The editors commented that even Ben-Gurion's colleague
in Rafi, Moshe Dayan, did not concur with the criticism.

42 On the parade affair and the Alterman poem see U. Narkis, *Akhat Yerushalayim (Jerusalem is One)*, Tel Aviv: Am Oved, 1976, pp. 14–20; see also Haber,
ha-Yom Tifrotz Milkhama (Today War will Break Out), Tel Aviv: Idanim,
1988, pp. 145–148.

43 *FRUS*, 1964–1968, Vol. 19, Doc. 5.

44 Rabin, *Pinkes Sherut (Service Notebook)*, A, Tel Aviv: Maariv, 1979, p. 134.
Vague information was conveyed to the Chief of Staff prior to this, on the night
of 14/15 May. Ibid.

12 The start of the crisis

1 Meir Amit, head of the Mossad (1963–1968), lists among the negative results
of the Sinai Campaign 'a fathomless crisis with Egypt'. Amit, *Rosh be-Rosh
(Head On)*, Tel Aviv: Hed Artzi, 1999, p. 79.

2 Bar-Zohar, *Ben-Gurion*, C, Tel Aviv: Zmora Bitan, 1975, pp. 1526–1529.

3 Amit, *Head On*, pp. 204–228. For an opposing view see Y. Karoz, *ha-Ish Baal
Shnei ha-Kovaim (The Man with Two Hats)*, Tel Aviv: Ministry of Defence,
2002, pp. 184–186. For the Minutes of a meeting with the head of the Mossad
on this issue see Z. Shalom, 'A missed opportunity', *ha-Tziyonut (Zionism)*, 22
(2001), pp. 321–353.

4 On the Rotem affair see Rabin, *Pinkes Sherut (Service Notebook)*, A, pp.
106–108 and Z. Tzahor, 'It all depends on the Air Force: the Rotem affair, February 1960', in Z. Lakhish and M. Amitai (eds) *Asor lo Shaket (An Unquiet
Decade)*, Tel Aviv: Ministry of Defence, 1995, pp. 225–248. See also stenographic minutes of a discussion at the Dayan Centre (16 December 1987) on
the Rotem affair of 1960 as a stage on the way to the May 1967 crisis, Dayan
Centre library, Tel Aviv University, and U. Bar-Joseph, 'Rotem: the forgotten
crisis on the road to the 1967 war', *Journal of Contemporary History*, 1996,
Vol. 31 (3), pp. 547–566.

5 Amer's scheme was known to the General Staff at the beginning of December
1966. Rabin at a study day on 'The waiting period' held at Yad Tabenkin, Efal,

on 4 September 1989. See also S. Yitzhaki, *be-Einei ha-Aravim (In Arab Eyes)*, Tel Aviv: Ministry of Defence, 196, p. 95.

6 Rabin, *Service Notebook*, A, pp. 134–135.

7 This was in accordance with the security doctrine. See Y. Tal, *Bitakhon Leumi (National Security)*, Tel Aviv: Dvir, 1996, pp. 85–88.

8 IDF History Department (classified internal research) *Supreme Command Post*, p. 183. Testimony of Rabin's bureau chief Col. Rafi Efrat on the events of 16 May 1967.

9 Eshkol at government meeting, 16 May 1967. Compare 'The main Intelligence evaluations' for this period, IDF History Department (classified internal research), *ha-Oyev, ha-Um veha-Maatzamot (The Enemy, the UN and the Powers)*, B, pp. 12–13.

10 Eban at government meeting, 16 May 1967.

11 Aran and Eshkol, ibid. Between 8 and 12 May, Fatah's terror acts included mining of roads in the Galilee, firing on a bus on the main road to Jerusalem, and a mine laid near Kibbutz Amatzia.

12 On the evacuation of the UNEF force, see I.J. Rikhye, *The Sinai Blunder*, New Delhi: Oxford and *IBH*, 1978, pp. 14–22. For a serious attempt to clarify the background and the Egyptian intentions behind the demand for evacuation, see R. Parker, *The Politics of Miscalculation in the Middle East*, Bloomington: Indiana University Press, 1993, pp. 63–71. See also U Thant's report to the Security Council, 27 May. Cited in Laqueur, pp. 253–281.

13 Rabin's testimony, *IDF Archive*, 192/74/1168.

14 Dayan at the Foreign Affairs and Security Committee, 17 May 1967. See summary of Eshkol–Bunche meeting (6 July 1966) and a document on 'Israel's position on UNEF', *IDF Archive*, 9/96/57.

15 Eshkol at Foreign Affairs and Security Committee, 17 May 1967.

16 Knesset members at the Foreign Affairs and Security Committee, 17 May 1967.

17 Eshkol at Foreign Affairs and Security Committee, 17 May 1967.

18 Foreign Minister's briefing of political correspondents, 17 May 1967, *IDF Archive*, 117/70/114.

19 Regular television broadcasts were introduced in Israel only in 1968.

20 Testimony of Efrat on events of 17 May 1967. See also *Khel ha-Avir be-Milkhemet Sheshet ha-Yamim (The Air Force in the Six Day War)*, Air Force Command (classified internal research), pp. 117–119.

21 Efrat's testimony on events of 17 May 1967.

22 IDF History Department, *Supreme Command Post*, p. 193.

23 Ibid., p. 195.

24 Ibid.

25 Efrat's testimony on events of 18 May 1967. Rabin's report at the government meeting, 21 May 1967. I.J. Rikhye, *The Sinai Blunder*, New Delhi: Oxford and IBH, 1978, pp. 30–35.

26 Efrat's testimony on events of 18 May 1967.

13 The era of diplomacy

1 From the outset, the goal of Israeli diplomacy was to avert war and not to prepare the diplomatic conditions for a military operation. See Y. Ben-Meir, *Civil–Military Relations in Israel*, New York: Columbia, 1995, p. 93.

2 The expression 'noble steeds' applied to senior officers eager for battle was coined by Moshe Dayan. *Yoman Maarekhet Sinai (Sinai Campaign Diary)*, Tel Aviv: Am Hasefer, 1965, p. 85.

3 A detailed and well-documented description of the crisis and of Israel's decision-

making from Eban's viewpoint, with emphasis on the political and diplomatic echelon, appears in the ms. of his book, *Abba Eban, The Six Day War*, 1969. The ms. which I received thanks to Dr Benjamin Geist, comprises more than 500 pages, including numerous documents. The book was never published and part of it was integrated into Eban's autobiography, *Pirkei Hayim (Chapters in a Life)*, B, Tel Aviv: Maariv, 1978. Important studies in this sphere include M. Brecher, *Decisions in Crisis*, Berkeley: University of California, 1980; B. Geist, 'The Six Day War – a study in the setting and the process of foreign policy decision making under crisis conditions' (Dissertation), Jerusalem: The Hebrew University, 1974. J. Gross Stein and R. Tanter, *Rational Decision-making: Israel's Security Choices 1967*, Columbus: Ohio University Press, 1980. Y. Bar-Simantov, *Israel, the Superpowers and the War in the Middle East*, New York: Praeger, 1987, pp. 85–145. See also Bar-Zohar, *ha-Khodesh ha-Arokh be-Yoter (The Longest Month)*, Tel Aviv: Lewin-Epstein, 1968.

4 On this see in particular D. Neff, *Warriors for Jerusalem*, New York: Linden Press, 1984; R. Parker, *The Politics of Miscalculation in the Middle East*, Bloomington: Indiana University Press, 1993 and W.B. Quandt, *Peace Process*, Washington, DC: Brookings Institute, 1993. See also *FRUS*, 1964–1968, Vols 18 and 19.

5 On the worsening of relations between Nasser and Johnson, see Parker, *Miscalculation*, pp. 225–249 and Heikal, *Cairo Documents*, pp. 99–122. On the Soviet definition of Lyndon Johnson as a dangerous man capable of becoming involved in adventures, see Heikal, *ha-Sphinx veha-Commissar (The Sphinx and the Commissar)*, p. 29 and see pp. 167, 154 and 172. On US–Egypt contacts see *FRUS*, 1964–1968, Vol. 18, Doc. 20, 96–98, 110–111, 115, 125–132, 193–198, 217, 378, 390, 412, 417.

6 The evidence from various sources on aggressive Egyptian intentions is resounding. There were apparently orders for a surprise Egyptian attack on 27 May which were cancelled at the last moment, probably because of the US warning. One of the sources of evidence is the Egyptian Chief of Staff General Fawzi. See Quandt, *Peace Process*, p. 512, n. 38, and M. Oren, *Six Days of War*, Oxford: Oxford University Press, 2002, pp. 92–97, 119–121.

7 *FRUS*, 1964–1968, Vol. 19, Doc. 8.

8 For a description of the evolvement of Johnson's stand from 'red light' to 'yellow light' during the crisis see W. Quandt, 'Lyndon Johnson and the June 1967 war: what colour was the light?', *Middle East Journal*, 46(2) (spring 1992), pp. 198–228.

9 Eshkol letter to Johnson, 18 May 1967, *Eshkol Archive*.

10 The 'editors' committee' was a closed, select forum, which consisted of editors of newspapers and radio networks (TV broadcasts began only in 1968). In July 1966 an agreement was signed between the Chief of Staff and the committee, which replaced a previous agreement from 1951. See M. Zak, 'The censor and the press in five wars', *Kesher*, 13 May 1993, pp. 5–20. On the Six Day War, ibid., pp. 12–13.

11 Eshkol to editors' committee, 18 May 1967, *Eshkol Archive*.

12 Report of Foreign Ministry to legations, 19 May 1967, *Eshkol Archive*.

13 P. Seale, *Assad*, Tel Aviv: Maarakhot, 1994, p. 137. See also Quandt, *Peace Process*, pp. 28–30, and Mutawi, p. 94.

14 Eban at General Staff meeting, 21 May 1967. Perusal of the press at the time reveals that the editors did in fact cooperate. Only on 22 May was a brief item published, quoting Radio Cairo, on Israel's communications to the Western Powers, informing them that it would resort to military force if Egypt blocked the Straits of Tiran. *Yediot Aharonot*, 22 May 1967.

15 Eban at Ministerial Committee on Security, 21 May 1967. On the quiet diplomatic campaign warning against the possibility of blocking of the Straits, see Eban, *Six Day War*, pp. 63–69.

16 Cable from Eban to Harman and Raphael, 20 May 1967, *Eshkol Archive*.

17 Cable from Eban to Raphael, 21 May 1967, *Eshkol Archive*.

18 In a conversation with US Ambassador Barbour and emissary McPherson when war broke out, the head of the Mossad, Meir Amit, mentioned this message conveyed to Nasser before the blocking of the Straits. Cable from Bitan to Harman, Evron and Raphael, 5 June 1967, *Eshkol Archive*.

19 On the US commitments on freedom of shipping given to Israel in return for consent to full withdrawal from all territory conquered during the Sinai Campaign, and Foreign Minister Golda Meir's pronouncements on this issue at the UN on 1 March 1957, see Bar On, *Gates of Gaza*, pp. 352–368; see also G. Meir, *Khayai (My Life)*, Tel Aviv: Maariv, 1975, pp. 218–225.

20 Eban at Ministerial Committee on Security, 21 May 1967.

21 Quandt believes that the administration in Washington could have warned Nasser more firmly against closing the Straits, but adopted an over-cautious approach both on freedom of shipping and on commitment to Israel's security. Quandt, *Peace Process*, pp. 28–30.

22 The Foreign Minister cabled the Ambassador in Washington in response to his report: 'We must protest vehemently against the comment of [Assistant Secretary of State Lucius] Battle that the time is not right for expedition of the supply of the agreed security needs', and emphasized that this could be 'psychologically and politically destructive'. Eban to Harman and Raphael, 20 May 1967, *Eshkol Archive*.

23 Ambassador Barbour pleaded with Israel not to rule out the principle of the presence of a 'symbolic part' of the UN force on Israeli soil. Bitan to Harman, 22 May 1967, *Eshkol Archive*.

24 Eshkol and Eban at the Ministerial Committee on Security, 21 May 1967. At the time the US administration approved a 'package' of economic and security aid requested by Israel, which included one hundred armoured cars, considerate credit for the purchase of Patton tanks and Hawk missiles, spare parts for tanks and supply of surplus foodstuffs. Cables from Evron to the Foreign Ministry, 21 May 1967 and 23 May 1967, *Eshkol Archive*.

25 Bitan to Harman, 21 May 1967, *Eshkol Archive*. The sensitivity of the administration on this issue is attested to by an appeal by Rostow on behalf of the President to Jewish associates to do everything in order to moderate public opinion in the US. Evron to the Ministry, 22 May 1967, *Eshkol Archive*. On the Jewish impact on Johnson see H. Saunders, 'The White House, US Jewry and the Six Day War' in A. Sheshar (ed.) *Shisha Yamim – Shloshim Shana (Six Days – Thirty Years)*, Tel Aviv: Am Oved, 1999, pp. 137–142.

26 Eban at Ministerial Committee on Security, 21 May 1967, *Eshkol Archive*.

27 After the Sinai Campaign Israel revoked unilaterally the armistice agreement with Egypt. See M. Bar-On, *Shaarei Aza (The Gates of Gaza)*, Tel Aviv: Am Oved, 1992, p. 318. Ben-Gurion, *Yihud ve-Yeud (Singularity and Mission)*, Tel Aviv: Maarakhot, 1971, pp. 269–270.

28 Minutes of the meeting reveal that Eshkol did not read out this prepared summary, *Eshkol Archive*.

29 In addition to the Egyptian reconnaissance sortie over Dimona on 17 May, mentioned above, a more daring photography flight was carried out on 26 May (see below).

30 Interview with Azaryahu Arnan, Galili's aide, 12 August 1998.

31 See also statement by Rabin (Chapter 2 above): 'There is an object in the south

of the country, the ideal object for limited reaction [on the part of Egypt] for which it would receive the total support of the whole world.'
32 The Minister of Transport Moshe Carmel, who was also not a champion of Dimona, was more anxious at the prospect of the bombing of airfields. See his remarks at the Ministerial Committee on Security, 21 May 1967.
33 There is no indication that Israel took any clandestine action to warn Egypt against attacking the reactor. See also A. Cohen, *Israel and the Bomb*, New York: Columbia Press, 1998, pp. 259–276.
34 Ministerial Committee on Security, 21 May 1967.
35 Eban at General Staff meeting, 21 May 1967.
36 *Haaretz*, 22 May 1967.
37 Ministerial Committee on Security, 21 May 1967.
38 Ibid.
39 On the discussion in the Knesset and Ben-Gurion's attempt, which failed, to transfer the discussion to the Foreign Affairs and Security Committee, see S. Nakdimon, *li-Kraat Shaat ha-Efes (Towards Zero Hour)*, Tel Aviv: Ramdor, 1968, pp. 31–40.

14 The revision of Intelligence evaluations and the shift to Intelligence planning

1 Testimony of Efrat, on 19 May 1967.
2 This was the last General Staff discussion in the customary form in the conference room of the General Staff. Immediately afterwards the bureaux of the Chief of Staff, Chief of Operations and Chief of Intelligence moved to the supreme command post ('the Pit').
3 Yariv at General Staff meeting, 19 May 1967.
4 For details see IDF History Department, *Supreme Command Post*, pp. 201–206.
5 Yariv at General Staff meeting, 19 May 1967.
6 The comparison which naturally comes to mind is the conduct of Intelligence Chief Brigadier General Eli Zeira in October 1973. Zeira refused to modify his evaluation that Egypt and Syria would not start a war despite overwhelming information to the contrary.
7 Rabin at General Staff meeting, 19 May 1967.
8 Efrat's testimony on 19 May 1967.
9 For details see IDF History Department, *Supreme Command Post*, pp. 215, 209.
10 Ben-Gurion Diaries, 22 May 1967.
11 Rabin, *Pinkes Sherut (Service Notebook)*, A, Tel Aviv: Maariv, 1979, pp. 144–145.
12 IDF History Department, *Supreme Command Post*, A, p. 217 (according to testimony of Deputy Chief of Staff Southern Command, Aryeh Shahar).
13 Hofi lectured to the Staff College on 28 July 1971 on 'The operational plans which preceded the Six Day War', *IDF Archive*, 192/74/981.
14 For Kilshon, including maps and assignment of forces and tasks, see IDF History Department, *Supreme Command Post*, A, pp. 12–128.
15 For a description of the logistic problems of Pitchfork see remarks of representative of the Quartermaster Branch in a discussion with the Chief of the Operations Department on 20 May 1967, IDF History Department, *Supreme Command Post*, A, pp. 219–239.
16 For the main points of the plan presented by Hofi to Weizman see IDF History Department, *Supreme Command Post*, A, p. 219.

17 Allon's notes on submission of the plans, *IDF History Department Archive*, 20 May 1967.
18 Testimony of Tal, *IDF Archive*, 192/74/405.
19 Testimonies of Gavish, *IDF Archive*, 192/74/998 and of Sharon, *IDF Archive*, 192/74/1038 and 192/74/205.
20 Dayan, *Avnei Derekh (Milestones)*, Tel Aviv: Idanim, 1977, p. 402.

15 *Casus belli*

1 For the full text of Nasser's speech see W. Laqueur, *The Road to War 1967*, London: Weidenfeld & Nicolson, 1968, pp. 288–293.
2 For Nasser's version of the Sinai Campaign in 1956 see his article in the *Egyptian Gazette*, 6 December 1956, translated and edited by M. Shemesh, *Iyunim bi-Tkumat Yisrael (Israel Independence Studies)*, 4 (1994), pp. 98–116.
3 For Lior's version of events see Haber, *ha-Yom Tifrotz Milkhama (Today War Will Break Out)*, Tel Aviv: Idanim, 1988, pp. 163–165.
4 Press headlines reflect the atmosphere. See e.g. *Maariv*, 23 May 1967. The immediate mobilization of reserves intensified the atmosphere of emergency.
5 Testimony of Efrat for 23 May 1967. See also IDF History Department, *Supreme Command Post*, A, pp. 240–241 and note on page 241.
6 That same day Johnson issued a statement denouncing the blocking of the Straits and supporting freedom of shipping, and Eugene Rostov met with Harman and Evron and informed them that the US had approved an 'aid package' requested by Israel including, among other things, one hundred armoured cars, spare parts for tanks, and considerable credit (US$214 million) for purchase of Patton tanks and Hawk missiles, surplus foodstuffs and so on. Cables of Ambassador and Minister in Washington, 23 May 1967, *IDF Archive*.
7 The summary of Rabin's remarks according to the diary of Efrat, his bureau chief, for 23 May 1967.
8 Ibid. According to Lior, Rabin predicted 'tremendous damage' to the northern settlements since Israel had no immediate response to offer to Syrian artillery. Lior's summary, *Eshkol Archive*.
9 An oil-tanker from Iran, bearing the Liberian flag, was due at Eilat on 29 May. It changed its destination.
10 Lior's summary 'Consultations in Supreme Command Post', 23 May 1967, *Eshkol Archive*. Efrat wrote in his diary that he had gained the impression that the Prime Minister had not yet decided whether to take action. Efrat's testimony for 23 May 1967. See also Haber, pp. 163–165.
11 This is evident in the Minutes of the meeting of the Ministerial Committee on Security, 23 May 1967. For a detailed description of the meeting by Lior, see Haber, *Today*, pp. 165–170 and cf. M. Gilboa, *Shesh Shanim Shisha Yamim (Six Years Six Days)*, Tel Aviv: Am Oved 1968, pp. 128–129.
12 Several of the participants in the meetings proposed sending a non-official figure to the US, for example, Golda Meir, former Foreign Minister. Eban threatened to resign and the proposal was rejected. Rabin, *Service Notebook*, A, p. 155.
13 Minutes of meeting with representatives of the opposition, 23 May 1967, *Eshkol Archive*.
14 Testimony of Efrat for 23 May 1967.
15 Ibid. Efrat commented: 'The Chief of Operations exerted more pressure than the Chief of Staff'.
16 Ibid. Rabin was voicing his doubts as to the ability of the IAF to achieve superi-

ority in the air rapidly. The government's fears at the prospect of bombarding of settlements in the north are also reflected in his remarks.

17 Haber, *Today*, p. 173.
18 Efrat's testimony for 23 May 1967.
19 S. Nakdimon, *li-Kraat Shaat ha-Efes (Towards Zero Hour)*, Tel Aviv: Ramdor, 1968, pp. 56–57.

16 The army pressures the government

1 The IDF pressure was expressed, *inter alia*, in a briefing for military correspondents. See e.g. Zeev Schiff, *Haaretz*, 24 May 1967: 'It's not the British who will break the blockade for us nor the Sixth Fleet. The blockade is like a rotten tooth to be extracted, otherwise the whole body will be affected.'
2 Weizman, *Lekha Shamayim Lekha Aretz (Heaven and Earth are Yours)*, Tel Aviv: Maariv, 1975, p. 259.
3 Weizman's testimony, *IDF Archive*, 192/74/1157. Testimony of Gavish, *IDF Archive*, 192/74/998.
4 'Summary of a conversation between the Prime Minister and the Chief of Operations', 24 May 1967, *Eshkol Archive*.
5 Haber, *ha-Yom Tifrotz Milkhama (Today War will Break Out)*, Tel Aviv: Idanim, 1988, pp. 174–175.
6 Barlev, who had spent the day – the first since his return from Paris the previous evening – studying the IDF plans, expressed his support for Kardom 2 as presented by Weizman. After the presentation to Eshkol, Barlev visited Rabin, briefed him and reassured him. Barlev's testimony, *IDF Archive*, 192/74/1232.
7 Testimony of Efrat for 24 May 1967.
8 This transpires from Weizman's order to move forces that night. See also Rabin, *Pinkes Sherut (Service Notebook)*, Tel Aviv: Maariv, 1979, A, p. 160.
9 Haber, *Today War will Break Out*, pp. 175–176.
10 On details of movements see testimonies of Gavish and Tal, *IDF Archive*, 192/74/998 and 192/74/974.
11 Sharon's testimony, *IDF Archive*, 192/74/1038. Testimony of Gavish, *IDF Archive*, 192/74/998.
12 Testimony of Barlev, *IDF Archive*, 192/74/1232. See also Weizman, *Heaven and Earth are Yours*, pp. 262–263.
13 Rabin, *Service Notebook*, A, p. 152.
14 Rabin, *Service Notebook*, A, p. 159. Weizman, *Heaven and Earth*, pp. 258–259. Haber, *Today*, pp. 174–175.
15 Argov to Bitan, 24 May 1967, *Eshkol Archive*.
16 Argov to the Foreign Ministry, 24 May 1967, *Eshkol Archive*. Barbour's response suggests that he understood from Argov that the army was liable to act on its own initiative.
17 The Commander of the IAF, Motti Hod, claims that it was clear to him and to most of the General Staff that the pressure exerted by the IDF commanders 'doesn't reach the political echelon the way we phrase it but through Yitzhak Rabin and it sounds different when coming from him', *IDF Archive*, 192/74/1156.
18 Haber, *Today*, p. 176.
19 On the content of the discussion see Rabin, *Service Notebook*, A, p. 161.
20 Testimony of Efrat for 25 May 1967. Summary of the meeting by Lior, *Eshkol Archive*.
21 Summary of the meeting by Lior, *Eshkol Archive*.
22 The Egyptian Minister of War, Shams Badran, left for Moscow on 24 May for

two days with the aim of military coordination and supply. Heikal, *ha-Sphinx veha-Commissar (The Sphinx and the Commissar)*, Tel Aviv: Am Oved, 1981, pp. 27, 178–180.

23 The text of the cables sent on 25 May to the Foreign Minister is cited in Yariv's testimony, *IDF Archive*, 192/74/1323.

24 On the Eban–de Gaulle meeting on 24 May in the Elysee Palace see, for details, Gilboa, *Shesh Shanim Shisha Yamin (Six Years Six Days)*, Tel Aviv: Am Oved, 1968, pp. 136–141 and Eban, *Pirkei Khayim (Chapters in a Life)*, B, Tel Aviv: Maariv, 1978, pp. 337–340. Bar-Zohar, *ha-Khodesh ha-Arokh be-Yoter (The Longest Month)*, Tel Aviv: Lewin-Epstein, 1968, pp. 101–107.

25 On the views for and against Eban's trip see Gilboa, *Six Years*, pp. 130–132 and Nakdimon, *li-Kraat Shaat ha-Efes (Towards Zero Hour)*, Tel Aviv: Ramdor, 1968, pp. 57–58, 61–62.

26 Eban, *Chapters in a Life*, B, pp. 344–349, makes critical mention of the cables. See also Rabin, *Service Notebook*, A, pp. 161–165.

27 Weizman noted that on his return on 25 May, Rabin 'was different to what he had been in the past'. Weizman, *Heaven and Earth*, p. 262.

28 Efrat's testimony for 25 May 1967.

29 M. Oren, *Six Days of War*, New York: Oxford University Press, 2000, pp. 119–121. See also W. Quandt, *Peace Process*, Washington, DC: Brookings Institute, 1993, p. 512, fn. 38.

30 A summary of the meeting of the Chief of Staff, Chiefs of Operations and Intelligence and Brigadier-General Barlev with the PM, 25 May 1967, *Eshkol Archive*.

31 On receiving the cable after arrival in Washington, Eban immediately requested that his meeting with Secretary of State Dean Rusk be brought forward. At the meeting on 25 May in the afternoon, Eban read out the text of the cable. Rusk, taken by surprise, immediately cut short the meeting in order to report to the President and the Secretary of Defence. Eban, *Six Day War* (ms. 1969), pp. 114–115. *FRUS*, 1964–1968, Vol. 19, Doc. 64.

32 Report by the General Director of the Foreign Ministry Arie Levavi at the meeting of the Ministerial Committee on Security, 26 May 1967. The words 'suicide' and 'US commitment to Israel's security' do not appear in the State Department telegram to Cairo, but were probably expressed by Rostow during his meeting with Kamel. See *FRUS*, 1964–1968, Vol. 19, Doc. 65.

33 Heikal claims, for example, that Johnson terrified the Soviets, and the Secretary General of the Communist Party Leonid Brekhnev told the UN Secretary-General: 'This man is ready to undertake any adventure. The world should beware him!' Heikal, *The Sphinx and the Commissar*, p. 29; see also ibid., pp. 154, 167, 172.

34 Eban's report on his meetings in Washington, government meeting, 27 May 1967. *FRUS*, 1964–1968, Vol. 19, Doc. 69, 72, 76, 79.

35 Minutes of government meetings, 27–28 May 1967. See also Eban, *Chapters*, B, pp. 344–349.

36 Eban did not evaluate correctly the significance of the US warning to Egypt. He believed that because of the cables he lost the first round of the battle. Ibid., p. 349.

37 See chapter on the Six Day War headed 'The trap' in Heikal's book, *The Sphinx*, pp. 172–198.

38 *FRUS*, 1964–1968, Vol. 19, Doc. 84, 88, 90.

39 Heikal, *The Sphinx*, pp. 181–182.

17 The politicians' quandry

1 Rabin, *Pinkes Sherut (Service Notebook)*, Tel Aviv: Maariv, 1979, p. 163.
2 Minutes of meeting of the Alignment Party Political Committee, 25 May 1967, *Eshkol Archive*.
3 At a meeting with Eshkol on 25 May, Shapira demanded that the government be expanded and the appointment of Ben-Gurion, or at least Dayan, as Minister of Defence. Eshkol remained adamant. He was surprised at Shapira's contradictory stand: 'You want Dayan and you don't want war?' Minutes of Alignment Party Political Committee, 26 May, 1967, *Eshkol Archive*.
4 Haber, *ha-Yom Tifrotz Milkhama (Today War will Break Out)*, Tel Aviv: Idanim, 1988.
5 Testimony of Tal, *IDF Archive*, 192/74/974. Rabin, *Service Notebook*, A, p. 162.
6 The forum consisted of the Prime Minister, Ministers Allon, Galili, Aranne and Sasson, the Mapai Secretary Golda Meir and Shaul Avigur. Minutes of the political committee meeting, 25 May 1967, *Eshkol Archive*.
7 Ibid.
8 Minutes of consultations, 25 May 1967, *Eshkol Archive*. The meeting was attended by Eshkol, Levavi, Tekoah, Dinstein, Yaffe, and later also by Amit and Yariv.
9 Ibid.
10 According to Amit, the CIA man said: 'Help us to help you!' Ibid.
11 Summary of PM s consultation with his advisers, 25 May 1967, *Eshkol Archive*.
12 Many years later Moshe Carmel recalled the 'stunned shock' of the ministers when they learned, during that government meeting, that 'a squadron of Egyptian fighter planes was over the Dimona reactor'. Carmel at a study day on 'The waiting period', Yad Tabenkin, 4 September 1989.
13 Participating in the consultations were Eshkol, Rabin, Weizman, Herzog and Lior. Lior's summary of the meeting, 26 May 1967, *Eshkol Archive*.
14 Ibid and testimony of Efrat for 26 May 1967 on the government resolutions as conveyed to him by the PM's military secretary.
15 Efrat's testimony for 26 May 1967. Minutes of government meeting, 27/28 May 1967.
16 The term 'fateful conversation' is taken from Efrat's diary. Efrat's testimony for 26 May 1967.
17 Ibid. President Johnson was angered by the atmosphere of pressure created by Eban, and wanted to postpone the meeting. See Quandt, *Peace Process*, Washington, DC: Brookings Institute, 1993, p. 37, and a cable from Minister Evron to the Prime Minister, 26 May 1967, *Eshkol Archive*.

18 The height of the diplomatic campaign and the outcome

1 Eban's report at the government meeting, 27 May 1967. W.B. Quandt, *Peace Process*, Washington, DC: Brookings Institute, 1993, pp. 35–41.
2 According to Evron's cable to the Prime Minister, 26 May 1967, *Eshkol Archive*. Cf. *FRUS*, 1964–1968, Vol. 19, Doc. 64.
3 Evron to the PM, 26 May 1967, *Eshkol Archive*.
4 Remez to Foreign Ministry, 26 May 1967, *Eshkol Archive*.
5 Geva to Rabin, 26 May 1967, *Eshkol Archive*. Geva to Intelligence Branch, 26 May 1967, *Eshkol Archive*.
6 The information on the Johnson–Eban meeting in this chapter is based on an

almost verbatim report of the talks in the file for 26 May 1967, *Eshkol Archive.*
Compare *FRUS, 1964–1968,* Vol. 19, Doc. 77.

7 Ibid.

8 The text of Bulganin's letter to Ben-Gurion may be found in Bar-On, *Shaarei Aza (The Gates of Gaza),* Tel Aviv: Am Oved, 1992 pp. 316–317.

9 Kosygin to Eshkol, 26 May 1967, *Eshkol Archive.*

10 Cable from Ambassador in Moscow to Foreign Ministry, 27 May 1967, *Eshkol Archive.*

11 See remarks of Egyptian and Russian participants on the Soviet role in the Six Day War at a symposium marking its twenty-fifth anniversary. R. Parker (ed.) *The Six Day War – a Retrospective,* Gainesville: University Press of Florida, 1996 (throughout the book); see also Heikal, *ha-Sphinx veh A-commissar (The Sphinx and the Commissar),* Tel Aviv: Am Oved, 1981, pp. 178–182.

12 The text of Nasser' speech appears in Document 1 in T. Draper, *Israel and World Politics – Roots of the Third Arab–Israeli War,* New York: Viking Press, 1968.

13 Harman to Foreign Ministry, *Eshkol Archive,* 27 May 1967. Ibid.

14 Rikhye, *The Sinai Blunder,* New Delhi: Oxford and IBH, 1978, pp. 63–86.

15 Details of deliberations – government meeting, 27–28 May 1967.

16 On US efforts in Cairo during the crisis see mainly R. Parker, *The Politics of Miscalculation in the Middle East,* Bloomington: Indiana University Press, pp. 225–226, 233–238.

17 Sapir did not specify Peres by name, but his meaning was clear. Peres did in fact meet with Sapir that day (27 May). Nakdimon, *li-Kraat Shaat ha-Efes (Towards Zero Hour),* Tel Aviv: Ramdor, 1968, p. 113.

18 The following details are cited from the Minutes of the meeting, 28 May 1967.

19 The US commitment of 1957 to Egyptian freedom of shipping through the Straits of Tiran, in light of the Israel government resolution to withdraw from Sinai, was qualified to the effect that it would not conflict with a possible ruling of the International Court at The Hague. See Memorandum from Secretary of State Dulles to Ambassador Eban on 11 February 1957. B. Reich and A. Gottfeld, *Artzot ha-Brit veha-Sikhsukh ha-Yisraeli–Aravi (The US and the Israel–Arab Dispute),* Tel Aviv: Maarakhot, 1977, pp. 127–128. Israel feared that the issue might be submitted to The Hague while the Straits were blocked. Nasser told U Thant that he was willing to accept international arbitration on the Straits question, including The Hague Court, but displayed no readiness to revoke the blockade. Rikhye, *The Sinai Blunder,* pp. 70–79.

19 Waiting

1 IDF History Department, *Mutzav Pikud Elyon (Supreme Command Post),* A, p. 278. Gavish testimony, *IDF Archive,* 192/74/998.

2 The Armistice agreement between Israel and Egypt was signed on 24 February 1949. Eilat was captured on 10 March.

3 Muhammad Hasanin Heikal described the creation of a buffer between 'the Arab East and the Arab West' as the gravest consequence of the 1948 war. I. Asia, *Tismonet Dayan (The Dayan Syndrome),* Tel Aviv: Yediot Aharonot 1995, pp. 7, 137–140. Egyptian documents captured during the war included operational orders to cut off the southern part of the Negev. *IDF Archive,* 192/74/33.

4 IDF History Department, *Supreme Command Post,* A, pp. 273, 300.

5 Efrat's testimony for 27 May 1967. This was apparently the first statement of the political echelon in the course of the crisis in favour of capturing the Golan Heights.

6 IDF History Department, *Supreme Command Post*, A, p. 279. IDF Archive, 192/74/1232.
7 Sharon's testimony, *IDF Archive*, 192/74/1038.
8 After the government meeting, Minister of Finance Pinhas Sapir proposed that Eshkol should not wait until the following day in order to address the public which 'felt a little neglected', but should broadcast that evening to the nation. Government meeting, 28 May 1967.
9 On the broadcast, its circumstances and outcome see Haber, *ha-Yom Tifrotz Milkhama (Today War will Break Out)*, Tel Aviv: Idanim, 1988 pp. 193–194, Nakdimon, *li-Kraat Shaat ha-Efes (Towards Zero Hour)*, Tel Aviv: Ramdor, 1968, pp. 128–131, Gilboa, *Shesh Shanim Shisha Yamim (Six Years Six Days)*, Tel Aviv: Am Oved, 1968, pp. 168–170. The shorthand typist Mitka Yaffe blamed herself for typing the speech in small letters. T. Lipkin-Shahak, 'The muse of history', *Maariv*, 30 January 1998.
10 The full text of the speech may be found in Gilboa, *Six Years*, pp. 169–170.
11 Shlomo Shamgar, *Yediot Aharonot*, 30 May 1967. Uri Avneri, *Haolam Hazeh*, 31 May 1967.
12 Eilon's notes on the discussions, *IDF History Department Archive*, Haber, pp. 194–198.
13 Haber, ibid. See also Asia, *The Dayan Syndrome*, pp. 149–150.
14 Haber, p. 198 and Lior's note, 28 May 1967, *Eshkol Archive*.
15 Efrat's testimony for 28 May 1967. Eilon's notes, *IDF History Department Archive*.
16 Haber, *Today*, p. 193.
17 Testimony of Tal, *IDF Archive*, 192/74/974. Testimony of Gavish, *IDF Archive*, 192/74/404. Testimony of Sharon, *IDF Archive*, 192/74/1038.
18 Eilon's notes on the discussion with the Chief of Staff, 29 May 1967, *IDF History Department Archive*.
19 Testimony of Yariv, *IDF Archive*, 192/74/1155.
20 The document is in the *IDF Archive*, 192/74/1176.
21 Ibid. This is the only explicit reference I have found to the possibility that Egypt might employ radioactive weapons. It will be recalled that the view was expressed in Israel that Nasser possessed 'a secret weapon'. Bar-Zohar, *ha-Khodesh ha-Arokh be-Yoter (The Longest Month)*, p. 140. This was also the conclusion of the US Embassy in Cairo. R. Parker, *The Politics of Miscalculation in the Middle East*, Bloomington: Indiana University Press, 1993, p. 90.

20 Establishment of a national unity government: the military aspect

1 'I decided in my heart: history! – whatever you want to do – do it fast!', Eshkol told party members. Minutes of Mapai Secretariate meeting, 1 June 1967, *Eshkol Archive*.
2 For a detailed survey of the evolvement of events in the political establishment from 22 May to the formation of the extended government, see S. Nakdimon, *li-Kraat Shaat ha-Efes (Towards Zero Hour)*, Tel Aviv: Ramdor, 1968.
3 A document summarizing the stages up to Dayan's appointment, *Eshkol Archive*.
4 Ibid., M. Dayan, *Avnei Derekh (Milestones)*, Tel Aviv: Idanim, 1977, p. 420. Nakdimon, *Towards Zero Hour*, p. 102.
5 Nakdimon, *Towards Zero Hour*, p. 165. Wahrhaftig claims that the preference for Ben-Gurion and Dayan was due to Ben-Gurion's stand, similar to that of the National Religious Party, against an initiated attack. Author's interview with Wahrhaftig, 24 August 1998.

6 Nakdimon, *Towards Zero Hour*, p. 138.
7 Ibid., pp. 183–184.
8 Record of a telephone converaation between Eshkol and Shapira, 31 May 1967, *Eshkol Archive*. Government meeting 31 May 1967.
9 On 24 May Begin met on his initiative with Eshkol and proposed the establishment of an emergency government headed by Ben-Gurion or, alternatively, the appointment of Ben-Gurion as Minister of Defence. Eshkol rejected the proposal outright, saying: 'These two horses will never again be able to pull a single wagon.' Nakdimon, pp. 68–70. Gilboa, pp. 160–161.
10 Herut originated in the Revisionist Movement whose map of Eretz Israel on both banks of the Jordan, included no Egyptian territory, apart from the Gaza Strip which was then under Egyptian domination.
11 Nakdimon points out in his book that circles in Mapai were convinced that Minister of the Interior Shapira thought that Dayan and Begin would constitute a moderate factor security-wise. Nakdimon, *Towards Zero Hour*, p. 184.
12 Y. Peri, *Between Battles and Ballots*, Cambridge: Cambridge University Press, 1983, pp. 249–251.
13 General Rehavam Ze'evi says that if it had depended on his colleagues at the General Staff, Allon would have been preferred to Dayan. Interview of author with Ze'evi, 3 September 1989. See also Nakdimon, *Towards Zero Hour*, p. 180.
14 See Tevet, *Moshe Dayan*, p. 428.
15 Testimony of Narkis, *IDF Archive* 192/74/1336 Nakdimon, *Towards Zero Hour*, p. 256.
16 This is Peri's view. See Peri, *Between Battles and Ballots*, pp. 249–251.
17 Nakdimon, *Towards Zero Hour*, p. 141, 253.
18 Ibid., p. 256.
19 Ibid., p. 140. The words 'military coup' do not appear in the fragmented quote cited by Nakdimon, but they are clearly implied from the context. In his book, Abba Eban refers critically to Eshkol's meeting with the generals, and notes that 'there was even talk of a military coup'. Eban, *The Six Day War* (manuscript 1969), pp. 165–168.
20 Nakdimon, *Towards Zero Hour*, pp. 145–146. Nakdimon notes that Ben-Gurion's moderate statement contained an echo of much more extreme remarks which he had voiced previously at a meeting of the Rafi faction. See also central item in *Haaretz*, 30 May 1967.
21 Nakdimon, ibid., p. 184.
22 Ibid., pp. 245, 254.
23 Ibid., pp. 251–257.
24 Ibid., pp. 179–180. In the summary it was noted that the Prime Minister 'left after a commotion'. Summary of Alignment faction meeting, 30 May 1967, *Eshkol Archive*.
25 Minutes of the morning meeting of the Alignment leadership, 31 May 1967, *Eshkol Archive*. Gilboa, *Shesh Shanim Shisha Yamim (Six Years Six Days)*, Tel Aviv: Am Oved, 1968, pp. 175–176 and Nakdimon, *Towards Zero Hour*, pp. 181–183.
26 Minutes of afternoon meeting of the Alignment leadership, 31 May 1967, *Eshkol Archive*. Dayan, *Milestones*, p. 416, Nakdimon, *Towards Zero Hour*, pp. 187–188, 209–211.
27 Dayan, ibid., Nakdimon, ibid., pp. 188–189.
28 This was also the opinion of General Rehavam Ze'evi. Author's interview with Ze'evi, 3 September 1998.
29 Government meeting, 31 May 1967. Dayan, ibid. Rabin, *Service Notebook*, A, pp. 175–176. Conversation with Gavish, *IDF Archive*, 192/74/1379.

30 Rabin's condition was an open secret in the General Staff. Rehavam Ze'evi did not go into detail on the subject but his remarks imply that he and other members of the General Staff guarded and protected Rabin during the crisis. Interview of author with Ze'evi, 3 September 1998.

31 Government meeting, 31 May 1967.

32 On the stormy meeting on 1 June 1967, see full stenographic report in *Nakdimon, Towards the Zero Hour*, pp. 205–220, 223–242. Note Eshkol's remarks, ibid., pp. 205–217.

33 Ibid., pp. 220–223.

34 Ibid., pp. 244–245.

35 Ibid., pp. 242–243. When women supporters of Rafi demonstrated outside the Mapai Central Office in support of Dayan, Eshkol nicknamed them 'the merry wives of Windsor'. Dayan, ibid., p. 420.

36 Nakdimon, ibid., p. 259. Eshkol reported to the Alignment ministers that the Chief of Staff was being 'roasted on the spit' by the generals because of his proposal to appoint Dayan as CO Southern Command. Minutes of the meeting, 1 June 1967, *Eshkol Archive*.

37 Hazan and his party claimed that the defence portfolio should be retained by Eshkol, but Hazan understood that his party alone could not counter the demand for the replacement of the Minister of Defence. Gilboa, *Six Years*, pp. 186–187. Nakdimon, ibid., p. 245.

38 Weizman, *Lekha Shamayim Lekha Aretz (Heaven and Earth are Yours)*, Tel Aviv: Maariv, 1975, p. 263.

39 Haber, *ha Yom Tifrotz Milkhama (Today War will Break Out)*, Tel Aviv: Idanim, 1988, p. 203. Weizman himself provides a milder and slightly different version of the event in, *Heaven and Earth*, p. 264.

40 The coopting of Dayan as representative of Rafi was the logical outcome of the political reality, but Eshkol cited an additional reason – fear that Rafi might decide to appoint Shimon Peres as its representative in the new government. Minutes of Alignment ministers' meeting, 1 June 1967, *Eshkol Archive*. The resentment against Peres, the moving spirit in Rafi, who had conducted the savage propaganda campaign against the government, was often reflected in statements by Eshkol and other ministers.

41 Ibid. See also Dayan, *Milestones*, p. 418. Nakdimon, *Towards Zero Hour*, p. 245.

42 Dayan promised BG: 'I will come to you morning and night.' He declared that one of his aims in joining the government was for 'Ben-Gurion to be ready to be at my side in all weighty calculations … I will regard this guidance as no less significant than the weighty things I will do as minister of defence'. Nakdimon, ibid., pp. 254–255, 263. It was a meaningless promise. From the moment Dayan was appointed he found no time for Ben-Gurion. The latter's attempts up to the end of the war to meet with Dayan and influence his decision-making bordered on the pathetic. *Ben-Gurion's Diary*, 5–11 June 1967.

43 The candidature of Begin, leader of the Herut movement and Chairman of Gahal, was self-evident. The Liberal Party, the second component of Gahal, did not choose Yosef Sapir as its representative until the following day. Hence only Begin attended the first session of the new government on 1 June 1967.

44 Two of the senior party members, Golda Meir and Shaul Avigur, did not attend, probably in protest at not having been consulted. Nakdimon, *Towards Zero Hour*, p. 246. Eshkol asked Golda Meir to join the government but she refused. Minutes of Mapai Secretariate meeting, 1 June 1967, *Eshkol Archive*. Nakdimon, ibid., p. 259.

45 Nakdimon, ibid., pp. 246–248.

46 The government subsequently took the decision to accept Eshkol's request to release him from his position as Minister of Defence, to bring in Dayan and Begin as ministers and to empower the Prime Minister to bring in an additional minister from Gahal. Government meeting, 1 June 1967.

47 Ibid.

48 Ibid.

49 The entry of foreign forces into Jordan, and in particular into the West Bank, was regarded as one of the pretexts for war which would require Israel's military intervention. M. Behr, *Kavim Adumim b'Astrategiat ha Hartaah ha-Yisraelit (Red Lines in Israel's Deterrent Strategy)*, Tel Aviv: Maarakhot, 1990.

50 Meeting of the Ministerial Committee on Security, 1 June 1967.

21 The strategic turning point: the Egypt–Jordan defence pact

1 A detailed description by King Hussein of his trip to Cairo, its background and outcome appears in his book *Milhamti Be- yisrael (My War with Israel)* (translated into Hebrew and edited by A. Kam), Tel Aviv: Maarakhot, 1974, pp. 47–55. The text of the Jordanian–Egyptian pact appears in S. Segev, *Sadin Adom (Red Sheet)*, Tel Aviv: Tversky, 1967, pp. 269–271. On Jordan's predicament, and the constraints and internal pressures which left it no alternative but to link up with Egypt, see S.A. Mutawi, *Jordan in the 1967 War*, Cambridge: Cambridge University Press, 1987, pp. 85–122; see also Chapter 8 (above).

2 Y. Allon, *Masakh shel Hol (Curtain of Sand)*, Tel Aviv: Hakibbutz Hameuhad, 1959, pp. 373–378.

3 It is noteworthy that Lyndon Johnson too in his memoirs attributes Israel's decision to go to war to the Jordanian–Egyptian pact: fear of entry of Iraqi troops into Jordan, assignment of an Egyptian commander in Jordan and the threat of commando action against Israeli airfields. See L.B. Johnson, *The Vantage Point*, New York: Holt, Reinhart & Winston, 1971, p. 296. Similar comments are made by Rusk, justifying Israel's preventive action. D. Rusk, *As I Saw It*, New York: W.W. Norton, 1990, p. 387.

4 Hussein himself explained to the US Ambassador in Amman that he was flying to Egypt to obtain 'life insurance'. Harman's report for 1 June 1967 on his talk with Eugene Rostow, 31 May 1967, *Eshkol Archive*.

5 There are echoes of this hope in a talk between the British Ambassador Michael Hadow and Eban. The Ambassador reported that he had heard from his counterpart in Jordan that Hussein's situation was very bad and he felt the end was near, and the British Foreign Office was surprised that Israel had not taken immediate action when Nasser announced the blocking of the Straits. Report of Eban–Hadow meeting, 29 May 1967, *Eshkol Archive*.

6 The day before the war began, Eban said that he had checked all the reports and found that 'since the Egyptian–Jordanian pact, no US statement has repeated the question of restraining etc'. Minutes of Ministerial Committee for Security 4 June 1967, *Eshkol Archive*.

7 IDF History Department, *Mutzav Pikud Elyon (Supreme Command Post)*, A, p. 298. Rabin even said that he was ready to risk losing settlements in the Galilee Panhandle and the Jordan Valley as the result of a sudden Syrian attack if it averted danger from the West Bank. In any event, he emphasized, the main thing would be the blow to the Egyptian army. Eilon's reports on General Staff discussions, 31 May 1967, *IDF History Department Archives*. Peri, *Between Battles and Ballots*, Cambridge: Cambridge University Press, 1983, pp. 249–250.

8 Peri, ibid., pp. 249–250.

9 Rabin said: 'The main enemy is Egypt and therefore no other arena should divert us from the main issue.' Notes by Eilon on General Staff discussions, 31 May 1967, *IDF History Department Archive*, and see Dayan's remarks to Uzi Narkis, CO Central Command, on 1 June 1967, U. Narkis, *Akhat Yerushalayim (Jerusalem is One)*, Tel Aviv: Am Oved, 1976, pp. 79–80.

10 Eban, *Pirkei Khayim (Chapters in a Life)*, B, Tel Aviv: Maariv, 1978, p. 401. The messages to Hussein were transmitted through three channels: military liaison through Lt. Col. S. Gat and Colonel Daud; through the head of the UN Observers General Odd Bull; and through the US Embassy in Israel. Rabin, *Pinkes Sherut (Service Notebook)*, A, Tel Aviv: Maariv, 1979, p. 188.

11 IDF actions on the Jordanian front on the first day of the war were conducted for tactical purposes and were aimed in the main at removing Jordanian artillery in the Jenin sector from the range which threatened the IAF base at Ramat David; in south Jerusalem on taking over the the the UN Headquarters at Commissioner's Palace which the Jordanian army had taken over, and to capture the 'sausage' positions and the village of Zur Baher in order to cut off Jerusalem from Bethlehem and the Hebron mountains; in northern Jerusalem the objective was to link up – through the Police Academy position, Ammunition Hill stronghold and the quarter of Sheikh Jarah – with the Mount Scopus enclave whose safety was feared for, and to break through the Radar positions, Sheikh Abdel Azizi and Bidu towards tel el-Ful in order to cut off Jerusalem from Ramallah and Samaria. In addition, the small Jordanian air force was destroyed (some thirty planes) after it had bombed targets inside Israel. On the war on the Jordanian front see IDF History Department, *ha-Maarakha ba-Zirah ha-Yardenit (The Battle in the Jordanian Arena)*, pp. 133–413.

12 Eilon's notes on the discussions, 30 May 1967, *IDF History Department Archive*.

13 See details, IDF History Department, *Supreme Command Post*, A, pp. 299–300.

14 Ibid. In the afternoon of the same day the Head of the Operations Department held an additional discussion for a more detailed formulation of the plan to conquer the West Bank. Eilon's notes on the discussions, 30 May 1967, *IDF History Department Archive*.

15 Narkis' testimony, *IDF Archive*, 192/74/1336. On Ben-Gurion's decision to limit IDF intervention, in the event that Hussein was deposed and foreign forces entered the West Bank, to a link-up to Mount Scopus see also Narkis, *Jerusalem is One*, p. 52.

16 IDF History Department, *Supreme Command Post*, A, pp. 300–304.

17 Ibid., p. 318. Eilon's notes on presentation of plans to the Chief of Operations, 31 May 1967, *IDF History Department Archive*.

18 Eilon's notes on the discussion, 31 May 1967, *IDF History Department Archive*.

19 IDF History Department, *Supreme Command Post*, A, pp. 323–324. The following day the *Sadan* deployment for the Jordanian sector was presented to the Chief of Staff in the war room. Rabin then conferred with the CO Central Command to discuss Jerusalem. Efrat testimony for 1 June 1967. At this meeting, Narkis requested the further postponement of the fortnightly convoy to Mount Scopus which had already been delayed, lest it serve as 'a match to a barrel of fuel'. Rabin agreed. Narkis, *Jerusalem is One*, p. 77.

20 *Pargol* – planning order, *IDF Archive*, 192/74/1176.

21 Testimony of Efrat for 1 June 1967. Efrat adds: '[CO IAF] Motti [Hod] tells us that by the evening no bomb will fall on Israel from the air.' The CO of the IAF was implying that by the first evening of the war the IAF would have completed the task on neutralizing the Arab air forces and they would no longer be able to attack Israel. Hod wanted to bolster Rabin's confidence and disperse his doubts in the IAF abilities. Hod's testimony, *IDF Archive*, 192/74/1156.

22 Efrat's testimony for 1 June 1967. Eban, *Chapters of a Life*, B, pp. 380–381.
23 Bar-Zohar, *ha-Khodesh ha-Arokh be-Yoter (The Longest Month)*, Tel Aviv: Lewin-Epstein, 1968, pp. 102–107. M. Zur, *Moka Limon*, Tel Aviv: Maariv, 1989, pp. 115–116.
24 Eshkol himself thought it would be better to send Golda, under guise of a fund-raising mission so that the trip would appear unofficial. See Nakdimon, *li-Kraat Shaat ha-Efes (Towards Zero Hour)*, Tel Aviv: Ramdor, 1968. p. 56.
25 In the government, as noted above, Allon was Eban's sharpest critic and also reflected the views of the General Staff. The Gahal and Rafi representatives, convened by Eshkol on 23 May for consultations without telling them about Eban's mission, felt they had been deceived. Nakdimon, ibid., pp. 57–58. Knesset members from Eban's party rallied against him. MKs Aryeh Eliav, Aharon Yadlin and Gabi Cohen defined themselves as 'the counter-balance to Eban's five-stage missile [i.e. the US plan for lifting the blockade as presented by Eban] which would never be launched'. See ibid., pp. 179, 185–187.
26 It was Minister of Justice Yaakov Shimshon Shapira, Eban's fellow party member, who proposed this at a meeting of the Alignment Party Political Committee on 31 May. According to this proposal, Eban was to receive the impressive and empty title of 'deputy prime minister'. Eban announced that he would resign, and the proposal collapsed. Moshe Haim Shapira and Moshe Kol hastened to his defence. See ibid., pp. 179, 183–184, and Gilboa, *Shesh Shanim Shisha Yamin (Six Years Six Days)*, Tel Aviv: Am Oved, 1968, p. 175.
27 Gilboa, ibid., p. 154. Bar-Zohar, *Longest Month*, p. 143.
28 Minutes of government meeting, 27 May 1967. See also Gilboa, ibid., p. 173.
29 In his talk with Eban in the White House on 26 May, Johnson said: 'I'm not a feeble mouse or a coward, and we're going to try. What we need is a group, five or four or less, or if we can't do that, then on our own.' See Chapter 18 (above), and Gilboa, ibid., p. 154.
30 In his communication to Johnson on 29 May, formulated by Eban, Eshkol welcomed the US promise to adopt 'any and all measures' to open the Straits of Tiran. Walk Rostow expressed reservations and commented to Evron that this formula could be interpreted as exceeding the President's authority. Eban claims that he was basing himself on Johnson's positive answer to the question of whether he had decided to make 'every possible effort' to guarantee freedom of shipping. He saw no fundamental difference between the two phrases. Eban, *The Six Day War* (ms.), 1969, pp. 196–199. The American reservation made a poor impression and Eban was blamed. E. Haber, *ha-Yom Tifrotz Milkhama (Today War will Break Out)*, p. 201. Rabin, *Service Notebook*, A, pp. 177–178.

22 The decisive meeting in the Pit: the Ministerial Committee versus the General Staff

1 Eshkol at government meeting, 1 June 1967.
2 The impact of their meeting with the senior command on Friday was evident in the remarks of the ministers at Sunday's government session. Minutes of government meeting, 4 June 1967.
3 The content of the 2 June meeting of the Ministerial Committee with the General Staff forum as quoted below is based on the Minutes of the meeting, *IDF Archive*, 192/74/1201; and cf. Haber, *ha-Yom Tifrotz Milkhama (Today War will Break Out)*, Tel Aviv: Idanim, 1988, pp. 204–212.
4 Reference was to Jewish influence on the administration. See H. McPherson, 'The White House, US Jewry and the Six Day War', *Shisha Yamim, Shloshim Shana (Six Years, Six Days)*, Tel Aviv: Am Oved, 1999, pp. 137–142.

5 In practice this was an indirect admission that Israel should not wait, even for economic reasons, more than a few days.
6 There were, however, differences of opinion between Dayan and Allon. The latter favoured reaching the Canal, conquering the Gaza Strip and transferring its refugees to Sinai. Dayan objected. See Dayan, *Avnei Derekh (Milestones)*, Tel Aviv: Idanim, 1977, p. 422.
7 Efrat's testimony about 2 June 1967.
8 For characterization of a political culture as 'mature' where the level of military intervention in politics is the lowest, see A.S. Feiner, *ha-Ish al Gav ha-Soos (The Man on the Horse)*, Tel Aviv: Maarakhot, 1982, pp. 24–182.
9 See A. Perlmutter, *The Military and Politics in Modern Times*, New Haven: Yale University Press, p. 14.
10 Z. Schiff, '1967 – the General Staff in the government's Eyes', *Haaretz*, 6 June 1997.
11 Wahrhaftig related that during a tour of the Gaza Strip border he conferred with representatives of settlements and the Deputy CO of the Eighty-fourth Division, Herzl Shafir. Offensive epithets were directed at the government 'as if to say: you are fools!' Author's interview with Wahrhaftig, 24 August 1998.
12 The economic recession and the deterioration in security during the second half of 1966 and the first half of 1967 affected the public mood and created an atmosphere of depression across the country. Many Israelis emigrated to Europe and America, and a popular joke at the time was that 'the last to leave is requested to switch off the light at Lod [later Ben-Gurion] airport'.
13 In order to prevent slackening of tension, it was decided, as noted above, to defer release of reserve units, a decision which was misinterpreted by the Prime Minister's office. Haber, *Today War will Break Out*, p. 193.
14 S. Nakdimon, 'The generals revolt 67', *Yediot Aharonot*, 15 September 1985.
15 Remarks of Tal, Narkis and Elazar at the stormy meeting with the Prime Minister on 28 May. IDF History Department, *Supreme Command Post*, A, pp. 288–289. Haber, *Today War Will Break Out*, pp. 196–197.
16 Eshkol's widow, Miriam Eshkol, in press interviews, used the word 'putsch'. The members of the 1967 senior command reject her version of events and admit only that there was a 'sharp conflict' between them and the politicians, and no more. S. Nakdimon, 'The generals revolt 67', *Yediot Aharonot*, 15 September 1985.
17 Weizman is quoted as follows: 'I don't believe that a military coup could have taken place, but we were never closer'; see J. Larteguy, *The Walls of Israel*, New York: Evans & Co, 1968, p. 75.
18 B.S. Hersh, *Bereirat Shimshon (Samson's Choice)*, Tel Aviv: Yediot Aharonot, 1992, p. 125.
19 Sharon's testimony, *IDF Archive*, 192/74/1038. A senior military correspondent heard from a certain general (apparently Sharon) that he thought it was possible to lock the ministers in another room and carry out a clean coup. Z. Schiff, '1967 – the General Staff in government eyes', *Haaretz*, 6 June 1967.
20 S. Huntington, *The Soldier and the State*, Cambridge: Cambridge University Press, 1957, pp. 74–79.
21 Dayan, *Milestones*, pp. 422–423.
22 Another of Eshkol's fears, which Dayan tried to calm, was of 'beheadings' in the Ministry of Defence. Minutes of meeting of Alignment ministers, 1 June 1967, *Eshkol Archive*. Lior describes the situation differently. Haber, *Today War Will Break Out*, pp. 145–185.
23 Minutes of government meeting, 8 June 1967. Dayan, *Milestones*, pp. 474–475.
24 IDF History Department, *Supreme Command Post*, A, p. 353.

25 Ibid.

26 Ibid. See also Dayan, *Milestones*, p. 423.

27 The war did not proceed according to Dayan's instructions, and he himself approved the seizing of strongholds beside the Suez Canal in order to block the Egyptian escape routes from Sinai. Moreover, after the war Dayan regretted not having ordered the IDF to hold on to the West Bank of the Canal (and the East bank of the Jordan). Dayan at a gathering to sum up the lessons of the war, 28 February 1968, *IDF Archive*, 192/74/987.

28 Eilon notes on 2 June 1967, *Archives of IDF History Department*.

23 The decisive stage: war

1 Cables of Washington Embassy, 30 May 1967, *Eshkol Archive*.

2 *FRUS*, 1964–1968, Vol. 19, Doc. 2, 5.

3 *FRUS*, 1964–1968, Vol. 19, Doc. 13.

4 *FRUS*, 1964–1968, Vol. 19, Doc. 18, 19.

5 *FRUS*, 1964–1968, Vol. 19, Doc. 36.

6 *FRUS*, 1964–1968, Vol. 19, Doc. 30.

7 *FRUS*, 1964–1968, Vol. 19, Doc. 34.

8 *FRUS*, 1964–1968, Vol. 19, Doc. 31. Goldberg recommended to U Thant that he also visit Tel Aviv and Damascus. U Thant ignored the recommendation.

9 *FRUS*, 1964–1968, Vol. 19, Doc. 40, 41.

10 *FRUS*, 1964–1968, Vol. 19, Doc. 49.

11 *FRUS*, 1964–1968, Vol. 19, Doc. 51.

12 *FRUS*, 1964–1968, Vol. 19, Doc. 57, 58, 62, 133. De Gaulle unquestionably wanted to exploit the crisis in order to gain France a central role in solution of international problems as the intermediary between West and East, and to promote French interests in the Middle East.

13 *FRUS*, 1964–1968, Vol. 19, Doc. 53, 54.

14 Rusk himself explained to the President, before meeting with Eban, that Eban needed something 'solid' to appease the 'hawks'. *FRUS*, 1964–1968, Vol. 19, Doc. 71.

15 On 31 May Johnson ordered the establishment in the State Department of a 'task force' to consider urgently other solutions. *FRUS*, 1964–1968, Doc. 106.

16 *FRUS*, 1964–1968, Vol. 19, Doc. 58, 68, 91, 130.

17 *FRUS*, 1964–1968, Vol. 19, Doc. 61, 76, 142.

18 *FRUS*, 1964–1968, Vol. 19, Doc. 79.

19 Note from Johnson to Kosygin, *FRUS*, 1964–1968, Vol. 19, Doc. 88. Eban–Rusk meeting, *FRUS*, 1964–1968, Vol. 19, Doc. 64.

20 *FRUS*, 1964–1968, Vol. 19, Doc. 54, 61, 79, 130. The US Ambassador to Moscow, Thomas Thomson, deduced, on the other hand, that the Russians had known about the Egyptian moves which had generated the crisis, but not about the intention to block the Straits. *FRUS*, 1964–1968, Vol. 19, Doc. 59.

21 *FRUS*, 1964–1968, Vol. 19, Doc. 50, 69, 98.

22 *FRUS*, 1964–1968, Vol. 19, Doc. 71.

23 *FRUS*, 1964–1968, Vol. 19, Doc. 64, 71.

24 *FRUS*, 1964–1968, Vol. 19, Doc. 69, 98.

25 *FRUS*, 1964–1968, Vol. 19, Doc. 131.

26 *FRUS*, 1964–1968, Vol. 19, Doc. 99.

27 *FRUS*, Vol 19, Doc. 108, Doc. 122.

28 *FRUS*, 1964–1968, Vol. 19, Doc. 56, 67, 107.

29 Nolte even proposed a package deal whereby Israel would grant the Palestinian refugees the choice between return and full compensation, and agree to inter-

nationalization of Jerusalem and discussion of its borders on the basis of the 1947 UN partition plan. In return, the Arabs would recognize its existence 'in effect', permit passage through the Bay of Aqaba and end the boycott. *FRUS*, 1964–1968, Vol. 19, Doc. 67.

30 *FRUS*, 1964–1968, Vol. 19, Doc. 117.

31 *FRUS*, 1964–1968, Vol. 19, Doc. 91, 114, 115, 137, 143.

32 *FRUS*, 1964–1968, Vol. 19, Doc. 125, 141.

33 *FRUS*, Vol. 19, Doc. 144.

34 M. Bar-On, *Gates of Gaza*, pp. 130–138.

35 *FRUS*, 1964–1968, Vol. 19, Doc. 100, 119, 128.

36 *FRUS*, 1964–1968, Vol. 19, Doc. 123, 129, 134, 145.

37 *FRUS*, 1964–1968, Vol. 19, Doc. 144. The Americans and British also discussed the possibility of appointing a mediator, and even mentioned the name of Gus Lindt, Swiss Ambassador to Moscow. *FRUS*, 1964–1968, Vol. 19, Doc. 130.

38 *FRUS*, 1964–1968, Vol. 19, Doc. 77.

39 Preparations in Washington for the visit of Mohi al-Din and his meeting with President Johnson began on 4 June. *FRUS*, 1964–1968, Vol. 19, Doc. 148.

40 *FRUS*, 1964–1968, Vol. 19, Doc. 114.

41 *FRUS*, 1964–1968, Vol. 19, Doc. 141.

42 Amit confirmed this at a study day at Yad Tabenkin on 4 September 1989 devoted to the waiting period.

43 Zeev Schiff defined Amit's mission as a 'question mark' concerning everything that Eban had brought back. Schiff at a study day on the Six Day War, Tel Aviv University, 20 March 1996. See also Haber, *ha-Yom Tifrotz Milkhama (Today War will Break Out)*, Tel Aviv: Idanim, 1988, p. 216, and Bar-Zohar, *ha-Khodesh ha-Arokh be-Yoter (The Longest Month)*, Tel Aviv: Lewin-Epstein, 1968, p. 143.

44 This is also Amit's view. See *Maarakhot*, No. 325 (June–July 1992), p. 12. Eban claims that the decision to send Amit was taken jointly by himself and Eshkol. Eban (ms. 1989), p. 199.

45 Amit related at the study day at Yad Tabenkin on 4 September 1989 that the plane in which he travelled to the United States was full of passengers fleeing Israel.

46 Amit's description of the meeting, ibid., and expanded remarks in Amit, *Rosh be-Rosh (Head On)*, Tel Aviv: Hed Artzi, 1999, pp. 237–243. *FRUS*, 1964–1968, Vol. 19, Doc. 124.

47 At the beginning of the crisis the Israeli Embassy in Washington already estimated that 'the problem is Zvulun'. Evron to Bitan, 20 May 1967, *Eshkol Archive*. 'Zvulun' was the code-name for Rusk in confidential Foreign Ministry correspondence.

48 Harman to the Foreign Minister, 2 June 1967, *Eshkol Archive*. Rusk, it seems, did not accept Israel's stand that the concentration of forces and blocking of the Straits were an act of aggression to which Israel had the right to respond with gunfire.

49 Evron to Deputy Minister of Defence, 3 June 1967, *Eshkol Archive*. Bitan to Evron, 3 June 1967, *Eshkol Archive*. The fact that the Dolphin was anchored at Massawa ready to sail for Eilat was mentioned by Ambassador Harman in a talk with Rusk and Rostow on 2 June. *FRUS*, 1964–1968, Vol. 19, Doc. 132.

50 Clark Clifford, Head of the President's Foreign Intelligence Advisory Board, described this as a 'personal view' in a talk with Evron. Evron to Foreign Minister, 1 June 1967, *Eshkol Archive*. Johnson's friend, the Jewish Justice Abe

Fortas, told Ambassador Harman that it was vital for Israel to avoid firing the first shot. Harman to Foreign Minister, 2 June 1967, *Eshkol Archive.*

51 Johnson's note to Eshkol, 3 June 1967, *Eshkol Archive.*

52 The meeting was also attended by Deputy Defence Minister Zvi Dinstein, Foreign Minister Eban and his Director-General Levavi, Yigal Allon, the PM's Adviser Ygael Yadin and PM Office Director-General Yaakov Herzog. Summary of meeting, 3 June 1967, *Eshkol Archive.*

53 Ibid.

54 Summary of meeting at PM's home with Amit and Harman, night of 3–4 June 1967, *Eshkol Archive.*

55 *Rabin Report*, p. 172. Efrat's testimony for 3 June 1967. See also Haber, *Today War will Break Out*, pp. 215–218.

56 See below and testimony of Lior, ibid., p. 219.

57 Meeting of Ministerial Committee on Security, 4 June 1967. See also Haber, ibid., 1988, p. 215.

58 Eban said: 'I checked all the material from three to four days ago, and in effect since the pact between Egypt and Jordan no American talk has repeated the talk of self-control, restraint.' Meeting of the Ministerial Committee on Security, 4 June 1967.

59 Eshkol's military secretary, Yisrael Lior, was the first to greet the Prime Minister when he arrived in his office on the morning of 4 June before the meeting of the Ministerial Committee. He sensed that Eshkol was again suffering last-minute indecision. Lior's summary, 4 June 1967, *Eshkol Archive.*

60 Dayan ridiculed the very thought that the Sixth Fleet might guarantee Israel's safety: 'Two thousand Marines from the Sixth Fleet won't do more than two hundred [Egyptian] tanks in Eilat.' Allon too dismissed the idea, claiming that it would turn Israel into a dependant state and a victim of appeasement. Ministerial Committee on Security, 4 June 1967.

61 Ibid.

62 On the agenda of the government, whose session was 'camouflaged' as a regular meeting, were additional clauses for discussion apart from the 'security situation'. For example, Israel's participation in the diplomatic conference in Stockholm, the ratification of an Israel–Belgium cultural agreement, the coopting of Knesset member Yosef Sapir into the government, and of Begin, Dayan and Sapir on to the Ministerial Committee on Security. Government meeting, 4 June 1967.

63 The French embargo had been proclaimed two days previously, on 2 June. A US declaration on the stoppage of arms consignments to the region was expected once fighting began.

64 Government decision, 4 June 1967.

65 In hindsight, Rabin said that as a result of the waiting, the reserve forces entered the fight as a regular army with regard to training, organization and integration in the fighting force. Rabin at study day on the waiting period, Yad Tabenkin, 4 September 1989.

66 See Irit Keinan, 'The Six Day War as the mirror of a bygone media era' in Sessar (ed.) *Shisha Yamim – Shloshim Shana (Six Days – Thirty Years)*, Tel Aviv: Am Oved, 1999, pp. 209–221.

67 H. Herzog, *ha-Yamim ha-Gdolim (The Great Times)*, Tel Aviv: Maariv, 1969. Herzog's broadcasts won him tremendous popularity and natioal standing, which later promoted his election as Israel's sixth President (1983–1993).

68 See A. Yariv, 'War of alternatives – war of no alternatives', in *Milkhemet Brera (War with Alternatives)*, Tel Aviv: Hakibbutz Hameuhad, 1985, pp. 9–29.

69 IDF History Department, *Supreme Command Post*, A, pp. 380–385.

70 For details of the reasons for choosing 07:45 as the zero hour, see IDF History Department, *Supreme Command Post*, A, p. 378.
71 IDF History Department, *Supreme Command Post*, A, p. 396. This is according to the operational ledgers. General Ze'evi claimed in an interview that he gave the order 'Red Sheet' – the code-name for Operation Nakhshonim. Interview of the author with Ze'evi, 3 September 1998.

Afterword

1 Government decision, 4 June 1967.
2 Government meeting, 5 June 1967.
3 *Ben-Gurion's Diary*, 6 June 1967.
4 Lior's summary of a meeting in the PM's office, night of 5/6 June 1967.
5 Meeting of Ministerial Committee on Security, 8 June 1967. H. Bartov, *Dado*, A, Tel Aviv: Maariv, 1978, p. 136.
6 Reuven Pedatzur, *Nitzahon ha-mevukha (The Triumph of Confusion)*, Tel Aviv: Yad Tabenkin, 1966, pp. 39–40.
7 Ze'evi document, 'Political settlement for the West Bank', 15 June 1967. Ami Gluska, *Gandhi's Heritage*, B, *Maariv*, 24 October 2001.
8 Pedatzur, *Triumph of Confusion*, 1996, pp. 47–57. The September 1967 Arab summit in Khartoum decided on the famous three 'No's': no negotiation, no recognition and no peace with Israel.
9 *Maariv*, 13 June 1967.
10 Pedatzur, *Triumph and Confusion*, pp. 117–121.
11 The Six Day War cut short a historical process of 'Jordanization' of the Palestine problem, whose fruition could have finally integrated the two banks of the Jordan. The Jordanian option was open to Israel for twenty years, between 1967 and 1987, until the first Intifade broke out, following which King Hussein renounced responsibility for the West Bank. Failure to take advantage of the Jordanian solution left Israel in direct and cruel confrontation with the insoluble Palestinian problem.

Appendix

1 Yisrael Tal, CO of the Armoured Corps under Rabin, described him as the supreme authority, 'guide and mentor' of the entire IDF command, 'an unparalleled expert', 'erudite', and the man who built up the army. Author's interview with Tal, 19 October 1998. See also *Maarakhot*, 344–345 (December 1995), pp. 4–5. Rehavam Ze'evi, Deputy Chief of Operations, lavishly praised Rabin as the best and profoundest of his commanders in the IDF, who taught him more than anyone else – author's interview with Ze'evi, 3 September 1998. Elsewhere he described him as 'head and shoulders above others'. See M. Sheshar, *Sikhot im Rehavam Zeevi (Conversations with Rehavam Zeevi)*, Tel Aviv: Yediot Aharonot, 1992, pp. 116 and 165. See also testimony of Eshkol's military secretary, Yisrael Lior, Haber, *ha-Yom Tifrotz Milkhama (Today War will Break Out)*, Tel Aviv: Idanim, 1988, pp. 41–42, 97.
2 Moshe Dayan's biographer, Shabtai Tevet, wrote that it was Rabin who used the English phrase 'He is a user of force, not a builder of one' about Dayan – Tevet, *Moshe Dayan*, Jerusalem and Tel Aviv: Schocken, 1973, p. 405. Rabin, on the other hand, was more a builder of force than a user of force. Unlike Dayan, he did not believe in improvisation but only in precise planning. D. Horovitz, *Mesima Bilti Gemura – Khayav u-Moto shel Yitzhak Rabin (Unfinished Mission – the Life and Death of Yitzhak Rabin)*, Or Yehuda: Maariv, 1996, pp. 42–43.

3 See also Peri, *Between Battles and Ballots*, Cambridge: Cambridge University Press, 1983, pp. 162–163.
4 Testimony of Narkis, *IDF Archive*, 192/74/1149. Testimony of Hod, *IDF Archive*, 192/74/1156.
5 Rabin interview by Ronel Fisher, *Hadashot*, 22 May 1992.
6 Rabin, *Pinkes Sherut (Service Notebook)*, Tel Aviv: Maariv, 1979, pp. 149–150.
7 Assistant to the Minister of Defence Haim Yisraeli says that Rabin did not request Eshkol's approval for his meeting with Ben-Gurion. Author's interview with Yisraeli, 12 November 1998.
8 Rabin, *Service Book*, 1979, p. 150. *Hadashot*, 22 May 1992.
9 *Ben-Gurion's Diary*, 22 May 1967.
10 M. Dayan, *Avnei Derekh (Milestones)*, Tel Aviv: Idanim, 1977, pp. 399–400.
11 Ibid., p. 399.
12 Rabin, *Service Book*, pp. 156–158.
13 Haber, *Today*, p. 173.
14 Testimony of Efrat for 23 May 1967.
15 Leah Rabin, *Kol ha-Zman Ishto (Always his Wife)*, Tel Aviv: Idanim, 1988, p. 112.
16 Weizman memo of 6 November 1967 – published in *Haaretz*, 22 April 1974.
17 Weizman, *Lekha Shamayim Lekha Aretz (Heaven and Earth are Yours)*, Tel Aviv: Maariv, 1975, pp. 258–259. Weizman's mention of a second meeting with Rabin contradicts Leah Rabin's report that her husband received sedation and slept until the following afternoon. It is possible that Rabin got up in the morning, met Weizman and then went back to sleep.
18 Rabin, *Service Notebook*, p. 159.
19 In an interview twenty-five years later, Rabin said that he had indeed offered Weizman command over the IDF, but did not remember if he had meant until he recovered or more than that: *Hadashot*, 22 May 1992.
20 Rabin, *Service Notebook*, p. 159. See also *Haaretz*, 22 April 1974.
21 Weizman, *Heaven and Earth*, p. 262.
22 This is the impression gained from the documents, but it was denied by Ze'evi. He claimed that 'Barlev did not push Rabin aside. Rabin chose to remain aside.' Author's interview with Ze'evi, 3 September 1998.
23 Weizman, *Heaven and Earth*, p. 258. Author's interview with Ze'evi, 3 September 1998. Weizman memo in *Haaretz*, 22 April 1974. Rabin denied it: 'There was no problem with my functioning from 24 May onward.' *Hadashot*, 22 May 1992. Barlev said cautiously that Rabin 'until the end of the war . . . was not in full form'. C. Guy, *Barlev*, Tel Aviv: Am Oved, 1998, p. 125.
24 Minutes of meeting of Alignment Party ministers, 31 May 1967, *Eshkol Archive*. See also Bar-Zohar, *ha-Khodesh ha-Arokh be-Yoter (The Longest Month)*, Tel Aviv: Lewin-Epstein, 1968, p. 84. Author's interview with Wahrhaftig, 24 August 1998.
25 Mati Peled commented: 'It was obvious that Rabin was relieved when Dayan was appointed Minister of Defence. He was freed of the burden of a Chief of Staff who was in effect also fulfilling the role of minister of defence.' Nakdimon, 'The Generals' Revolt 67', *Yediot Aharonot*, 15 September 1985.
26 See Ben-Meir, *Civil–Military Relations in Israel*, New York: Columbia University Press, 1995, pp. 107–108, 128.
27 See e.g. Amos Keinan's article, 'Yitzhak Rabin, hero of Israel', *Yediot Aharonot*, 10 June 1967, and a profile by Raphael Bashan, *Yediot Aharonot*, 13 June 1967.

Select English bibliography

Books

Abu-Lughod, Ibrahim (ed.). *The Arab–Israeli Confrontation of June 1967: An Arab Perspective*, North Western University Press, Evanston, 1970.

Ajammi, Fouad. *The Arab Predicament*, Cambridge University Press, Cambridge, 1981.

Aronson, Shlomo. *Israel's Nuclear Programme, the Six Day War and its Ramifications*, Kings College, London, 1998.

Bar-Siman-Tov, Yaacov. *Israel, The Superpowers and The War In the Middle East*, Praeger, New York, 1987.

Ben Meir, Yehuda. *Civil–Military Relations in Israel*, Columbia University Press, New York, 1995.

Bialer, Uri. *Between East and West; Israel's Foreign Policy Orientation 1948–1956*, Cambridge University Press, Cambridge, 1990.

Brecher, Michael *Decisions in Israel's Foreign Policy*, Oxford University Press, London, 1974.

Brecher, Michael (with Benjamin Geist). *Decisions in Crisis – Israel 1976 and 1973*, University of California Press, Berkeley, 1980.

Bull, Odd. *War and Peace in the Middle East*, Leo Cooper, London, 1973.

Cockburn, Andrew and Leslie. *Dangerous Liaison*, HarperCollins, New York, 1991.

Cohen, Avner. *Israel and the Bomb*, Columbia University Press, New York, 1998.

Draper, Theodore. *Israel and World Politics – Roots of the Third Arab–Israeli War*, Viking Press, New York, 1968.

Evron, Yair. *Israel's Nuclear Dilema*, Routledge, London, 1994.

Gazit, Mordechai. *President Kennedy's Policy toward the Arab States and Israel*, Tel Aviv University Press, Tel Aviv, 1983.

Glassman, Jon D. *Arms for the Middle East – The Soviet Union and War in the Middle East*, Johns Hopkins University Press, Baltimore, MD, 1975.

Golan, Galia. *Soviet Policies in the Middle East from World War Two to Gorbachev*, Cambridge University Press, Cambridge, 1990.

Gross-Stein, Janice and Tanter, Robert. *Rational Decision-making: Israel Security Choices 1967*, Ohio University Press, Columbus, 1980.

Hahn, Peter L. *The United States, Great Britain and Egypt 1945–1956*, North Carolina University Press, Chapel Hill, 1991.

Heikal, Mohamed H. *The Sphinx and the Commissar*, Harper & Row, New York, 1978. *The Cairo Documents*, Doubleday, New York, 1973.

Hirst, David. *The Gun and the Olive Branch*, Faber & Faber, London, 1977.

Huntington, Samuel. *The Soldier and the State*, Cambridge, 1957.

Janowitz, Morris. *The Professional Soldier*, Free Press, New York, 1971.

Johnson, Lyndon B. *The Vantage Point*, Holt, Reinhart & Winston, New York, 1971.

Kerr, Malcolm. *The Arab Cold War 1958–1967*, Oxford University Press, Oxford, 1967.

Lacouture, Jean. *Nasser*, A.A. Knopf, New York, 1973.

Lall, Arthur. *The U.N. and the Middle East Crisis 1967*, Columbia University Press, New York, 1968.

Laquuer, Walter. *The Road to War 1967*, Weidenfeld & Nicolson, London, 1968.

Larteguy, Jean. *The Walls of Israel*, Evans & Co, New York, 1968.

Luttwak, Edward and Horowitz, Dan. *The Israeli Army*, Allen Lane, London, 1975.

Medzini, Michael. *Israel's Foreign Relations – Selected Documents*, The Ministry of Foregn Affairs, Jerusalem, 1976.

Mutawi, Samir, A. *Jordan in the 1967 War*, Cambridge University Press, Cambridge, 1987.

Nassif, R. *U Thant in New York*, Hurstand Co, London, 1986.

Neff, Donald. *Warriors for Jerusalem*, Linden Press, New York, 1984.

Nutting, Anthony. *Nasser*, Constable, London, 1972.

Oren, Michael. *Six Days of War*, Oxford University Press, New York, 2000.

Palumbo, Michael. *Imperial Israel*, Bloomsbury, London, 1992.

Parker, Richard. *The Politics of Miscalculation in the Middle East*, Indiana University Press, Bloomington, 1993.

—— (ed.). *The Six Day War – A Retrospective*, University Press of Florida, Gainesville, 1996.

Peri, Yoram. *Between Battles and Ballots*, Cambridge University Press, Cambridge, 1983.

Perlmutter, Amos. *Military and Politics in Israel*, Frank Cass, London, 1969.

—— *The Military and Politics in Modern Times*, Yale University Press, New Haven, CT, 1977.

Perlmutter, Amos and Bennet, V. (eds). *The Political Influence of the Military*, Yale University Press, New Haven, CT, 1980.

Quantdt, William. *Decade of Decisions*, University of California Press, Berkeley, 1977.

Quandt, William B. *Peace Process*, The Brookings Institute, Washington, DC, 1993.

Rabin, Yitzhak. *The Rabin Memoirs*, Steimatzky, Bnei-Brak, 1994.

Rabinovich, Itamar. *Syria Under the Baath*, Israel University Press, Jerusalem, 1972.

Rahmy, A.A. *The Egyptian Policy in The Arab World*, University Press of America, Washington. DC, 1983.

Reich, Bernard. *Quest for Peace: U.S.–Israel Relations and the Arab–Israeli Conflict*, Transaction Books, New Brunswick, 1977.

Riad, Mahmoud. *The Struggle for Peace in the Middle East*, Quartet Books, London and New York, 1981.

Rikhye, Indar Jit. *The Sinai Blunder*, Oxford University Press and IBH, New Delhi, 1978.

Rostow, Eugine. *Peace in the Balance*, Simon & Schuster, New York, 1972.

Rusk, Dean. *As I Saw It*, W.W. Norton, New York, 1991.

Sacher, Howard M. *A History of Israel*, Alfred A. Knope, New York, 1969.

—— *Egypt and Israel*, Marek, New York, 1981.

Sadat, Anwar. *In Search of Identity*, Harper & Row, New York, 1977.

Safran, Nadav. *Israel – The Embattled Ally*, Harvard University Press, Cambridge, MA, 1978.

Segev, Shmuel. *The Iranian Triangle*, Free Press, New York, 1988.

Shemesh, Moshe. *The Palestinian Entity 1959–1974*, Frank Cass, London, 1988.

Shlaim, Avi. *Collusion Across the Jordan*, Columbia University Press, New York, 1988.

Wilson, Harold. *The Chariot of Israel*, Weidenfeld & Nicolson, London, 1981.

Yaniv, Avner. *Deterrence Without the Bomb – The Politics of Israeli Strategy*, Lexington Books, New York, 1984.

Young, Peter. *The Israeli Campaign 1967*, William Kimber, London, 1967.

Articles

Benjamini, Haim. 'The Six Day War, Israel 1967: decisions, coalitions, consequences – a sociological view' in M. Lissak (ed.) *Israeli Society and Its Defence Establishment*, Frank Cass, London, 1984.

Bentwich, Norman. 'The Israel–Syrian Armistice Agreement', *International Relations*, 3 (October 1967), pp. 253–258.

Brown, C.L. 'Nasser and the June war: plan or improvisation?' in Samir Seikaly *et al.* (eds) *Quest for Understanding*, American University of Beirut, Beirut, 1991.

Cohen, Avner. 'Nuclear weapons, opacity and Israeli democracy' in A. Yariv (ed.) *National Security and Democracy in Israel*, Boulder, CO: Lynne Riennner, 1993, pp. 197–225.

—— 'Cairo, Dimona and the June 1967 war', *Middle East Journal*, 50(2) (spring 1996).

Gera, Gideon. 'Israel and the June 1967 war: 25 years later', *Middle East Journal*, 46(2), pp. 229–243.

Hahn, Peter L. 'Containment and Egyptian nationalism: the unsuccessful effort to establish the Middle East command', *Diplomatic History* (winter 1987), pp. 23–40.

Handel, Michael. 'The development of the Israeli political-military doctrine' in F.B. Horton *et al.* (eds) *Comparative Defence Policy*, Johns Hopkins University Press, Baltimore, MD, 1974, pp. 279–289.

Horowitz, Dan. 'The control of limited military operations, the Israeli experience' in Y. Evron (ed.) *International Violence: Terrorism, Surprise and Control*, The Leonard Davis Institute, Jerusalem, 1979, pp. 258–276.

—— 'The Israel defence forces: a civilianized military in a partially militarized society' in R. Kolkowicz and A. Korbonski (eds) *Soldiers, Peasants and Bureaucrats*, George Allen & Unwin, London, 1980.

Hourani, Albert. 'The June war' in A.R. Taylor and R.N. Tetlie (eds) *Palestine: A Search for Truth*, Public Affairs Press, Washington, DC, 1970, pp. 159–165.

Lapidoth, Ruth. 'The Security Council in the May 1967 crisis: a study in frustration', *Israel Law Review*, 4(4) (October 1969).

Lissak, Moshe. 'Paradoxes of Israeli civil–military relations' in Moshe Lissak (ed.) *Israeli Society and Its Defence Establishment*, Frank Cass, London, 1984.

Luttwak, Edward. 'Defense planning in Israel: a brief retrospective' in G. Newman (ed.) *Defense Planning in Less-indusrialized States*, Lexington Books, Lexington MA, 1984, pp. 131–144.

Parker, Richard. B. 'The June 1967 war: some mysteries explored', *Middle East Journal*, 46(2) (Spring 1992), pp. 177–197.

Perlmutter, Amos. 'The Israeli army in politics: the persistence of the civilian over the military', *World Politics*, 20(4) (July 1968), pp. 606–643.

—— 'The military and politics in Israel' in F.B. Horton *et al.* (eds) *Comparative Defense Policy*, Johns Hopkins University Press, Baltimore, MD, 1974, pp. 88–97.

Quandt, William B. 'Lyndon Johnson and the June 1967 war: what color was the light?', *Middle East Journal*, 46(2), pp. 198–228.

Yost, Charles W. 'The June 1967 war: how it began' in M.D. Khadduri (ed.) *The Arab–Israeli Impasse*, Robert B. Luce, Washington, DC, 1968.

Index

The arrangement is letter-by-letter.
References to notes are prefixed by n.
References to bibliographic notes are
suffixed with *b*.
Italic page numbers indicate
illustrations, tables and plates not
included in the text page range.

Lightning Source UK Ltd.
Milton Keynes UK
UKHW020123241222
414416UK00004B/9